THE RISE OF RELIGIOUS LIBERTY
IN AMERICA

THE

RISE OF RELIGIOUS LIBERTY
IN AMERICA

A History

BY

SANFORD H. COBB

HERE the free spirit of mankind, at length,
Throws its last fetters off.
— BRYANT

COOPER SQUARE PUBLISHERS, INC.
NEW YORK
1968

TO

THE COLONIAL CLUB

𝔒𝔣 𝔊𝔯𝔞𝔫𝔡 ℜ𝔞𝔭𝔦𝔡𝔰, 𝔐𝔦𝔠𝔥𝔦𝔤𝔞𝔫

WITH AN AFFECTION UNDIMINISHED

BY TIME AND DISTANCE

Originally Published 1902
Published by Cooper Square Publishers, Inc.
59 Fourth Avenue, New York, N. Y. 10003
Library of Congress Catalog Card No. 68-27517

Printed in the United States of America
by Noble Offset Printers, Inc., New York, N. Y. 10003

PREFACE

THOUGH the title of this work suggests a topic having a religious aspect, yet the book itself offers no history of the churches or of religion in America. That field is well occupied by such works as those of Baird, Dorchester, Bacon, and others, and by denominational histories. The aim of the present work is political rather than religious. It attempts a systematic narrative — so far as the author is aware, not hitherto published — of that historical development through which the civil law in America came at last, after much struggle, to the decree of entire liberty of conscience and of worship. It is thus purely historical, and confines itself rigidly to those incidents in colonial history which are closely related to this special theme. The purpose is to exhibit in proper historical sequence those influences and events which guided the American republics to their unique solution of the world-old problem of Church and State — a solution so unique, so far-reaching, and so markedly diverse from European principles as to constitute the most striking contribution of America to the science of government.

With such aim and for the double purpose of correcting certain popular misconceptions and of placing plainly before the mind the complete goal of this historical progress, it has seemed desirable to define in the first chapter the elements of a pure religious liberty, as that principle has embedded itself in the American mind and law. Besides, in order that this principle and its development might be shown in true historical relations, it seemed further needful to describe in the second chapter, so briefly as possible, the genesis and growth of the " Old World Idea " in regard to Church and State, which obtained in full force in every European government at the time of American colonization, with which the American liberty stands in so sharp a contrast, and from the bonds of which the story will show the colonies gradually setting themselves free.

As to works cited, it is proper to specially note that the citations from Bancroft's " History of the United States " refer to the 23d (8 vol.) edition, Boston, 1864 ; also, that in the sketch of the " Old World Idea," in view of its special place in this treatise, the author has felt at liberty to depend largely upon the very acute and comprehensive monograph, " Church and State," by A. Innes of Edinburgh, whose page is cited in every instance of direct quotation.

TABLE OF CONTENTS

I

THE AMERICAN PRINCIPLE

II

THE OLD WORLD IDEA

V

PURITAN ESTABLISHMENTS

1. *Plymouth*

2. *The Massachusetts Theocracy*

AUTHORITIES

BANCROFT. *History of the United States*, 23d (8 vol.) edition, Boston, 1864.

MCMASTER. *History of the People of the United States.*

SCHOULER. *History of the United States.*

VON HOLST. *Constitutional and Political History of the United States.*

FELT. *Ecclesiastical History of New England.*

LIEBER. *Civil Liberty and Self-government.*

PAINE. *Rights of Man.*

PRICE. *Observations on the American Revolution.*

WILLIAMS. *The Bloody Tenent of Persecution.*

    "   *Letters.*

E. G. SCOTT. *Constitutional Liberties.*

L. W. BACON. *American Christianity.*

STORY. *Commentaries on the Constitution of the United States.*

KENT. *Commentaries on American Law.*

BRYCE. *American Commonwealth.*

    "   *Holy Roman Empire.*

RAWLE. *View of the Constitution of the United States.*

COOLEY. *Constitutional Limitations.*

BLACKSTONE. *Commentaries.*

INNES. *Church and State.*

HOOKER. *Ecclesiastical Polity.*

RANKE. *History of the Popes.*

KURTZ. *Church History.*

FISHER. *History of the Christian Church.*

    "   *Colonial Era.*

ELLIOT. *State and Church.*

FOWLER. *Life of John Locke.*

MORLEY. *Life of Burke.*

SCHAFF. *Religious Liberty.* (Article in Pub. of Am. Hist. Assoc., 1886–1887.)

ANDERSON. *History of the Colonial Church.*

HAWKS. *Contributions to Ecclesiastical History.*

CAMPBELL. *History of Virginia.*

FISKE. *Beginnings of New England.*

" *Old Virginia and her Neighbors.*

" *Dutch and Quaker Colonies.*

FORCE. *Historical Tracts.*

MASSACHUSETTS HISTORICAL SOCIETY: *Collections.*

HENING. *Statutes of Virginia.*

STITH. *History of Virginia.*

BURKE. *History of Virginia.*

HOWISON. *History of Virginia.*

VIRGINIA HISTORICAL SOCIETY : *Collections.*

MEADE. *Old Churches and Families of Virginia.*

FOOTE. *Sketches of Virginia.*

SPRAGUE. *Annals of the American Pulpit.*

Johns Hopkins Studies.

NORTH CAROLINA : *Records.*

SOUTH CAROLINA : *Statutes.*

BYRD. *Manuscripts.*

LORD BACON. *Works.*

HUTCHINSON. *History of Massachusetts Bay.*

" *Collections.*

PLYMOUTH COLONY : *Laws.*

PALFREY. *Compendious History of New England.*

YOUNG. *Chronicles of the Pilgrim Fathers.*

" *Chronicles of Massachusetts.*

BRADFORD. *History of Plymouth.*

BARRY. *History of Massachusetts.*

WINTHROP, R. C. *Life and Letters of John Winthrop.*

WINTHROP, JOHN. *Journal.*

MORTON. *Memorial.*

LOWELL INSTITUTE : *Lectures.*

PRINCE. *Annals.*

ADAMS. *Three Episodes in Massachusetts History.*

DOYLE. *The English in America.*

WEEDEN. *Social and Economic History of New England.*

DAVENPORT. *Life of John Cotton.*

MASSACHUSETTS : *Records.*

MASSACHUSETTS : *Colony Laws.*

ELLIS. *Puritan Age.*

PARKER. *Massachusetts and her Early History.*

ARNOLD. *History of Rhode Island.*

Colonial History of New York.

Documentary History of New York.

ADAMS. *Emancipation of Massachusetts.*

MATHER. *Magnalia*

SEWELL. *Diary.*

BAIRD. *Religion in America.*

CONNECTICUT : *Colonial Record.*

CONNECTICUT HISTORICAL SOCIETY : *Collections.*

NEW HAVEN HISTORICAL SOCIETY : *Papers.*

Cambridge and Saybrook Platforms.

Letters to Connecticut Governors.

BARBER. *Historical Collections.*

ANDREWS. *Moravians in Kent.* (Am. Church Rev., 1880.)

NEW HAVEN : *Colonial Records.*

JOHNSTON. *History of Connecticut.*

WOLCOTT. *Memorial of Connecticut.*

STANLEY. *Westminster Abbey.*

BARSTOW. *History of New Hampshire.*

NEW HAMPSHIRE HISTORICAL SOCIETY : *Collections.*

BELKNAP. *History of New Hampshire.*

McCLINTOCK. *History of New Hampshire.*

NEW HAMPSHIRE : *Provincial Papers.*

O'CALLAGHAN. *History of New Netherland.*

Laws of New Netherland.

CORWIN. *History of the Reformed Church.*

SMITH. *History of New York.*

COBB. *Story of the Palatines.*

Colonial Laws of New York.

NEW YORK : *Legislative Journal.*

HOFFMAN. *Ecclesiastical Law in the State of New York.*

STRONG. *History of Flatbush.*

JOHNSON. *Foundation of Maryland.*

MARYLAND : *Acts of Assembly.*

MARYLAND HISTORICAL SOCIETY : *Publications.*

SCHARF. *History of Maryland.*

PERRY. *Historical Collections.*

SMITH. *History of New Jersey.*

NEW JERSEY : *Archives.*

STEVENS. *History of Georgia.*

HUBBARD. *History of New England.*

PENNSYLVANIA : *Charter and Laws.*

PENNSYLVANIA : *Colonial Records.*

PENNSYLVANIA : *Archives.*

PROUD. *History of Pennsylvania.*

STILLÉ. *Religious Tests in Pennsylvania.* (Penn. Hist. Mag. IX.)

Laws of Delaware.

DEMAREST. *History of the Reformed Church.*

BEARDSLEY. *The Episcopal Church in Connecticut.*

Letters by an Anti-Episcopalian.

CHANDLER. *Appeal in behalf of the Church of England in America.*

DE TOCQUEVILLE. *Democracy in America.*

JOHN ADAMS. *Works.*

JONATHAN EDWARDS. *Works.*

ALLEN. *Life of Edwards.*

RIVES. *Life of Madison.*

JEFFERSON. *Works.*

ELLIOTT. *Debates.*

SHEPHERD. *Statutes at Large.*

SERGEANT AND RAWLE. *Reports.*

STIMSON. *American Statute Law.*

WINSOR. *Narrative and Critical History of the United States.*

ROOSEVELT. *Life of Gouverneur Morris.*

TYLER, M. C. *Life of Patrick Henry.*

RISE OF RELIGIOUS LIBERTY

I

THE AMERICAN PRINCIPLE

THE history of religion and the Church in America, as these stand related to the civil government, presents features unparalleled in the rest of Christendom, and marks a sharp contrast with the religious and ecclesiastical history of Europe. Its resultant principle of Liberty on which religious institutions and life in the United States are founded to-day, is thus a peculiarly American production. This principle, cutting right across that which the Old World had for all the Christian centuries regarded as axiomatic, illustrates, better than aught else, the profound remark of Bancroft : —

" American law was the growth of necessity, not the wisdom of individuals. It was not an acquisition from abroad; it was begotten from the American mind, of which it was a natural and inevitable, but also a slow and gradual development." [1] America explicitly set aside all the old-time theories of Church and State. In varying forms these had obtained universal rule. There were differing policies of union or of control; of alliance, as of two equal parties; of Church dictation to the state, of state government over the Church; of interference by both with the conscience and faith of the individual. The basic idea of them all assumed the necessity of a vital relation between Church and State; an idea accepted by European churchmen, theologians, statesmen, jurists, and publicists, with scarce an exception, from the

Church and State.

[1] *History of the United States*, VII, 354, 23rd (8 vol.) edition, Boston, 1864.

1

time of Constantine to that of Jefferson. In clear denial of
all such theories, the American principle declared them and
their fundamental idea to be oppressions of conscience and
abridgments of that liberty which God and nature had conferred on every living soul.

Definition.

With such denial, this new principle defined that, neither
should the Church dictate to the state, as having peremptory
spiritual jurisdiction over things civil; nor should the state
interfere with the Church in its freedom of creed or of worship, in its exercise of ordination and spiritual discipline;
nor yet again should the individual be subjected to any
influence from the civil government toward the formation
or refusal of religious opinions or as regards his conduct
thereunder, unless such conduct should endanger the moral
order or safety of society.

Thus by whatever causes promoted, into which it will be
our study to look, this revolutionary principle, declarative
of the complete separation of Church from state, so startlingly
in contrast with the principles which had dominated the past
— this pure Religious Liberty — may be confidently reckoned
as of distinctly American origin. Individuals there had
been, whose thought had reached to the natural right of this
principle; governments and peoples had asserted and maintained for themselves freedom from all alien religious dictation; but it was reserved for the people and governments of
this last settled among the lands to announce the religious
equality of all men and all creeds before the law, without
preference and without distinction or disqualification. Here,
among all the benefits to mankind to which this soil has
given rise, this pure religious liberty may be justly rated as
the great gift of America to civilization and the world, having among principles of governmental policy no equal for
moral insight, and for recognition both of the dignity of the
human soul and the spiritual majesty of the Church of God.

An Ameri-
can idea.

To the average American citizen of to-day it may not at
once appear that this religious liberty, as defined in the law

and life of this land, is to be thus characterized as of distinctly American origin. We have been born and nurtured in its atmosphere, without questioning its source or analyzing its constituents. As with other natural rights, no doubt has affected the mind with regard to its propriety and justice. It is like the air we breathe, breathed and unthought of, save when some hostile element asserts itself. For the most part, its coming into the public life was so gradual and in so quiet fashion, that no challenge was given to the attention of the people. Save in New England, where Puritan exclusiveness struggled to hinder its approach; and in Virginia, where the "gentlemanly conformity to the Church of England" was impatient of dissent ; and yet again, for two short periods, in New York, where the fanatical folly of Dutch and English governors led to cruelty and oppression, — the people of the colonies at large were scarce cognizant of the process by which this principle was gradually taking such place in their thought and life, that in the ripeness of time it should be crystallized in the fundamental law.

Happily for the people, their rights of conscience were never forced in this country to appeal to arms, and the soil of America was never drenched, as were so many battle- Persecution. fields in the Old World, with the blood of men fighting and dying for conscience and creed. There were some cases of wicked cruelty. Colonial law, judicial action, and official spite were not always free from the spirit and the severe act of persecution. But the instances were rare, and bore no comparison with the ruthless and sweeping cruelty which turned Holland, England, and Scotland into houses of mourning. Of these few instances of colonial persecution it is folly to speak in apologetic terms. The significant thing about them is, that they were speedily followed by such a revulsion of the public mind that the after-occurrence of similar cruelties was made forever impossible.

So it was that the religious liberty of America grew quietly. Differentiating itself from all systems of mutual relationship between religion and law ever known in the world before, save for a short period in the age of Constantine, it came to its right and place almost without observation. It also did its work so well as to put upon its conclusions the force and effect of axioms, assuming to the universal American mind so self-evident and natural demonstration as to promote surprise that there should be any to deny their value and necessity.

Of course, this idea of growth implies that the principle of liberty in religious matters did not assert itself, save in one

Growth. instance, at once that American colonization was begun. For the most part, the founders of the various colonies came to this country imbued with the ideas concerning the relations between government and religion, which had been universal in Europe. He who voiced the exception noted, stood in marked contrast with all churchmen and all statesmen of his time. They, with one consent, agreed that the lines of civil and ecclesiastical establishment should intersect, with more or less of dependence of one upon the other, and more or less of direction of one by the other. As we shall see in the next chapter, there were differing phases of this general and underlying principle, according as one or other factor rose to the ascendancy.

This principle was not called in question by the Reformation, which lost so many provinces to Rome. It met only the dissent of despised Anabaptists and Separatists. It lay in the general mind as an axiom not to be doubted for a moment, and with the force of its unquestioned assumption the fathers of New England, New York, Virginia, and Carolina, laid the foundations of their new home and government on these western shores.

Roger Williams. This makes the attitude of our American exception, Roger Williams, the more striking and significant. More than one hundred years in advance of his time, he denied the entire theory and practice of the past. To his mind it was alike unphilosophical and unchristian; on the one hand, an invasion of the natural spiritual liberty of man, and on the other, an unwarranted intrusion of human authority into realms where the divine sovereignty should alone hold sway.

Because he was so far in advance of his age, it is not surprising that Williams had not fully thought out all the details of his revolutionary principle and in some respects failed, at the outset of his colonial efforts, to discern some of the limitations needful to the integrity and solidarity of society.[1] Nor is it surprising that, in the first decades of Providence and Rhode Island, there should have resorted thither, not only the serious dissenters from the surrounding theocracies of New England, but also many whose restless spirits were hostile to all wholesome restraint. The excess of their ideas of liberty prevented that fraternal union which is a necessity for all organization, whether civil or religious. In some instances there was an impatience of all law, and an unwillingness to submit to that subordination, which is a condition not only of social permanence but also of the continuance of liberty itself.

The occurrence of such unrest in these early years of Williams' colony, though all the circumstances of the age made it both natural and inevitable, has often seemed to obscure the glory of this great apostle of spiritual liberty. But this is notably unjust. Not in a day will the enunciation of a new principle, especially if it be radical and revolutionary, lodge itself in the minds of men with all those details of regulated application to which only experience can give form and authority. To the glory of Williams it remains true, that far deeper than any men of his age he looked into the laws of God and spiritual life and into the human soul; that, as a voice crying in the wilderness, he hesitated not to proclaim a truth, against which the powers of Church and State were alike arrayed; that he refused not to endure cold and hunger and nakedness, and the loss of friends and home, for the sake of this truth; and that in the very early days of this western world he lifted up an ensign for the

[1] Felt, *Ecclesiastical History of New England*, II, 294.

people to proclaim true liberty of soul.   There is nothing to detract from that glory—the glory of the prophet who afar off tells of the blessing which is to come.

It is significant, with an import unequalled by any other element in colonial conditions, that at the very beginning this standard should be raised, to be at first derided and driven out; then to be tolerated; and at last, as the promise of what the spiritual mission of America was to be, to win to itself the fealty and following of every portion of the land.   To have discovered and preached that truth of the liberty of soul, so that in the blessing of it all after generations have rejoiced, places Williams among the few great benefactors of the race, and among the earlier founders of the American Republic, with whatever equals, surely without any superior.

Contents of Liberty.

The idea of a pure religious liberty, such as obtains in the United States and is guaranteed in the national constitution and the constitutions of the various states, seems at the first glance to be simple.   Resting upon the fundamental truth that God alone is Lord of the conscience, all its consequents flow naturally and logically therefrom.   In the light of history, however, with the countless interferences of the civil power, and with the age-long struggle to ascertain and effect this liberty, the idea has become complex and demands some points of definition.

Freedom of Conscience.

A not uncommon confusion of thought holds Freedom of Conscience as a synonym for this liberty.   But they are not the same.   To establish the parallel we need to add to this freedom of conscience its exercise in outward expression.   In reality the conscience is always free, and the mind is free.   No power on earth can compel the conscience or the mind.

> "The man convinced against his will
> Is of the same opinion still."

The civil power may reach to silencing the expression of that opinion, but cannot force the intellectual espousal of its opposite.   It may compel conformity to the expression of a creed and the exercise of a certain form of worship, but it cannot transmute unbelief into faith, or to the inner consciousness change the nature of moral convictions.

On this point Dr. Francis Lieber well and tersely says:—

"Conscience lies beyond the reach of government. 'Thoughts are free,' is an old German Law. The same must be said of feelings and conscience. That which government, even the most despotic, can alone interfere with, is the *profession* of religion, worship, and church government."[1]

In the "Political Tractate" of Spinoza, published after his death, is a very curious appeal to this inalienable freedom of conscience, as a reason for submission by the citizen to governmental regulation of outward religious matters. Having urged that the safety of society required that the state should direct all public faith and worship, he meets the argument from conscience with the words, "The *mind* of the individual belongs to himself, not to the state. Wherever I am, I can worship God and cultivate religion in my heart, and can look after my own conduct; and that is the business of the private citizen. The care of spreading that religion is to be handed over to God and to the supreme powers, for to them alone it belongs to care for the community." The sophistical character of this argument is abundantly evident, yet the distinction made as to the inalienable freedom of mind is true as it is acute. Only when the outspeaking of faith or thought demands that it be untrammelled by civil power, and only when the demand of conscience reaches to the outward exercise of worship in whatever forms shall seem best to the worshipper, does the freedom of conscience assume the larger dignity of religious liberty.

Another mistaken conception, not unfrequently coming to speech, is the likening of religious liberty to Toleration. This mistake is gross, for the two things are irreconcilably at odds. It may be true enough that a toleration may be so

Toleration.

----

[1] *Civil Liberty and Self Government*, I, 118, *Note.*

broad as to furnish both safety and comfort to the followers of a tolerated religion, and yet the principle on which that toleration is granted, is the precise denial of the principle which underlies the idea of religious liberty. Religious liberty asserts the equality of all; that in the matters of religion all men are equal before God and the law. Quite opposite from this, toleration assumes that all are not equal, that one form of religion has a better right, while for the sake of peace it consents that they who differ from it shall be allowed to worship as shall best please themselves.

Toleration, then, is a gift from a superior to one who is supposed to occupy a lower station in the scale of rights. We are compelled at times to tolerate that which is incontestably evil, for the reason simply that we cannot abate it. Indeed, this is in the very meaning of the word. To tolerate is to endure — to bear a burden, from which one would gladly be freed. The follower of any religion in a hostile environment may be very thankful for the toleration which permits the free exercise of his worship, with whatever limitation of civil rights it may involve. But if he understands himself, the nature of religion, and the true foundation of human rights, he will recognize in that toleration itself an unjust burden, the imposition of which is an outrage to the dignity of the soul. He will bear that burden only so long as he must, and will labor and pray unsatisfied until, in the recognition of his equal right with all, he shall deem himself to have obtained outwardly as inwardly, that liberty with which Christ makes His people free.

This thought of toleration was finely expressed by Lord Stanhope in the house of lords, during the debate of 1827, on the bill for the repeal of the " Test and Corporation Acts." " The time was," he said, " when toleration was craved by dissenters as a boon; it is now demanded as a right; but the time will come when it will be spurned as an insult." Says Paine, " Toleration is not the opposite of intolerance, but is the counterfeit of it. Both are despotisms: the one assumes to itself the right of withholding liberty of conscience, the other of granting it." [1]

" In liberty of conscience I include much more than toleration. Christ has established a perfect equality among His followers. It is therefore presumption in any of them to claim a right to any supremacy or preëminence over their brethren. Such a claim is implied whenever any of them pretend to *tolerate* the rest. Toleration can take place only when there is a civil establishment of a particular mode of religion . . . (which) thinks fit to suffer the exercise of other modes." [2]

There were times in the colonial history of America when the word *toleration* could be used in description of the governmental attitude towards certain forms of religious faith and worship. Thus, after many struggles, the authorities of Massachusetts concluded to tolerate Episcopalians and Baptists, while the Presbyterians were compelled to be satisfied for many years with the more or less liberal toleration of New York and Virginia. But for over a hundred years there has been neither place nor need for toleration in these states, where the religious equality of all men before the law is made a corner-stone in the foundation of rights.

The true definition of religious liberty is to be sought in two things: its origination in the will of God as Maker of the human soul, and its relation to the civil law. That God so breathed the living spirit into man as to constitute Himself the only law-giver of its life, may be here assumed without discussion. Our proper discussion arises about what civil society and law may have to say touching the exercise of this inalienable right conferred by God upon His creature. In every community it is the attitude of the law which defines Relation to the measure of religious liberty enjoyed. According as the Civil Law. civil law interferes with religious matters by direct control; by establishment of a State-Church; by preference of one

[1] *Rights of Man*, p. 58.
[2] Price, *Observations on the American Revolution*, p. 28.

form of religious organization to the prejudice of others ; by
exclusion from civil rights of the followers of any specified
form of religion ; or as it expressly abstains from all such
interference, preference or control, will the measure of
religious liberty be declared.

This relation to the civil law must be emphasized, as a not
infrequent confusion of thought grafts upon the idea of
religious liberty that which does not belong to it. By some
persons it is assumed that any process, of any kind, against
preachers of so-called heretical doctrine is an invasion of
Heresy. religious liberty. An ecclesiastical trial or sentence for heresy
is sometimes thus spoken of ; but there is no propriety in
such representation, which confounds two different relation-
ships. A man's membership in a church is not the same as
citizenship ; and yet there is this likeness, that both demand
loyalty. If he break the civil law, he is rightly punished. So
if he prove false to the Church, of which he is a member, he
can justly be proceeded against. While the civil law has no
jurisdiction in religious matters, it yet must hold true that the
Church must have its own law to guard and maintain its
purity. So long as no law compels a man to be in a Church,
there is no injustice in the requirement that, while he is in a
Church, he shall not teach doctrine subversive of its faith or
polity. Such requirement is for the protection of the Church
itself and is in no sense an oppression of conscience. The
man is at liberty to withdraw. But of all this the civil law
takes no cognizance in this country.

Interfer- There are many degrees of interference by the civil law
ences. represented in the Christendom of to-day. At one extreme
Russia. stands Russia, with so exclusive an ecclesiastical establishment, under the direct and personal rule of the czar, that no
form of dissent is tolerated, save the Lutheranism of Finland;
while other religionists, such as the Stundists, are subjected
to the cruelties of a persecution almost equal to the bitterness
of fire and sword. At the other extreme is England, where,
though the individual finds no bonds to the following of any

faith and worship which his mind and conscience may approve, yet an established Church, existent by act of parliament and supported by public tax, marks a measure of state interference with religious matters notably below the standard of a pure religious liberty, such as the American understands that liberty to be.[1]

It needs to be noted, however, that while this relation to the civil government necessarily involves such interferences, and while the interferences are directly antagonistic to our American idea of liberty of the Church, yet it affects the Church only as an organization, and never, save in the lightest and most remote way, works aught that savors of religious oppression. Indeed, so far as concerns individual excursions into the outlying regions of faith, the tendency is towards a broader comprehensiveness than would be likely to obtain in a self-governing organization.

Thus, there is in the Church of England a singular com- England. pound of bondage and liberty; bondage to the state with respect to external order and function, and freedom to the individual in matters of faith. The result from centuries of growth, the home also of much that is sweetest and best in the treasures of spiritual life, the Church of England has endeared itself to the vast majority of Englishmen. Though to the American mind it presents many features which seem abatements from a true liberty of faith, it is yet not difficult to understand the mistaken lament of D'Israeli over the dis-

---

[1] It is a curious fact that in England, while the establishment of the Anglican Church determines the governmental preference and entails for its followers many valuable perquisites, yet by reason of that very establishment the Anglican Church, as a religious organization, is far less free than the dissenting Churches. Thus, it is not a self-governing body. It cannot alter its articles of faith or form of worship; it cannot choose its bishops and archbishops; it cannot issue to final decision any but the most insignificant cases of discipline; and it cannot cast out the most blatant heretic from its communion, be he infidel or pagan, without the appointment or approval of the civil government, or a formal act of parliament. From any sentence of its spiritual courts an appeal may lie to the king in council, whose decision either in approval or reversal is alone final.

establishment of the Irish Church in 1868, which he described as, "destroying that sacred union between Church and State which has hitherto been the chief means of our civilization, and is the only security for our religious liberty."

In distinction from all the degrees of union and mutual dependence between Church and State, which have ever obtained in the past or now exist in various parts of the Christian world, the American principle asserts an entire independence and separation, both as the Church might seek to control the organic action of the state, and as the state might affect to interfere with the faith or function of the Church.

Limitations. In their mutual relation, the Church is limited to the cultivation in the citizen of those virtues of order, truth, and righteousness, which shall mould good citizenship, and through that a righteous nation; while the state is confined to adjudication of such questions as involve the rights of property and of ecclesiastical corporations voluntarily formed under the statute law. The implied duty herein of the Church arises from the moral quality of its mission as a teacher of righteousness; while the duty of the state comes, not from religious considerations, but from its place as guardian of the good order of society.

The independence here asserted is complete in respect to all matters of faith, worship, and ecclesiastical action. The grounds of this independence may be well stated in the words of Roger Williams. Despite the occasional quaintness of his language, the one hundred years of struggle after his day and the following century of experiment and proof have not produced a better statement of the principle. Perhaps we might desire to change a phrase or two as possibly suggestive of exaggeration, but the general principle stands clear and is well defended.

"All civil states," writes Williams, "with their officers of justice, in their respective constitutions and administrations, are . . . *essentially civil*, and therefore not judges, governors, or defenders of the Spiritual, or Christian, State and worship. . . . It is the will and command of God that, since the coming of His Son, the Lord Jesus, a permission of the most Paganish, Jewish, Turkish, or anti-Christian consciences and worship be granted to all men, in all nations and countries; and they are only to be fought against with that sword which is only, in Soul matters able to conquer, to wit; the sword of the Spirit — the Word of God. . . . God requireth not an uniformity of religion to be enacted and enforced in any civil state; which enforced uniformity, sooner or later, is the greatest occasion of civil war, ravishing consciences, ⌐ersecution of Christ Jesus in His servants, and of the hypocrisy and destruction of millions of souls. . . . An enforced uniformity of religion throughout a nation or civil state confounds the civil and religious, denies the principles of Christianity and civility, and that Jesus Christ is come in the flesh." [1]

On a foundation so deep and broad as this did Williams essay the building of institutions wherein a universal and comprehensive liberty should dwell. " His work in life seems to have been that of transforming this sentiment [freedom of conscience] into a living force, and to him is due the honor of being the first who recognized it as a constitutional principle, and who actually created a polity that had it for a foundation stone." [2]

As is well known, these principles were far from meeting, in Williams' day, with general recognition and approval. Rather were they reprobated by the majority of colonists, while their teacher was subjected to exile and much affliction on their account. But he sowed his seed in good soil, wherein it took root and grew, until the whole land now dwells under the shadow of its stately tree of life. To the aid of his doctrine presently came Calvert, of whom it is hardly unjust to say, that the motive of his prescription of religious liberty may have been one rather of shrewd policy than of necessary

[1] *Bloody Tenent of Persecution*, 1, 2.
[2] Scott's *Constitutional Liberty*, p. 107.

moral principle. Within the half century Penn added his testimony of charity, clearly recognizing the principle of religious freedom and lifting up its standard in the heart of the colonies, though with some inconsistent restrictions.

From such beginnings the leaven worked throughout the whole lump of colonial life, gradually bringing under its influence, with but very few and weak exceptions, the mind of the entire people. There were many fostering circumstances. The conditions of life and society in the new world, where men had to found *de novo* their institutions, at great distance from the straitening influence of age-long prescription and custom, had much in them to abet impatience with whatever should seek to fetter free expansion. The character of much of the immigration went for the issue of liberty. The adventurous spirit out of which came, first, more or less of dissatisfaction with home conditions; and second, voluntary exile into new climes to meet hardness and danger, insensibly fitted the mind to the propositions of liberty. Almost from the very beginning the colonists assumed a larger political liberty than they had known, as the plain necessity of their colonial life. It is not strange that, in harmony with this new spirit, the conscience should presently seek to free itself from all bonds of human authority.

To this was added a natural resentment towards the foolish and arbitrary actions of the civil authorities in many questions of religious import. The unwise severity of theocratic Massachusetts revolted many of her own citizens. The brutalities of Berkeley in Virginia, and the impudent arrogance of Fletcher and Cornbury in New York, had large influence in preparing the people for the separation of religion from the care of the civil power. At the same time, the neglect of the Church of England in the colonies by the ecclesiastical authorities at home, the shameful personal character of the majority of its clergy in Maryland and Virginia, together with the absence of anything like efficient episcopal jurisdiction, resulted in strengthening the same feeling. To these

Marginal note: Fostering circumstances.

still another factor was added in the number of sects, no one
of which, outside of Massachusetts and Connecticut, embraced the majority of the population, so that it was impossible
to continue to any one the preference of the civil power,
without entailing the animosity of all the rest. Doubtless
also much was due to the religious indifference so widely
existent in the period of the later colonial and the revolutionary eras.[1]

By reason of such general and many minor influences, the
education of the people in the principles of religious liberty
was equal-paced with that which issued in political independence; so that together with the doctrine, that the American
state should no longer owe allegiance to the mother country,
was also uttered the new and startling declaration, that the
American Church should henceforth be free from all dictation
and interference by the state.

It is well to bear in mind the several points of distinction *Points of*
which make up the American idea of religious liberty. Its *distinction.*
complete separation of state from Church involves that: —

1. The civil power has no authority in, or over, the individual or the Church, touching matters of faith, worship,
   order, discipline, or polity.
2. The Church has no power in the state to direct its policy
   or action, otherwise than its influence may be felt in
   the persuasion of the public mind towards the principles it teaches.
3. The state cannot appropriate public moneys to the
   Church, or for the propagation of religion, or any
   particular form of religion.
4. The Church cannot look to the state for any support of
   its worship or institutions, otherwise than, like all
   other corporations, it may appeal, and must submit,
   to legislation and judicial decisions in matters of
   pecuniary trusts and foundations, the ground of

[1] See Bacon's *American Christianity*, p. 221.

which legislation and decisions is not at all religious,
but strictly civil.

5. The civil power cannot exercise any preference among
the various churches or sects, but must hold all as
having equal rights under the law, and as equally
entitled to whatever protection under the law circumstances may furnish need for.

6. The civil power may not make any distinction among
citizens on account of religion, unless the following
thereof is dangerous to society. Neither the right to
vote nor to hold office is to be invalidated because of
opinions on the matter of religion. Nor, again, is a
citizen's right to bear witness, or to inherit property
to be called in question for reasons of religion.

Thus the severance of state from Church — of the civil power
from all efficient concernment for religion — is made thorough
to the minutest detail. As Story somewhat boldly phrases
it,[1] "The Catholic and the Protestant, the Calvinist and the
Arminian, the Jew and the Infidel may sit down at the common table of the National Councils without any inquisition
into their faith and mode of worship."

Such is the peculiar contribution of America to the formative ideas of civilization, the rise of which and its formulation
in the fundamental law afford a study of great and varied interest. "Of all the differences between the Old World and
the New this is perhaps the most salient."[2] It is interesting
to note how thoroughly it permeated the social life and institutions of the people, and how, under the influence of its
beneficial ministry of a century and a quarter, it has so justified itself as to take in the mind of American jurists and publicists the form and dignity of inherent and self-evident truth.

Lieber. Thus writes Dr. Lieber,[3] "Liberty of Conscience, or, as it

[1] On *The Constitution*, Sec. 1880.
[2] Bryce, *American Commonwealth*, II, 554.
[3] *Civil Liberty and Self Government*, I, 118.

ought to be called more properly, the liberty of worship, is one of the primordial rights of man, and no system of liberty can be considered comprehensive, which does not include guarantees for the exercise of this right. It belongs to American liberty to separate entirely from the political government the institution which has for its object the support and diffusion of religion." In like manner, Kent declares,[1] Kent. "The free exercise and enjoyment of religious profession and worship may be considered as one of the absolute rights of the individual, recognized in our American Constitution and secured by law. Civil and religious liberty generally go hand in hand, and the suppression of either of them, for any length of time, will terminate the existence of the other." With similar thought Rawle, discoursing about statutory interfer- Rawle. ence with religion, says,[2] "Thus a human government interposes between the Creator and His creature, intercepts the devotion of the latter, or condescends to permit it only under political regulations. From injustice so gross and impiety so manifest multitudes sought an asylum in America, and hence she ought to be the hospitable and benign receiver of every variety of religious opinion." Thus also Judge Cooley writes, Cooley. "Nothing is more fully set forth or more plainly expressed (in the American Constitutions) than the determination of their authors to preserve and perpetuate religious liberty, and to guard against the slightest approach towards the establishment of any inequality in the civil and political rights of citizens, which shall have for its basis only their differences of religious belief. The American people came to the work of framing their fundamental laws after centuries of religious oppression and persecution — sometimes by one party or sect and sometimes by another — had taught the utter futility of all attempts to propagate religion by the rewards, penalties, or terrors of human law. They could not fail to perceive also that a union of Church and State like that which existed in

[1] *Commentaries*,— Part 4, Sec. 24.
[2] Rawle on *The Constitution*, p. 117.

England, if not wholly impracticable in America, was certainly opposed to the spirit of our institutions, and that any domineering of one sect over another was repressing to the energies of the people, and must necessarily tend to discontent and disorder." [1]

Such is the American principle of religious liberty, unique among the governmental policies of the world, the evolution of which in the colonial era it is the purpose of this present work to trace. In order to observe its spring and progress in true historical perspective, we shall do well to note some of the antecedent conditions, and to review the development and chief elements of the Old World Idea, in as brief space as the subject will permit.

[1] Cooley, *Constitutional Limitations*, p. 371. Cf. von Holst, *Constitutional History of U. S.*, v. 103, vi. 260.

II

THE OLD WORLD IDEA

THAT questions as to the relation between things religious and things political have occupied large space in the history of Europe, is evident to the most casual reader. It will be difficult, indeed, to find any other question so important, so insistent for solution, so widely affecting society, and so efficient in guiding historic development. Thus, in very emphatic words, Ranke declares, " The whole life and character of Western Christendom consists of the constant action and counteraction of Church and State." From the beginning of the Christian state it was assumed that, among its first duties and missions was care for the interests of the Church or submission to its demands; and it was soon made evident that the union between the two was so intimate that, whatever became of interest to the one was matter for action by the other. In all matters of peace and war, in all arrangements of society, in all movements and policies of government, and in all popular ferments, the loudest and most imperative voice came either from this settled principle of union, or from the determined efforts to shake off its bonds.

This thought is expressed by Story in perhaps somewhat exaggerated language : [1] " Half the calamities, with which the human race has been scourged, have arisen from the Union of Church and State." If the view were confined to that portion of the race which has dwelt under European institutions, we might accept the statement without great reduction of its terms. Such is the more guarded expression of Bryce : [2]

[1] On the *Constitution of United States*, Sec. 622.
[2] *American Commonwealth*, II, 554.

19

"Half the wars of Europe, half the internal troubles that have vexed the European States, from the Monophysite controversies in the Roman Empire of the fifth century down to the Kultur Kampf in the German Empire of the nineteenth, have arisen from theological differences, or from rival claims of Church and State."

To thoroughly understand, then, the character of the unique development of the American principle of entire separation, and to appreciate the gravity of the revolution thereby introduced, the student must hold in mind the more salient features of the European principle and its development. At the outset, also, it must be noted that the study is necessarily confined almost entirely to western Christendom. The eastern Church, resigned to the protection of the empire, sank into dependence and subsequent decadence, alien to those movements of thought and purpose out of which struggle and advancement come. It was content to be the servant and creature of the state.

Quite diversely, the western Church, cast on its own resources of courage, faith, and resolution by the destruction of the empire, grew increasingly virile and ambitious as the centuries advanced. The sole saviour of society in the midst of the chaos of empire, it found itself guide and arbiter in countless matters other than those which concerned faith and worship. It is not strange that its ambition, thus nurtured, should reach to the complete mastership over kings, governments, and people. Nor is it strange that, with the resettlement of society and the growing consciousness of national life, there should arise struggle and revolt against an exacting ecclesiasticism — a revolt to which the Renaissance of art and letters, with its logical consequent of the Reformation, added both strength and variety.

A Christian Problem. From the nature of the case the problem of Church and State is entirely Christian. It could arise only within the pale of a Christian society, more or less civilized and advanced. To the Hebrew *cultus* it was unknown, and its propositions would be unintelligible. The Hebrew State and Church were one, merged together, not as by union of two distinct entities, but as the component factors of one substance, neither of which could exist without the other. This finds illustration throughout Hebrew history, both in that divine institution wherein the civil and the ecclesiastical law are seen to be identical, and in those results of recurrent impiety, which instantly entailed rational degradation only to be retrieved by a revival of religion. Thus, the Hebrew state was set as the embodiment of the supreme religion. God was declared the Ruler and Head, not only as He is the Governor of all the nations, but as the recognized *constitutional* Source of all authority for the Hebrew in things secular and things religious. David was the viceroy of the true King of Israel, and his realm constituted the visible Church of God — a genuine Theocracy. *The Hebrew Theocracy.*

In the heathen world other conditions were exclusive of our Christian problem. Religions were many, differing not alone in service and customs in different lands, but also in the names and characters of the gods and goddesses who dwelt in the mythological heavens. Their literature was an aggregation of myth and fable, here and there underlaid by a more or less recondite philosophy. But of institutional character, with system of doctrine, and channels of settled polity, the religion was entirely destitute. Making no pretence to a divine statement or foundation, the religion of a people was at the caprice of superstition and of the conditions of life under various climes. Out of the cold north, sterile and forbidding, issued Odin and Thor, with their hammer and fire; while Aphrodite, rising from the southern sea, invited the lusts of Olympus. In the far east, the Persian and Vedantic philosophies reached to immensely higher principles and, discoursing on the meaning of life, sought to nurture the moral powers of men. But in all there was no such thing as systematized organization, nothing that resembled the embodied Church. What religious *institutions* *Pagan Conditions.*

existed in any land were the creation of the governing power.

It was only when Christ came, establishing a kingdom in the world, which should be amid the kingdoms of earth and as leaven penetrate throughout them all, and yet saying, "My kingdom is not of this world," that the possibility arose of any such question as that of the mutual relations of Church and State.

The question, indeed, did not come to expression at the beginning of the Church. The conditions of the problem required the existence, side by side, of the two institutions of Church and State, each recognizing the other, and each having an inherent right to be and to exercise its functions, with more or less of independence, according as the prevalent solution or compact should decide. But such conditions did not obtain during the first three centuries of the Church. The state did not recognize the Church, seeing in it no institution with inherent right to be. Its very existence was an infraction of the imperial edict against associations. Its assemblies were simply gatherings of the followers of a pestilent and dangerous doctrine, which should be forbidden and destroyed — a *religio illicita*. Thus, for three hundred years the only relation between the two was that of disapproval and denunciation by the civil power, asserting itself with varying intensity as the dispositions of successive emperors desired; now in long periods of inactive contempt, and again in waves of most cruel and widespread persecution.

Meanwhile, the doctrine spread itself throughout the empire; "So mightily the word of God grew and prevailed."[1] It penetrated among all the provinces, claimed its votaries in the imperial palace, honey-combed the army, and counted its adherents by the hundred thousand.

It had founded, also, and elaborated a permanent polity and order with episcopal and presbyterial powers, vigorous with life, — an organization that had clearly come into the world to

---

[1] *Acts* xix, 20.

stay, and making no secret of its mission and desire to reclaim that world to the service of its own Master. Never was
an aim more glorious and never a progress more magnificent.
Undeterred by the prohibitions of law or the cruelties of fire
and sword, bearing the burden of persecution without a
thought of violent resistance, it yet lifted up its testimony for
Christ after so persuasive fashion, that it were difficult to tell
whether at the end of the third century the people of the
Roman Empire were more heathen or Christian.

Out of either the recognition or the fear of this situation
came the persecution of Diocletian, the last of the persecutions Diocletian.
and the most severe in its terms and acts. In this it was like
the dying throes of a monster, whose bitterness of spirit
increases as his power wanes. In the year 303 Diocletian
issued a series of edicts, the terms of which indicate the
despairing and yet determined effort to root out every vestige
of the Christian faith and Church. " By these enactments all
Christian assemblies were prohibited ; all churches were to be
demolished ; all copies of the Scriptures to be burned ; all
Christians who held rank or office to be degraded ; all of
whatever rank to lose their citizenship, and be liable like
slaves to the torture ; Christian slaves were to be incapable
of receiving freedom ; all bishops and clergy were to be thrown
into prison and there compelled to sacrifice ; and all Christians
everywhere ordered publicly to worship the gods, under the
usual penalty of torture and death." [1]

The severity of these edicts marks the extreme of imperial
proscription, giving way in a few years to a liberal policy of
toleration equally extreme and sudden. This change of atti- Toleration
tude and disposition is indicated by the edict of Galerius in of Galerius.
the year 311, which at once put an end to persecution, and
opened the new era of toleration and freedom. The edict,
while declaring the purity of motive, " to regulate everything
according to the ancient laws and public discipline of the
Romans," as a justifying reason for the persecution, at the

[1] Innes, *Church and State*, p. 19.

same time acknowledges that the Christians had become so numerous and were so tenacious of their faith, as to render futile all efforts towards the repression of their religion. Therefore, the edict recites, " We have come to the conclusion that the most frank and open toleration should be extended to them, to the effect that they may now again be allowed to be Christians, and gather together in their societies; provided, however, that they take no action against the religion of the State." [1]

This was a long step towards the freedom of the Church, a complete liberty of conscience and worship to whomsoever should elect to be Christian. Christianity, long proscribed, now takes its place by the side of Judaism as a *religio licita*.

But not long did it remain in such condition of humble sufferance by a heathen power. The strides by which the Church passed from the state of bondage to that of emancipation, and thence to empire, were few and rapid. Hardly had Galerius published his edict of toleration when death removed Constantine. him from the throne; and in the next year, 312, Constantine, having conquered his rival Maxentius in the battle of the Milvian Bridge, ascended the throne as sole emperor of the west. It is in the night before the battle that legend places the vision of the cross with its motto, " *In hoc signo vinces.*" However much truth the legend holds, it seems to be the fact that in the battle the soldiers of Constantine bore a banner with the sign of the cross. Without any such vision it might well be that such banner should appear in an army, a large constituency of which was Christian, while Constantine himself was disposed, not only to toleration, but to the Christian faith.

Educated in the principles of Neo-Platonism, he had no faith in the gods of Rome and Greece, and was ready to accord to Christianity a broad and philosophic tolerance at the very outset of his career. His high order of statesmanship at once recognized it as an element to be reckoned with, not with the

[1] Innes, p. 22.

sword of repression, but with such enactments of law as should assert its right to come into the public life, and to open for its doctrine the fullest freedom of speech and discipleship. Nor was it long before his own mind, convinced of the truth of that doctrine, led him to give the adhesion of his personal faith.

It is to be noted that, while the edict of Galerius gave to Christianity the fullest toleration, yet Paganism still remained the religion of the state, the *established* religion, so far as the thought of establishment can be applied to the situation. This condition continued but two years. In the year 313 Constantine met at Milan Licinius, the emperor of the east, and then the two monarchs issued the famous proclamation known as the "Edict of Milan." By this edict was established the fullest Edict of toleration of all religions and freedom of worship, without Milan. hindrance from the state and without preference by the state of one religion before another. Its terms are most broad and explicit. It gives "both to the Christians and to all others free power of following whatever religion each man may have preferred. . . . The absolute power is to be denied to no one to give himself either to the worship of the Christians, or to that religion which he thinks most suited to himself, . . . that each may have the free liberty of the worship which he prefers; for we desire that no religion may have its honor diminished by us." The edict not only declares this freedom of the individual conscience and worship, but accords it to all religious associations and institutions, and in addition ordains that the losses of property sustained by the Churches in the recent persecutions should be made good to them.

By this edict was "introduced a universal and unconditional religious freedom," in the enactment of which, as Innes remarks, "two points are to be noticed: 1st. It was the chief act of disestablishment in history. Paganism was disestablished throughout the Empire. 2d. No religion is established by it."[1]

[1] *Church and State*, p. 25.

This may be recognized as the ordination of the fullest religious liberty the world has known until the foundation of the American republic. Its enactment is one of the marvels of history, so diverse from all that had preceded and from all that followed. Its continuance of the policy was short lived, enduring but little longer than a single generation, but it remains an object-lesson to all subsequent history.

Though the edict of Milan was issued in the name of both emperors, it expressed the will of Constantine alone, whose greater force of character had overborne Licinius. Despite this enforced consent of Licinius to the principles of toleration, he remained attached to the pagan religion, and in his own dominion of the east took many measures hostile to religious freedom and to Christianity. He encouraged the exercise of heathen worship and endeavored to suppress the Christian, sentencing many Christians to exile and slavery. This anti-Christian attitude of Licinius served as fuel to the flame of jealousy between Constantine and himself, and became a strong cause of the war between the two emperors, which broke out in 323, and in which Constantine completely destroyed the power of Licinius, uniting in his own person the empire of the entire Roman world.

He was now in a position to give world-wide effect to his views of religious policy. Himself more pronouncedly Christtian than in the past, confessing his faith in God and in Jesus Christ, he yet stands clear from all narrowness of view as to individual liberty of religion. At once that he assumed the sovereignty of the empire of Licinius he issued the famous "Proclamation to the Peoples of the East," in which he emphasized the principles of toleration in the edict of Milan, and explained them with larger and more exact detail. The form of the proclamation is unique. It is not couched in the ordinary terms of a governmental edict, but in the forms of religious address, conveying the expression of the emperor's own faith and the religious reasons which controlled his action. Thus, the immediate address of the edict is not to

Proclamation to the Peoples of the East.

the people, but to God Himself, and it becomes on the part of Constantine a covenant with God for the policy his government assumes towards questions of religion. The specially significant passages to be here cited are as follows : —

"I hasten, O God, to put my shoulder to the work of restoring Thy most holy house, which profane and impious princes have marred by their violence. But I desire that my people should live at peace and in concord, and that for the common good of the world and for the advantage of mankind. Let the followers of error enjoy the same peace and security with those who believe : this very restoration of common privileges will be powerful to lead men towards the road of truth. Let no one molest his neighbor. What the soul of each man counsels him, that let him do. Only let men of sound judgment be assured that those alone will live a life of holiness and purity whom Thou callest to find rest in Thy holy laws. But for the others, who keep apart from us, let them, if they please, retain the temples of falsehood. We have the resplendent house of Thy truth given us as our inheritance. But this we pray for them also, that they may come to share the gladness of a common belief. . . . Let all men henceforth enjoy the privilege placed within our reach, *i.e.* the blessing of peace ; and let us keep our consciences far from what might hinder it. Whatever truth a man has received and been persuaded of, let him not smite his neighbor with it. Rather, whatever he has himself seen and understood, let him help his neighbor with it, if that is possible ; if it is not, let him desist from the attempt. For it is one thing to voluntarily undertake to wrestle for immortality ; it is another to constrain others to it by fear. These are my words, and I have enlarged on this more than my forbearance would have prompted, because I was unwilling that my trust in the true faith should remain secret and hidden." [1]

The terms of this proclamation leave nothing to be desired, and the reader of it is impressed alike by its breadth and the

[1] Innes, p. 30.

deep spiritual insight it declares. That the privilege of freedom would "lead men towards the road of truth"; that "to
constrain by fear" is no proper means of conversion; and that
conscience demands for all men what it demands for itself;
are truths which speak to us out of the turmoil of the fourth
century with startling accents, soon condemned to silence
until fourteen hundred years should give them voice again,
in a far distant land.

For the most part Constantine adhered to this policy of
religious liberty with admirable consistency. The most glaring
infraction was legislation against conversion to Judaism,
threatening such converts with "deserved pains." This was
accompanied by the denunciation of death to Jews for stoning
converts from their own faith to Christianity and may be
looked upon as reprisal for their persecuting actions. Moreover, it was issued in the year 315, after the edict of Milan,
but eight years before the broader Proclamation to the Peoples
of the East.

Undoubtedly the strong moral influence of Constantine was
exerted for the furtherance of Christianity. He founded
Constantinople on the site of old Byzantium as a Christian
city. He turned "to Christian uses the revenues of some of
the less frequented heathen temples." He presided in Church
councils and often brought his personal power to bear in the
decision of controversies in the Church. But he never
attempted to constrain the religious preferences of his subjects, never forbade heathen sacrifices or service, and never
established Christianity as the religion of the state.

At the same time, it is true that his personal influence
towards the furtherance of the Christian faith had been so
constantly exerted, that the whole moral weight of government, devoid of all enactment, was thrown into that scale.
Beyond that he could not go. Of a profoundly philosophical
habit of mind, he was far removed from the disposition of the
persecutor. He reverenced not only the majesty, but the
dignity of human nature, and though with advancing years

his own persuasion of the Christian truth became constantly firmer, he yet maintained and defended the rights of the individual conscience. This makes the attitude of Constantine altogether unique in history, until it is resembled by Williams and American statesmen of the eighteenth century. Desirous as a Christian ruler that all his subjects should be enlightened by the gospel, he yet never resorted to his imperial power to force that issue, recognizing the fundamental truth, to which the following centuries were blind, that only by the inner persuasion of the mind could the truth prevail.

It was impossible that the successors of Constantine should have equally broad conceptions. Of far lower powers, to them the personal addiction of their father to the Christian faith seemed by logical and natural consequence to demand resort to power for its advancement, and to those measures of repression and enactment from which he had scrupulously abstained. He died A.D. 337, leaving the throne to his sons Constans and Constantius, who almost at once began to draw upon their imperial power to discourage paganism and advance the Christian doctrine. Thus, four years after their father's death, they issued the first decree against the old religion; "Let superstition cease; let the madness of sacrifices be abolished." In 353 Constantius alone ordered that all the heathen temples should be closed, saying, "We will that all abstain from sacrifices: if any be found doing otherwise, let him be slain with the sword." [1] Repression of Heathenism.

The natural issue of such policy was the formal establishment of Christianity as the religion of the state, but it was delayed for a quarter of a century. A slight reaction followed under Julian, whose preferences for the pagan religion endeavored to make themselves felt, though the shortness of his reign hindered his efforts from their desired effectiveness. His successors, Jovian in the east and Valentinian in the west, reasserted the just balance instituted by Constantine, and not until 380 did the Christian doctrine assume the purple. In

[1] Innes, p. 33.

that year Theodosius the Great, being baptized, accompanied
the confession of his personal faith with a decree establishing
Christianity as the religion of the whole empire.   This edict,
in which Gratian and Valentinian were associated with Theo-

Establish-
ment of
Christian-
ity.

dosius, declared, " We will that all the nations who are ruled
over by our moderation and clemency, shall cultivate and
exercise that religion which the divine Apostle Peter originally introduced and has since handed down to the inhabitants
of Rome, and which is publicly professed by the Pontiff
Damasus and by Peter, Bishop of Alexandria, . . . the belief of the one God-head of the Father, and the Son
and the Holy Spirit, under an equal majesty and under a
pious trinity, according to the teaching of the apostles and the
doctrine of the gospels. . . . Those who follow this doctrine
we authorize to assume the name of Catholic Christians ; and
all others, judging them to be senseless and insane, we
ordain to bear the infamy of holding heretical dogma ; nor
must their congregations assume the name of Churches.   On
the contrary, they must expect to be visited first by the divine
vengeance, and then by that also of the authority which
we have received from the will of heaven." [1]

The senate of Rome, which city remained predominantly
heathen, urged upon the emperors that liberty of sacrifice
should be allowed to the Romans.   This, it would seem, they
were at first disposed to grant, but gave way to the argument

Ambrose.

of the celebrated Ambrose of Milan : " Wrong is done to
none of your subjects when Almighty God is preferred before
him.   To Him belong your convictions, and you must carry
them out. . . .   If you advise pagan sacrifices, if you decree
sacrifices on the Roman altars you really offer those sacrifices
yourself; and after that idolatry the Church cannot receive
you.   Choose ; for you cannot serve two masters." [2]

Thus, for the first time, and that by the most masterful
Christian voice of the age, was uttered the specious principle
that the conscience of kings must be the law to the conscience

[1] Innes, pp. 35, 47.   [2] Innes, p. 37.

of subjects; that for kings alone among men their faith is as
well public as personal; and that upon them must rest
the responsibility for whatsoever errors in faith and practice
any of their subjects may be guilty of, unless they exert their
authority for the abatement and punishment of such errors.
This principle we shall see appearing in various guise, the informing principle in all effective union of Church and State.

The argument of the great bishop was effective. The
desire of the Roman senate was denied; and in the next few
years the emperors proceeded to enforce their decree of establishment. Valentinian, for the west, in 391 forbade any one to
"pollute himself by sacrifices," and punished the frequenters
of the temples. On the death of Valentinian, A.D. 392,
Theodosius made a law for the whole empire, defining sacrificing and soothsaying as public crimes, "like high treason."
Says Innes: "The wheel had now come almost full circle; for
not only was Christianity now established, as Paganism had
been before, but the open exercise of the one religion was declared a crime against the state in the same way, and even in
the same words, in which in the previous century the law had
bent itself against the profession of the other." [1]

By the end of the fourth century Christianity thus became
the religion of the state, and the domain of the one was considered coterminous with the dominion of the other. The
character of the relation between the Church and State, however, differed materially from that which in later centuries
marked divisions in Christendom itself. The Church was
one in all lands, subject to jealousies and rivalries of contending episcopal jurisdictions. It was subject also to heresies,
which precipitated fierce disputes and demanded ecumenical
councils, and in the settlement of which the imperial government often exercised its power. Even before the establishment of Christianity the authority of the emperors had
been invoked. The councils of Nicæa, Ephesus, and Chalce-
don, were called by imperial rescripts, their decrees largely

---

[1] *Church and State*, p. 38.

shaped by the emperor's sympathies and enforced by his authority. The exile and recall of Arius and of Athanasius illustrate the varying sympathies of the throne and the effectiveness of its interference. A like illustration is seen in the progress of the Donatist controversy through its century of strife. But it is to be noted that these interferences were on the appeal of the Church, without which appeal the emperors did not assume to intervene until after the Christian establishment.

Even then the controlling attitude was that of a Christian empire facing the heathenism out of which itself had lately emerged, covenanted, not to the maintenance of one distinctive Christian Church among others — for there were no others —but to the maintenance of the general Christian faith as against all the forms of heathenism, which it doomed to extirpation. With the arms of the empire went the preacher of the cross. Far in advance of its legions the Christian apostles penetrated into the north and west. In the wreck of the western empire the Church maintained its seat and subdued to its faith the Gothic hordes. Goth, Visigoth, Vandal, Frank, alike bowed to the majesty of the faith. The empire of the west owed its continuity to the Church, and remained Christian against all forms of invading paganism.

Alliance.   For centuries the relation between Church and State was one rather of alliance and mutual helpfulness than of organic union. The two institutions existed side by side, for the most part mutually independent as to functions and order, the one not attempting interference with those matters which were peculiarly the property of the other. Held in the bond of a common faith, each contented itself with such measure of influence on the other as would secure from the crown the exercise of power in defence of the Church, and from the Church the voice of spiritual authority to constrain peoples to obedience and rulers towards righteous enactments.

But the seeds were early sown, which in later years should blossom and bear fruit in those colossal struggles between the two which make up the history of mediæval Europe. When the empire had just declared itself Christian the great Augustine. tine came to his African bishopric; and while that transition was yet new and was seeking ways of legitimate expression, he was employing all the powers of his profound and subtle mind and all the energies of his fervid heart in defining both the terms of Christian doctrine and the relationship of the Church to the state. Incontestably the greatest of the early fathers, his influence on the human mind has been more profound and enduring than that of any other man since the day of Paul. The Augustinian theology still holds the faith and affections of millions, while the Augustinian view of the " City of God " remains to this day the chief ground for every system of union between Church and State. His theory of the new civic and religious system revealed in the Church, as it is embosomed in society and the state, has proved the most elastic of human speculations and capable of endless applications. Defining " the duty of the powers of earth to buttress the invisible City of God," it laid the foundation for all religious persecution in subsequent ages. It was seized on by the papacy as the strongest weapon for ecclesiastical aggrandizement. In the age of the Reformation it was accepted as axiomatic by all the Reformed Churches; and in this dawn of the twentieth century every religious establishment must appeal to it as justifying its principles and methods.

While the great African bishop was thus laying the foundation for all after efforts towards ecclesiastical imperialism, and all appeals of the Church to the secular arm for the protection of the faith and suppression of heresy, there very early appeared another element — the *widening of the episcopal* Episcopal *jurisdiction.* In the circumstances of the time this was a Power. matter almost of necessity. Though the empire had established the Christian religion, and had thrown its powerful influence towards the furtherance of the faith, it had yet taken no legislative action for the support of the Church. After that establishment, as before, the financial support of the Church came from individual benefactions, the difference being that, while formerly such benefactions had been forbidden, under the Christian empire they were both allowed and encouraged. To this were added the frequent gifts of imperial favor; many times, indeed, drawn from the public treasury, but bestowed in the name of the emperor. For Christian uses, under the control of the Church, were also appropriated the confiscated revenues of many heathen temples.

Thus, though not for centuries arose the legislative taxation, or tithe, for the support of religious institutions, there soon came into the possession of the Church large funds and endowments, which, either by the tacit consent or the direction of the emperor, were committed to the care and administration of the bishops, whose duties and powers connected therewith added a semi-civic function to the religious character of their office. To this chamberlainship the bishops soon aspired to add judicial powers, especially in all cases in which the rights of the clergy, either general or individual, were involved. In the vast majority of instances, especially in the western empire, such an episcopal court was not only desirable, but also necessitated; for in that chaotic condition of society which followed the irruption of the northern hordes, the only hope of wisdom or justice was found in the Church.

But while this grafting of civil function on the episcopal office may thus be considered a necessity of the age, at the same time it is evident as a foundation for those lofty ambitions which afterwards moulded the papal policy. Here is the seed of that ecclesiastical arrogance which for centuries refused to the civil law the right of judgment upon offences by the clergy. Here, also, is the seed of that tremendous struggle over the right of investiture, which convulsed the eleventh and twelfth centuries. In view of the growth of episcopal power with functions reaching into civil and judicial matters, it was inevitable that the bishop should become in certain important particulars an officer of the state, in whose appointment the emperor should claim to be considered as having authority. This claim the Church, as it grew in power and ambition, was increasingly ready to resist, until at Canossa it obtained its greatest triumph.

Meanwhile, the Church of the west was the saviour of society. In the downfall of the empire and the wreck of all social and civil institutions, towards the Church alone turned the hopes of men, the only stable thing in the midst of universal ruin, the only anchor in the storm. It was a city of refuge for the fugitive and the oppressed. It listened to the cry of the afflicted. It stretched out the hand of authority or uttered the voice of persuasion, to check many turbulences and to make many crooked things straight. As society recast itself after the violence of the storm, the moulding hand of the Church was everywhere present, as the sole possessor of light and knowledge, the constant witness for law and righteousness. The Church saves Society.

" Though the tone of the Church remained humble, her strength waxed greater, nor were occasions wanting which revealed the future that was in store for her. The resistance and final triumph of Athanasius proved that the new society could put forth a power of opinion such as had never been known before; the abasement of Theodosius, the emperor, before Ambrose, the archbishop, admitted the supremacy of spiritual authority. In the decrepitude of old institutions, in the barrenness of literature and the feebleness of art, it was to the Church that the life and feelings of the people sought more and more to attach themselves; and when in the fifth century the horizon grew black with clouds of ruin, those who watched with despair or apathy the approach of irresistible foes, fled for comfort to the shrine of a religion which even those foes revered.

" But that which above all we are concerned to remark here is, that this Church system, demanding a more rigid uniformity in doctrine and organization, making more and more vital the notion of a visible body of worshippers united by participation in the same sacraments, maintained and propagated afresh the feeling of a single Roman people throughout

the world. Christianity as well as civilization became con-
terminous with the Roman Empire."[1]

Rome.

The prestige of the Eternal City was also a colossal force,
both as holding the veneration of the people and directing
the ambitious policy of the Roman bishops. The Augustan
City had administered the affairs of the empire in a dominion
which the bishops of Rome claimed as a pattern for their own.
Already, with the proclamation of Theodosius, had begun the
dispute for supremacy between the Churches of the east and
the west, never settled indeed by any concord between the two,
but confirming in the western mind the claims of the Roman
see. Long before the final rupture, the entire Church of the
west had accorded the primacy of Rome and the universal
authority of its bishop. Thus to the evident tokens of inherent power, on the beneficent action of which the very life
of society and civilization had depended, was added the conscious ambition to become the vicegerent of God upon the
earth. With such inspiration and with a system built up by
centuries of spiritual guidance and of wise statecraft, Rome
at last presented an institution, with which, when the kings of
the earth attempted to cross swords, the struggle was as a
battle of the gods.

Epochs.

The periods of development may be roughly noted as
follows : —

1. That of *Alliance*, from Theodosius and Augustine to
   Gregory the Great.
2. That of *ecclesiastical effort for supremacy*, from Gregory
   the Great to Charlemagne.
3. That of the distinct *Supremacy of the State*, from
   Charlemagne to Hildebrand.
4. That of *Church Imperialism*, from Hildebrand to Boniface VIII.
5. That of *Nationalism*, from the time of Boniface VIII.
   to the present day.

[1] Bryce, *Holy Roman Empire*, pp. 12, 13.

The change from one to other, save as regards the revolution wrought by Hildebrand, was by slow steps and ever subject to fluctuations, with issues unsuspected at the beginnings. Thus, it is impossible to suppose that Augustine divined the historical sequence of his theories. His principles, that the civil power should constrain unity of faith, and should subserve the interest of the Church, did not reveal at once their baneful possibilities. They were potent in present usefulness for the resettlement of society and securing of peace, of salutary effect in almost all applications. So long as the two institutions, Church and State, were content to live in the early spirit of alliance, each regardful for the other, and each practically independent in its own internal administration, there could arise few reasons for friction. These reasons were brought forth when either party, forgetting the rights and dignity of the other, attempted interference and dictation.

Out of such attempts came the first change in the form of the question of Church and State, and in the attitude of one to the other. No longer satisfied with a mutually respecting alliance, each sought a superiority. Especially did the Church learn to resent and deny all theories of equality. Confessedly a divinely instituted power, it early claimed precedence of all earthly kingdoms. Keeper of the king's personal conscience, it claimed direction of his civil rule. It took to itself the words of Wisdom, " By me kings reign, and princes decree justice." (Prov. viii. 15.) Thus, in the full outcome of its claims, it demanded from kings homage for their crowns; interfered at pleasure with the internal affairs of kingdoms, and even presumed to absolve from allegiance the subjects of monarchs bold enough to resist the authority of the pope, who affected to be a king of kings. The complete claim is seen in Boniface VIII. (A.D. 1300), seated on the throne, crowned with the tiara and girt with a sword, exclaiming, " I am Cæsar. I am Emperor." In such increasing claim of universal dominion in things secular as religious, the

Claims of the Church.

Church by degrees outlined and finally enforced an imperialism vaster and further-reaching than that of the proudest Cæsars.

For this issue affairs were in long training and with many fluctuations, until the culmination of papal ambition was reached in the audacity of Boniface VIII. The beginnings of it may be found in Gregory the Great, who, coming to the pontificate, A.D. 590, exercised vast influence, chiefly moral, in the pacification of political affairs in Italy and the west, and showed an example of genius for government, which his able successors were not slow to emulate. The success of their pretensions was due, fully so much as to their ability, to the disorder of society and the weakness of the princes. This process of papal aggrandizement thus begun, received a long and decided check from the power of Charlemagne, though at the same time his benefactions to the Church laid the foundation of further progress.

Gregory the Great.

This greatest of Frankish kings had compacted under his sceptre the whole of western Europe, conquered Italy and Rome, revived the empire of the west, of which in the year 800 he was, at Rome and by the pope, crowned emperor. Himself devoted to the Church, he confirmed the hierarchical system to which he abandoned the government of the Church; sanctioned the canon law; constituted the " States of the Church," as representing the temporal sovereignty of the popes; and established throughout his empire " the tithe, a tax on land, one third of which went to support the bishops and clergy, one third to maintain the edifices of the Church, and one third to the poor." At the same time he reserved to himself the convoking of synods and the confirming of their actions; the appointment of bishops whom he regarded as vassals of the crown; and the final decision as to the legislation of the Church.

Charlemagne.

Far in advance of former rulers, Charlemagne asserted a supremacy of the state over the Church, and initiated a policy which continued operative with more or less effectiveness for two centuries. He regarded his own office as equally spiritual as secular, and his empire as a theocracy. "Among his intimate friends he chose to be called by the name of David, exercising in reality all the (theocratic) powers of the Jewish King, presiding over the kingdom of God upon earth." " There are letters of his extant, in which he lectures Pope Leo in a tone of easy superiority, admonishes him to obey the holy canons, and bids him pray earnestly for the success of the efforts which it is the monarch's duty to make for the subjugation of pagans and the establishment of sound doctrine throughout the Church. Nay, subsequent popes themselves admitted and applauded the despotic superintendence of matters spiritual which he was wont to exercise, and which led some one to give him playfully a title that had once been applied to the pope himself, ' *Episcopus episcoporum.*' . . . Within his own dominions his sway assumed a sacred character; his unwearied and comprehensive activity made him, throughout his reign, an ecclesiastical, no less than a civil, ruler; summoning and sitting in councils, examining and appointing bishops, settling by capitularies the smallest points of Church discipline and polity." [1] His immediate successors were weak, and his dominions were divided for nearly half a century, but the empire was reconstituted, as the " Holy Roman Empire," in 852, by the Saxon Otto the Great, who added to the policy of Charlemagne the demand that no pontiff should be elected at Rome without the emperor's consent. This demand could not be refused, and " The pope became a secular subject to the emperor." The weakness of succeeding Franconian emperors suffered the papacy to fall under the power of Italian princes until, in 1046, Henry III. entered Italy with an army, and calling a synod, deposed three contending popes and secured for himself the right of nomination, a right exercised in the appointment of three successive pontiffs.

This marked the extreme of the supremacy of the state,

Otto.

[1] *Holy Roman Empire*, pp. 64, 66.

the power of which after the death of Henry, waned rapidly, in consequence, partly of the long minority of Henry IV. and chiefly of the character and power of Hildebrand. Of this pope writes Ranke in graphic words: "Gregory VII. was a man of bold, bigoted, and aspiring spirit; straightforward as a scholastic system, invincible in the stronghold of logical consequence, and no less dexterous in parrying just and well-grounded objections with specious arguments. . . . He resolved to emancipate the papal power from the imperial yoke. . . . The bond between both was the right of investiture. The determination that this ancient right should be wrested from the emperor was of the nature of a revolution."[1] Hildebrand, first as counsellor to Popes Victor, Stephen, Nicholas II., and Alexander II., and afterwards as Gregory VII., was the ablest of the long line of pontiffs. Taking advantage of the minority of Henry, he succeeded not only in setting aside the nomination of the pontiff by the emperor, but in removing the election of the pope from the clergy and citizens of Rome to the college of cardinals. Further than this, he asserted the right of the popes to inquire into the civil administration of the empire. This was a tremendous stride of ecclesiastical ambition, for the taking of which an immediate event gave occasion.

The young Henry had attained to his majority, and in the exercise of his power had been so arbitrary that many of his subjects appealed to the pope, who summoned him to Rome to answer the complaints. To this summons Henry replied with a synod of the German Church at Worms, which called on Gregory to retire from the pontificate as having abused his office. Gregory's response was terrific. Nothing like it had ever been attempted by any bishop of Rome, and could hope to be effective only by reason of the Church's hold upon the mind and affection of the people. He excommunicated Henry and released from allegiance all his subjects. Henry was forced to submit, illustrating his penitence by standing

Hildebrand. (margin)

Henry IV. (margin)

[1] *History of the Popes*, p. 24.

for three days barefoot in the snow at Canossa, until the proud Canossa.
Gregory was willing to receive his confession. It is true that
this severity brought a reaction; that Henry's indignation at
this insulting treatment was shared in by the majority of his
subjects; that he conquered Rudolph, who with the pope's
approval had usurped his throne; and, invading Italy, captured Rome and shut up Gregory in the castle of St. Angelo.
Thus Henry revenged his wrongs and asserted his power.
But none the less the action of Gregory had given to the
theory of state supremacy a shock from which it never
recovered. Though Gregory, having escaped to Salerno,
died there in the following year, his successors held fast to
his claims.

Closely allied thereto was the question of *investiture*. On Investiture.
the one hand, the emperors claimed that, inasmuch as bishops
exercised many civil functions, and in many cases were princes
with temporal jurisdiction, the right of appointment and investiture with the insignia of office belonged to the crown;
and that the pope was bound to consecrate to the spiritual
office the appointees of the secular power. On the other hand,
the Church claimed that, inasmuch as the episcopal function
was predominantly spiritual, the crown was obliged to acquiesce in such appointments as the Church should make.
The state refused as vassals those over whom it could exercise no authority; and the Church refused as spiritual officers
those whose title came from a secular source. On this issue
battle royal was joined, the varying features of which it is not
needful here to recount. It is only needful to note that on
this, as on other questions, the policy of Hildebrand was
carried on by his successors, to the general triumph of the
ecclesiastical power.

The effective application of that policy is illustrated in the
Emperor Lothair holding the stirrup of Pope Adrian, and in
many acts of Innocent III., whose ambition was greater than Innocent III.
Hildebrand's and whose exercise of power met with less resistance. Innocent insisted that all kings should do him

homage for their crowns; that their title by inheritance was not good until ratified by him. He insisted on his right as supreme lord to interfere in any kingdom for the redress of wrong, himself being the sole judge. "He excommunicated Sweno for usurping the throne of Sweden." He laid an interdict on Spain, because the king of Leon had married his cousin. He commanded Philip to take back his divorced wife, and on the king's refusal, laid an interdict on all France. All religious services ceased: "the dead were unburied; the living were unblessed." He threatened John of England with deposition and an interdict, and annulled *Magna Charta*. In the theory of Innocent, all kings and emperors were temporal vassals of the pope. "He declared explicitly that as the power and property of the realm belonged to the Roman Church, its vassal-king could make no change in its condition, to the Church's prejudice." [1]

Church Supremacy.

This was the high-water mark of Church supremacy. It remained practically stationary for one hundred years, though during that period were increasing tokens that the ebb could not be long delayed. The second Frederic — a man of great powers and great vices — carried on long battle with Gregory IX. and Innocent IV. Twice excommunicated, he "appealed to the indelible rights of Cæsar, and denounced his foe as the anti-Christ of the New Testament. He scoffed at anathema, upbraided the avarice of the Church, and treated her soldiery, the friars, with a severity not seldom ferocious." [2] At the end he was forced to a qualified submission, and died under the ban of the Church.

The death of Frederic brought the end of the empire as a world power, and seemed thus to remove from the stage the greatest obstacle to papal ambition. In reality it made way for conditions which efficiently checked that ambition, and put a term to ecclesiastical supremacy. The NATION was beginning to appear. France and England, under the rule of

Nation-alism.

[1] Innes, pp. 81, 82.
[2] *Holy Roman Empire*, p. 210.

vigorous monarchs, were presenting the spectacle of emergence from the confusion and rivalries of feudalism into the higher state of national life, which grew instantly more and more impatient of papal dictation. The dawn of the Renaissance was bringing to the mind glimmerings of liberty. " It was already indicative of the dawn of the new epoch that the national languages arose everywhere at the same time. Hitherto the Church had been predominant over the sense of nationality." [1] This rising sense of a special, individual national life, with speech and aims of its own, gradually bred a profound impatience of dictation, which, however religious, clearly demonstrated the domination of a foreign and selfish power. Men were beginning to question the secular aims of the Church, and some to suspect even certain of its religious dogmas. Europe was making its first unconscious movements, which were to result in the great upheavals of the sixteenth century.

It is in such beginnings of change that we find the reason of the failure of Boniface VIII. on the field where Hildebrand, Innocent, and Gregory IX. had been successful. More audacious than they all, he failed to read the tokens of changing times. When he joined issue with Edward I. and Philip the Fair, he found facing him wills strong as his own and peoples who refused to be absolved from loyalty by a papal bull. On this last factor he had not counted, nor dreamed that the popular mind could be less submissive to the pontiff's will than in the past.

In the struggle of Boniface with Philip and Edward, a struggle induced by his interference with their taxation of the clergy, there was brought to expression the theory of *Nationalism*. For this St. Louis in his Pragmatic Sanction, A.D. 1269, had prepared the way in France, defining that the election of bishops should be free from the control of the pope, and that no money should be levied for the pope without the consent of the Church and king. This was the first

[1] Ranke, *History of the Popes*, p. 26.

assertion of what afterwards came to be called " the Gallican Liberties." [1]

Both Edward and Philip for their respective kingdoms declared also their entire independence of the pope in things political, and their right to levy upon the already enormous wealth of the clergy. To the remonstrances of Boniface and his threats of interdict and excommunication they paid no regard, in which attitude they were sustained by the estates of their realms. The bull, "Unam Sanctam," declared that the acknowledgment of the universal lordship of the pope was necessary to salvation. Philip publicly burned the bull and declared his independence; forbade his clergy to go to Rome; imprisoned the papal legate, a French bishop, for insolent behavior and quoted the scripture, "Render unto Cæsar the things which are Cæsar's." [2] The battle was long, bequeathed from king to king and from pope to pope. Boniface was captured at Anagni by Philip, and never recovered from the humiliation, dying broken-hearted. His ambitious claims also lost their power. Though they were repeated by his successors down to the opening of the eighteenth century, they were not admitted or submitted to by any considerable secular power.

The spirit of opposition here involved rapidly assumed power and wide influence in the greater nations. Beginning in France, it spread to England, as we have seen, where the policy of Edward I. became as a law to the kingdom, by reason of which the third Edward refused the payment of tribute to Rome, and was sustained by his parliament.

---

[1] The contrast between the papal claim and the opposing Gallicanism is very aptly drawn by Hodge : "The indirect power of the papacy over civil affairs was founded on the claim that the Church only had a right to judge whether any civil decrees interfered with doctrine and discipline." *Church Polity*, p. 108. On the other hand, the Gallican position claimed for the king "a right to judge whether the acts or decisions of the Church were consistent with the rights and interests of the state," and that the royal *placet* was necessary to give them force in his realm.

[2] Kurtz, *Church History*, Sec. 110, 156. Fisher, *Church History*, p. 240. Innes, p. 94. Ranke, p. 26.

Germany came next, and " The electors assembled at Reuss to concert measures in common for manifesting the honor and dignity of the empire."

Thus the principle of nationalism intrenched itself firmly in the policy of states. The papal imperialism came to an end. In place of it was the assertion of entire freedom of the state in all secular affairs, and the integrity of the national Church, as a branch of the Church universal, with powers of self-government free from the dictation of Rome. What was further-reaching than all these, Nationalism — or Gallicanism — as defined by the assembly called by Louis XIV., A. D. 1682, insisted that the pope himself was subject to the general councils, both as to authority and as to judgment in matters of doctrine.

In this long dispute the aid of the schoolmen was sought by both sides. Their battle was second only to that of the princes in its fury, and had larger consequence, in that it broke up that lethargy of mind which had made the schools willing captives to the hierarchy. William of Occam, the " Invincible Doctor," saying to Louis, "Defend me with the sword and I will defend you with the pen;" Egidius de Colonna, and John of Paris, to whom may be added the immortal Dante, opposed the extravagant demands of the papacy and defended the independence of the kings.

It is to be noted that in this development of nationalism no room was made for such a thing as liberty of conscience. The kings, who most stoutly resisted the pretensions of Rome to political domination, were as fully bent on maintaining the unity of the faith. The movement, undoubtedly, as loosening the mind from one of the trammels of the past, had something of a casual relation to the Reformation, and certainly prepared a solution for some of the problems brought up by that struggle; but with that cardinal principle which lay at the heart of the Reformation, the Right of Private Judgment, the new nationalism had no sympathy whatever. This is abundantly evidenced by the Spanish Inquisition; the slaughter of the

No Freedom of Conscience.

Albigenses, the death of Huss, and, most notably, the attitude of Henry VIII. of England, who, while carrying the theory to the furthest extreme, abjuring the pope and making himself head of the Church of England, yet persecuted on the one hand those who maintained allegiance to Rome, and on the other those who denied the Roman dogmas.

It is a remarkable illustration of the possible narrowness of human judgment that none of the publicists, statesmen, and theologians of the Reformation era, and none of the princes, save William of Orange, were able to follow this principle of revolt to its logical issue in the freedom of the individual conscience. While the Protestant disallowed the faith and the authority of Rome, yet he insisted as stoutly as any Romanist that unity of faith was essential to the integrity of the government. In despite of the rights of mind, it was the practical axiom of the day that the accident of birth and political denizenship must control the form and expression of religious faith.

This, indeed, needs emphasis. While the Reformation broke the power of the papacy and severed some of the nations from the Roman Church, it did not introduce liberty. It made a way for liberty by which, in the fulness of time, she should come to proclaim the dignity and rights of the individual soul. But the recognition thereof by the princes and governments delayed for more than two centuries, while in certain parts of Christendom they are not recognized to-day. The principle of nationalism, already defined as triumphant over the papacy before the Reformation, was at once seized upon by the Protestant princes as the regulative principle which should constitute and control ecclesiastical affairs in their dominions.

Protestant-
ism.

A new element also was added to the old question of Church and State. Hitherto the Church had been one, and the sole question had been as to the relation between this one Church, having its head at Rome, and the state. Now is added another question: Which Church shall be followed?

For the one Church is broken asunder, and a new faith presses itself upon the mind and conscience, demanding the obedience of princes and peoples. It was given to them to choose — Romanist or Protestant — which shall the nation be? Undoubtedly the choice of Protestantism was dictated not only by the preference of princes, but as well by their recognition of the wide spread among their people of the new faith; but once that the choice was made, the Church became a national Church, in many matters of control subject to the dictation of the state.

This is further illustrated by the division in the ranks of Protestantism. While in the past there had been but one Church, the Roman, known in western Europe; and while among those nations, which after the Reformation remained faithful to the Roman See, the Church was still one, so that, despite the claims of political freedom, the religious faith of France, Spain, Italy, and southern Germany was unified under the spiritual organization of Rome, yet from the beginnings of Protestant ecclesiasticism the fact of division appeared.

The Protestant Church was not one. Though united by common sympathy of opposition to Rome, the Lutheran and Reformed faiths made for themselves sharp lines of separation from each other.[1] Thus the choice of the Protestant prince called for yet another decision — whether in the Reformation he should follow Luther or Calvin. There was nothing like organic union between these two great churches of the Reformation. More than that, there was no such union of similar churches in different countries, either Lutheran or Reformed. There was no organization common to the Lutheran churches of Saxony and Sweden, or to the Reformed churches of Holland and Scotland. Each Church of the Reformation was distinctly national. Says Ranke,[1] "Religion was diversely seized by the nations in the several modifications of its dogmatic forms; the chosen body of dogmas became blended with the feelings of nationality. It became

Lutheran and Reformed.

[1] *History of the Popes*, p. 327.

the first question respecting each country, What was the dominant religion there? "

Hence arose the maxim, universal in the Reformation period and not altogether disallowed to-day, succinctly put into the words, " *Cujus regio, ejus religio.*" [1] It defines the duty and right of the prince to choose and direct the religion for his people. To this was necessarily added, as a logical consequence, that it is the duty of the prince to root out heresy. This duty and right many a Protestant prince obeyed, under-standing as heresy, not only the peculiar doctrines of Rome, but as well also the differing views of other forms of the Protestant faith, or the reluctance to conform to the special ecclesiasticism which the prince had ordained. So the Covenanter was slain because he could not accept either Episcopacy or the National Kirk, and the Pilgrims came across the sea because they could not conform.

The argument in support of this supremacy of the state was very simple. Religion and morality were understood to lie at the foundation of the state, while of morality religion was the base. Therefore it became the first duty of the princes and magistrates to take order for the support of religion and the defence of its purity. It was taken for granted that two forms of religion, though both might be Protestant, could not co-exist in the same state without peril to civil institutions. The Church throughout Protestant Europe was thus shorn of its divine character in popular estimation and made an adjunct of the state, while the individual conscience was put outside of the law. This is true even of the Scottish Kirk, which, while insisting in its symbols on the "alone Headship of Jesus Christ," at the same time demanded the secular power for its own support, and made itself an establishment under the crown.

One of the most remarkable things in that most marvellous age of the Reformation is the tenacity with which the general Protestant mind clung to the idea that an intimate union

The power of princes.

---

[1] " Whose is the government, his is the religion."

of Church and State was necessary to the purity of religion and the perpetuity of government. This was the universal opinion, the exceptions to which can be counted on less than the fingers of one hand. It was formulated as general law. The Peace of Augsburg made the religion of a community Augsburg. determinable by the religion of the prince. The ruler thus became supreme, with a clerical synod, or consistorial body, as his advisors. The only relief to dissenters from the religion of the prince was that of emigration from his dominions.[1] So long as a man remained under the rule of a prince he was bound to conform in matters of religion.

This position of the Augsburg Peace is less liberal than that of the Confession, and was reached as a compromise between Roman and Lutheran princes. The Confession, published twenty-five years before, in 1530, attempted to define the practical independence of Church and State. "The administration of civil affairs has to deal with other matters than the gospel deals with. . . . The ecclesiastical and civil powers are not to be confounded. The ecclesiastical has its own command to preach the gospel and to administer the sacraments. Let it not intrude into the office of another than itself." The chief stress in the distinction is laid upon the impropriety of ecclesiastical interference in civil affairs, which was the special aspect of the question at that day. It fails to warn the state against interference with the Church, though it in no place recognizes that the civil power has a duty against heresy, In these respects the Augsburg Confession was far in advance of the later confessions of the Reformed churches.

Written by Melanchthon under the influence of Luther, it is Luther. clearly expressive of their mind. Luther undoubtedly held in theory the independence and self-government of the Church, but he "considered the Germans too rough, turbulent, and unpractised to take ecclesiastical government into their hands at once." The princes, as principal members of the Church, should take the lead and the people must follow. In the cir-

[1] Fisher, p. 415.

cumstances of the time, that was an easy step by which this moral leadership passed into the requirement of conformity. Luther saw this and was embarrassed by it; but he saw no way of escape from the necessity of reliance to some extent upon the civil power. The practical need was enforced to his mind by the disorders induced by some of the Anabaptists and by the Peasants' War, which called him from the Wartburg. This accounts for contradictory expressions by Luther. In one place he says, "Whenever the temporal power presumes to legislate for the soul, it encroaches;" and in another, "Since it is not good that in one parish the people should be exposed to contradictory preaching, he (the magistrate) should order to be silent whatever side does not consist with the Scripture!" Of course, this constitutes the magistrate the judge of Scripture and doctrine, and installs him as supreme in the Church. Long before Luther's death the princes had become the real governors of the Church, which was organized and regulated entirely by their will. The Lutheran consistory, which governs the Church to-day, was organized in 1540, a body of jurists and theologians, appointed by, and responsible to, the crown, and exercising all the powers of church government and discipline. Luther did not like it, but he knew not how to mend it. "Satan remains Satan," he said. "Under the pope he pushed the Church into the State; now he wishes to push the State into the Church." [1]

Calvin.

Calvin, the great leader of the Reformed, while vindicating the independence of the Church as to its order and discipline, yet explicitly demanded the coercive power of the state for suppressing heresy and vice. Differences occurred between Calvin and the Genevan authorities as to the delimitation of the respective powers of the civil and religious authorities, with the result that the Reformer and his friends were banished from Geneva for a short time. Their return was a virtual triumph for Calvin on the matters at issue, and thereafter the government of the Church, with its relation to the civil power,

[1] Innes, pp. 130-135 ; Fisher, *Church History*, p. 415.

was on the lines laid down by Calvin. The regulations of Calvin involved a severe regimen both as to morals and faith, under which offences called for both spiritual censure by the Church and material punishment by the state. Whatever censures were imposed by the consistory were regularly reported to the city council for such action under the civil law as that body might order. To what extreme of persecution that body could go with the consent of Calvin, is shown in the martyrdom of Servetus for denying the doctrine of the Trinity.

The position of the Swiss Reformers is tersely expressed in the First Helvetic Confession, A.D. 1536, "The chief office of the magistrate is to defend religion, and to take care that the word of God be purely preached." The same thought is in the French Confession, written by Calvin in 1559, "God hath put the sword into the hands of magistrates to suppress crimes against the first, as well as the second, table of the law of God." This doctrine is somewhat modified in the Second Helvetic Confession, which, defining the chief office of the magistrate as procuring " the peace and tranquillity of mankind," adds, " we hold also that the care of religion is a first duty of a *religious* magistrate." [1]

First Helvetic Confession.

French Confession.

Second Helvetic Confession.

Under the influence of Zwinglius, readiest among all the reformers to appeal to civil and military power, the situation at Zurich was so moulded that Church and State were practically identical. Ecclesiastical power was lodged in the Great Council, which governed the civil affairs of the city. To this absorption Calvin made a strenuous objection. He argued that the state had no right to absorb the Church, but was bound to coöperate with the Church, enforce its decrees, and give effect to its discipline. [2]

Zwinglius.

[1] What might be the duty of a non-religious magistrate is not intimated, but the subjection of religious offences to civil penalty is clearly stated. Probably the phrase, " religious magistrate," was not used in the sense of distinguishing between men as religious or irreligious. Every one in those days was supposed to be of some religion, and the kind of magistrate here indicated is one who religiously or faithfully sought to do his duty.

[2] Fisher, p. 417.

In the Netherlands, strange as it appears to us, notwith-standing the untold sufferings to which the people were sub-jected by reason of Philip's claim that he could dictate the religion of his subjects, the fathers of the Reformed Church did not hesitate to declare in the Belgic Confession, A.D. 1561, that the magistrate was vested with power not only to guard the state, but to maintain religion and the Church, and " to remove and destroy all idolatry and false service of God." Practically, indeed, though the Reformed Church was es-tablished in Holland and so remains to this day, this theory of repression of other faiths but once attempted enforcement. A large toleration was the unwritten law, as long as religious divergence did not entail disturbances of public order. Their great leader, William of Orange, while himself of the Calvin-istic faith, held firmly to the principles of toleration. In this he was broad enough to comprehend Anabaptists. Under him it was impossible for the theoretical demands of the Confession for the magistrate's interference to find any expression in act. As Fisher aptly remarks, " In the last years of the war with Spain the Calvinists learned that, by reason of their sins, they could not all be reduced to one and the same religion." [1]

Belgic Confession.

There is indeed one great exception to be found in the action of the state toward the Arminians. Finding that they could not remain in the established Church, they petitioned for toleration outside of it. The contention grew fierce and the States forbade controversy. Under the influence of Maurice, the Stadtholder, Grotius was cast into prison and Oldenbarneveldt beheaded. The Synod of Dort in 1618 con-demned the heresy, without allowing to its followers a liberty of debate, and deposed them from the ministry. To this the States added a decree forbidding them to preach, on pain of banishment from the country.

Arminius.

If we cross the channel into England, we find a situation quite unique as compared with continental countries, though the

[1] *Church History*, p. 344.

same rule of state supremacy obtains and with greater force. Save that the teachings of Wycliffe had so affected the popular mind as to predispose it to acquiesce in the separation from Rome, the Reformation in England was a movement set afoot, not as in other countries by the conscience of the people, but by the policy of government. Henry VIII., the most despotic of English kings, threw off the yoke of Roman authority; while in matters of faith he was as much of a Romanist as ever, putting himself at the head of the English Church, a virtual pope. In later years he gave a more open ear to the Reformed doctrine, so that under his son Edward, guided by the shifty Cranmer, England ranged itself with the Reformed countries of Europe. The violent reaction by which Mary sought to return the kingdom to Rome was short-lived, but illustrated the fact that the principles of the Reformation had taken firm hold upon the people. This Elizabeth recognized, while she retained in her own hand the reins of government over the Church as well as over the state. The form of the Church of England remains to-day substan- Church of tially the same as it became under the moulding hand of the England. great queen — a creation of the civil power and subject for creed, government, and discipline to the final authority of the magistrate.

The position taken by Elliot [1] on the origin of the Church of England cannot be maintained. He says: " The Church never was established. The institution grew in the same way that other parts of the constitution grew. . . . It does not owe its origin as an institution to any definite act of the legislature or other sovereign authority." This confounds the two characteristics of the Church as a body of believers, and as an organization under law. It is true that the legislature did not originate the Church as a body of believers. But it is equally true that the legislature did originate that organized institution known as the Church of England. Previous to the rupture by Henry there was in the organic

[1] *State and Church*, p. 3.

sense no such thing as a Church of England. There was
a Church in England, but it was an integral part of the one
Church of Rome. As a distinct institution the Church of
England owes its existence to the act of parliament, 1538,
declaring separation from Rome and the supreme headship as
resident in the king. In the reign of Elizabeth the "Articles
of Religion," *i.e.* the Church Creed and the Prayer-book,
were approved by acts of parliament, without which action of
the civil power the Church had, no legal right to so believe
or so pray. It is difficult to imagine how the idea of
"establishment" could be more clearly defined in act.

The several elements, or features, of this establishment
are : —

1. The supremacy of the crown.
    All high offices in the Church are matters of royal
    gift.
2. Complete control of parliament over the Church, as to
    articles of faith, order, worship, and discipline.
3. Membership of bishops in the upper house of legis-
    lature.
4. National support of the Church.
5. The broad membership in the Church, conditioned on
    citizenship and not on personal faith or character.
6. Patronage in the Church — the right of presentation
    to livings without regard to the wishes of parish-
    ioners.

In no country is the idea of establishment more strikingly
presented than in England, even the England of to-day.
The civil and ecclesiastical administration are closely blended,
having the same head and united on many lines of mutual
dependence, justifying the words of Burke, "The ideas of
Church and State are inseparable in our view."

In the history of this establishment after the age of Elizabeth, though there was no general persecution of individuals

for conscience' sake, there was very stringent application of the " Acts of Uniformity." Dissenting ministers were, time and again, silenced and turned out of their parishes. Dissenting laymen were excluded from office and from the universities. No one could enter parliament without taking the Test Oath, which required subscription to the Thirty-nine Articles and communicating according to the rites of the Church of England. Romanist, Jew, Independent, Presbyterian, were alike disabled. Especially was the cry of " Popery " like shaking a red rag before a bull. In these acts of uniformity is to be found the beginnings of America. Under their stress the Pilgrims went to Holland in 1609, and in 1628 the first band of Puritans crossed the sea.

It is abundantly evident that the controlling idea in this establishment was political, rather than religious, not seeking so much the furtherance of a particular form of faith and worship for the sake of religion as the maintenance of the chosen form as an adjunct of the state. Uniformity was insisted on, not as a thing of religion, but a matter of civil order. Dissent was reprobated because, to the mind of the authorities, it was pregnant with public disorder. This is most tersely exhibited by Blackstone : " The sin of schism, as such, is by no means the object of temporal coercion and punishment. The civil magistrate has nothing to do with it, unless their (the dissenters') tenets and practices are such as threaten ruin or disturbance of the State. He is bound, indeed, to protect the Established Church, and if this can be better effected by admitting none but its general members to offices of trust and emolument, he is certainly at liberty so to do, the disposal of offices being matter of favor and discretion. But this point being once secured, all persecution for diversity of opinions, however absurd or ridiculous they may be, is contrary to every principle of sound policy and civil freedom." [1]

[1] Most of these disabilities remained until well into the present century. The parliamentary test was not set aside until 1826. The compulsory pay-

Scotland.

Among the confessional utterances of the Reformation era, that of Scotland is not behind those already cited, in conceding to the state a duty and power concerning religion. John Knox was not averse to demanding that the civil power should support Christ's Kirk and Covenant, and should suppress opponents thereto. He did, indeed, emphasize the independence, of each other, of Church and State, with God supreme over both. Yet the assembly of 1560, which formed the First Confession, and "set forth God's glory and the weal of His Kirk in this realm," reported their work to the parliament, by which body it was ratified as the true doctrine, and authorized as the law of the land. Thus was the Presbytery established in Scotland, and its confession asserted, "To kings, princes, rulers, and magistrates we affirm, that chiefly, and most principally, the conservation and purgation of the religion appertains." A religious function is thus asserted as the first duty of the magistrate. On the abdication of Mary, among the legal steps taken were acts of parliament, confessing the Protestant doctrine, forbidding the mass, declaring the Church, whose confession was ratified seven years before, to be "the only true and holy Kirk of Jesus Christ within this realm"; and framing for the sovereign a new coronation oath, binding him "to maintain the true religion and withstand the false," and to banish from the kingdom — "root out" — "all heretics and enemies to the true worship

ment of Church rates by dissenters, as well as churchmen, was not abolished until 1868. The universities were opened to dissenters in 1854, but denied to them university honors and emoluments until 1871. The admission to parliament of dissenters involves the possibility that they at some time might have the majority, with the anomalous result that the Church would be ruled by its foes! Such a condition would force disestablishment. It is worthy of remark that, the old-time disabilities being removed, the only sufferer under the establishment is the Church itself. Completely deprived of autonomy and subject to civil dictation in most important matters, whatever may have been its work of grace and good, it yet lacks the inherent dignity and self-government which should ever belong to the Church of God.

of God, that shall be convict by the true Kirk of God of the foresaid crimes."[1]

Thus in the immediate Reformation era there was in all the Protestant churches a practical unanimity of opinion, that to the civil magistrate belonged a religious function, in some, intimately related to the very life of the Church, in others, restricted to the suppression of heresy.

In the next century, after one hundred years had cumulated their illustrations of this principle, after the expatriation of Pilgrim and Puritan, the Westminster Assembly delivered itself as follows : " The civil magistrate may not assume to himself the administration of the word and sacraments, or the power of the keys of the kingdom of heaven; yet he hath authority, and it is his duty to take order that unity and peace be preserved in the Church, that the truth of God be kept pure and entire, that all blasphemies and heresies be suppressed, all corruptions and abuses in worship and discipline prevented or reformed, and all the ordinances of God duly settled, administered, and observed. For the better effecting whereof, he hath power to call synods, to be present at them, and to provide that whatever is transacted in them be according to the word of God." *West-minster.*

Nothing, in all the utterances of the period, can better than these words illustrate the tenacity of the principle, that the civil power should perform a religious function. Emancipated from the Roman tyranny which depended on that principle, these men of England had been learning for a century that only an exchange of masters was being made, as they struggled against prelacy. Now the long-oppressed dissent comes to places of power and at once adopts the same principle in its own defence. There is no wonder that the satirist wrote, —

---

[1] It is to be noted that the Church of Scotland possessed under the establishment an autonomy not existent in the Church of England. Though it sought the approval of the estates, and demanded their support, it was yet self-originated and was not subject to the civil power, in matters of order, faith, or discipline.

" New Presbyter is but old Priest writ large ! "

It is evident that, while the assembly was unable to free itself from that moss-grown principle, it was yet conscious of confusion and inconsistency. It solemnly declares that " God alone is Lord of the conscience," and then proceeds to put that conscience at the discretion of the magistrate. Fearing that the magistrate may use his power unjustly, it empowers [1] him to call synods, but leaves to his judgment the question, whether the transactions of the synods are according to the word of God, and therefore binding on him, as guardian of the pure word, and suppressor of heresy. In reality, by this deliverance, the assembly bound the Church, hand and foot, under the power of the magistrate. Though formulated more than one hundred years after the opening of the Reformation, the Westminster Confession was more subservient than any of the precedent creeds of that epoch. The reign of Presbyterianism in England was very short, and no occasion of civil oppression by it is recorded. It is probable that in any event the enlarged sense of religious liberty would have forestalled any gross exercise of this restraining power ; but at the same time the state was hereby, in set terms, put into possession of a power over the Church fully so great as that involved in the supremacy of Henry VIII.

To this testimony of the creeds of Protestantism, all of which speak substantially with the same voice, as to the religious function of the civil power, there may be added that of the great company of writers, philosophers, jurists, theologians of the age, who with but little variation agree thereto.

Erastus.

Erastus, who was court physician to the Elector Palatine, and whose name has been borrowed to express that theory which denies all self-government to the Church, taught that there was no power of discipline in the Church, and that sins

---

[1] This " empower " does not direct. He may act without a synod, if he so please.

of its members should be punished by the civil magistrate, "for that is his duty and office." Hugo Grotius, the great Grotius. leader of the Arminians, notwithstanding the fact that himself was persecuted for opinion's sake, taught that, while the civil magistrate could not himself exercise sacred functions (administering the word and sacraments), yet he could enforce their exercise by those properly commissioned. Thus it was in the power of the state to abolish false religion and punish its disciples; to establish and control a State-Church.

Spinoza, while pleading for toleration and "liberty of phi- Spinoza. losophizing," yet maintains that "authority about sacred things should be wholly in the supreme power of the State, and that, if we wish rightly to obey God, we should conform our outward worship with a view to the peace of the republic"— "a piety accommodated by the decree of the State to public utility."

Hobbes held that a Church without warrant from the sover- Hobbes. eign was unlawful, the sovereign being supreme pastor and head of the Church. As such he could preach and administer sacraments by himself or others.

Cartwright, professor of divinity at Cambridge, 1580, main- Cartwright. tained that while the Scripture was the only rule of faith and government, and that the management of Church affairs belonged to the Church itself, yet the Church may call upon the civil power to root out heresy and to preserve the purity of religion.

The theory of Hooker, 1594, merged Church and State to- Hooker. gether. On this he justifies the control of the crown and parliament over the Church, "Seeing that there is not a man of the Church of England but the same man is also a member of the commonwealth; nor any man a member of the commonwealth which is not also of the Church of England." Hooker was not in sympathy with the cruel proscription, with which Elizabeth in her later years pursued the non-conformists, and his essay on *Ecclesiastical Polity*, while attempting a reasonable foundation for the royal supremacy, offers no defence of persecution.

Thus it appears that for well-nigh two hundred years the general trend of opinion set one way, with variations as to extent and severity, but all agreeing that the state had a right of greater or less supremacy over the Church. Bossuet was substantially correct in saying that on one point all Christians had long been unanimous — the right of the civil magistrate to propagate truth by the sword; that even heretics were orthodox on this point. For the most part, Romanist and Protestant alike would as soon think of assailing any other principle of government as of calling in question this religious function of the civil ruler.

Exceptions. The exceptions were very few. As already noted, William of Orange desired a comprehensive toleration, but it does not appear that he was opposed to a state establishment. In England the only voice lifted for freedom of conscience and worship was that of the Brownists and Barrowists. Barrow and others were executed on the pretext of attacking the ecclesiastical system, which action was held to be treasonable. The majority fled to Holland. Later in the seventeenth century, the great Cromwell showed himself to be more liberal than most men of his age. He had doubts as to hard and fast lines of ecclesiastical policy. "Is it ingenuous," he said, "to ask for liberty and not to give it?" Yet under the commonwealth, while the persecution of Romanists was relaxed, they could neither vote nor hold office; and the use of the book of prayer was forbidden.[1]

Cromwell.

By far the most advanced man of his time was Sir Harry Vane. He had suffered somewhat from the intolerance of Massachusetts, and, returning to England, had thrown his energies into the struggle against the king. But, whether from king or commonwealth, he did not approve of interference with religion. In 1656 he published *A Healing Question*, in which he took the ground that "the magistrate had no

Vane.

[1] Fisher, pp. 484, 485.

right to go beyond matters of outward practice, converse, and dealings in the things of this life between man and man." In this same essay he also maintained that the army should be subject to parliament, for which he was haled before Cromwell and thrown into prison.

In the same decade arose the sect of the Quakers, Quakers. whose "Inward Light," resenting all external interference with religion, proclaimed the largest liberty of conscience. But their extreme "iconoclasm," which would destroy all forms, institutions, and sacraments, added to their many wild vagaries of conduct, brought their vital truth into contempt. Fox was not recognized as a leader, save of visionaries.

John Locke stands highest in this list of individual ex- Locke. ceptions. In the year of the accession of William and Mary, 1689, the great Toleration Act of England was passed. With this Locke was delighted, though far from satisfied.[1] His famous first *Letter on Toleration* written to his friend Limborch, said: "Toleration has indeed been granted, but not with that latitude which you and men like you would desire. But it is something to have got thus far." This letter was written in Latin and not designed for publication; but William Popple, a London merchant, in some way coming into possession of a copy, translated it into English and published it, much to the annoyance of Locke, who thought the time not ripe for so open utterance. In the preface to the translation Popple used the words, which have been wrongly attributed to Locke, "Absolute liberty, just and true liberty, equal and impartial liberty, is the thing that we stand in need of."

In fact, however, these words did not misrepresent the opinions of Locke, as appears from his subsequent letters on the same subject. Thus he wrote, "People will always differ from one another about religion, and carry on constant strife and war, until the right of every one to perfect liberty in

[1] Fowler, *Life of John Locke*, pp. 57, 59.

these matters is conceded, and they can be united in one body by a bond of mutual charity." [1]   Again, speaking of the State and Church as related to each other, he said: " The boundaries on both sides are fixed and immovable.   He jumbles heaven and earth together, the things most remote and opposite, who mixes these societies, which are in their original end, business, and in everything, perfectly distinct and infinitely different from each other." [2]

Toleration Act.

On William's Toleration Act, Innes remarks: [3] " To the nineteenth century this seems a narrow and grudging piece of legislation.   But it was a great step from Tudor and Stuart despotism, and from all that went before.   For the first time since England was a nation, the worship of God was permitted outside the law, and a Church was tolerated outside the Church which the State selected for support."   The Toleration Act, great as was the relief afforded, only recognized the right of non-confirming worship, and did not relax in any particular the civil disabilities to which its followers were subjected.   Under these the non-conformists suffered for yet a hundred years and more; while in Ireland, where the Protestants were in a very small minority of the population, the Romanists suffered extreme oppression.   They could not vote, or hold any office whatever.   They could not plead, or even sue, in court.   They could not teach, or be taught by, a Protestant, and could not go abroad for education.   If a Romanist married a Protestant, the union was set aside, and the officiating priest was to be hanged.   Priests and monks not registered were banished, and if they returned, were hanged.   John Morley says, " The severity of the persecution against the Catholics exceeded that of the ten historic persecutions of the Christian Church." [4]   This is

[1] Fowler, *Life of John Locke*, pp. 57, 162.

[2] Such breadth of view is not quite consistent with Locke's *Fundamental Constitutions for Carolina*, by which, together with great liberty of religion and worship, the Church of England was yet established in that colony.   But the twenty years since writing the constitutions had given ample time for expansion of view.

[3] Innes, p. 193.   [4] *Life of Burke*, p. 108.

overstrained, yet the lot of the Irish Romanists appeals to the compassion of the centuries.

The grudging toleration of William, with its slow after expansions, illustrates most strikingly the slowness with which the general mind came to the conception of true liberty, whether religious or civil. Burke, writing of the French Revolution, put the conception in words that have never been excelled:[1] "The liberty I mean is *social* freedom. It is that state of things in which liberty is secured by equality of restraint. This kind of liberty is, indeed, but another name for justice. *Whenever a separation is made between liberty and justice, neither is in my opinion safe.*" This acute remark is equally true of religious as of civil liberty, and it makes another comment on the tardiness of human progress to note that the very man, whose profound mind thus declared the nature of true liberty, opposed with all the force of his impassioned speech the first attempt to lighten the burdens on the English non-conformists. Men not seldom, while discerning abstract principles, fall lamentably short in their application of them to concrete matters of life.

But among the few and scattered European voices for religious liberty, heard in the two hundred and fifty years from the day of Luther, the place of honor is undoubtedly to be accorded to the Anabaptists. Their doctrine is one of the most remarkable things which appeared in that wonderful age. It comes to speech with a clearness and fulness which suggest a revelation, just as to Luther dawned justification by faith, soul enlightening and uplifting. And, no less notable, this doctrine came at the very opening of the Reformation, in the year 1524, just after the famous Diet of Worms and while Luther was secluded in the Wartburg.

The doctrine,[2] making a thorough distinction between the kingdom of nature and the kingdom of grace, insisted that freedom of conscience and of worship was fundamental,

Marginal notes: Burke. Anabaptists.

[1] *Life of Burke*, p. 144.
[2] Kurtz, II, 393; Fisher, p. 425.

and that religion should be entirely exempt from the regulation or interference of the civil power, so that a man's religion should not work his civil disability. Besides this, they declared also that the Church should be composed exclusively of the regenerate, membership therein to be conditioned, not upon residence or birth, but upon the work of grace in the heart. In this last point they anticipated, by more than two centuries, that distinction by Edwards which shattered the union of Church and State in America.

There can be but one mind as to the grandeur of the doctrine thus propounded by the Anabaptists, nor as to the immense blessings which it finally conferred upon the world. This is the great contribution to Christian thought made by this one among the Protestant sects. To the honor of its descendants it should also be noted that they ever clung tenaciously to these principles so early declared. Thus, the English Baptists at Amsterdam, in 1611, made it an article of faith that — " The magistrate is not to meddle with religion or matters of conscience, nor compel men to this or that form of religion; because Christ is the King and Lawgiver of the Church and conscience." And when, in the following century, the struggle for religious liberty took place in America, among the various Churches the Baptists were most strenuous and sturdy in its defence. They divide the honors, indeed, with the Quakers. But while the Quakers were immovable in their passive resistance to intolerance, the Baptists added to such virtue the active energy which overcomes.

But upon the world of the early Anabaptists their doctrine smote with a voice of alarm. In Romanist and Protestant alike it aroused disgust and anger, seeming to strike at the foundations of both Church and State. And not without reason. It was too radical, and neither princes nor people were ready to recognize its vital and enlightening principle. For them it meant disorder and revolution without good ends or stable aims, merely for disorder's sake.

Moreover, the doctrine was too great even for these first proclaimers. It was as though the effect upon them overwhelmed and unbalanced the mind. They lacked a great leader, a Luther or Calvin, who could bear so great a revelation, and with clear vision and firm hand discern and impose those just limitations which true liberty is glad to own. Consequently, they almost at once brought their doctrine into deserved reproach by running off into the wildest and most fantastic vagaries and disorders. They declared that the state was an evil to be endured only so long as there were unregenerate people; that a community of Christians needs no civil magistracy, for law concerns only evil-doers, and the only valid legislation for Christians is the Bible. Princes were to be dethroned; the enemies of the gospel were to be destroyed. John of Leyden, under such fanaticism, attempted to set up at Munster the new " Kingdom of Zion," in which all things were to be common, and which was to usher in the millennium. He was guilty of many atrocities. All Europe was alarmed, and most stringent measures were adopted. The poor enthusiasts were hunted and slain like wild beasts. With curious and bitter irony, the Protestant Canton of Zurich decreed that all " rebaptizers and rebaptized," should be *drowned*. Thus the new and glorious life was eclipsed to reappear after long waiting in America.

The Old World Idea, developed and illustrated in the passage of sixteen centuries, had thus in all lands, both those under the Roman See and those divided between the followers of Luther and Calvin, this common principle — a root out of which came many variations — that the state should legislate for the benefit of the Church; that the Church should look to the state for support and defence; and that the state should recognize and establish a particular Church as the representative of the only legally authorized form of religion and worship. Such was the almost universal mind of Christendom at the time when the Pilgrims, fleeing from persecution, went first to Holland and, eleven years after, to New England.

And when, nearly a hundred years later, the first act of toleration was passed in modern times, it was not as a concession of justice and right, but a grudging dole extorted by clamor too instant for resistance.[1]

[1] It is in place, as of interest, to here note that this principle is still dominant in Europe, with but small exceptions. The only country where religious liberty in the American sense obtains, is Ireland. Up to 1869 the Church of England was established in Ireland, the people being "forced to support a religion professed only by a very small minority." In that year the Church was disestablished, the *Regium Donum* to the Presbyterians and Catholic endowment of Maynooth were discontinued, and all churches were put on a footing of perfect equality before the law. On the continent, Switzerland approaches nearest to the United States. The Constitution of 1874 declares the freedom of conscience and worship to be inviolable, and that no one can be compelled to accept or support a religion or be punished on account of religion. At the same time the constitution excludes Jesuits and forbids establishment of convents and religious orders, while each canton has its own established Church controlled by the civil magistrate.

(A very full statement of present European attitudes on this subject is contained in a pamphlet by Philip Schaff on "Religious Liberty," in the publications of the American Historical Association for 1886–1887.)

III

It is thus evident that, at the period when American colonization began, the Church and State in Europe were substantially of one mind as to this fundamental principle, that the prosperity of both depended upon a union more or less intimate and vital. To but very few individuals had the thought of true liberty occurred, while in no country had even a grudging toleration of other than the State-Church been made the rule of law.

We need not be surprised, then, to find the most of the colonists in hearty sympathy with that principle. Some of them, indeed, had suffered through its application; but in their view that suffering was a consequence, not of a vicious principle, but of a wicked application of a principle which was very right and necessary. These men had no doubt as to the propriety of a legal insistence upon a prescribed form of worship, supposing that form to be the true form of worship. The impropriety and wrong of persecution were to be decided, not by any inherent vice of persecution itself, but by the character of the doctrine persecuted. If the doctrine were false then persecution of it were justified. If the doctrine were true, persecution became wicked. Thus, to the minds of the fathers of Massachusetts it was clear, both that the English authorities were criminal in persecuting them, and that they were right in their measures against the Brownes and Mrs. Hutchinson; because they, both as persecuted and as persecutors, represented the truth. [1]

It is very true that the Pilgrim fathers, landing on the

[1] Fisher, *Colonial Era.*

"stern and rock-bound coast" of New England, sought and
obtained "freedom to worship God." But the usual understanding of Mrs. Hemans's famous lines, that they desired to
establish anything like a general religious liberty, is very far
from the truth. Their conscious desire was freedom for
themselves, never dreaming of extending an equal freedom
to such as differed from them in religious opinion; though to
the honor of the Pilgrims it should be noted, that they were
afterward far more lenient and tolerant toward dissentients
than were their neighbors of Massachusetts, and that they
never were guilty of great harshness.

New
England
intolerance.

To the early leaders of Massachusetts, especially the religious leaders, toleration of dissent from the "established
order" of religious worship was as sedition in the state and
sin against God. John Cotton declared that "it was Toleration that made the world anti-Christian." There are many
choice specimens of this repressive spirit in Nathaniel Ward's

Simple
Cobler.

(1645) "Simple Cobler of Aggawam in America."[1] "I take
upon me," he says, "to proclaim to all Familists, Antinomians (&c.), to keep away from us; and such as will come, to
be gone; the sooner the better." "Polipiety (a variety of
sects) is the greatest impiety in the world." One other
specimen of the Cobler's spirit should not fail of quotation,
"He that is willing to tolerate any unsound opinion, that
his own may be tolerated, though never so sound, will for a
need hang God's Bible at the Devil's girdle."

This sentiment showed a marvellous tenacity, very slowly
yielding to the influences of more liberal thought; and so
late as 1673 President Oakes,[2] of Harvard College, said in an
election sermon, "I look upon unbounded Toleration as the
first-born of all abominations."

There is to the mind of to-day something of amazement at
the process by which these men justified their harsh measures.
When Sir Richard Saltonstall, by far the broadest-minded

[1] Force, *Historical Tracts.*
[2] Felt, *Ecclesiastical History of New England*, II, 504-506.

among the early Puritans, remonstrated against the Boston persecutions, on the ground that by such proceedings "many are made hypocrites," Wilson and Cotton replied: "Better be hypocrites than profane persons! There is a great difference between God's inventions and men's inventions. We compel none to men's inventions." Cotton, answering Cotton. Williams's "Bloody Tenent," quite outdoes himself: "It is not right to persecute any for conscience' sake *rightly informed;* for in persecuting such Christ Himself is persecuted in them. . . . For an erroneous and blind conscience (even in fundamental and weighty points) it is not lawful to persecute any, till after admonition once or twice. . . . The word of God in such things is so clear, that he *cannot but be convinced* in conscience of the dangerous error of his way, after once or twice admonition wisely and faithfully dispensed. . . . If such a man, after such admonition, shall still persist in the error of his way and be punished, he is not persecuted for cause of conscience, but *for sinning against his own conscience.*" The arrogance of spiritual inquisition and tyranny could hardly go farther than that in specious defence of its principles.

The powerful presence of such principles has to be constantly noticed in the early history of New England, operative with more or less strictness and severity in all the colonies, except Rhode Island, the corner-stone of which was the explicit denial of this very principle; indeed, without the memory of this religious attitude of the New England colonies much of their history through the first century will become an unconnected and unmeaning jumble of events. To attempt to read into that history the settled principles of a later day, or to apologize to posterity for ancestral oppressions, is absurd and confusing. These men need no apology. They stood in their lot, in their own age of the world, working out their problem, blindly and blunderingly enough at times, but surely. The issue, to the light and blessing of which their children came, was quite other than their thought, and yet the Religious Liberty of a later day owed much to the sharp-cut illustrations furnished by the New England Theocracy.

A similar thing may be said of the establishments in the colonies in the South. In these, notably exhibited in the story of Virginia, the attitude of the civil government toward the Church and religion was solely due to a secular or political motive, quite different from the Puritan, whose motive was purely religious. The Puritan insisted on conformity because he wanted to make the state religious and to preserve the true religion in its purity. The Virginian insisted on conformity, because the Church was a department of the state, and all dissent was indicative of civil disorder and insubordination. This contrast is very marked; and it is among the things of special interest to note how from these two diverse grounds the question of Church and State came to simultaneous solutions in America, one religious and the other secular. On the one hand, the Puritan experiment demonstrates that the effect of the union is essentially irreligious; while on the other, the Virginian makes it clear that the law of conformity is the fruitful mother of disorder.

Indeed, there were three separate answers coming to speech and exhibition at the same time. Massachusetts set up its theocratic state with its chief interest centred in the Church; Virginia established its civil state, with the Church as a subject member, a conformity to which was the mark of a good citizen; while Rhode Island boldly denied the purposes and premises of both, placing an impassable gulf between the State and the Church, and relegating to the individual conscience and to voluntary association all concern and action touching the Church and religious matters.

These are the three extreme types about which all the other colonies may be grouped with more or less of similarity to their several patterns. In the one group with Massachusetts are Plymouth, New Haven, Connecticut, and New Hampshire, with their Congregational establishments. Among these it will be observed that theocratic Massachusetts and New

Haven were more closely akin in the strictness of their religious requirements; that Plymouth and Connecticut were more liberal in spirit and enactments; while New Hampshire was organized so long after the period of severity had waned that it furnishes few illustrations of our theme.

In another group are Virginia and the two Carolinas, in which the Church of England was established at their foundation and continued the State-Church until into the era of the Revolution, displaying at times strong and bitter feeling against all forms of dissent.

A third group is composed of New York, New Jersey, Maryland, and Georgia, in which occurred changes of attitude toward the Church. Maryland began with religious freedom, under Roman Catholic auspices, and was afterward dragooned into establishing the Church of England. In New York and New Jersey, the violence of English officials endeavored to force the same Church on a Dutch Reformed foundation, but never secured for it a legal establishment. The charter of Georgia declared liberty of worship, but on its abrogation the Church of England was established by royal edict and legislative enactment, a few years before the Revolution.

The fourth group comprises Rhode Island, Pennsylvania, and Delaware. The last-named, however, was for so long a time a part of Pennsylvania that its history on the religious question is merged with that of the larger colony. In these colonies no Church was ever established. More than that, the impropriety of a religious establishment was explicitly declared. Of the two, Rhode Island was far broader than Pennsylvania. The Quaker, notwithstanding his voice for liberty of conscience, could yet make no civic room for the infidel, and insisted on certain religious restrictions. Strangely enough, even to-day, Pennsylvania, by terms of its constitution, is unique among the United States, in that it restricts its civic privileges to believers in " an Almighty and Eternal God." Rhode Island from the beginning imposed no religious restrictions whatever upon its citizenship, and allowed no

question by the civil law as to the belief or unbelief of any
one.   The civil law knew neither theist nor atheist, neither
Jew nor Christian, neither Romanist nor Protestant, neither
Episcopalian nor Baptist, neither Congregationalist nor Presbyterian.   There has never been a more perfect equality of religious beliefs before the law than was enacted in Rhode
Island at its very beginning — a revelation and pattern to all
the other colonies ; by them for a long period despised and
derided, but to the likeness of which they were glad at last
to come.

The stress of conflict was in Massachusetts, Virginia,
Maryland, and New York, because of exceptional enthusiasm
on the part of religionists meeting with exceptional determination of the civil power ; or yet again of peculiar historical
developments with which religious questions became mingled.
Of the one the story of the Quakers in Massachusetts, and of
the other the change from Dutch to English rule in New
York, may serve as illustrations.   For this reason our attention
will be mainly directed to the history of these four colonies.

In that study another and striking contrast will appear,
arising from the *origin* of the respective establishments.   In
Virginia was a Church imposed on the colony by the civil
authorities without any suggestion that the people should be
consulted in regard to it.   It was simply a branch plucked
from the Church at home and planted in the soil of Virginia,
though afterward ratified by the colony.   In Massachusetts was
a Church native to the soil, not owing descent from any
establishment across the sea, the choice of the people, by
them organized and vested with the powers of the civil
magistrate.   In both the religious establishment was of positive character, while in Massachusetts the union of Church
and State was far closer, and its spirit more inquisitorial,
than in Virginia.

Yet again, in New York, after a half century of existence
under the lax superintendence of the Reformed Church of
Holland, was a perverse attempt — never legally successful —

Origin of
colonial
establish-
ments.

to force a foreign Church upon a people, nine-tenths of whom were opposed to its policy and methods. In Maryland, also, will be seen a unique situation. Begun under the notable tolerance of a Roman Catholic proprietor with freedom not less than that of Pennsylvania, the religious life of the colony was subjected to many troublesome variations — some of them through the rivalry of Puritan and Cavalier, and others through political changes in government.

One other thing to be frequently noted is that, so far as the direct influence of the English government could affect the character of religious institutions in the colonies, the judgment was almost invariable that such institutions should be in vital relation with the Church at home. This judgment appears in charters and in frequent "instructions" to governors, often very peremptory in their terms. It found practical effect in America in all places where a stronger adverse religious sentiment of colonists did not oppose it.

With these preliminary observations we turn to the history of the different colonies. The special peculiarities require that each narrative should cover the entire colonial period without break, inasmuch as each possesses distinctions peculiarly its own. One of the most marked features of the history is in these distinctions, pronouncing often the sharpest contrast between colonies, the borders of which touched each other.

We may, however, on the line of a similarity already suggested, observe the groups into which the colonies fall by reason of the general character of their governmental attitudes toward religion and the Church. As so classed we may consider their respective stories, without rigid regard to the chronological succession in the planting of the colonies.

IV

THE CHURCH OF ENGLAND ESTABLISHMENTS

THE first group is of those colonies in which the Church of England was established by charter at the beginning, was formally established also by enactment of the colonial legislatures, and remained the State-Church until the Revolution. They are *Virginia* and the *Carolinas*.

I. *Virginia*

Religious motive.

The profession of a religious motive in the founding of Virginia, as of other colonies, was very pronounced. Remembering how a similar motive was declared by the Spaniard in the Floridas, by the French in Canada, by the perpetrators of countless atrocities, such as Menendez, who hanged the Port Royalists, "not as Frenchmen, but as Lutherans," we need not inquire over accurately into its sincerity. But it stands on record as a motive and aim.

Raleigh.

To Sir Walter Raleigh, planning the settlement of the province which he had named Virginia in honor of his queen, Hakluyt writes a letter, deploring that "the fewest number" of explorers seek "the glorie of God and the saving of the soules of the poore and blinded infidels," and expressing pleasure in Raleigh's project, because "you meane to sende some such good Churchman thither (to Virginia) as may truly say with the Apostles to the Sauvages, wee seeke not yours but you."

The same motive finds place in the first Virginia charter, given by James I., 1606, which recites the hope and intention that, "so noble a worke may by the Providence of Almighty God hereafter tend to the glorie of his Divine Majesty in the

74

propagating of the Christian religion to such people as yet live in darkness." To this admirable Christian and missionary motive the charter, after outlining the method of colonial administration, adds a prescription, " that the said presidents, councils, and the ministers should provide that the Word and Science of God be preached, planted, and used, not only in the said colonies, but also as much as might be among the savages bordering among them, according to the rites and doctrine of the Church of England." [1] Thus at the very beginning and in the foundation of the new community was the Church of England established in Virginia.

Church established.

The first expedition, which left England in December of 1606 and reached Virginia in the following April, brought the Rev. Robert Hunt, who was specially chosen for the service by the archbishop of Canterbury and for whose support the company voted £500. He is variously described as well fitted for his position — "a pious, disinterested, resolute, and exemplary man" — "a man of piety, scholarship, and devotion." [2] The colonists settled Jamestown, built Fort James, and "for a Church they nailed a board between two trees to serve as a reading desk, and stretched a canvas awning over it, and there the Rev. Robert Hunt, a highminded and courageous divine, first clergyman of English America, read the Episcopal service and preached a sermon twice on every Sunday." [3]

Robert Hunt.

The second charter of 1609 repeated the terms of ecclesiastical establishment. It also licensed the company to take to Virginia "all persons wishing to go thither, who would take the oath of supremacy." This clearly marks the desire that no non-conformists should be settled in the new colony. At the same time it opened the door to a far more undesirable class of people, as says the *New Life of Virginia*,[4] " By which

---

[1] Anderson, *History of Colonial Church*, I, 199.

[2] Hawks, *Contributions to Ecclesiastical History*, I. Campbell, *History of Virginia*, p. 52.

[3] Fiske, *Old Virginia*, I, 93.   [4] Force, *Historical Tracts*.

means the body of the plantation was now augmented with such numbers of irregular persons . . . they displayed their condition in all kinds of looseness." To such admission of " irregular persons," who would not scruple at the oath of supremacy, the government attempted shortly afterward to add the forcible importation of convicts.[1] Setting out to enforce the Act 39 Eliz., " that such rogues as are dangerous to the common people be banished the realm," the king commanded the Virginia company to receive one hundred " dissolute persons " and send them to Virginia. The company resisted, but the transportation of at least fifty was insisted on. Later, in 1617, there was an order in council for the delivery of five prisoners in Oxford gaol to Sir Thomas Smyth, for transportation to Virginia.[2] On this policy wrote Stith, " It hath laid the finest countries in America under just scandall of being a mere hell upon earth."

Whitaker.

There is no need for us to follow the general fortunes of the infant colony. The short ministerial service of Hunt was followed by the ministry of Alexander Whitaker, " the Apostle of Virginia," who wrote the "*Good News from Virginia.*" Of him, W. Crashawe, in the "*Epistle Dedicatorie,*" says that he was " a scholler, a graduate, a preacher, wellborne and friended in England; not in debt or disgrace, but competently provided-for; not in want, but rich in possession and more in possibility; of himself, without any persuasion (but God's and his own heart), he did voluntary leave his warme nest, and undertooke this hard — heroical resolution to go to Virginia and helpe to beare the name of God unto the Gentiles."[3]

Governor Dale.

Whitaker's "*Good News*" was published in 1612, the year after Sir Thomas Dale came to the governor's office. Dale was sent out by the company to correct the disorders which jealousies, a false system, and lax morality had caused in the

---

[1] Anderson, *Colonial Church*, I, 324.
[2] *Massachusetts Historical Collections*, IV, 9; I.
[3] Force, *Historical Tracts;* Hawks' *Contributions to Ecclesiastical History.*

colony, a work to which the stern soldier set himself with a firm hand. Whitaker describes him as "a man of great knowledge in divinity, and of a good conscience in all things, both which be rare in a martial man." The first act of Dale was to destroy the communal system of land tenure and labor, and by giving personal titles to land and to rewards of labor to infuse life and hope into an almost dying community.

The next step was the attempted correction of the moral and religious slackness of the settlers, to accomplish which he ordained the "Lawes Divine, Moral and Martial." These laws "had been copied, for the most part, from the Laws observed during the wars in the Low Countries, in which Dale had himself served." [1] Like the laws of Draco, they were of a severity far exceeding any of the more famous Puritan restrictions in New England. The extreme harshness of them can only be accounted for by the supposition of the great laxity in the young community, described in "*Virginia's Cure*" — a letter written by R. G. to the Bishop of London: "Through the licentious lives of many of them the Christian religion is like still to be dishonored, and the name of God blasphemed among the Heathen, who are near them and oft among them, and consequently their conversion hindered." [2]

Lawes Divine.

---

[1] Force, *Historical Tracts*, III; Anderson, *History of Colonial Church*, I, 282.

[2] Force, *Tracts*, III. It is notable that, while Dale was sent to Virginia with a purpose of reforming abuses, by reason of which "the plantation had fallen into discredit" at home, he yet brought with him a large instalment of the class of people whose errors he was to correct. Himself writes that the people were "Such as they were enforced to take — gathering them in riotous, lazy, and infected places; such disordered persons, so profane, so riotous, so full of mutiny and treasonable intendments, that in a parcel of three hundred not many gave testimony, beside their names, that they were Christians." (*Massachusetts Historical Collections*, IV, 9; I, note.) Sir Thomas Smyth vindicates the severity of Dale's code as needful to keep the disorderly elements in check. He speaks of many among them as dissolute and convicts, and states that, so late as 1620, the city of London contributed £500 toward the expense of transporting one hundred youth, "in order to rid itself of the burden of them." In fact, this compulsory colonization was frequent until the end of the century, though, happily, its victims were not always of the disorderly class.

The sections of Dale's Code, which have reference to religion, are briefly as follows:[1]—

1. To speak impiously of the Trinity or one of the Divine Persons, or against the known articles of Christian faith, was punishable with death.
2. The same penalty of death was to avenge "blaspheming God's holy Name."
3. To curse or "banne"—for the first offence some severe punishment; for the second a "bodkin should be thrust through the tongue"; if the culprit was incorrigible, he should suffer death.
4. To say or do anything "to the derision or despight of God's holy word," or in disrespect to any Minister, exposed the offender to be "openly whipt 3 times, and to ask public forgiveness in the assembly of the congregation, 3 several Saboth daies."
5. Non-attendance on religious services entailed a penalty, for the first offence, of the stoppage of allowance; for the second, whipping; for the third, the galleys for six months.
6. For Sabbath-breaking the first offence brought the stoppage of allowance; the second, whipping; and the third, death.
7. Preachers and ministers were enjoined to faithfulness in the conduct of regular services on pain "of losing their entertainment."
8. Every person in the colony, or who should come into it, was required to repair to the Minister for examination in the faith. If he should be unsound, he was to be instructed. If any refused to go to the minister, he should be whipt; on a second refusal he should be whipt twice and compelled to "acknowledge his fault on Saboth day in the assembly of the congregation"; for a third refusal he should be "whipt every day until he makes acknowledgment."

[1] Force, *Historical Tracts*, III.

Notwithstanding the atrocity of these requirements, it does not appear that their severer penalties were ever enforced by Dale. His "bark was worse than his bite," and the fulmination of such orders was doubtless with the view of frightening the lawless elements into decency.

Dale's successor, Argal, who came to office in 1616, a man of "indiscriminate rapacity and vices," was not so gentle. The "bloody code" spoke his mind, and he made use of its severity, and more, to further his own greed and passion. " The condition of Virginia became intolerable ; the labor of the settlers was perverted to the benefit of the governor ; servitude for a limited period was the common penalty annexed to trifling offences ; life itself was insecure against his capricious passions." [1] Finally, his ferocity in condemning Captain Brewster to death brought a general outcry from the colonists. Appeal was taken to England, the "Lawes Divine, Moral and Martial," were abrogated by the company, and Argal was superseded by Yeardley, whose inefficient administration was, after three years, terminated by the appointment of Sir Francis Wyatt. *Argal.*

Hitherto, the government of Virginia had been a practical despotism by the company in London and by the governors. Wyatt brought with him in 1621 new ordinances of government, which transformed the entire system. Adding to the governor a council and a general assembly, meeting annually, the new system was practically as free and self-governing as that established by the Massachusetts Puritans. Nor was it in any essential particular modified by the abrogation of the company's patent in 1624 and the assumption of the colony as a royal province. It was meant to conserve " the greatest comfort and benefit of the people, and the prevention of injustices, grievances, and oppressions." [2] *Wyatt.* *Royal province.*

The first article of " Instructions " to the new government, as of prime importance, directs the authorities " to take into their special regard the service of Almighty God and the *Care for the Church.*

[1] Bancroft, I, 152.   [2] *Ibid.*, I, 158.

observance of His divine Laws; and that the people should be trained up in true religion and virtue . . . to the Order and Administration of Divine Service according to the form and discipline of the Church of England; carefully to avoid all factions and needless novelties, which only tended to the disturbance of peace and unity; and to cause that the Ministers should be duly respected and maintained." [1]

Under these ordinances, which also provided that no decree from England should have the force of law in Virginia until ratified by the general assembly, the care for religion and the establishment was made a prime duty of the government — a duty which the legislature set itself repeatedly to perform.

The first assembly, whose acts have been preserved, was that of 1623. Among its earliest actions was a rather comprehensive measure in regard to religious matters. [2] It enacted that "there should be in every plantation, where the people are to meet, for the worship of God, a house or room sequestered for that purpose, and not to be for any temporal use whatever." Also, "there should be a uniformity in our Church as near as may be to the Canons in England, both in substance and in circumstance, and that all persons yield readie obedience under pain of censure." [3]

Religious legislation.

---

[1] Anderson, *Colonial Church*, I, 328.

[2] Hening, *Statutes*, I, 122.

[3] The act provided penalties : for absence of one Sunday from Church a fine of five pounds of tobacco ; for speaking "disparagingly of any minister without proof," a fine of 500 pounds of tobacco. The act also forbade ministers to be absent from their parishes, under penalty ; and forbade the people to sell any tobacco or corn until the claims of the minister were paid out of the best of both crops.

The care which the assembly thus assumed for things ecclesiastical finds constant expression in after years. As to the clergy, it took many measures for their support and behaviour. It gave them glebes, "which glebes were, in the first instance, to be cultivated by six tenants placed on each of them at the public expense." The annual support of a minister was fixed at 1500 pounds of tobacco and 16 barrels of corn, to be assessed at the rate of 10

The assembly was very careful for the standing, reputation, behaviour, and efficiency of the clergy. Thus in 1629 it was ordered that " All ministers conforme themselves to the canons of the Church of England."[1] Further, "noe man shall disparage a mynister, whereby the myndes of his parishoners may be alienated from him, and his mynistrie prove less effectuall, upon payne of the severe censure of the governor and council."[2] Not only must the people be restrained from such disrespect for the ministry, but the clergy must be forbidden all conduct which could justify disparagement. It would appear that, already forgetting the examples of the saintly Hunt and Whitaker, the Virginia clergy had begun to assume that indecorous conduct which was the cause of so much lamentation in after years. Thus the statute reads,[3] " Mynisters shall not give themselves to excesse in drinking or ryott, spending the time idelie by day or by night, playing at dice, cards, or any other unlawful game, but at all tymes convenient they shall heare or reade somewhat of the holy scriptures, shall occupie themselves with some other honest studies or exercise, always doing the things which shall appertayne to honestie and endeavor to profitt the Church of God, having

Ministers.

pounds of tobacco and one bushel of corn *per* head for every man and boy over sixteen years. This stipend, estimated at the value of £200, was the highest amount payable to a minister. If in any parish the quota was less than this amount, the stipend should be reduced ; if greater, the stipend should not be increased ; but the ratio of assessment should be reduced (Stith's *Virginia*). In 1629 the assembly declared (Hening, I, 144) that "it is thought fitt that all who worke in the ground, of what qualitie or condition soever, should pay tithes to the minister." In 1632 the assembly ordered that the minister's tobacco and corn be deposited " in such place as he may appoynt, before any other tobacco of any man's cropp be disposed of ; " also, " because of the low rates of tobacco," that there should be given to the minister " the 20th calfe, the 20th kidd of goates, and the 20th pigge." The minister's fees, " petty duties," were fixed at two shillings for marrying, and one shilling for churching and for burying. Christening must be performed *gratis*. It was also ordered that the church-wardens should collect all ministerial dues and be themselves responsible on failures. (Hening, I, 144, 149, 207.)

[1] Hening, I, 149.   [2] *Ibid.*, I, 156.   [3] *Ibid.*, I, 158, 183.

alwayes in minde that they ought to excell all others in
puritie of life, and should be examples to the people, to live
well and christianlie."

As to services, the assembly ordained, in 1631 and 1632, [1]
that every minister "shall preach one sermon, every Sunday
in the year," and " shall, halfe an hower before every prayer,
examine and instruct the youth." He must also visit " the
dangerouslie sick "; and must administer the sacrament
" thrice in the year." It also commanded that " all preaching,
administrynge the communion, and marriage shall be *in* the
Church, except in cases of necessitie."

Baltimore.   In 1628 Lord Baltimore came to Virginia, intending only
to make that colony a place of temporary sojourn while arranging for his own colony under the king's patent. But he
was not suffered to remain. The governor and council insisted that, even for so short a time as his purposes required,
he must take the oath of supremacy. As a Roman Catholic,
it was impossible for him to acknowledge the ecclesiastical
headship of the king of England, but he offered to take a
modified oath covering all necessary questions of allegiance.
This the Virginians were not willing to accept, and Baltimore,
though a personal friend of Charles, was not allowed to remain
in the colony. We may very strongly suspect that this action
was due, less to ardor for the royal prerogative and the maintenance of the established Church, than to jealousy of a new
proprietor who designed to found another and rival colony on
the borders of Virginia.

However this may be, the incident may be credited with
inciting a renewal of zeal for the establishment, which expressed itself in a new act of uniformity by the assembly of
1631.[2] The act ordained the observance " throughout this
colony " of " the canons and constitution of the Church of
England — upon penaltie of the paynes and forfeitures in
that case appoynted." This act was repeated in the next
assembly. Absentees from Church services were fined one

[1] Hening, I, 157, 158.   [2] *Ibid.*, I, 155.

shilling for each offence, while "all commanders, captaynes, and church-wardens" were solemnly charged to "see this good and wholesome lawe" observed; and the church-wardens were required to take oath to faithfully discharge their duties and watch over the conduct of the people under the statute.

So far as the terms of law went, Virginia, both under the company and under the king, was not liberal in matters of religion. Practically, however, while the laws were rigid, the authorities were lax in their enforcement up to the time of Berkeley. This action in regard to Lord Baltimore was the first case recorded of molestation for conscience' sake.[1] There occurred also under Governor Harvey an instance of ministerial subjection to the civil power. A certain Mr. White, a minister, was silenced by Harvey "for cursing those of his own parish."[2] This action was presently used as an accusation against Harvey. He defended himself by saying that White never produced any credentials of ordination, though he had two years in which to obtain them. Harvey cited the commandment of Archbishop Laud that no man should be taken as a minister to Virginia, until his orders were approved by the bishop of London. The practical rule, however, was tolerant, though it is probable that, had any avowed Romanist come to the colony with purpose of domicile, he would have been expelled, as among all Protestants of the time there was an abiding hatred of all things "papistical." *Early tolerance.*

To such animosity the Puritans were not obnoxious for the first thirty years of Virginia history. Indeed, until about 1640, the Puritans in England considered themselves, and were considered by others, as having right and place in the Church of England. Winthrop and his companions bade a tender farewell to their "own Mother Church," as they set sail for America. Not until they set about their own Church-making in New England did they separate from the dear *Puritans in Virginia.*

[1] See Burke's *History of Virginia*, I, 304.
[2] *Massachusetts Historical Collections*, IV, 9, 133, note.

English mother. Thus in Virginia there was a considerable sprinkling of Puritans, who could without scruple take the oath of supremacy. A considerable number came over in Wyatt's term. The apostle Whitaker was himself a Puritan. " Here," said he, " neither surplice nor subscription is spoken of." [1] Even the Pilgrims (Separatists) of Plymouth would have met a welcome in Virginia had they accepted the invitation sent after their first hard winter. [2]

A change in the attitude of Virginia toward the Puritans appeared about 1639, during Wyatt's second term, as a reflection of the struggle in England. There the Puritans had espoused the side of the parliament, and the cause of the king and Church had become identical. Already had Archbishops Bancroft and Laud fulminated against allowing Puritans in the royal province of Virginia, distinguished by its statutory zeal for Church and king ; and Charles had issued a proclamation forbidding their admission into the colony. For this reason the Virginia authorities, looking on the Puritans in England as rebels, soon learned to consider all Puritans everywhere as heretics, and became anxious to take such steps as would " prevent the infection from reaching this colony" in larger measure than was already present.

Severer measures.

The first action, in 1642, was to strengthen the establishment against all opponents. To this end the legislature

---

[1] Bancroft, I, 206 ; Fiske, *Old Virginia*, I, 301.

[2] Occasionally, an act of punishment took place for disrespect toward the establishment. Thus, in 1634, Henry Coleman was sentenced to excommunication for forty days, for " using scornful speeches and putting on his hat in Church." At the end of that period he was ordered to publicly acknowledge his offence and ask forgiveness. (Anderson, *Colonial Church*, II, 144.) The notable thing in the act is that the civil court imposed a spiritual penalty. Later, Stephen Reek, for ridiculing Archbishop Laud, was condemned to two hours in the pillory, a fine of £50, and to be jailed at the governor's pleasure. (Howison, *Virginia*, II, 148.) But such actions had no relation to the spirit of intolerance, and were doubtless approved by the Puritans themselves, who, on their coming to Virginia, had found no reason to separate from the Church in which they were at home in England. They were forced into dissent altogether against their will.

enacted an elaborate law for the government of the Church. [1]
This provided for a rigid performance of the Church of
England "liturgie, according to the booke of common prayer,
allowed by his Ma'tie and confirmed by consent of parliament."
It also provided for a "yearly meeting of the ministers and
church-wardens before the commander and commissioners of
every county court, in the nature of a visitation." This act
was accompanied by another against the Romanists. Such were Romanists.
to be disfranchised, and any priests, coming into the colony,
were to be expelled within five days. [2] The latter action was
to guard against the danger of "infection" from Roman
Catholic Maryland.

It may be doubted whether the above demand for conformity would have disturbed the Puritan element already in
Virginia had not the scarcity and quality of the established
clergy compelled them to look elsewhere for religious teachers.
The number of the clergy was very small, and supposing
them to be of the most devoted spirit, they were far too few
to minister to the people, who were not gathered in towns,
but scattered on plantations. In recognition of this lack of
ministers, the legislature at sundry times made efforts to increase their number by urging emigration and offering rewards
for their importation. The quality of the clergy, also, had
already begun to express those scandalous features, of which
at a later day so much complaint was made.

Because of such conditions the Puritans in Nansemond
County, leaders among whom were Richard Bennett and
Daniel Gookin, bethought them of sending to Boston for
religious aid. [3] Philip Bennett, a ship-master, carried to the
governor of Massachusetts a letter descriptive of the religious
needs, and asking that ministers be sent to Virginia. This
"Macedonian Cry" stirred the hearts of the New England

[1] Hening's *Statutes*, I, 240.

[2] *Ibid.*, I, 269.

[3] Bancroft, *United States*, I, 206; Bacon, *American Christianity*, p. 48;
Campbell, *Virginia*, p. 212; Fiske, *Old Virginia*, I, 303.

Puritans, who in solemn conclave deputed three ministers to the mission. They were William Thomson of Braintree, John Knowles of Watertown, and Thomas James of New Haven. They immediately departed for Virginia, taking with them a letter from Governor Winthrop to the governor of Virginia, Sir William Berkeley.

Berkeley. Berkeley had just come to the province, and brought with him a spirit "very malignant to the way of the Churches in New England," believing that "to tolerate Puritanism was to resist the king." To such feeling he gave sharp expression in his reception of the New England ministers, who were at once made to understand that they were very unwelcome in the colony.[1]

The visiting ministers were not discouraged by the churlish behaviour of Berkeley, but began their proposed work in Nansemond, and thereupon the governor procured the passage of a law requiring the "governor and council to take care that all non-conformists be compelled to depart the collony with all conveniencie."[2] This act of expulsion was at once obeyed by Knowles and James, who retired into Maryland and afterward to New England. Thomson remained for several months, laboring with success, until he also was forced to leave. A Mr. Durand, apparently a minister, was also banished by the governor; and Richard Bennett, who had been instrumental in bringing the New England ministers, found it desirable to accept the invitation of Lord Baltimore to a refuge in Maryland. The controversy was not long sustained, as, in view of the scattered population, it was difficult to make head against the despotic Berkeley. But Puritan sentiments continued to be quietly disseminated,

---

[1] Berkeley's chaplain, Thomas Harrison, at first joined the governor in opposing the missionaries, but was afterward won to their side and became a Puritan, thus offending the governor, who dismissed him, saying that he did "not want so grave a chaplain." Subsequently Harrison crossed into Nansemond County and preached among the Puritan settlers, and eventually was expelled from the colony. (Felt, *Ecclesiastical History of New England*, II, 7.)   [2] Hening, I, 277.

and Harrison, on his departure from Virginia (1648), reported that "one thousand of the people, by conjecture, were of similar mind." [1]   Fiske notes that the Indian massacre of 1644 was variously considered as a divine judgment for harboring, or persecuting, the Puritans.

It would appear that even some of the established clergy had become infected by the poison of Puritanism,[2] as in 1645 the assembly enacted a law to punish such *clergymen* as should refuse to read the common prayer, or conduct service "according to the Church of England."   The delinquents were mulcted in a fine of five hundred pounds of tobacco.   It was also laid upon parents and masters, under penalties, to compel children and servants to attend church and "catechizing."

In one respect there was a disturbing influence in the bosom of the Church itself.   This came from the ambition of the Church vestries.   These bodies were the subject of frequent legislation.   Owing to social conditions, they were often called upon to discharge semi-civil functions, and were ambitious of more power than the government was willing to concede.   Especially were they impatient at the governor's claim to the right of presentation to all parishes, insisting that it belonged to them to choose and settle the ministers.   To this insistence the government was forced to yield, and in 1642 the same legislature which denied liberty outside of the Church declared the right of the people in the Church by conceding the claim of the vestries, "provided that it shall be lawful for the *Governor*, for the time being, to admit and elect such a minister as he shall allow of in James Citty parish." [3]   The governor was minded to have a decisive voice in the selection of his own minister.

This loss of patronage by the governor gave great offence to the "ardent and narrow-minded" Nicholson, nearly fifty years later, and he endeavored to restore the right to the

Vestries and patronage.

[1] Campbell's *Virginia*, p. 211.
[2] Hening, I, 311.
[3] *Ibid.*, I, 240.

governor's office. An extreme high-churchman, he carried
the matter to England and secured from Attorney General
Northey an opinion against the act of 1642, which he sent
to all the vestries in the colony. But they were too firmly
intrenched in their position by time and use to be disturbed
or affected.[1] They went on their own way and too often
used their power to the disadvantage of the Church and
people. Much complaint was made of their proceedings
from time to time, especially for frequent refusal to install
ministers as rectors, preferring to *hire* them from year to year,
in order " to make slaves of them." Godwyn's letter to
Berkeley complained that: " Ministers are most miserably
handled by their Plebeian Juntos, the Vesteries ; " that they
were browbeaten and poorly paid, and there was no inducement for good men to come from England.[2]

The specially notable feature in this situation, aside from
its influence on the state of religion, is the fact that it marks
the first step towards disestablishment, unconsciously taken,
indeed, and with no thought of such an issue. At the same
time it was a stride towards the freedom of the Church, the
first and successful protest in the Church itself against the
interference of the civil power.

Despite the presence of this unsuspected seed of disunion,
the leaders in Virginia seem to have felt that, with the
Puritan services suppressed, the condition of the Church was
prosperous in Berkeley's first term as governor. A tract
published in London in 1649, entitled, " *A Perfect Description of Virginia*," [3] says : " They have twenty Churches in
Virginia, and the Doctrines and orders after the Church of
England. The Ministers' Livings are esteemed worth at least
£100 *per annum ;* they are paid by each planter so much
Tobacco *per* Pole and so many bushels of corn ; they live all
in peace and love."

[1] Campbell, *Virginia*, p. 367.
[2] Anderson, *Colonial Church*, II, 559.
[3] Force, *Historical Tracts*, II.

With the accession of Cromwell to power in England, the Cromwell. intolerance of Virginia received a temporary check. Commissioners from the commonwealth, one of whom, Bennett, succeeded Berkeley as governor, came out to visit the colonies and regulate their affairs. By an agreement between them and the colonial legislature, all oppressions were forbidden, and "the use of the book of common-prayer permitted for one year, save the prayers for the King."[1] It does not appear, however, that the limit of one year was regarded. The Anglican service was connived at and continued through the commonwealth period, while non-conformists were unmolested. The direction of Church affairs was left to the people, and in relation thereto but two laws were passed, in 1655 and 1657.[2] The one ordered that tithes in a vacant parish should be paid to the county court. The other formally committed to the vestries and people the care of ecclesiastical affairs, an act which would possibly have soon issued in an entire separation of Church from State, had not the restoration of the kingdom put an end to its validity.

The liberalizing tendency of the period, however, was Quakers. not universal, and in 1659 Virginia ranged herself with Massachusetts and New York in persecuting Quakers. The strange zeal which brought the early followers of Fox into every place where a chance of persecution offered, led some of their number to Virginia, where at once they were proscribed. We have no such detailed account of proceedings against them as exists in the annals of Massachusetts, but the laws to suppress them were surpassed in severity by the northern colony only in its imposition of the death penalty. In 1659[3] the legislature enacted its first law against the sect. Not anticipating their coming, as did Massachusetts, Virginia waited until the arrival of the dreaded agitators. Then the house of burgesses proceeded against "that unreasonable and turbulent sort of people, comonly

[1] Burke, *Virginia*, II, 90 ; Anderson, *Colonial Church*, II, 151–159.
[2] Hening, I, 400, 433.   [3] *Ibid.*, I, 532.

called Quakers." Shipmasters were forbidden to bring them
to the colony under a penalty of £100. The same penalty
was ordered for any person "entertaining" any Quaker.
No person could publish or dispose of their books. All members of the sect in the colony were to be arrested and imprisoned until "they abjure the country," and then were to
depart with all speed and not return again.[1] If banished
Quakers should return, they were to be punished as "con-
temners of the law and magistrates," and if they should be
"a third time so audacious and impudent as to return hither,"
they were "to be proceeded against as felons."

That was what Virginia had to say to Quakers under the
commonwealth. Under the Restoration, when Berkeley had
returned as governor, the repressive laws were reënacted,
though with somewhat less severe penalties.[2] In 1661 it was
ordered that Quakers not attending the Church service should
be fined "under the statute 23^d Elizabeth"; and any person
attending a Quaker meeting should be fined one hundred
pounds of tobacco. Again, in 1663, the act of 1659 was
substantially repassed, with the substitution of tobacco for
pounds sterling in the description of penalty. The failure
of a magistrate to enforce the law was punishable by a fine
of two thousand pounds of tobacco.

This clause of urgency on the magistrates is a clear indication that the practical severity of proceedings against the
Quakers was relaxing; of which the act gives another token
in a clause permitting the release of Quakers on giving
security not to assemble to worship. It shows that the authorities, however hostile in feeling to the sect, had recognized the fact that their exclusion from the colony had become
impossible.[3]

---

[1] Under this law William Robinson, who was soon afterward hanged at
Boston, was imprisoned for several months.

[2] Hening, II, 48, 181, 198.

[3] Of this hostile feeling the house of burgesses gave a sharp exhibition in
their treatment of John Porter, the member from Norfolk. He opposed the
act of 1663, and the house promptly vacated his seat, "for being loving to

But the Quakers held their ground, though with many vexations for some years. Especially did the petulant Berkeley endeavor to make things unpleasant for them.[1] A large number of them were from time to time arraigned and fined. One of them, Owen, said, "Tender consciences must obey the law of God, however they suffer"; to be met by Berkeley with the reply, "There is no toleration for wicked consciences." In 1672 William Edmundson sought from Berkeley a kinder treatment of the Friends, but could obtain no satisfaction. On his complaining to Major General Bennett that the governor "was very peevish and brittle," the General asked, "Did he call you dog, rogue?"—"No," said Edmundson. "Then," was the reply, "you took him in his best humor, those being his usual terms when he is very angry; for he is an enemy to every appearance of good."

After Berkeley's time we read of no further molestation of the Quakers, though it was not until the next century that they obtained from legislation that relief in the matter of tithes, oaths, and military service, which their consciences demanded.[2] It is notable that the final act of exemption from all proscriptive penalties, an act which classes them with the Mennonites as "those peaceable and industrious people," was not passed until 1783.

The Restoration put an end to the qualified liberty which the commonwealth had allowed in Virginia, and Berkeley returned to his government fully prepared to assert the claims of the Church of England. His instructions from the king enjoined him to "special care that the Common Prayer, The Restoration.

---

the Quakers." Such a proceeding looks like a high-handed interference with the limited liberty of debate which obtained in deliberative bodies of the day, but it is probable that Porter had given, outside of the house, other evidence of friendliness to the proscribed sect. On his purgation he was offered the oaths of allegiance and supremacy and he refused them, to be at once expelled.

[1] Bancroft, *United States*, II, 201.

[2] Hening, *Statutes*, III, 298; VIII, 242; IX, 34; X, 201, 314, 334, 362, 417; XI, 252, 503.

as now established, be read each Sunday and Holy Day, and the blessed Sacraments administered according to the *Rights* of the Church of England." He was ordered to care for the Churches, and have more built; to see also that the ministers were supported, homes built for them with glebes of one hundred acres each.[1] In edifying contrast with the usual intent of the establishment, and also with the legislation immediately enacted in the colony, the king's instructions further declared: "and because we are willing to give all possible encouragement to persons of different persuasions in matters of Religion to transport themselves thither with their stock, You are not to suffer any man to be molested or disquieted in the exercise of his Religion, so he be content with a quiet and peaceable enjoying it, and not giving therein offence or scandall to the Government."

Berkeley, it would seem, considered that to himself, as the government, any non-Anglican worship was so great an offence as to negative all the tolerance of his instructions. His first legislation in 1661[2] enacted stringent laws. The old law of 1642 was revived, and to it were added requirements, that "the whole liturgy of the Church of England should be *thoroughly* read every Sunday"; that the ministers should preach every Sunday, and administer the Lord's Supper at least twice a year, and that no catechism should be used other than that appointed by the canons. Another law declared that no ministers, "but such as were ordained by some Bishop in England," could be allowed in the colony. All others were to be sent away. Still another statute limited the right of performing the marriage service to ministers of the Church of England, and declared the children of marriages by other ministers illegitimate. In the following year the legislature vented its wrath against the "many schismatical persons, so averse to the established religion and so

Stringent laws.

---

[1] *Virginia Historical Society*, July, 1895, p. 15 ; Anderson, *Colonial Church*, II, 548.

[2] Hening, II, 46, 47, 49.

filled with the new-fangled conceits of their own heretical inventions, as to refuse to have their children baptized." Then followed penalties for such refusal, and it was ordered that no non-conformist could teach, even in private, under pain of banishment.[1] The same session made a new vestry law, constituting a vestry of twelve in each parish, giving power to levy all taxes, and also to fill all vacancies in their own body. Thus "the control passes from the parish to a close corporation which the parish could neither alter nor direct."

These severe measures reinstated bigotry in greater force than it had ever held in Virginia, and many of the more liberal minded, specially from the Puritans in Nansemond, went over into North Carolina. This with the previous departure of Puritans to Maryland, estimated (probably over-estimated) by Howison as to the number of one thousand, reacted on the colony to its very serious moral and religious loss. All accounts agree that the condition of religious affairs was deplorable. Besides the departure of the non-conformist element, two other causes of this condition are noted. The one was the peculiar character of settlement, not in towns and villages, but on large plantations. The planter lived in the midst of his wide tract, surrounded by his family and servants, with no neighbors within miles. Frequent social or religious gatherings were difficult. The Church thus suffered, and the people were largely strangers to its services, with the consequences of much dissoluteness of life. Scattered settlements.

The pamphlet, *Virginia's Cure:*[2] *Discovering the true ground of that church's unhappiness, and the only true Remedy. Presented to the Bishop of London, 1661,* enlarges on the evils of this scattered condition. It calls this "settling remote from the Church" by the hard name of "Sacrilege," as causing "the Sin of robbing God of his Publick Worship and Service in the House of Prayer." It further complains "Virginia's Cure."

[1] Bancroft, *United States,* II, 201.   [2] Force, *Historical Tracts,* III.

of great destitution of Churches and ministers, that many
parishes were without Church buildings, and that not more
than one-fifth of the parishes were supplied with ministers.
As to the remedy, the " *Cure* " desired more and better ministers, with a bishop to direct them. This appears to be the
first outcry for an American episcopate so frequently heard in
after years. It is echoed in this same year, 1661, by the
Rev. Philip Mallory, who was sent to England to obtain
assistance for the Virginia Churches, and insisted that the
government should " send a bishop so soon as there should
be a city for a see." [1]

Clerical morals.   But the most baleful influence was in the moral character
of most of the ministers in the colony. The majority were
men of disrepute in England who had emigrated to Virginia,
either to retrieve their reputation or to indulge their vices
unchecked. They were profane swearers, brawlers, drunk-
ards, gamblers, and licentious. This shameful character
received statutory recognition in the laws of 1669 and 1705 [2]
against infidelity, blasphemy, swearing, Sabbath-breaking,
adultery, etc., which specially provided that " clergymen
guilty of any of these crimes " were not to be exempted from
the penalties of the law! To suppose that the moral character
of the clergy did not give reason for that provision, changes
the statute into a monstrous and gratuitous insult to the
Church and its ministry, — an impossible thing for a legislature imbued with reverence for the Church and its orders.

Morgan Godwyn, in the letter to Berkeley already quoted,
wrote, " Two thirds of the preachers are made up of leaden
lay priests of the vestry's ordination, and are both the shame
and grief of the rightly ordained clergy here." [3] This Godwyn was a clergyman, who spent some time in Virginia and
addressed the Bishops of England praying for a godly ministry. That address is lost. Godwyn was called by the Virginia agents in London, " an inconsiderable wretch," but an

[1] Campbell, *Virginia*, p. 251.   [2] Hening, III, 171, 358.
[3] Campbell, *Virginia*, p. 278.

abundance of other proof shows that his testimony in regard to the Virginia clergy is not to be invalidated.

Hammond's famous *Leah and Rachel*, or *Two Fruitful Sisters, Virginia and Maryland* (London, 1656),[1] uses strong language. Speaking of the efforts to obtain ministers from England, it says, " But Virginia savoring not handsomely in England, very few of good conversation would adventure thither (as thinking it a place wherein surely the fear of God was not), yet many came, such as wore Black Coats, and could babble in a Pulpit, roare in a Tavern, exact from their Parishioners, and rather by their dissoluteness destroy, than feed, their Flocks." The pamphlet further says that some of these reprobate persons were by the authorities " questioned, silenced, and forced to depart the country."

That such charges were just is further indicated by the acknowledgments of men with every inducement to prove them slanderous, if such proof were possible. Thus Anderson, a clergyman of the Church of England, and an historian giving many instances of special pleading for the claims and honor of the Church, writing of the sad condition of the Virginia establishment,[2] says, " Endowments by the Colonial Legislature only magnified the evil. They bribed to indolence ministers already settled in the province and attracted from the mother country others, who had long been a reproach to it. . . . Not a few of the clergy remained steadfast, . . . worthy, prudent, and pious, meeting with the love, respect, and encouragement that such men may deserve to expect. But these, it must be confessed, were exceptions to the general character of the clergy."

To this may be added the testimony of Meade,[3] Bishop of Virginia, 1829–1862: " Immense were the difficulties in getting a full supply of ministers of any character ; and of

[1] Force, *Historical Tracts*, III.
[2] *History of Colonial Church*, III, 217, 221.
[3] *Old Churches and Families of Virginia*, pp. 14–18 ; Hening, II, 157.

those who came how few were faithful and duly qualified for the station! . . . It is a well established fact that some, who were discarded from the English Church, yet obtained livings in Virginia. . . . There was not only defective preaching, but most evil living among the clergy. . . . One of them was for years president of a jockey club; another fought a duel in sight of the very Church in which he had performed the solemn offices of religion : another quarreled with his vestry violently, and on the next Sunday preached from the words of Nehemiah, 'And I contended with them, and cursed them, and smote certain of them, and plucked off their hair.'"

Governor Berkeley's testimony in the matter has been frequently quoted and is not to be set down to his constitutional bile. It is in his official reply to the annual "Inquiries" of 1671 from the home government as to the state of the province, and reads, "As to religious teaching — We have 48 parishes and our ministers are well paid, and by my consent should be better, if they would pray oftener and preach less. But as of all other commodities, so of this, the worst are sent us, and we had few that we could boast of since the persecution in Cromwell's tiranny drove divers worthy men hither."

The sole purpose in noting this degeneracy in the Virginia clergy is to mark it as a powerful factor in the question of Church and State. Accounts agree that the moral condition of the people generally was not of a high order, but even loose laymen object to clergymen whose morals are no better than their own. Says Meade, "It is not wonderful that disaffection should take place, and dissent begin." Long before the fall of the establishment in Virginia, the immense majority of the people were dissenters, many of them alienated from the Episcopal Church by this condition of its clergy.

Another less direct means may be found in the governmental restrictions on intellectual life. Schools were rarities, and printing was forbidden. Commissary Blair found

Schools and printing.

immense difficulty in founding his college at Williamsburg. Berkeley, in the above-quoted reply, exults over the lack : " But I thank God " — it is a consolation to him for the immorality of the clergy — " there are no free schools nor printing; and I hope we shall not have these hundred years : for learning has brought disobedience and heresy and sects into the world, and printing has divulged them and libels against the best government. God keep us from both ! " In 1682 Governor Culpepper and the council had before them a certain John Buckner, who had been guilty of printing the laws of 1680, and commanded him not to print anything ! The first evidence of printing thereafter in Virginia was in the Revised Laws, edition of 1733.[1] In 1683 Lord Howard of Effingham succeeded Culpepper in Virginia, and the royal instructions commanded him to " allow no person to use a printing press on any occasion whatsoever." [2]

In the year following the arrival of a governor, whose *instructions* were so narrow, there came into Virginia the man whose influence in the cause of religious liberty in the colonies must be reckoned as second to that of but few others. This was Francis Makemie, the first Presbyterian minister in America. Born and educated in Ireland, he was ordained in 1681 by the presbytery of Laggan to missionary work in the colonies. He went first to Barbadoes and soon thereafter came to Virginia. He settled in Accomac, where was his home until his death in 1708. A man of great devotion and courage, he not only labored diligently in the neighborhood of his home, but also spent much time in preaching tours, extending them into Carolina, and so far north as New York. It was in the latter colony that those experiences were suffered, which gave him his high place in the history of religious freedom, and which will be detailed when we come to tell the story of that province. He " durst not deny preaching and hoped he never should, while it was wanting and desired." [3]

Makemie.

---

[1] Hening, II, 518.   [2] Anderson, *Colonial Church*, II, 594.
[3] Campbell, *Virginia*, p. 371 ; Foote, *Sketches of Virginia*, p. 40.

In Virginia he suffered many annoyances from the authorities, but does not seem to have been subjected to any severity. He was the first dissenting minister in Virginia to obtain a certificate under the English toleration act of 1689, wherewith William and Mary signalized their accession to the throne. Together with this certificate Makemie obtained licenses for two houses in Accomac as places of dissenting worship, to which still another was added by 1704.[1]

The Virginia legislature was most grudgingly compelled to recognize the toleration act. Its first certificate, that to Makemie, was not issued until 1699; and in after years, as will presently appear, every new variety of religious worship was forced to extort its rights under the act, by dint of much effort and clamor, and, at times, of great suffering. Notwithstanding this, Beverly states that "liberty of conscience is given to all other congregations pretending to Christianity, on condition that they submit to the parish dues."[2]

In the following years, some exemptions from this condition were granted, because of special influence and spasms of unwonted legislative clemency. Many of the Huguenot refugees found their way to the colonies, and a number of those who came to Virginia were in 1700 organized by the governor and council into "The Huguenot Parish of King William"; of which parish it was ordered that "the inhabitants be left at their own liberty to agree with and pay their minister, as the circumstances will permit."[3] In 1730, through the influence of Governor Spotswood, the same exemption was granted to the German Lutherans of Germanna. But these favors were quite exceptional, and it does not appear

---

[1] Beverly in his *History of Virginia*, in an amusing effort to apologize for this success of dissenters, remarks : "Those counties, where the Presbyterian meetings are, produce very mean tobacco, and for that reason can not get an orthodox minister to stay amongst them : but whenever they could the people very orderly went to Church."

[2] *History of Virginia*, p. 226.

[3] Hening, III, 478 ; IV, 306 ; *Virginia Historical Collection*, V, 60.

that the other dissenters were relieved of Church rates until the Revolution brought the fall of the establishment.

For many years, indeed, though the sentiments of a large proportion of the people were averse to the established Church, there was yet little growth of dissenting bodies. Most of the aversion was due to irreligion, rather than to any force of conscience or desire for non-conforming worship. There was great neglect of worship, and the legislature was almost yearly exerting itself to force the people to attend services and to bring their children for baptism. Acts were multiplied to this end, and to create, divide, and unite parishes, in order to facilitate attendance on the established Church.[1] There was a strenuous governmental effort to counteract: first, the dissent of indifference ; and second, the spiritual dissent of the Presbyterian revival.

In 1702, there were reported forty-nine parishes with thirty-four ministers, three Quaker Meetings, and three Presbyterian congregations. Beyond these small numbers dissenting bodies did not greatly increase until the fifth decade of the century, and Governor Spotswood was able to write his famous report of 1710:[2] "This government is in perfect peace and tranquillity, under due obedience to royal authority and a gentlemanly conformity to the Church of England."

Occasionally there arose a desire for old-time persecution. Persecution. In 1722 the grand jury made thirteen presentments of absentees from divine service. At the same court Messrs. Mosley and Shelton were tried for baptizing a child, and required to give bonds for good behaviour, in default of which they were thrown into jail and condemned to suffer thirty-one stripes, "16 in the evening and 15 in the morning."[3]

Meanwhile there was a continual influx of elements of population which were eventually to bring the establishment

---

[1] Hening, *Statutes*, Vols. IV–VIII, *passim*.

[2] Bancroft, *United States*, III, 29.

[3] Anderson, *History of Colonial Church*, III, 216.

Baptists.   to grief. In 1714, a small number of English Baptists settled in the southeastern part of the province; and thirty years later a larger number came to the northwestern part and settled in the region of the Blue Ridge. These immigrations do not seem to have aroused the immediate opposition of the government.[1] It was not until the very end of the colonial period that the Virginia Baptists were driven to fight their noble battle for liberty of worship.

Other sects.   In 1729 began the immigration of sturdy Scotch Irish — almost to a man Presbyterian — which peopled much of the mountain regions about the head-waters of the Potomac, the Rappahannock, and the James.[2] To them were added many Germans, Lutheran and Reformed, first from the Palatinate and then from Pennsylvania. These Irish and Germans were fortunate in their location, so far as concerned their freedom of religion. Their distance from the seat of government served to obscure the offence of their non-conformity, while the government was anxious to have the frontier settled, as a " Barrier " against Indian attack, without close scrutiny into the religious preferences of the settlers.

Methodists.   Somewhat later the Methodists began to come into the colony, though they are not to be classed among the nonconformists or the strugglers for religious liberty. As in England, so in Virginia, they avowed their adherence to the established Church and, though they instituted an order of lay preachers, they insisted on the administration of ordinances by the hands of the regular clergy. They met with no opposition from the Virginia government, but identified themselves with the establishment, thus procuring to themselves no small portion of odium in the Revolution, as tories in politics and opponents to full freedom of worship.[3] It was because of this cordial regard between the Methodists

Whitefield.   and the establishment that Whitefield was permitted to freely

[1] Campbell, *Virginia*, p. 553 ; Howison, *Virginia*, II, 160.
[2] Foote, *Sketches of Virginia*, p. 99.
[3] Campbell, *Virginia*, p. 562.

preach in Virginia, during his visits to America; and it is to be noted that he so preached on the special invitation of Commissary Blair, the representative in Virginia of the bishop of London, to whom the care of the colonial Church had been committed by the government.[1] To this preaching of White-field is doubtless to be attributed an indirect influence in widening the limits of liberty. Its straightforward gospel teaching and its fervent eloquence made a profound impression in Virginia, as in other colonies, powerfully aiding in the introduction of a better moral and religious life.

Among its most notable immediate effects was the almost dramatic movement in which Morris and Winston were the principal figures. While there is no record that these men ever came into personal contact with the great preacher, we may take it as beyond doubt that they received their religious impulse from his work. With a few neighboring families in Hanover County, they withdrew themselves from the services of the established Church, and met at the house of Morris for worship. As their numbers grew, Morris built a reading-house for this express use.

This Samuel Morris is described as " a brick-layer, of singu- Morris. lar simplicity of character; sincere, devout, earnest." [2] He attempted no exercise of preaching, but read to the little congregation from such religious books as he could obtain — the Bible, a volume of Whitefield's Sermons, Luther's Table-Talk and Commentary on Galatians. The leaders of the movement, uninstructed in matters of Church polity and unguided by any minister, were at a loss to decide what to call themselves by way of religious denomination, and from their favorite author were at first disposed to assume the name of Lutherans.

These irregular religious services soon drew the attention of the authorities, and the leaders of the movement were summoned to answer before the governor and council. On

[1] Campbell, *Virginia*, p. 355.
[2] *Ibid.*, p. 438; Howison, *Virginia*, II, 170.

their way to such answer they found a copy of the Westminster Confession, with which they were so pleased that
they adopted it as their own, and presented it to the governor
as an exhibition of their creed and denomination. This book
was well known to Governor Gooch, who exclaimed, " These
men are Presbyterians," and acknowledged their rights under
the act of toleration.

Governor
Gooch.

Gooch was a man of unusual liberality of feeling, in marked
contrast with most of the royal governors. A letter of his is preserved in reply to one from the synod of Philadelphia, written
in 1738 to solicit the governor's kindly consideration for the
Presbyterians settled in the northern part of the province.
To this the governor answered: " You may be assured no
interference shall be given to any minister of their profession, who shall come among them, so as they conform themselves to the rules prescribed by the Act of Toleration in
England." [1]   In the opinion of Samuel Davies, had the governor been alone in power, the Presbyterians of Hanover
would have suffered little annoyance.[2] He wrote: " The
Hon. Sir William Gooch, our late governor, discovered a
ready disposition to allow us all claimable privileges, and the
greatest aversion to persecuting measures ; but, considering
the shocking reports spread abroad concerning us by officious
malignants, it is no great wonder the council discovered a
considerable reluctance to tolerate us. Had it not been for
this, I persuade myself that they would have shown themselves the guardians of our legal privileges."

The issue of this first action of the authorities seems to
have been without oppression, but the next few years brought
much opposition, and it is estimated that Morris paid more

[1] Foote, *Sketches of Virginia*, p. 103. Gooch was governor for twenty-two
years, and retired in 1749, " amid the regrets of the people. Notwithstanding some flexibility of principle, he was estimable in public and private character. His capacity and intelligence were of a high order, and were adorned
by uniform courtesy and dignity and a singular amenity of manners."
(Campbell, *History of Virginia*, p. 448.)

[2] Campbell, *History of Virginia*, p. 448.

than twenty fines for his steadfast adherence to the new movement.[1]

On the recognition of their rights by the governor the Hanover people at once declared themselves Presbyterians and applied to the synod of Philadelphia. The synod put the matter under the care of the presbytery of Newcastle, which sent William Robinson to organize a Church among them. He was the first non-Anglican minister to preach in Hanover County, and very shortly after so doing he was arrested for preaching without a license from the government; but he was soon released and permitted to continue his work. *Presbytery.*

In the next year, 1745, the presbytery sent two other ministers, John Blair and John Roan, the latter of whom was a man of unwisdom, and whose course may be charged with much of the responsibility for the subsequent annoyances suffered by the Presbyterians. Not content with preaching the gospel, Roan went out of his way to assail the character of the established clergy. However vulnerable that character might be, Roan's attack was both unnecessary and impolitic. The consequence was natural enough. The clergy were roused to great indignation, intensifying their opposition to this lately tolerated dissent. Their complaints, together with many "shocking reports of officious malignants," were hurried to the governor, whose sympathy was excited for the regular clergy : for, however he might be willing to tolerate an orderly dissent, he was too much of an Anglican to permit attacks on his own Church.

Gooch at once summoned the grand jury and denounced Roan and Joshua Morris, in whose house Roan had preached. In his charge to the jury the governor said, "It is not liberty of conscience, but freedom of speech, they so earnestly prosecute, and we are very sure that they have no manner of pretence to any shelter under the Acts of Toleration." [2] *Severe measures.*

[1] Howison, *Virginia*, II, 174.
[2] Foote, *Sketches*, p. 136 ; Burke, *Virginia*, III, 121.

The grand jury found a true bill, and the case was tried, with the result that Morris was heavily fined and Roan, who had fled to Philadelphia, was exiled.

The sequence to this trouble was continued annoyance to the Presbyterians; the authorities, with the exception of Gooch, making use of every opportunity to hamper and disturb. This they did by objecting to licenses for their ministers, granting some only after much struggle and refusing others altogether; by making much question also about the number of preaching houses, and seizing promptly upon the offence of preaching in a house not licensed. So long as Gooch remained governor, he acted as mediator between the Presbyterians and the council, but for a few years after his retirement in 1749, the new movement found itself "under the harrow."

Davies.

The man who exerted the greatest influence in securing their peaceful enjoyment of toleration, was Samuel Davies, than whose name the story of American Presbyterianism presents few more illustrious. Born at New Castle, Delaware, in 1723, he was educated in Pennsylvania, and, on his ordination at the age of twenty-three, was at once sent by the presbytery to Virginia. In 1746 he appeared at Williamsburg and sought a license to preach from the government, which the council at first refused, but by the governor were persuaded to grant.[1] With the license Davies went to Hanover, "and was received with joy, since on the Sunday before a notice had been fixed on Morris' Reading House forbidding itinerant preaching and warning people not to attend."[2]

Rodgers.

Davies settled near the Falls of the James, and in 1748 another minister, John Rodgers, was sent by the presbytery to join him. It is very probable that Rodgers ventured to

[1] Campbell, p. 446.

[2] Of Davies it is said, that "his fervid eloquence attracted large congregations, including many Churchmen." "Few who ever heard him preach," says Howison (*History of Virginia*, II, 180) "could entirely resist his influence." Patrick Henry declared that, by hearing him he was himself first taught what an orator should be.

preach without first obtaining a license, for such accusation was made against him when he applied for governmental permission. Gooch urged the Council to license him, but the majority refused, saying, " We have Mr. Rodgers out, and we are determined to keep him out." This determination was doubtless due to the ardent opposition of some of the established clergy, who followed Davies and Rodgers to Williamsburg, to combat the application.[1]

It is stated that Commissary Blair joined Gooch in urging the Council to give the license. " The young men insisted that they had asked nothing but a right, and not a privilege." But the effort failed, and Rodgers was forced to leave the province, entering on a career of distinguished usefulness in the north, as pastor for many years of the " Brick Church " in New York, and moderator of the first general assembly in America.[2]

Davies was thus left alone in Virginia, and presently his foes made new trouble for him by endeavoring to restrict his labors. It was a necessity of labor among such a widely scattered population that he should preach in many different stations, against which itineracy the legal point was made that his license allowed him to preach in only one place or house. This new action carried him to Williamsburg again, where it was sought to obtain an injunction from the court forbidding his scattered ministrations. Davies's answer contended that his course was justified by the grants of the toleration act, and the case turned upon the question as to whether the English act was of force in Virginia. The celebrated Peyton Randolph, the attorney-general, appeared in prosecution, while Davies pleaded his own cause, the court granting his request

---

[1] Foote (*Sketches of Virginia*, p. 165) relates of one of them, that he was so furious and vindictive as to extort from Gooch the rebuke: " I am surprised at you ! You profess to be a minister of Jesus Christ, and you come and complain of a man and wish me to punish him, for preaching the gospel. For shame, Sir ! Go home and mind your own duty. For such conduct you deserve to have your gown stripped from your shoulders."

[2] Sprague, *Annals of the American Pulpit.*

to be allowed to speak with some surprise that he should venture to cross swords with so famous an advocate. Not only did he win his case, but he astonished his auditors, some of whom said, " The attorney-general has met his match today." In 1753 Davies visited England and there obtained from Attorney-General Northey an opinion confirmatory of his own, to the effect that the toleration act of 1689 had the force of law in all parts of the British dominions. Thus the Presbyterians of Virginia secured their rights, so far as the statute did allow.[1]

Growing disaffection.

There is no doubt that the result of the Presbyterian contest was grateful to the majority of the people. The established Church was steadily losing ground in their affection and respect. They could see nothing but oppression in forbidding an irregular worship, where great distances made attendance on the established Church, to many a matter of much difficulty, and to others impossible. At the same time the failure of so many of the clergy to command respect still further emphasized their alienation, while the frequent oppressive acts of the authorities only served to nurture a growing popular indignation.

This feeling was not only shared by the common people, but found expression from many in the highest circles of society. Some of them, though in the communion of the established Church, were beginning to doubt the wisdom of the entire system of union between religion and the civil power. Thus, Lawrence Washington wrote to Governor Dinwiddie: [2] " It has been my opinion, and I hope ever will be, that restraints on conscience are cruel in regard to those on whom they are imposed, and injurious to the country imposing them."

[1] For Davies himself, who had thus valiantly and wisely been their champion, he remained in Virginia only a few years, being called to the presidency of the College of New Jersey, as successor to Jonathan Edwards. His tenure of that office was but for eighteen months, when death cut short his singularly brilliant life at the early age of thirty-six. (Sprague, *Annals.*)

[2] Campbell, *Virginia*, p. 453.

The letter had special reference to Germans contemplating settlement in Virginia, but deterred by fear of the established Church.   Mr. Washington wanted the governor, at that time in England, to secure some relief for them from the government, which Dinwiddie expressed his doubts of obtaining, though himself in favor of the desired exemption.   It was not until the opening of the Revolution that the relief sought, of exemption from Church rates, was accorded to dissenters by the colonial legislature.[1]

Dinwiddie, whose advent as governor was hailed by Davies   Dinwiddie. as a " happy omen," had been educated in the Church of Scotland, and had sincere regard for the Presbyterians.   In his office of governor he was guilty of no unfriendly acts, though he concerned himself, as his duty required, in the direction of affairs in the establishment.   Of this direction two curious incidents are preserved in his own letters.[2]   One is in a letter to St. Anne's Parish, December 13, 1751, presenting " the Bearer, the Rev. Mr. John Ramsay — I desire that you will receive and Entertain him as your Pastor."   The other is a letter to the bishop of London, September 12, 1757, in which the governor gives an account of a recent trial of a clergyman for immorality and " monstrous crimes."   The trial was before the governor and council and was really an ecclesiastical trial, for the man, having been found guilty, was by the governor deposed from the ministry and not otherwise punished.

The occurrence of the French and Indian war, with its excitements and alarms, so occupied the minds of the government that attention to Church affairs made in its period but few notes in legislation.   Nor do the courts seem to have bestowed much regard upon the continually increasing number of dissenters, who were practically left to follow their preferences without molestation.   Only two acts of the legislature during that period call for remark.

[1] Hening, IX, 164.
[2] *Virginia Historical Collection*, III, 14 ; IV, 695.

Papists.

One is the act of 1756,[1] "for Disarming Papists." All Papists were required to surrender their arms and ammunition, on penalty of three months' imprisonment, the loss of their arms, and fine. It is clear, however, that the measure, like a similar proposition in Pennsylvania, was more political than religious. The act observed that the "Papists were dangerous at this time" of war with their fellow-religionists. This does not explain another curious clause of the act, which forbade a Papist to keep a horse "above the value of £5, on pain of forfeiture." Only a desire to annoy would seem to account for that provision.

The other piece of legislation to be noted is the act of 1758, called the "Two-Penny Act," which stands in the history as having a powerful influence tending both to religious disestablishment and to political independence. It should be premised that a law of 1748 had fixed the minister's salary at sixteen thousand pounds of tobacco. At the ordinary price of tobacco at six pence *per* pound, this made the ministerial stipend exactly £400.

Two-Penny Act.

In 1755, and the following year,[2] the tobacco crop failed through drought, while the heavy taxes incident to the French war had added to the financial burdens of the people. Many complaints of the situation were carried to the legislature, and that body in 1758 enacted a law, "to run for ten months," that all debts payable in tobacco could be paid, either in tobacco, or in money at the rate of eighteen shillings and eight pence *per* one hundred pounds of tobacco. This reduced the price of tobacco, for the purpose of debt paying, to two pence *per* pound, and struck two-thirds from the ministerial salary. The act did not discriminate against the clergy, but applied to "all debts payable in tobacco," yet it affected the clergy more disastrously than others ; for, while afterward other contracts could be made on a money basis,

[1] Hening, *Statutes*, VII, 35.

[2] Campbell, *Virginia*, pp. 507-514 ; Foote, *Sketches*, p. 171 ; Hawks, *Ecclesiastical Contributions*, I, 120–126.

the clerical contract was by law fixed in terms of tobacco. Besides, the price of tobacco immediately rose above the usual rate, and the holders of it, compounding with the clergy at the ruinous reduction, really enriched themselves at the expense of the ministerial purse.

There can be no doubt that the act was thoroughly unjust, and no wonder is caused by the natural outcry of the clergy. Rev. John Camm, of York Hampton Parish, assailed the law in a pamphlet, *The Two-Penny Act*, which was answered by Colonels Bland and Carter. But no argument could justify the law. Sherlock, bishop of London, denounced the act; and the king in council refused to approve, though it does not appear that it was ever formally declared void.

Camm brought suit against his vestry for the full amount of salary for several years, at the rate of sixteen thousand pounds of tobacco at six pence *per* pound, the claim reaching to nearly £2400. On this the house of burgesses took the remarkable action of voting to support the vestry in its defence — a vote notable in two ways: first, that the interference of the legislature in such a matter was as unwarrantable as it was unprecedented; and second, that it notes the first legislative action of Virginia towards independence. The legislature was so bent on justifying its own law that it was blind to its own offence in thus interfering with the course of justice. The case went against Camm, who appealed to the king in council, but the appeal was dismissed on the ground of some informality, and "the clergy were left to take their chances in the Virginia courts."

The next suit was brought by Rev. Mr. Warrington, and the court awarded damages to him, while inconsistently declaring that the law of 1758 was valid! The suit of Rev. Alexander White had a similar issue. The great issue — great, both because of its utterly unexpected result and its lifting to the first position among orators a man unknown before — was joined in Hanover County court on the suit of Rev. James Maury in 1763. The court declared the act of

1758 invalid, as not approved by the king, and ordered that at the next term of court a jury should determine damages for the plaintiff.   The popular impression was, justly, that the whole question was practically decided in favor of the clergy, and at the next term the council for defendant, John Lewis, threw up the case.   No well-known lawyer could be found to take his place; and the case was well-nigh gone by default, when the defendants took for their advocate a young, un-known, awkward, unfledged lawyer, whose past had been spent in playing the fiddle, keeping a country store, swap-ping stories in taverns, and in desultory reading.   Perhaps never elsewhere has one action at once opened to a man such an avenue of usefulness, and crowned him with such imme-diate glory, as came then to Patrick Henry.   The incident is well known to all, and needs no detailed repetition here. The speech was the boldest yet made on American soil, maintaining that the act of 1758 was salutary and right, and arguing that a king, who could disallow a law designed for the relief of his distressed subjects, had forfeited his right to govern!   " The speech," says Hawks, " contained much more treason than logic — an appeal to men's passions, not to their understandings, and was managed with consummate skill."

It meant death to the " Parsons' Cause."   The jury, bound by the decision of the former term, brought in a verdict assessing damages at *one penny*.   That showed the mind of the people with sufficient clearness, and the clergy attempted no further suits.   It would have been well for them and for their Church, if they had attempted none at all, and, submit-ting to the immediate hardship of the time, had waited relief from a wiser legislature.   The damage they suffered was far greater than that represented by depleted stipends.   Immense force was added to the feeling against the establishment, the ministers of which were now described as having no concern for the poverty and burdens of the people, and only desirous of obtaining the last penny for themselves — " more anxious to enrich themselves than benefit the souls of men; and men

Marginal note: Patrick Henry.

began to admit the suspicion that the establishment was proving a burden instead of a blessing. It prepared the minds of men for the final blow struck in the stormy times of the Revolution." (Hawks.)

Before that blow was struck, another and justifying reason for it was given by the renewal of the spirit of persecution, in the most harsh and foolish actions of which the establishment was guilty. They are the more remarkable because coming after the gradual enlightenment of almost the entire colonial period and on the eve of the great struggle for freedom. So placed, the persecution of the Baptists may be rated as the worst and most inexcusable assault on freedom of conscience and worship, which our colonial history describes.[1]

Persecution of Baptists.

As before noted, Baptists began to come into the colony so early as 1714, settling quietly and undisturbed at Norfolk. Thirty years later, others began settlements in the northern part of the province, to which increasing numbers were added in the following years. In the same period numbers of Moravians and Mennonites also appeared in the Blue Ridge country. It is difficult to account for the outbreak of persecution which took place between 1765 and 1770. Twenty years before, Governor Gooch had issued a proclamation against the Moravians and Mennonites, but they do not appear to have been subjected to any more drastic measures. They quietly went about their own business and were undisturbed, sharing at last with the Quakers in the exemptions of 1766.[2]

Perhaps the bitter cup of persecution presented to the Baptists, at the same time that other sects were obtaining an enlargement of liberty, may be charged to their own violence of speech. It was a time of much religious excitement among the dissenting churches, especially in the north of

[1] Foote, *Sketches*, pp. 314, 318 ; Hawks, *Contributions*, I, 121 ; Campbell, *Virginia*, p. 553 ; Howison, *Virginia*, II, 160, 168.

[2] Hening, VIII, 242.

Virginia.[1]   The Presbyterians of the Shenandoah were
experiencing an almost constant revival through several
years, in the interest and fervor of which their Baptist brethren shared.   But the latter were not guided by the same
prudence of discussion or charity of speech which the Presbyterians observed.   Many of their preachers were illiterate :
they gave free rein to the language and manner of passion ;
and with their vehemence of gesticulation and a singularly
rasping quality of voice they wrought their hearers into a
high state of excitement.   With it all they did not scruple to
denounce the established Church and its clergy.   " There
was a bitterness," said Hawks, " in the hatred of this denomination towards the established Church, which surpassed that
of all others.   It was always prompt to avail itself of every
prejudice, which religious or political zeal could excite against
the Church. . . .   No dissenters in Virginia experienced for
a time harsher treatment than the Baptists.   They were
beaten and imprisoned, and cruelty taxed ingenuity to devise
new modes of punishment and annoyance."   It is but fair to
conclude that the former fact accounted for, though it could
not justify, the latter, in view of the peace and quietness
experienced at the time by all other dissenting churches.

The increase of the Baptists, with their impolitic freedom
of speech, excited alarm and stern opposition among churchmen.   The clergy of the establishment preached against them
as of the same sort as the Anabaptists of Munster, and the
local authorities learned to look upon them as disturbers of
the peace, to be suppressed by the civil power.

The climax came in 1768 when the sheriff of Spotsylvania
arrested John Waller, Lewis Craig, and James Childs, zealous
Baptist preachers.   On their appearance before the magistrate, release was offered if they would promise not to preach
in the county for a year and a day.   This promise was refused,
and the men were imprisoned.   Craig was released after four
weeks, but the two others lay in jail four weeks more.

[1] See Foote's *Sketches*.

It is to be noted that this persecution was entirely the act of local authorities. The colonial government had no hand in it and seems to have considered it unjust. That certainly was the mind of Governor Blair, who wrote a sharp rebuke to the sheriff of Spotsylvania County. "You may not molest these conscientious men," he wrote, "so long as they behave themselves in a manner becoming pious Christians. I am told that they differ in nothing from our Church but in (the manner of) Baptism, and their renewing of the ancient discipline, by which they have reformed some sinners and brought them to be truly penitent. . . . If this be their behaviour, it were to be wished we had some of it among us."

At the trial of Waller and Childs, which the rebuke of the governor had no power to stay, some notable things occurred. The prosecuting attorney bore testimony to their zeal in his opening words: "May it please your worship, these men are great disturbers of the peace : they can not meet a man upon the road, but they must ram a text of scripture down his throat!" The indictment charged them with "preaching the gospel contrary to law." This astonishing charge furnished to Patrick Henry the second opportunity of dramatic exhibition before a court. He offered his services to defend the poor preachers, and tradition has it that he rode fifty miles to do so. In his speech he so dwelt upon the folly and wickedness of attempting "to punish a man for preaching the gospel of the Son of God," that he overwhelmed the court and secured the immediate discharge of his clients.

But the issue of this case did not end the persecution. In 1770 two other Baptist preachers, William Webber and Joseph Anthony, were thrown into Chesterfield County jail, and there "they did much execution by preaching through the grates of their windows." In Middlesex County several Baptist ministers were imprisoned and treated like criminals. So late as 1772 a letter in the *Virginia Gazette* justified the persecution, charging the Baptists with heresy and hateful doctrines, and with disturbing the peace of religion, and denying that they were entitled to the benefit of the toleration act. This was strange language at the very time when Virginia was ringing with the cry for freedom. But it was unheeded. The end of the persecution had come, and of all persecution in America.

Fall of the establishment. Presently there was to pass into oblivion the religious establishment, in whose interest such oppression was instituted. The Church in Virginia had grown almost obsolete; its methods, its claims, its arrogance alike hateful to the great majority of the people. The causes of this issue are not far to seek. The unwillingness of the Church to permit any other worship than its own, with the consequence that many of the scattered population were deprived of all religious services; its indifference to the spiritual good of the people; the corrupt character of many of its clergy; its rancor in prosecuting any dissent; the growing sense of injustice in taxing people for the support of a religion not their own; the ill-starred Parsons' Cause, which left upon the clergy and the Church a heavy, though unjust, burden of ridicule and contempt; the persecution of the Baptists, as the last throe of a dying tyrant; and finally the ill-judged effort to establish an American episcopate — an effort to be hereinafter detailed — all together forced the Church of England in Virginia to a dishonored fall, far different from the fate which, as shall be seen, the theocratic establishment of Massachusetts met with dignity and composure.

While we can have no sympathy with the spiritual tyranny of early Massachusetts, nor approve its oppressive measures; at the same time we cannot fail to reverence the high religious motives of its leaders, by whom God's honor was chiefly to be sought; the learning and pure character of its ministry; its care for a "godly ministry" in every vicinage; and the decorous gravity with which it adapted itself, though unwillingly, to the growing liberty of mind. We look in vain for such traits in the Virginia establishment; a mere appendage of the state, with no higher demand than an outward conformity to its law, and no more earnest purpose than to secure its own perquisites and emoluments.

Thus the difference between the two institutions was immense. The Theocracy represented a magnificent dream, which had in it more of heaven than of earth — a superb effort to realize in the world the purity and duty of the City of God. The Virginia establishment debased the things of God into a mere setting for the sordidness of earth. In its fall there were few to mourn.

The details of its disestablishment will be noted in our study of the Revolutionary Period and the Final Settlements.

II. *The Carolinas*

The earliest settlers in the territory of the Carolinas came across the southern border of Virginia. Some of them were non-conformists who desired to escape from the intolerant measures of Berkeley. Some were Quakers; one of whose preachers, Edmundson, was the first man to preach the gospel in Carolina. Others, without any religious motive, sought "more and better land." This desire, according to Professor Weeks,[1] "and not that for religious liberty, was the leading factor in the settlement of North Carolina."

Governor Berkeley of Virginia had already assumed to grant property rights so far to the south as Cape Fear, but the first formal and legal action toward colonial institution in the territory was by charter, granted in 1663 by Charles Charter. II. to Lords Clarendon, Albemarle, Craven, Berkeley and Ashley, Sir George Carteret, Sir William Berkeley (governor of Virginia), and Sir John Colleton.[2] The charter constituted these eight men proprietaries of all the territory now included in the two Carolinas, with all privileges and powers

[1] *Johns Hopkins Studies*, X.

[2] Of this number Lord Berkeley and Sir George Carteret, ten years later, became proprietaries of New Jersey.

possessed by "any Bishop of Durham in the County Palatine, or Bishoprick, of Durham in our Kingdom of England." The authority thus conferred was almost regal, and was equalled among colonial charters only by that given to Baltimore, as will be noted in our sketch of Maryland. The title of "Palatine" went with these charters, and was always used by the chief of the Carolina proprietaries until the surrender of the province to the immediate government of the King; but it early fell into disuse by Baltimore.[1]

Church.

By these charters was given the right of "patronage and advowsons of all Chappells and Churches . . . according to the ecclesiastical law of our Kingdom of England."[2] We will hereafter note the peculiar construction that Baltimore put upon this right. Unlike him, the Carolina proprietaries evidently considered it as giving to the Church of England the status of an establishment in their colony. What was lacking for that end in the charter was afterward supplied in the "Fundamental Constitutions," presently to be noted.

Toleration.

At the same time the charter accorded large liberty to those "who cannot conform to . . . the liturgy, forms, and ceremonies of the Church of England, or take and subscribe the oaths and articles." To such persons the proprietaries "have full and free license, liberty and authority, by such legal ways and means as they shall think fit, to give and grant . . . such indulgences and dispensations, for and during such time and times, and with such limitations and restrictions, as they shall in their discretion think fit and reasonable."

Under this charter the proprietaries at once issued a "Declaration and Proposal,"[3] inviting emigrants to the new colony, declaring among other things, "We will grant, in as ample manner as the undertakers shall desire, freedom and liberty of conscience in all religious and spiritual things,

---

[1] Fiske, *Old Virginia and Her Neighbors*, I, 255.
[2] *North Carolina Records*, I, 22–32.
[3] *Ibid.*, I, 43.

and to be kept inviolably with them, we having power in our charter so to do." In the following year (1664) the proprietaries entered into an "Agreement" with certain "adventurers," desiring to go from Barbadoes and elsewhere to Carolina.[1] In this agreement they declared: "8. No person . . . shall be any ways molested, punished, or called in question, for any difference in opinion or practice in matters of religious concernment, who do not actually disturb the civil peace, . . . but all and every person and persons may, from time to time and at all times, freely and fully have and enjoye his and their judgments and contiences in matters of religion throughout all the Province, they behaving themselves peaceable and quietly, and not using this liberty to Lycentiousnesse, nor to the Civill Injury or outward disturbance of others; any Law, Statute or clause, usage or custom of this realm of England to the contrary hereof in any wise notwithstanding.

"9. No pretence shall be made from the charter right of advowsons to infringe the liberty above conceded . . . and we grant unto the General Assembly power to appoint ministers and establish maintenance. Giving liberty besides to any person or persons to keepe and mainteyne w^t preachers or Ministers they please."

In 1665 Charles issued a second charter in which the concession of religious liberties was repeated.[2] From both instruments and from the declaration and agreement it is evident that the foundation of Carolina designed both to establish the Church of England, and, while conceding a modified liberty to dissenters, to so put religious control in the hands of the proprietary government that at any time, in their discretion, such privilege could be withdrawn. Though the phrase "to be kept inviolably" makes promise of security, yet other portions of the instruments and the subsequent conduct of the proprietary government make it clear that

Religious control.

[1] *North Carolina Records*, I, 80.
[2] *Ibid.*, I, 102.

the authorities had no intention of abridging their own power in religious and ecclesiastical affairs. Thus, the first person appointed as governor, Sir John Yeamans, was instructed to observe the promise of religious liberty, and also to use his influence to dissuade non-conformists from settling in the colony.[1] This may be regarded merely as an indication of the proprietaries' desire, never expressed in any exclusive prescriptions. The fact was, that with their wish to obtain settlers in the colony, they were forced to content themselves with such as came, the main drift of whom were from sources outside of the Church of England. For the first twenty years the immense majority of the immigration was composed of dissenters. The Quakers scattered themselves over the whole province, but settled in largest numbers in the northern division, acquiring very considerable political power and furnishing to the proprietaries and the High Church party a constant exasperation. Joseph Blake, brother of the great admiral,

Dissenters. led a large company of English dissenters to the settlement of Charleston. Thither, also, came many Huguenots, who located themselves in that city and on the banks of the Cooper and Santee.[2] Scotland also sent many of her Presbyterians, fleeing from Claverhouse to find a refuge in North Carolina and become the fathers of those sturdy men who, in the Mecklenberg Declaration, sounded the first clear trumpet of American Independence. Baptists also appeared. Some of that faith were in Blake's Company, and in 1684 a Baptist Church migrated from Massachusetts under the lead of their pastor, William Screven. The Dutch Reformed added to the number, two shiploads of them going to Carolina from New York, in resentment of the course pursued by the English authorities on ecclesiastical questions.[3] These made the great volume of immigration. Clearly, the tide of dissent was too strong and too valuable for the proprietaries

[1] *Johns Hopkins Studies*, X (Weeks).
[2] Bancroft, *United States*, II, 172, 181.
[3] Bacon, *American Christianity*, p. 63. See also our sketch of New York.

to stem ; and with too much power to permit the success of subsequent schemes to aggrandize the Church of England. Though that Church was legally established in the Carolinas, yet it never laid hold upon the religious affections of the people at large ; and only once, and then disastrously for themselves, did the authorities venture on any measure of proscription toward dissenters.

The formal establishment of the Church was effected by the famous "Fundamental Constitutions," the most singular and fantastic instrument of government ever devised by the human mind.   It essayed to combine relics of a dead feudalism with institutions of the new popular power in a mixture both absurd and unserviceable.   In practical working the scheme proved itself impossible and in less than fifteen years was formally annulled.   The only permanent impress left on the colony was in the Church established and the laws relating to dissent.   For this reason, and also because of the unique terms and details in which the religious sections are expressed, its provisions may be here very properly recited. *Fundamental constitutions.*

The credit of framing the fundamental Constitutions has been generally given to the philosopher Locke.   If this attribution is just, it may well serve to illustrate the fact that the deepest philosophic mind may be at fault, when called to deal with practical affairs and the uncertain quantities possible in human nature and will.   The latest biographer of Locke [1] questions this usually alleged authorship, and accounts for it by the facts, that Locke was an intimate personal friend of Ashley, for many years an inmate of his lordship's household, and at the same time the secretary of the associated proprietaries.   The scheme of political government, with its palatine, landgraves, barons, and caciques, Fowler judges must have been impossible for Locke to conceive and distasteful to him when suggested by others. He concedes that it is easy to discern Locke's hand in the articles on religion, which especially concern us here. *Locke.*

[1] Fowler, *Life of Locke*, p. 22 (*English Men of Letters*).

These articles are eleven in number, entering into matters of detail with a notable particularity, and, while extending a large liberty to certain sorts of dissent, putting other sorts under a sharp ban.[1] The first specification excludes atheists and non-religionists: " 95. No man shall be permitted to be a freeman of Carolina, or to have any estate or habitation within it, that doth not acknowledge a God, and that God is publicly and solemnly to be worshipped." The next article establishes the Church of England: " 96. As the country comes to be sufficiently planted . . . it shall belong to the parliament to take care for the building of Churches and the public maintenance of divines, to be employed in the exercise of religion according to the Church of England, which, being the only true and orthodox and the natural religion of all the King's dominions, is so also of Carolina ; and, therefore, it alone shall be allowed to receive public maintenance by grant of parliament."

The next article is in form the most remarkable decree of toleration on record: " 97. But since the natives of that place . . . are utterly strangers to Christianity, whose idolatry, ignorance, or mistake gives us no reason to expel or use them ill ; and those, who remove from other parts there, will unavoidably be of different opinions concerning matters of religion, the liberty whereof they will expect to have allowed them, and it will not be reasonable for us on this account to keep them out: that civil liberty may be obtained amidst diversity of opinions, and our agreement and compact with all men may be duly and faithfully observed ; the violation whereof, upon what pretence soever, cannot be without great offence to Almighty God and great scandal to the true religion which we profess ; and also that Jews, Heathens, and other dissenters from the purity of the Christian religion may not be scared and kept at a distance from it, but, having an opportunity of acquainting themselves with the truth and reasonableness of its doctrine, and the peaceableness and in-

Atheism excluded.

Church of England.

Dissent allowed.

[1] *South Carolina Statutes*, I, 53, 54.

offensiveness of its professors, may, by good usage and persuasion and all those convincing methods of gentleness and meekness suitable to the rules and designs of the gospel, be won over to embrace and unfeignedly receive the truth:—Therefore, any Seven or more persons, agreeing in any religion, shall constitute a Church or profession, to which they shall give some name to distinguish it from others."

Certain rules for the formation and faith of such dissenting Churches are next imposed. "98. The terms of admittance and communion with any Church or profession shall be written in a book, and therein be subscribed by all members of said Church or profession, which book shall be kept by the public Register of the Precinct wherein they reside. 99. The time of every one's subscription and admittance shall be dated in the said book of religious record.

Rules for dissenting Churches.

"100. In the terms of communion of every Church or profession these following shall be there, without which no agreement or assembly of men upon pretence of religion shall be accounted a Church or profession within these rules : —

1. That there is a God ;
2. That God is publickly to be worshipped ;
3. That it is lawful and the duty of every man, being thereunto called by them that govern, to bear witness to truth; and that every Church or profession shall in their terms of communion set down the eternal way whereby they witness a truth as in the presence of God ; whether it be by laying hands on, or kissing, the bible, as in the Church of England, or by holding up the hand, or any other sensible way.

"104. Any person subscribing the terms of communion . . . before the precinct Register and any five members of said Church, or profession, shall be thereby made a member."

"108. Associations, upon any pretence whatsoever, not observing or performing the above rules, shall not be esteemed as Churches, but unlawful meetings, and be punished as other riots."

There is provision made that slaves can be members of the Church or profession, but shall "not thereby be freed from the civil dominion of their masters."

Two sections forbid molestation:

"106. No person shall use any reproachful, reviling, or abusive language against any religion of any Church or profession."

Molestation. "109. No person whatsoever shall disturb, molest, or persecute another for his special opinions in religion or his way of worship."

But the most remarkable of all the requirements is the section which outlaws an irreligious person: "101. No person above seventeen years of age shall have any Irreligion benefit or protection of the law, or be capable of any place outlawed. of profit or honor, who is not a member of some Church or profession."

This last provision is altogether unique, having no parallel in other colonial statute. The intent of it was to force an outwardly religious community, and the principle was the same as that which still operates in some European establishments, requiring confirmation and communion for every grown youth. But nowhere else can be found a formal law putting non-communicants outside the pale of law. Even in countries demanding rigid conformity to a State-Church, so long as an individual did not profess an opposing faith, a position of indifference was not counted for a crime. Of this Carolina requirement the specially novel element is that, while a broad dissent is allowed to the very limit of theism, every citizen must have some religion and be a communicant in some Church, or be an outlaw.

All the religious requirements of the "Constitutions" make a notable medley of stringency and liberty and may well take their place, along with the rules for civil foundation, among the curiosities of history. As with the civil regulations, these religious rules, save as regards the Church establishment, soon proved but an ideal which the proprietaries were unable to realize in the colony. It does not appear that the regulations governing dissent were observed with any strictness, or their method followed in the organizing of dissenting Churches. Nor does it appear that any irreligious person was ever put out of the colony, or under the ban, because of his lack of religion.

In fact, it is safe to say that no small proportion of the people must have been without any definite religion. This was specially true of North Carolina. Though the Church was established at the beginning, yet more than twenty years passed before its first clergyman was settled.[1] The settlers in South Carolina were of a higher type as regards religion, but there was a long-continued lack of ministers and the conveniences for public worship. The Quakers, not depending on a consecrated ministry, held their meetings with some approach to frequency, but for most of the people for many years there was a total destitution of ministry and Churches. So late as 1729, Colonel William Byrd wrote of Edenton, the then capital of North Carolina: "I believe this is the only metropolis in the Christian or Mohammedan world where there is neither Church, Chapel, Mosque, Synagogue, or any other place of worship of any sect or religion whatever. . . . They pay no tribute either to God or to Cæsar."[2] One wonders whether this destitution of Churches may have caused the peculiar form of the colonial law of 1691, relating to the Sabbath. It makes no allusion, as do similar statutes in other colonies, to attendance on Church services, but, forbidding all secular work, requires that "all and every person and persons shall on every Lord's Day apply themselves to the observance of the same by exercising themselves of piety and true religion."[3]

Destitution.

[1] Anderson, *Colonial Church*, II, 529.
[2] Byrd Mss., I, 59, 65.
[3] *South Carolina Statutes*, II, 69.

Anglican immigration.

Before the end of the century a large number of people attached to the Church of England emigrated to Carolina. Many of them were of gentle birth, and, with the sympathies of the proprietaries, soon founded an oligarchy, grasping after political power to be controlled in the interest of the Church.[1] Their schemes precipitated an intense political strife almost entirely on religious lines. The method pursued was such as to indicate a digested conspiracy against the liberties of the people.

Plot against dissenters.

Its first step was the specious act of 1696 giving "liberty of the Province to Aliens," which ran : "All Christians . . . (Papists only excepted) shall enjoy the full, free, and undisturbed exercise of their consciences, so as to be in the exercise of their worship according to the professed rules of their religion, without any lett, hindrance, or molestation by any power either ecclesiastical or civil whatever."[2] The purpose of the act would seem to have been that of forestalling clamor against further intended steps and to create the impression of the widest spirit of toleration. At the same time the act is silent as to the matter of civil rights, and thus is a contradiction of the promises in the now abandoned Fundamental Constitutions.

It is noticeable that, while that abandonment seemed to the colonial authorities to make necessary this assertion of religious freedom, it did not suggest the reëstablishment of the Church by formal statute. Rather was it at first taken for granted that the principle stated in the constitutions, that the Church of England was "the only true and orthodox religion and the natural religion in all the king's dominions, and so in Carolina," was a sound principle. Certainly, the high-Church party accepted the establishment as thus founded and proposed no other statutes to buttress it until 1704.

The first act of detail under the establishment, to settle the maintenance of a minister, was passed in 1698.[3] This

---

[1] Bancroft, III, 13.   [2] *South Carolina Statutes*, II, 131.

[3] *Ibid.*, II, 135 ; Anderson, *Colonial Church*, II, 688.

was for the settlement at Charleston of Samuel Marshall, First clergyman. the first clergyman of the Church of England in Carolina. Anderson says that the legislature was moved to the action by its special pleasure in Mr. Marshall's character and conduct. The act appropriated to him and his successors forever a yearly salary of £150; and for his peculiar benefit directed "that a negro man and woman, and four cows and calves be purchased for his use and paid for out of the public treasury."

The next step of the Church party was perhaps the most high-handed legislation ever perpetrated in the colonies. This was in the astonishing acts of 1704, establishing the Church and disfranchising non-conformists.[1] Previously to this action, the contest between the Church party and its opponents — almost three-fourths of the population — had pronounced itself with no little bitterness, and the strife had run so high that the proprietaries had been compelled to so far yield to popular clamor as to appoint the Quaker Arch- Archdale. dale, himself one of the proprietaries, to the office of governor. Archdale's policy was wise. He organized his council in such proportions that the high-Church party had but one-third of its membership, and his administration was for the most part peaceful.

After composing the difficulties in the colony Archdale returned to England, and on his absence the Church party found the opportunity of accomplishing their designs. By a majority of one in a small house the assembly of 1704 passed two acts which were a direct outrage upon the majority of the people. The first was entitled an " Act for the Pro- Dissenters disfranchised. tection of Government," and required that all members of the legislature should be of the Church of England and should have taken the sacrament in that Church, at least once in the year past. The second act was "for establishing Religious worship according to the Church of England," and entered

---

[1] *South Carolina Statutes*, II, 232, 236 ; Bancroft, *United States*, III, 18 ; *North Carolina Reports*, I, 635, 638, 642, 643.

into much detail as to erection of Churches, support of ministers, glebes, parishes, and the choice of ministers, vestries,
clerks, and sextons, fixing even the salaries of clerk and
sexton at £10 and £5. To these matters of routine the act
added an astounding feature in providing for an ecclesiastical

A lay eccle-
siastical
court.

court, to be composed of twenty *laymen,* having almost episcopal powers of supervision and direction in all Church affairs.
They were made competent to settle disputes, to exercise
discipline, and remove ministers " for cause."

In the next two years the assembly enacted : first, another
law of establishment, but providing that nothing in the act
should take away the right of dissenting ministers to baptize,
marry, and bury; and second, an act creating a parish in the
French settlement on the Santee, on condition that "they
conform to the Church of England, and use a French translation of the Book of Common Prayer." [1] The spirit of these
acts was at the same time well illustrated by the legislative
response to a petition from some dissenters living near
Pamphlico River. They informed the authorities that, "trust-
ing to the assurances of liberty," they had settled in the
colony and desired permission to engage a minister of their
own faith. The request was denied, " though they offered with
cheerfulness to be at the Charge of maintaining them." [2]

That such legislation would raise a storm among such a
people as that of Carolina was so certain, that one marvels at
the audacity of the Church party in venturing the action.
Doubtless, knowing the attachment of all the proprietaries,
except Archdale, to the Church and their desire for a full
establishment in the colony, they presumed that the proprietaries' influence in London would win the royal approval,
and thus the dissenters would be coerced into submission.

The people.

As to the people to be coerced, Commissary Blair of Virginia wrote a suggestive description in 1704: [3] " The country
is divided in four sorts: 1st, The Quakers, who are the most

[1] *South Carolina Statutes*, II, 259, 268.   [3] *Ibid.*, I, 601.
[2] *North Carolina Reports*, I, 604.

powerful enemies to Church government, but very ignorant of what they profess; 2d, A great many who have no
religion, but would be Quakers if they would not be obliged
to lead a more moral life; 3d, A sort something like Presbyterians, upheld by some idle fellows who have left employment to preach and baptize, without any orders from any
sect; and 4th, Those who are zealous for the interest of
the Church." Blair's description is of the people in the
northern division, and he says that the Churchmen were by
far the fewest in number and were opposed by the other three,
" with common consent to prevent anything that will be
chargeable to them, as they think all Church government
will be."

Of course, the Quakers were as ready in Carolina as else- Quakers.
where to resist all imposition of tithes and all forms of establishment. Governor Spotswood of Virginia wrote of them in
1711 that they were " not only the principal fomenters of the
distractions in Carolina, but made it their business to instil
the like pernicious notions into the minds of his majesty's
subjects in Virginia." [1] To this settled principle of the
Quakers must be added not only the resistance of the sober-
minded dissenters of other sects, but also the aversion to
Church taxes on the part of a large number, who had no
religion at all.

These elements of opposition were not slow in making
their voice heard across the water. Archdale protested
against the acts of 1704 in the association of proprietaries, Acts of 1704
but a majority of that body sustained them. On this the annulled.
complainants went higher, and in a petition, signed by
Joseph Boone and others, laid their wrongs before parliament.
The petition cited the grants of liberty in the charter and the
" Fundamental Constitutions," and alleged that the great
majority of the inhabitants of Carolina were dissenters. To
this petition of the dissenters was added the opinion of the
only Church of England clergyman in the colony, Marshall

[1] *North Carolina Reports,* I, 782 ; Bancroft, *United States,* III, 21.

of Charleston, that the "high Ecclesiastical Commission Court (of the act of 1704) was destructive of the very Being and Essence of the Church of England, and to be had in utmost detestation and abhorrence by every man that is not an enemy to our Constitutions in Church and State."

The parliament met the petition with favor and presented the acts of 1704 to the Queen as "unwarranted by the Charter, unreasonable, and an Encouragement to Atheism and Irreligion." This opinion was sustained by the attorney-general and solicitor-general, who declared the acts "unreasonable, and against the Charter and English custom," whereupon the laws were voided by the Queen in Council in 1706. This issue was an overwhelming victory for the friends of liberty. The excitement had been so great, and the disapproval in England so loudly expressed, that the proprietary charter was in great danger for a while. To save the charter the proprietaries were forced to recede from their high-Church position; and to cause the legislature of 1706 to repeal the obnoxious statutes.[1] This ended all effort to infringe upon the civil rights of dissenters; while another act reëstablished the Church, without any invasion of their religious liberty, and without any lay court of supervision. Its features were of mere details of organization and maintenance, requiring no extended notice here.

But the province was still far from peace. The dissenters set about confirming their victory by the effort to secure a firm hold of political power. This effort was not always attended by success, but it was constantly amid a chorus of wails and complaints from the Church party. In 1708 the Rev. James Adams, a missionary of the "Society for the Propagation of the Gospel in Foreign Parts," wrote:[2] "The Quakers, though but one seventh of the people, through Archdale control the government. Their conjunction with the Presbyterians will bear down the Church.

Letters of
clergy.

---

[1] *South Carolina Statutes*, II, 281, 282.
[2] *North Carolina Reports*, I, 687.

Men are turned out of office because of the Church of England, and others put in because they are Quaker preachers and notorious blasphemers of the Church." In the same year Colonel Jennings, president of the Virginia council, wrote to the board of trade : " The proceedings (in Carolina) look liker the freaks of Madmen than the acts of men of reason." [1]

A Mr. Urmston, the first English clergyman settled in North Carolina and a man of no very savory reputation, overflowed with complaints. His letters were voluminous, and at times scornful, bitter, and alarmed.[2] At different times he wrote: "Here are many Quakers and many loose, disorderly professors of religion, factious, mutinous, and rebellious people, allied to the Quakers and at their beck ready to oppose either Church or State." Again : " The Assembly was made up of a strange mixture of men of various opinions and inclinations — a few Churchmen, many Presbyterians, Independents, but most anything-arians, some out of principle, others out of hopes of power and authority." "Our cowardice and Quaking principles render us the scorn and contempt of all our neighbors." If the opinion of Spotswood is to be received, the latter remark of Urmston is justified. The Virginia governor was sorely tried by what he saw across the border, and feared its influence on Virginia's "gentlemanly conformity." "I have been mightily embarrassed by a sett of Quakers, who broach Doctrines so monstrous as their Brethren in England have never owned, nor indeed can be suffered in any Government." [3]

As in Virginia, the established Church in North Carolina was heavily weighted by the character of its earlier ministers. Urmston was the only settled minister until after 1721, and at his departure Governor Eden wrote that there was not a clergyman of the Church in the whole colony.[4] The ministry of this man could not advantage a Church appealing to popular favor. He stands pilloried in the records of the society

Clerical morals.

[1] *North Carolina Reports*, I, 688.   [3] *Ibid.*, I, 814.
[2] *Ibid.*, I, 763, 769, 885.   [4] *Ibid.*, II, 430.

as, "wicked and scandalous, and a notorious drunkard."[1] "Like priest like people" also obtained, and the rector wrote of his own vestry, that they "met at an Ordinary, where rum was the chief of their business. They were most of them hot-headed."[2] In like criticism wrote a Rev. Mr. Gordon, a visitor, from Perkimans: "Here are twelve vestrymen, very ignorant, loose in their lives, and unconcerned as to religion." He says that their character had driven many of the people to the Quakers, and then attributes all the trouble of the situation to the Quaker "machinations"![3]

The absurd situation of a Church pretending to establishment is further illustrated by the almost total destitution of facilities for the services of the Church. This appears in many notes.[4] The vestry of Chowan wrote to the society: "We have a large parish, one hundred miles long, with many poor at a great Distance from each other, and but one sorry Church, which has never been finished." The secretary of the society reported in 1715, that there was but one clergyman in North Carolina and that those who were in South Carolina had mostly deserted. And in 1717 the wardens and vestry of Bath complained that they had never had a minister, that the missionaries never came to them, that the children were unbaptized, and that they were "kept from dissenting by the laws." The condition fully bears out the statement of Rev. Miles Gale, an English rector, in a letter to the bishop of London: "I am informed from my eldest son in North Carolina that the religion of that colony is at a very low ebb, and that the little stock carried over is in danger to be totally lost, without speedy care of sending ministers.[5]

Yet there would appear to be some concern for the religious proprieties on the part of magistrates, judging from various sentences for ungodly conduct. Among them that upon John Hassell is worth citation.[6] He was fined, in 1720, £25 for saying that he "had never been beholden to

No churches.

---

[1] *North Carolina Reports*, II, 431.   [2] *Ibid.*, I, 769.   [3] *Ibid.*, I, 711.
[4] *Ibid.*, II, 118, 200, 273.   [5] *Ibid.*, I, 867.   [6] *Ibid.*, II, 413.

God for anything." The court judged the offence worthy of punishment because tending "to the dishonor of God Almighty and his Attributes, and against the holy written Profession and Religion, now allowed and profest by authority in his now Majesty of Great Britain's Dominions, and subverting of all the faithful and true believers and professors of the Protestant Church and Religion now by Law Established and Confirmed."

All that remains is simply to note that until the Revolution the care of the legislature was frequently directed toward the affairs of the establishment,[1] both as affecting the colony at large and as touching individual parishes. In 1715 a new law of establishment was enacted, in which one clause bears witness to the influence of Jacobitism. It required every vestryman to make oath, "I do declare that it is not lawful on any pretence whatever to take up Arms against the King, and that I will not apugne the Liturgy of the Church of England." The act also assessed five shillings " per Poll on all taxable persons " for support of the ministry, and imposed fines on all persons, " not dissenters," refusing to serve as wardens and vestrymen, when elected. The act of 1722 increased the stipend of country parsons from £50 to £100, and if this were not paid within twenty-one days, the parson was authorized to sue the receiver-general. This was in South Carolina, after the annulling of the charter in 1720, the institution of the royal government, and the division of the province. By the South Carolina act of 1756 the " Chapel on James Island is established as a Chapel of Ease in the parish of St. Andrew, and the rector of said parish is hereby obliged, enjoined, and required to preach and perform divine service in said Chapel of Ease, every fourth Sunday." If he, or any other person enjoined to serve in any Chapel of Ease, should neglect the duty, " the Public treasurer of the Province shall deduct £10 " from the salary for every occasion of neglect.

Charter annulled and province divided, 1720.

[1] *North Carolina Reports*, II, 207 ; VIII, 4, 45 ; IX, 1010 ; *South Carolina Statutes*, II, 339, 352 ; III, 11, 174, 485, 531, 650 ; IV, 3, 25.

The last act of civil authority over the Church in the southern division was so late as 1785, increasing the powers of the vestries in the parishes of St. Paul and St. Andrew, and *requiring* the vestry of the latter parish to repair their Church building.[1] In North Carolina the last ecclesiastical act of the legislature was in 1774, and organized the parish of St. Bartholomew. In the fifty years preceding there had been various similar acts and others continuing the statute of establishment, but nothing of distinguishing character.

In the entire province after 1706, while the legislature consistently maintained the idea of a State-Church in various acts such as noted above, there was never again an approach to any other oppression than that which was involved in the tithes. The two parties struggled for power in the state with varying success, the line of partition between them being largely that of religious affiliations, yet they never again locked horns on the religious question. The dissenters in power respected the establishment, and the Churchmen respected the rights of dissent. As the decades passed away, and the country became more thickly settled, the asperities of the early contests ceased. The disproportion between the establishment and dissenters constantly increased and with it the popular unwillingness to pay taxes for a Church not their own. This was specially true of North Carolina. In the southern colony, the hold of the Church of England was much stronger, owing to the facts that its early settlers were of a more religious disposition, and that the English clergy were of a much higher character. But even in South Carolina the inequity of taxing three-fourths of the people, to support the Church of the other fourth, failed not to impress the minds of the leaders. Thus the province was prepared for that disestablishment, which followed soon upon the Revolution.

[1] *South Carolina Statutes*, IV, 703.

V

THE PURITAN ESTABLISHMENTS

UNDER this head are grouped all the New England colonies, with the exception of Rhode Island. In them all the Congregational Church was established by law, with more or less of proscription of other forms of worship. This establishment was not by charter or by imposition of external authority, but by act of the colonial legislature at the beginning of the colonies, in conformity with the will of the great majority of the people. Each colony had a spirit of its own in its regard for the established order, in some instances sharply contrasting it with its neighbors. Theocratic Massachusetts and New Haven reverenced the order as the chosen instrument of God, with which a man could interfere only to his peril, and on conformity to which all civil rights depended. Plymouth and Connecticut loved it as a seemly thing and as conducive to religious and social prosperity, but at the same time recognized the claims of charity toward men of other minds. Of this spirit also was New Hampshire, though for half a century merged with Massachusetts, and afterward vexed by foolish royal governors attempting forcible conversion to the Church of England.

I. *Plymouth*

When the men of Scrooby fled to Holland from English persecution, they had no thought of giving up their English citizenship. From 1609 to 1617 they remained in quiet enjoyment of Dutch toleration. But, though never disturbed by the authorities for the sake of religion, they were unsatisfied to remain in a foreign land and become merged in popu-

lation alien to their own English stock. Though driven out
of England, they were still English at heart and desired to
live and to bring up their children under the English flag.

With this desire strong within them they greeted the news
of the planting of Virginia with the hope that in the bounds
of this infant colony there might be found for them a place,
where they could at once be subjects of their own king and
enjoy religious freedom. So moved, in 1617, they sent Carver and Cushing to London with propositions toward settlement in Virginia. These propositions, while not evading the
Separatist view of Church polity, yet asserted their agreement with the creed of the Anglican Church and their desire
of spiritual communion with its members. In civil matters
they declared their entire subjection to the king, with " obedience in all things ; active, if the thing commanded be not
against God's word ; or passive, if it be." This first informal
application to the Virginia company was favorably received,
under the kindly influence of the secretary, Sir Edwin Sandys,
a man of large liberality of spirit.

On the report of their agents the Pilgrims at Leyden, in
December of the same year, transmitted by the hands of
Robinson and Brewster their formal request of the company
to be allowed to embark for Virginia. With this request
was coupled a petition to the king, which brought temporary
disaster to their enterprise. The petition sought a formal
allowance to them of liberty in religious matters in their con-
templated settlement in America. Strange to say, James,
whose hatred for presbytery and addiction to prelacy were
well known, hesitated as to the character of his reply. Both
the king and Villiers seem at first to have looked upon the
request with some degree of favor. At all events, they were
unwilling to return a negative without advice. This advice
they sought from the greatest man of the age, Lord Bacon,
whose greatness was equalled, according to the epigram, by
his meanness. His courtier-like sycophancy was abundantly
able to silence a principle, which his philosophical intellect

Attempts to
emigrate to
America.

Bacon.

might discern, in order to give voice to sentiments more pleasing to his royal master. It is hard to believe that so wise a man as Bacon could have failed to see that toleration at least could be demanded as a natural right; but he failed to express any such thought in his "Letter of Advice" — a letter which both disappointed the Pilgrims and established the administrative policy in religious matters through the colonial era. He says: "Discipline by bishops is fittest for monarchy of all others. The tenets of separatists and sectaries are full of schism and inconsistent with monarchy. The king will beware of Anabaptists, Brownists, and others of their kinds: a little connivency sets them on fire. For the discipline of the Church in those parts (the colonies) it will be necessary that it agree with that which is settled in England, else it will make a schism and rent in Christ's coat, which must be seamless, . . . and for that purpose it will be fit that they be subordinate to some bishop or bishoprick of this realm. . . . If any transplant themselves into plantations abroad who are known schismatics, outlaws, or criminal persons, they should be sent back upon the first notice: such persons are not fit to lay the foundation of a new colony."[1] So Bacon demeaned himself to compose a variation on his master's favorite theme: "No Bishop, no King." James listened only too willingly to this advice and refused the petition of the Pilgrims.

But they were not discouraged by this failure, nor disposed to give up their project of removal to America. They presently entered into arrangements with a number of London merchants, as yet not incorporated into a chartered company, who were to act as agents for the colony. These merchants, afterward chartered as the "Plymouth Company," were to Plymouth provide means of transportation and to attend to matters of Company. supply and the sale of such produce as the emigrants should send to England. They presumed upon no steps of government, nor marked out for the colonists any lines of either

[1] Bacon, *Works*, VI, 438; Bancroft, *History of United States*, I, 304.

civil or ecclesiastical procedure.   Under such purely business arrangement with their London principals, the Pilgrims set out upon their voyage to New England; without any charter but their own will, without any consent or cognizance of the king, free to decide for themselves as to their local civil and religious institutions.   They owed nothing to grants of power or to royal favor: but went forth in sublime confidence that God would be their guide and defence.

As to their churchly condition, it must be borne in mind that their emigration was that of a Church already constituted.   In their own intention that band of men and women, who filled the cabins of the Mayflower, were but the advance company of the Church of English Separatists at Leyden, whose remaining brethren were to follow them as soon as might be possible.   Their beloved pastor Robinson, who longed for America and " died without the sight," remained at Leyden only for the sake of that portion of the flock which was left.   So we do not read of any organization of a Church when the Pilgrims arrived at Plymouth.   " These first inhabitants immediately formed themselves into a body politic, but they did not embody into a new Church state, looking upon it as unnecessary, as being a branch of the English Church at Leyden; and they expected the pastor and rest of the Church to follow them into the wilderness." This is the language of J. Cotton, Esq., in his " *Narrative of the Plymouth Church*," printed in 1760.[1]   He also says that the failure of the expected balance of the Church was due to the " opposition of several of the merchant adventurers in England, who, not liking their principles or strictness in religion, would not provide shipping and money."

Emigration as a Church.

Mayflower Compact.   The famous Mayflower compact, made when already the stern coast of New England had lifted itself in wintry garb before their sight, was solely for the direction of their civil affairs.   So far as their local government was concerned this compact was an ordinance of a pure democracy.   By it, they

[1] *Massachusetts Historical Collections,* I, 4 ; 108, 109.

say, "we solemnly and mutually, in the presence of God and one of another, covenant and combine ourselves together into a civil body politic." With the general purpose and practice under this compact, the Plymouth company, chartered by the king in the following year, did not interfere. Under it for the first score of years the governing body of the colony was the gathering of all the colonists. This simple device afterward gave way for convenience' sake to the general court, composed of deputies from the several towns.

Hutchinson, speaking of the Mayflower compact, says:[1] "Some of the inferior class among them muttered that, when they should get ashore, one man would be as good as another, and they would do what seemed good in their own eyes. This led the graver sort to counsel how to prevent it. One great reason of this covenant seems to have been of a mere moral nature, that they might remove all scruples of inflicting necessary punishments, even capital ones, seeing that all had voluntarily subjected themselves to them."[2]

With the exception of the English statutes touching religious matters, the Plymouth men were well content to accept the opinion of Lord Chief Justice Holt, that, in case of an uninhabited country newly found out and settled by English subjects, all laws in force in England are in force there.

---

[1] *History of Massachusetts Bay*, II, 407, 409.

[2] This undoubtedly expresses the spirit of the leaders, who were men of gentleness and in no instance approached the severity, which finds so many illustrations in the early history of Massachusetts and was not foreign to the colonists of New Haven. Quite otherwise, they exercised great patience and hesitated to inflict the severer penalties. Thus in 1630, a murder having occurred, they had doubt as to their power to award death to the criminal. This doubt arose, partly from their own aversion to exercising so supreme power, and partly from the restrictions of the Plymouth company in England. Their patent did not give to that company the power of life and death, and consequently they could not confer such power upon the colonists. In this dilemma Bradford and his associates took counsel with the recently arrived Puritans of Massachusetts, whose advice, given by Winthrop after consulting with "the ablest gentlemen there," was that the man ought to die, and "the land to be purged from blood." (*History of Massachusetts Bay*, II, 413.)

They, as Mr. Hubbard said, were "willing to be subject unto them, though in a foreign land," only adding thereto "some particular municipal laws of their own, suitable to their constitution." "They seem cautiously to have preserved as much of their natural liberty as could be consistent with the maintenance of government and order." (Hutchinson.)

As to the rights of conscience and worship, they remained true to the principles, which in England gave them the name of Separatists [1] (as separating from the establishment), and which caused their afflictions and exile. Happily for them, they were not greatly tried during the early period by questions of dissent from the religious and Church order, under which by common consent they lived. They never established that order by any civil law, and what the magistrates did in Church affairs was in their character of Church members and not in their civil capacity.

Moreover, they never, after the example of the Puritans, made Church membership a condition of citizenship.[2] At first, in their colonial democratic assemblies every man could speak his mind and vote. Afterward it was ordered that candidates for the franchise should be propounded by the deputies to the general court, " being such as were approved by the freemen of the town where they live." The law of Freeman's law. 1671 said that none should be admitted freemen but "such as were 21 years old, of sober and peaceable conversation, orthodox in fundamentals, and of £20 ratable estate." [3]

The purpose of the Plymouth colony was, indeed, predominantly religious, but it was uniquely confined to obtaining for themselves the freedom which had been denied at home.

[1] Many writers of the day use Separatist and Brownist as convertible terms, the latter from the name of the early leader. But the Pilgrims looked upon Brownist as offensive, in view of some of Brown's principles, which they disclaimed ; and specially offensive afterward, when Brown renounced Separatism and returned to Episcopacy.

[2] Myles Standish was not a member of the Plymouth Church, though very prominent as a citizen.

[3] Plymouth Colony Laws. Edition 1836, p. 258.

Satisfied with this, they abstained from dogmatizing and from Tolerant
all attempts to force on others their own peculiar views. spirit.
Their design did not look toward the building up of a large
and populous colony, but rather to the preservation of " a
pure and distinct congregation." Had not the colony of Massachusetts Bay settled near them in a few years, it is probable
that Plymouth would have seen a much larger influx of new-
comers. As it was, the population at Plymouth remained
small and almost entirely homogeneous, while the great stream
of immigration was directed to the Bay.[1]

Thus the occasions of discord were not many at Plymouth,
nor were there frequent temptations to the exercise of severity; while there are several tokens that the men of Plymouth
looked with disapproval upon some of the severer actions of
their brethren to the north. They granted to Mrs. Hutchinson, banished from Massachusetts, leave to settle on Aquidneck (Rhode Island), then in the Plymouth patent, although
they did not approve of her teachings any more than did the
magistrates at Boston. They were kindly to Roger Williams;
went far to a charitable construction of the motives of Maverick and Childs, and distinctly disapproved of the cruelties
visited on the Quakers. Indeed, the liberality of Plymouth
was so offensive to the rulers of Massachusetts, that at one
time it threatened to break up the New England Confederacy. " However rigid the Plymouth colonists may have
been at their first separation from the Church of England,
they never discovered that persecuting spirit which we have
seen in Massachusetts." [2] To this liberality Bancroft suggests
that their sojourn in Leyden may have led them.[3] " Their residence in Holland had made them acquainted with various
forms of Christianity; a wide experience had emancipated
them from bigotry, and they were never betrayed into ex-
cesses of religious persecution."

[1] Palfrey, *History of New England*, I, 141.
[2] Hutchinson, *History of Massachusetts Bay*, II, 421.
[3] *History of United States*, I, 322.

Religious
legislation.

In the *Colonial Records* of Plymouth there is a conspicuous
absence of legislation on matters of religion.   The general
court did not take order for the formation of Churches, or
building of meeting houses, or the payment of ministers, or to
compel attendance on divine services.   In 1646 the general
court resolved, "that something be done to mayntaine the
libertys of the Churches, without intermeddling or wronging
each other, according to the statute of England, that they
may live in peace."   But it does not appear that anything
further was done by the legislature.   In 1651 Arthur How-
land was presented by the grand jury " for not frequenting
the public assemblage on the Lord's Day."   But no trial is
recorded, and no law under which the presentment was made.

At the time of the " Presbyterian Cabal " (1643), of which
account will be given in the story of Massachusetts, and as a
part of the conspiracy, a proposition was made in the general

Presby-
terian
Cabal.

court[1] "for a full and free toleration of religion to all men,
without exception against Turk, Jew, Papist, Socinian, Fam-
ilist, or any other."   As it was afterward supposed to be
discovered, there was a political plot concerned with this motion, but the members of the Plymouth legislature did not
know it at the time, and were very favorably disposed to the
proposition.[2]

That there was a strong influence through general consent
leading to uniformity and to evenly distributed support of
religious services, seems clear, but there was no laying down
of rigid lines and no compulsion by the magistrate.[3]   This is
well illustrated by the reply of the Plymouth general court
to the commissioners of Charles II. in 1665.   The king had
demanded liberty of religious privileges for "all men of com-

---

[1] Bancroft, *History of United States*, I, 438.

[2] Winslow, who looked upon it with horror, wrote to Winthrop, " You
would have admired to have seen how sweet this carrion relished to the pal-
ate of the most of them."   Men of a later day can easily set down their feeling to the credit of the Pilgrims.

[3] Felt, *Ecclesiastical History of New England*, II, 525.

petent estates, knowledge, civil lives, and not scandalous."
To this the court replied, " We would not deny a liberty to any,
that are truly conscientious, although differing from us, they
maintaining an able preaching ministry for carrying on of
public Sabbath worship; and withdraw not from paying their
due proportion of maintenance to such ministers as are orderly
settled in the places where they live, until they have one of
their own, and that in such places as are capable of maintaining the worship of God in two distinct congregations." [1]

The liberal men of Plymouth were frequently criticised by
them of Massachusetts for too great laxity in matters of the
Church. Thus in 1656 [2] the governor and magistrates of the
latter colony addressed to the commissioners of the United
Colonies a solemn protest against the ecclesiastical indifference of Plymouth: " Our neighbor colony of Plymouth,
our beloved brethren, in a great part seem to be wanting to
themselves in a due acknowledgment and encouragement to
the ministry of the gospel." This complaint they justified on
the ground that the covenant of the United Colonies called
them " not only to strengthen the hearts and hands each of
other in appointing and maintaining of religion in its purity,
but also to be assistant each to other, where any deficiency in
such respects may appear."

The commissioners, of course, had no legislative capacity
and had to content themselves with some resolutions of an
advisory nature to act with moral pressure on the delinquent
colony. One of their resolutions enlarged on the necessity
of "an able orthodox ministry . . . to be duly sought out
in every society or township within the several jurisdictions ";
another dwelt upon the " competent maintenance (as) a debt
of justice . . . from the whole society jointly "; while a third
left (*per* force) the matter " to the wisdom of the general
court to draw up such conclusions and orders as may attain
the end desired." Then, as though it were an afterthought, the

Criticism by Massachu-setts.

---

[1] Hutchinson, *Massachusetts Bay*, I, 234.
[2] Hutchinson, *Collections*, p. 283.

commissioners resolved: "We do further propose to the general courts that all Quakers, Ranters, and other notorious heretics be prohibited coming into the United Colonies."

In this last action was Massachusetts' real objective. She was not content to submit to Plymouth's disapproval of her own cruelty to the Quakers, and thought to coerce the Pilgrims into sympathy. But the appeal was futile. The men of Plymouth took no very severe steps toward the sectaries, and went on in their own way of charity and peace.[1] The most that they could be brought to do was to rebuke any civil disorders. In John Cotton's *Account* it is stated that: "The Quakers much infested the country between the years 1650 and 1660, and proved very troublesome and subverted many. In the Church one family only was wholly led away. But Plymouth never made any sanguinary or capital laws against that sect."[2]

In this charitable disposition they were following the counsel of their beloved pastor, Robinson. In Holland they unhesitatingly communed with the Dutch and French Churches, and also with the Scotch, under his guidance; and on their departure for America he urged upon them a like liberal spirit, saying to them in his tender farewell, "there will be no difference between unconformable ministers and you, when they come to the practice of the ordinances of the kingdom."[3]

In "*Hypocricie Unmasked*," a tract written against Gorton by Edward Winslow, who himself frequently "exercised" as a preacher,[4] it is denied that the Pilgrims were ever un-

Quakers.

---

[1] Palfrey (*History of New England*, II, 37), without apparent warrant, states that Plymouth was more disturbed than any other colony, as to internal politics by the Quakers. Felt (*Ecclesiastical History of New England*, II, 168, 313) cites one whipping, a few fines, and banishments.

[2] *Massachusetts Historical Collections*, 3 ; III.

[3] Young, *Chronicles of Pilgrim Fathers*, pp. 392, 398.

[4] Winslow got into trouble for this exercise, when on an embassy to England in 1635. Archbishop Laud questioned him about his preaching and marrying, and threw him into the Fleet, where he was kept for seventeen

willing that Presbyterians should settle at Plymouth. Some
Presbyterians had written thither from Scotland, to learn if
they would be welcome " to freely exercise their Presbyterial
government amongst us ; and it was answered affirmatively,
they might." [1]

As further illustrating the liberal spirit of Plymouth
stands their action toward Charles Chauncy, who was after- Chauncy.
ward the president of Harvard College. He was called in
1638 as colleague to John Reyner, the pastor at Plymouth,
and preached there for three years. He refused, however,
to be installed or remain, because he was an immersionist.
But " the Church, being loth to lose a man of such eminency,
offered, in case he would settle, to suffer him to practice
according to his persuasion . . . provided he could peaceably
suffer Mr. Reyner to baptize according to the mode in general use." [2] This offer Mr. Chauncy did not accept.

The action of the Plymouth authorities against Lechford —
or Lyford [3] — though represented by the sufferer as for reli- Lyford.
gious exclusiveness, was in reality for misdemeanor as a
citizen. Thomas Lyford was an Episcopal minister, whose
experiences at Plymouth may be briefly related as illustrating the spirit of the Pilgrims.[4] He was sent over by the
company in 1623, to take the place of Robinson, whom
they were unwilling to send. Though such forcible supply of

weeks. (Hutchinson, *History of Massachusetts Bay*, II, 410 ; *Massachusetts Historical Collections*, IV, 3 ; 329.)

[1] Winslow mentions three ministers "of that way," who were not disturbed. (Young, " *Chronicles of Pilgrim Fathers*," p. 402.) One of these
three was Mr. Hubbard of Hingham, who is spoken of in Winthrop's History as having been forbidden to preach in Boston, because "his spirit was
averse to our ecclesiastical and civil government, and he was a bold man and Hubbard.
would speak his mind." The contrast between the prevailing spirits of
the two colonies finds few more apt illustrations.

[2] *Massachusetts Historical Collections*, I, 4 ; 111 (*Narrative* of John
Cotton, Esq.).

[3] Felt, *Ecclesiastical History of New England*, I, 442.

[4] Bradford, *History of Plymouth ; Massachusetts Historical Collections*,
IV, 3 ; 169 *et seq.*

Oldham.

their pastorate could not commend Lyford to the favor of the colonists, they received him amicably, provided for his support, and suffered him to teach. At the same time came John Oldham, one of a small number of emigrants, whom the company sent out under ill-defined peculiar relations to the body of settlers, and were thence called "particulars," and who were disposed to arrogate to themselves special dignity. Lyford and Oldham from the very beginning of their stay at Plymouth entertained sentiments hostile to the colony and its government, and conspired together to work "a reformation both in Church and State." To this end they wrote to the company in London malicious letters, abusing the colony and its magistrates, and gave voice to their feelings in the hearing of such of the colonists as they hoped to influence. The letters were intercepted by Bradford, and the men were soon brought to trial, the action being precipitated by riotous conduct on the part of Oldham. Presuming on his privilege as a "particular," he refused to do military duty and made no small disturbance, when the officers undertook to compel him. "The Governor, hearing the tumulte, sent to quiet him, but he ramped more like a ferocious beast than a man, and called them all treatours and rebells and other such foule language as I am ashamed to remember, but after he was clapt up for a while he came to himself."

On this the two men were arraigned, and the intercepted letters produced. Bradford upbraided them for their conduct, that they had been kindly received and entertained, but they had been ungrateful, acting "like the Hedgehogg, whom the conny in a stormy day in pittie received into her borrow, but would not be content to take part with her, but in the end with her sharp pricks forced the poore conny to forsake her own borrow: so these men with the like injustice indevored to doe ye same to those that entertained them."

Oldham met the charges with barefaced denials and hardihood, but Lyford "burst into tears and confest, and feared he was reprobate." Both were bidden to leave the colony within six months, but Lyford appeared so penitent and humble that he "was allowed to teach again," and some of the people were in favor of setting aside the sentence. Presently, however, he relapsed and was incontinently sent out of the colony. On arrival in England he possessed the ears of the company with sundry tales against the Plymouth people, which, with some asperity, they communicated to Bradford for explanation. One of the charges was that "there was diversitie about religion;" to which Bradford replied: "We knowe no shuch matter, for here was never any controversie or opposition, either publicke or private (to our knowledge)." Another charge was, "that the Church have none but themselves and separatists to live here"; to which the Governor answered: "They are willing and desirous y^t any honest man may live with them, that will carry himself peaceably, and seeke the comon good, or at least doe no harm." [1]

Somewhat later the company complained to Bradford for "receiving a man in their Church, who renounced all, universall, nationall, and diocessan Churches &c; by which it appears that though they deney the name of Brownists, yet they practiss the same &c; and therefore they should sin against God in building up such a people." This is another of Lyford's insinuations and seems to have been adopted by the company to justify their continued refusal to send Robinson to Plymouth. They insist that he should submit to the "French discipline" of Churches, and finally say, "Mr. Robinson and his company may not go over to our plantation, unless he and they will reconcile themselves to our Church by a recantation under their hands."

Meanwhile Lyford, in London, presses for justice and gets more than he wants: for on examination by a choice com-

---

[1] Bradford's final comment on Lyford is characteristic: "Shuch men (hypocritical ministers,) pretend much for poor souls, but they will look to their wages and conditions; if that be not to their content, let poor souls doe what they will, they will shift for themselves and seek poore souls somewhere els among richer bodys."

mittee he is proved to be of very loose morals, and is discarded. He did not return to Plymouth, but went to Virginia and there " died miserably." His pamphlet, "*Plaine Dealing*," published in London, 1641,[1] represents that he was persecuted at Plymouth as an Episcopalian, but the pamphlet abounds in so much malicious abuse of the people at Plymouth and the Bay, that the statement is not worthy of credence. He tells of a Mr. Doughty, a minister, who, in the gathering of a Church at Taunton, insisted that all children of baptized persons, according to the covenant of Abraham, were the children of Abraham, and so ought to be baptized. This was held to be a disturbance on his part, and the minister spoke to the magistrates to order him to be silent, "and the constable dragged him out;" and he and his family left the town. It does not appear, however, that the treatment of Doughty was due to any religious intolerance. It is quite possible, to-day, for disturbers of religious meetings to draw upon themselves the adverse action of the magistrate; and it is not at all unlikely that Doughty suffered, not as a religionist, but as a brawler.

Doughty.

Nor can we put much confidence in Thomas Morton's account of Lyford's afflictions. In his "*New English Canaan*" he says that Lyford's banishment was due to his refusal to submit to the " brethren at Plymouth, who would have him renounce his former episcopal ordination, and receive a new calling from them, after their fantastical invention." Morton's pamphlet is a conscious travesty, full of ridicule of the colonists, and with many flashes of very amusing wit.[2]

Thomas Morton.

Morton, indeed, had his own score to settle with both Plymouth and Massachusetts. He came over in 1622, as an agent for Gorges, and established himself at Merry Mount — in the present town of Quincy — and there led so easy and hilarious a life that he excited the pious horror of the Plymouth men. Bradford describes him as "setting up a schoole

[1] Force, *Historical Tracts.*
[2] *Ibid.*, II, 30; Barry, *History of Massachusetts*, I, 131; *Massachusetts Historical Collections*, III, 3; 80, 96.

of atheisme," as given to drink and "Maypole follies." He does not seem to have been disturbed, however, by the colonists, until he began teaching to the Indians the use of gunpowder and furnishing them with both guns and rum. This intensified the Plymouth horror into alarm, and in 1628 brought Myles Standish to Merry Mount to abate a dangerous nuisance. The settlement was broken up, and Morton was sent to England, only to return again in another year and presently draw down upon himself the repressive hand of the Bay authorities.[1]

It is unjust to credit the actions against Lyford and Morton to the spirit of religious intolerance. Of such spirit we look in vain through the early records of Plymouth for distinctly severe tokens, save in the exclusion of Romanists and Jesuits from the jurisdiction. How largely this freedom from intolerance was due to the comparative isolation of Plymouth we cannot say; nor can we declare what the action of that colony might have been, had it been tried by so frequent and incisive dissent as disturbed the peace of Massachusetts. For the most part such disturbing elements did not go to Plymouth, where the peace and contentment, natural to so religious and so notably homogeneous a society, gave small occasion for any restrictive action.

Doubtless the colony owed much of this peace to the wise influence of Bradford. Succeeding as governor to John Carver, Bradford. who fell a victim to the severities of the first winter, and reëlected year after year, he guided the fortunes of Plymouth with a discretion, moderation, and firmness, which reveal him as a man well qualified both in mind and character to be the leader of his fellows. He was a man to be trusted, followed, and loved. His Letter-Book and Narrative abound in illustrations of his wise vigor, and of a religious spirit which was simple as a child's. Occasionally he "drops into poetry," as witness the following from his "Poetical Account of New England ": —

[1] Fiske, *Beginnings of New England*, p. 91.

"But that which did 'bove all the rest excel,
  God in His word with us He here did dwell;
  Well ordered Churches in each place there were,
  And a learn'd ministry was planted here.

  .   .   .   .

  Men thought it happy and a blessed time
  To see how sweetly all things did agree:
  Both in Church and State there was an amity;
  Each to the other mutual help did lend;
  And to God's honor all their ways did tend;
  In love and peace His truth for to retain,
  And God's service how best for to maintain." [1]

Happy was that lot of Plymouth, which, while permitting
to them opportunity " to maintain God's service " in the way
most fitting to their mind and conscience, exposed them to
so infrequent contact with differing views. By reason of
such lot the historical incidents illustrative of our present
theme are few in number. In Plymouth abode a spirit of
broad tolerance, if not a legally defined religious liberty. It
was again her good fortune that, when the king in 1691
merged the colony with Massachusetts, the union did not
take place until the Bay theocracy had become little more
than a name and memory.

II. *The Massachusetts Theocracy*

Of quite different complexion was the early history of
Massachusetts. While in Plymouth peace abounded, in the
colony on the Bay discord did " much more abound."
Hardly had the colonists housed themselves and taken the
first steps toward settling their modes of life and government, when the voice of religious dissension made itself
heard, to be repressed by a severely persecuting hand and, in
one instance, in the midst of a controversy which shook the
very foundations of the commonwealth.

The history of the Bay settlement begins with the arrival
of Endicott and his company in 1628. There were a few

[1] *Massachusetts Historical Collections*, I, 3 ; 77.

scattered settlers before his coming: Thomas Walford at
Charlestown, William Blackstone at Shawmut, Samuel
Maverick on Noddle Island, and Morton's companions at
Merry Mount. These were all Churchmen and looked upon
the new comers with small degree of favor. Blackstone was
a minister and a recluse, desirous of a solitary life and somewhat of a dissenter. After the first settlement of affairs at
the Bay, with the Congregational Church establishment and
Shawmut occupied and renamed Boston, Blackstone felt
himself crowded out. He retired from the scene, complaining that he left England because he "did not like the Lord
Bishops," and now he could not join with the colonists because he "would not be under the Lord Brethren." These
men, on Endicott's arrival, showed considerable unwillingness
to allow his settlement or to submit to his authority. But
they were helpless and were persuaded to peace, from which
conclusion Endicott gave the name of "Salem" to the place   Salem.
chosen for this advance guard of the new colony.

Like the Plymouth Pilgrims, Endicott and his company
came in advance of a charter. They were hastened in their
departure by the company in England, which had already
made application for a charter, in order to anticipate the
schemes of Gorges. The charter was granted by Charles I.   Charter.
in the following year, and conferred upon the "Governor and
Company of Massachusetts Bay in New England" a power
of self-government, which the colony was not slow to use in
maintaining a practical independence. In this charter, differing from all charters given to colonies out of New England,
save that to Pennsylvania, there was nothing said about
ecclesiastical affairs. It was not stated that churches should
be founded "according to the laws of our kingdom of England." Nor was there anything said about religious liberty,
and "for a twofold reason: the crown would not have
granted it, and it was not what the grantees wanted. They
preferred to keep in their own hands the question as to how
much, or how little, religious liberty they should claim or

allow." [1] The charter did, indeed, contain a clause *authoriz-ing* the colonial magistrate to administer the oath of suprem-acy " to all persons who should pass into their plantation." But this was not required, being left to their discretion. It was also prescribed that the " Lawes and Ordinances (of the colony) be not contrarie or repugnant to the Lawes and Stat-utes of this our Realme of England." [2]

Religious attitude.

It is evident that the Puritans of Massachusetts were jeal-ous for their own freedom. They did not want the Church of England forced on them by the king, nor did they want religious liberty for any others than themselves. Whether this latter exclusiveness already lay in their mind when the charter was sought it is impossible to say, but, at once that their ecclesiastical regulations were formed, they appeared as sternly repressive of dissent as were the authorities of the English Church.

Their attitude toward the Church of England, as illus-trated by the ecclesiastical polity immediately established at the Bay, marks a strange and almost unreasonable change of mind. Up to the time of the settlement in Massachusetts the distinction between the Puritans and those who were afterward called Pilgrims was sharply drawn. The latter were Separatists whose conscience led them to withdraw from the national Church, in protest against her oppression

---

[1] Fiske, *Beginnings of New England*, p. 96.

[2] Anderson, in the *History of the Colonial Church* (II, 310), accuses the Puritans of bad faith and disloyalty for not conforming their Church to these terms of the charter. But this overstrains their intent, as comparison with various other charters shows. In them the royal desire to establish the Church of England in the colonies is expressed in specific language to that effect, and not left to any general inference from the laws obtaining in Eng-land. For this reason, as well as from the failure to make the oath of supremacy mandatory in the new plantation, the colonists were entirely jus-tified in holding that the reference to the laws and statutes of England had in view only the civil regulations which the colonists might enact. This cer-tainly was the opinion of Charles II., when, fifty years later, he wrote, " The principle and foundation of the charter of Massachusetts was the free-dom of liberty of conscience." (Bancroft, I, 343.)

and what they regarded as her corruptions. The Puritans, on the other hand, had never put themselves in such position, or withdrawn from the Church of England. Governor Hutchinson says of them:[1] "While they remained in England they continued in the communion of the Church. With some ceremonial parts all were more or less dissatisfied. The canons and rigid execution of them they accounted a grievous burden. The form of government in the Church was not a general subject of complaint, and they were very careful to distinguish themselves from the Brownists and other Separatists." In the general, the Puritans approved the creed and polity of the Church of England and professed undying affection for her communion, only desiring to reform from within the Church certain errors of service and practice.

These are the sentiments expressed by them to the last day of their lives in England, and with the expression of this tender love for their "Mother Church" they bade farewell to English shores, to seek their new home across the sea. Of such feeling nothing can be more expressive than the words of Winthrop and his companions in their farewell, written just as their ship was about to sail: "Reverend Fathers and Brethren," it says, "Howsoever your charitie may have met with discouragement through the misreport of our intentions or the indiscretions of some amongst us, yet we desire you would be pleased to take notice that the principals and body of our company esteem it our honour to call the Church of England, from whence wee rise, our deare mother, and cannot part from our native countrie, where she specially resideth, without much sadness of heart and many tears in our eyes; blessing God for the parentage and education, as members of the same body; and while we have breath we shall syncerely endeavor the continuance and abundance of her welfare."

Men possessed of hostile feelings toward the Church could send no such tender and loving message. It is not too much to suppose that, at the time of their departure from England,

[1] *History of Massachusetts Bay*, I, 417.

nothing was further from their minds than that attitude of separation from the Church of England immediately assumed on arrival in America.

The truth is, that the whole question of Church form was Endicott. settled for them by their forerunner, Endicott, and so settled that, in spite of past affiliations and preferences, their wisest course was rather to acquiesce than to overturn. If it were their purpose, as their farewell words suggest, to maintain cordial and fraternal relations to the Church of England, then Endicott was the wrong man to lead their first band and lay the first course of the new commonwealth's foundation. In him the sense of wrong in the Church had reached a deeper degree of dissent than in the most of the associates; while in character he was highly emotional, apt to give way to the strong impulse of the moment, sometimes in actions — like that of cutting the cross from the flag — which he soon found reason to regret. Withal, he was very devout, a man of rigid addiction to the sense of duty, and of a courage which no danger could alarm. Sent out by the company in advance as "a fit instrument to begin this wilderness work," he used the power and opportunity thus in his hand to so mould the new Church that it should express the principles of non-conformity to the Church of England, no less clearly than the Separatists of Scrooby, Leyden, and Plymouth. Yet even in the mind of Endicott himself it would seem that the purpose of entire and hostile separation must have formed itself after he left English shores, if we are to credit him with the sincerity which is his due, in the words of his farewell:[1] "We will not say as the Separatists, 'Farewell, Babylon! Farewell, Rome!' But we say, 'Farewell, dear England! Farewell, the Church of God in England!'"

It is but justice to suppose that the views of Endicott and his companions underwent some change during their long voyage, filled as it was with much religious counsel and exercise. With him came two ministers: Samuel Skelton,

[1] Young, *Chronicles of Pilgrim Fathers*, p. 398.

" a friend to the utmost equality of privileges in Church and State," and Francis Higginson, who had been deprived of his parish at Leicester for non-conformity. Through whatever motives they left England, the arrival of these men in their new home found them quite willing to commit themselves to a complete separation from the Church of England. It is possible also for them to have felt a practical unwisdom in making the order and discipline of their Church dependent on bishops three thousand miles away: a dependence which in after years furnished to the English establishments in America most exasperating and long-continued trouble.

Doubtless also the advice of Bradford had large influence with Endicott and his companions. It will be borne in mind that the Puritans of the Bay did not, as was the case with the Pilgrims, come to New England as an already organized Church. Members of the Church of England, they as individuals associated themselves for the purpose of a plantation in America. With very few exceptions, indeed, they were deeply religious men. Their aim in emigration was also chiefly religious. This aim is clearly expressed in the *Conclusions*, drawn up by the elder Winthrop and privately circulated in England. These stated that " former enterprises had aimed at profit: the present object is purity of religion ; the earlier settlements had been filled with a lawless multitude ; it is now proposed to form a peculiar government and to colonize the Best." [1] The younger Winthrop, on receipt of the *Conclusions*, wrote to his father signifying his hearty approval of its statements and purpose, and his own readiness to join the new enterprise : " For myself," he said, " I have seen so much of the vanity of the world, that I esteem no more the diversities of countries than of so many inns, whereof the traveller, that hath lodged in the best or in the worst, findeth no difference when he cometh to his journey's end : and I shall call that my country, where I may most glorify God and enjoy the presence of my dearest friends." [2]

[1] Bancroft, *History of the United States*, I, 351.
[2] Winthrop, *Life of Winthrop*, I, 307.

Planters'
Plea.

A like testimony of religious aim is very strongly stated in
" *The Planters' Plea: or the Grounds of Plantation Examined: a Manifestation of the Causes moving such as have
undertaken a Plantation in New England.*" This is the title
of a pamphlet published in London, 1630.[1] The heading of
Chapter V. runs, " That New England is a fit country for
the seating of a Colonie for the propagation of Religion."
The country is not rich and so is better for the religious
purpose. " If men desire people to degenerate speedily, and
to corrupt their minds and bodies too, and besides to *tole in*
theeves and spoilers from abroad, let them seek a rich soil,
which brings in much with little labor: but if they desire
that Piety and godliness shall prosper accompanied with
sobriety, justice, and love, let them choose a Country such
as this is — which may yield sufficiency with hard labor and
industry."

To our historical sense it would seem that inspiration itself could not have more clearly outlined one of the prime
conditions of New England's future greatness.[2]

Scottow's
Narrative.

Another and quaint description of the motive of colonization is contained in Scottow's " *Narrative of the Planting of
Massachusetts.*"[3] It was published at Boston in 1694, and
rivals productions of a hundred years before in its extravagant
language. " Neither Gold or Silver, nor French or Dutch
Trade of Peltry did Oil their Wheels; it was the Propagation of Piety and Religion to Posterity; and the secret Macedonian Call, COME OVER AND HELP US — the setting up

[1] Force, *Historical Tracts*, II.

[2] In another part of the *Plea* the author discourses as to the proper sort
of colonists and deprecates the notion that the worst characters in England
were fit for America. " It seems to be a common and gross error that colonies ought to be Emunctories or Sincks of State, to drayne away their filth."
Further, he notes "the principal scope whereat the Colonie aims; which
must be Religion; whether it be directed to the good of others for their Conversion, or of the Planters themselves, for their preservation and continuance
in a good condition, in which they cannot long subsist without Religion."

[3] *Massachusetts Historical Collections*, IV, 4; 287.

of Christ's Kingdom among the Heathens. . . . Infinite
Wisdom and Prudence contrived and directed this Mysteri-
ous Work of Providence: Divine Courage and Resolution
managed it; Superhumane Sedulity and Diligence attended
it, and Angelical Swiftness and Dispatch finished it. Its
Wheels stirred not but according to the HOLY SPIRIT'S
motion in them."

The religious aim is very clearly stated in the company's *Company's*
instructions to Endicott, April, 1629: "The propagation of *instructions.*
the Gospel we do profess above all to be our aim: we have
been careful to have a plentiful provision of godly ministers:
we trust that, not only those of our own nation will be built
up in the knowledge of God, but also that the Indians will
be reduced to the obedience of God and Christ." [1]

But the company made no suggestions as to the form which
the Church should take in the colony. They provided for the
support of the ministers, and that "convenient Churches"
should be built, one-half of the expense of which should be
borne by the company, and the other half by the planters.
Yet, strangely enough, as to Church polity they left the
colonists free to choose for themselves. It was competent
for the planters to adopt Independency, Presbytery, or
Episcopacy, with or without dependence on the Church of

[1] Young, *Chronicles of Massachusetts*, p. 142. Beyond this general aim
the Company go into some particulars: " We appoint that all . . . surcease
their labor every Saturday at three of the clock in the afternoon, and spend
the rest of that day in catechizing and preparation for the Sabbath, as
the ministers shall appoint. . . . Our earnest desire is that you take
special care, in settling these families that the chief in the family, at
least some of them, be grounded in religion ; whereby morning and evening family duties may be performed duly, and a watchful eye held over all
in each family by one or more in each family to *be appointed* thereto, that
so disorders may be prevented and ill weeds nipped before they take too
great a head. . . . Otherwise your government will be esteemed as a scare-
crow. Our desire is to use lenity ; but, in case of necessity, not to neglect
the other, knowing that correction is ordered for the fool's back." " We pray
you, make some good laws for the punishment of swearers. " (Young, *Chronicles of Massachusetts*, pp. 163, 167, 189.) Thus early was the foundation
laid for the inquisitorial methods and legislation of Massachusetts Bay.

England.   The only phrase of the instructions which could imply a thought of this matter is their language about the ministers: " For the manner of exercising their ministry, we leave that to themselves, hoping they will make God's word the rule of their actions." [1]

With this freedom of action it was suggested that counsel might well be sought at Plymouth.   Dr. Samuel Fuller wrote from Boston to Bradford in 1630 : " Here is a gentleman, one Mr. Cottington, who told me that Mr. Cotton's advice at Hampton was, that they should take advice of them at Plymouth and should do nothing to offend them." [2]   Upon this advice Endicott acted, when, shortly after landing, the scurvy broke out in the company.   He sent to Bradford for medical help, and the issue shows that by the same means he obtained help toward a Church foundation.   He wrote to Bradford : [3] " God's people are marked with one and the same mark, and sealed with one and the same seal, and have for the main one and the same heart, guided by one and the same Spirit of truth, and where this is there can be no discord — nay, there must needs be sweet harmony : and the same request (with you) I make unto the Lord, that we may as Christian Brethren be united by an heavenly and unfeigned love."

Salem
Church.

To the application thus lovingly made Bradford responded by sending Dr. Fuller to Salem as a competent adviser in the two matters in hand of healing the sick and organizing a Church.   It is safe to suppose that this angel of the Church at Plymouth acquainted the Salem brethren with the distinctive principles and teachings of the beloved Robinson, as illustrated in the Church of the Pilgrims.   According to this teaching " a company of faithful people in the covenant of God is a Church, though without any officers; and this Church has an interest in all the holy things of God *within itself, without any foreign assistance.*" [4]

---

[1] Young, *Chronicles of Massachusetts*, p. 142.
[2] *Massachusetts Historical Collections*, I, 3 ; 74.   [3] *Ibid.*, I, 3 ; 66.
[4] Robinson defined the Church as " a separation from the world into the

The advice given by Fuller seemed so sound that Endicott wrote to Bradford: "I rejoice that I am by him satisfied, touching your form of outward worship;" and on this pattern he and the godly of Salem proceeded to "form themselves into a Church state." Two fundamentals were at once laid down. The one was that the Church of Salem, though grateful for the advice received, should not "acknowledge any ecclesiastical jurisdiction in the Church of Plymouth." The other was that the "power of ordination should not exist in the clergy, but should depend entirely upon the free election of the Church." [1]

Thereupon the people of Salem proceeded to organize their Church, first adopting a Confession of Faith and a Covenant; and then, after a day of humiliation, choosing and ordaining their pastor and teacher; the two clergymen of the company having declared their readiness to renounce the episcopal ordination received by them in England. Of this proceeding Mr. Charles Gott wrote to Bradford; [2] first describing the *consensus* of opinion, that a minister must have two calls; the inward by the Spirit of God and the outward by the people; and then recounting the election, which was *by ballot.* "The most voice," he wrote, "was for Mr. Skelton to be pastor and Mr. Higginson to be teacher; and Mr. Higginson with three or four men of the gravest members of the Church laid their hands on Mr. Skelton, using prayer therewith: this

gospel and the covenant of Abraham"; and Bradford, as a voluntary association of persons, "whose hearts were touched with heavenly zeal for His truth, who shook off the yoke of anti-Christian bondage and joined themselves by a covenant of the Lord in a Church state." It was necessarily included in this that a Church should possess autonomy, that, as Robinson taught, "the members have equal power with the ministers and are to join in all the acts of the Church;" that the Church can choose, ordain, dismiss, and depose its own ministers. To this thorough independency the Cambridge Platform afterward added the mild restriction of Congregationalism, that, "when convenient, the neighboring Churches are to be advised with." (Morton, *Memorial*, pp. 411, 412, 423; Palfrey, *History of New England*, I, 285.)

[1] Morton, *Memorial*, p. 440.

[2] *Massachusetts Historical Collections*, IV, 3 ; 266.

being done, there was imposition of hands on Mr. Higginson. . . . Now good Sir, I hope that you and the rest of God's people (who are acquainted with the ways of God) with you will say that here was a right foundation laid, and that these two blessed servants of the Lord came in at the door, and not at the window." Whereon comments Bradford in his History, "Now came these people and quickly grew into Church order, and set themselves roundly to walk in all the ways of God."[1]

Thus was constituted the first Puritan Church in New England, approaching very closely in character to the Church of the Pilgrims. But the men of Salem could not break away from all bonds or concede freedom of conscience to the individual. "Because they foresaw this wilderness might be looked on as a place of liberty, and, therefore, might in time be troubled with erroneous spirits, therefore they did put in one article into the confession of faith on purpose, about the duty and power of the magistrate in matters of religion."[2]

Civil power over religion.

"This," says Judge Story, writing on the settlement of Salem, "was their fundamental error, — the necessity of a union between Church and State. To this they clung as to an ark of safety."[3] As we look at the matter, over so long a time and through so many lessons of experience, it is easy to detect this error, which became the fruitful source of so many woes in the young commonwealth. But to most men of that time legal exclusion of error, and even of "diversitie," was a prime condition of security. "It is by a mutual consent, through a special overruling Providence — to seek out a place of cohabitation and consortship, under a due form of government both civil and ecclesiastical."[4] So wrote Winthrop on shipboard, describing the purpose of the Puritan emigration in his "Model of Christian Charity" — a name

---

[1] *Massachusetts Historical Collections*, I, 3 ; 67.
[2] Morton, *Memorial*, p. 98.
[3] *Massachusetts and her Early History*, p. 34.
[4] *Lowell Institute Lectures*, p. 32.

which seems very much of a misnomer; for this expressed purpose, as illustrated in the immediately subsequent history, was quite distinct from that sufferance of opposing opinion, which a true Christian charity demands. Hutchinson expresses the purpose in clearer and more definite terms: "To obtain *for themselves* and their posterity the liberty of worshipping God in such manner as appeared to them to be most agreeable to the Sacred Scriptures."[1]

Immediately that this principle, denying all diversity and subjecting religious matters to the magistrate, was made a fundamental, the authorities found occasion to apply it. For the people were not altogether unanimous in the action. There was some dissent. How many were of that mind we are not told, but the party had very respectable leading in John and Samuel Browne. These brothers were among the substantial promoters of the plantation, entitled to respect and possessed of influence. Though decidedly Puritan, they still regarded the English Church and liturgy with affection, and were not willing to follow this abandonment of all her service. So with such as sympathized in this feeling they instituted a service of their own, using the book of common prayer and endeavoring to assert the continuance of their union with that "dear mother" in England. *The Brownes.*

But such liberty was not to be allowed.[2] To the mind of Endicott any dissent from the established order was a dangerous faction, to be put down with a strong hand. So he adopted an instant and imperious course, and, acting on his own authority alone, caused the Brownes to be put on a ship and returned to England. Thus early in the history do we find example of the then common inability of men to understand that liberty was a good thing for any others than them-

---

[1] *History of Massachusetts Bay*, I, 336. This definition would be still more exact through omission of the words "and their posterity," for the original planters, ordaining the manner of worship which pleased themselves, left to their posterity no liberty whatever in the matter.

[2] Palfrey, *History of New England*, I, 103.

selves. Endicott was deeply outraged by the law of conformity in England, but he found no objection to apply it in
America. The sole criterion of its right or wrong was in
the question as to who should suffer by it. When the
power lay in his own hand he had no objection to range
himself with the hated Laud.

The Brownes, thus summarily banished from New England, took home with them a deep sense of wrong, to which
on arrival they gave voice in complaint. But, while they
succeeded in creating much unfavorable comment about the
new settlers, they did not obtain from the company a redress
of their wrongs. The company, indeed, while avoiding
specific reference to their case, if indeed it had by that
time reached them, yet in their *Instructions* of 1629 already
quoted, use language which goes far to justify Endicott's
action.[1] " If fair means do not avail (against disorderly persons) we pray you to deal as in your discretions you shall
think fittest." They apologize for sending over Ralph
Smith (who afterward went to Plymouth), who, they say,
desired and obtained passage " before we knew of his difference in judgment in some things from our ministers."
Again, " It is often found that some busy persons, led more
by their will than by any good warrant out of God's word,
take opportunity by moving needless questions, to stir up
strife . . . from which small beginnings great mischiefs have
followed: we pray you, if any such disputes shall happen
among you, that you suppress them."

One curious sequent to this affair of the Brownes is preserved in a letter from Dudley to the Countess of Lincoln,[2]
written in December of 1630. He desired to defend the settlers
at the Bay from the charge of the Brownes that they " were
Brownists in religion and ill affected to our State at home ; "
and says, " I know no one person, who came over with us,
the last year, to be altered in judgment or affection, either

---

[1] *Chronicles of Massachusetts*, pp. 150, 151, 160.
[2] *Ibid.*, p. 331.

in ecclesiastical or civil respects." It is difficult to conceive how Dudley could have so written without a conscious perversion of the truth. There is documentary proof that, either these men grossly dissembled in their tender farewell to England and her Church, or else were radically "altered in judgment (and) affection in ecclesiastical affairs," on their arrival in the plantation. As to the term "Brownists," it is a dispute about a word, which was offensive to the Pilgrims themselves. But it is clear that, if the Pilgrims were Brownists, such also had the Puritans become in Massachusetts. They were Separatists from the Church of England as positively as the men of Scrooby, and differed only from the Pilgrims in that, having now the power, they merged Church and State together and suffered no dissent from their own opinions in matters of religious worship.

A more pleasing product of the time is preserved in Higginson's [1] "NEW ENGLAND'S PLANTATION, *or, a Short and True Description of the Commodities and Discommodities of the Country. Written by a rev. Divine now there resident.* Printed, London, 1630."

This is a pamphlet and concludes:

" But that which is our greatest comfort and meanes of defence above all others, is that we have here the true Religion and holy Ordinances of Almighty God taught amongst us.

> Thanks be to God! We have plentie of Preaching and diligent
> Catechizing with strict and careful exercise and good
> and commendable orders, to bring our People into
> a Christian conversation, with whom we have
> to do withal. And thus we doubt not
> but God will be with us, and, if
> God be with us, who can
> be against us ? "

Early in 1630 the larger company of Puritans, for whom Endicott had prepared the way, disembarked in Massachusetts. They brought with them the charter which enabled them to

---

[1] Force, *Historical Tracts*, I.

mould and establish a government of their own, without reference to a company in London or to king and parliament. So early was laid the foundation of American Independence.

Prominent in this company of seven hundred were John Winthrop, Thomas Dudley, and Sir Richard Saltonstall, the last of whom — unhappily for the colony, as we may think, because of his kind and liberal spirit — returned to England after a short sojourn in Massachusetts. Of these three Winthrop was easily the chief, a man who has had few equals in the history of America. A contemporary,[1] in language of enthusiasm, describes him as having "a more than ordinary measure of those Qualities which adorn an officer of human Society: His Justice was impartial; His Wisdom excellently tempered Things according to the Art of Governing: His Courage made Him dare to do right; All which Vertues he rendered the more illustrious by emblazoning them with the constant Liberality and Hospitality of a Gentleman. This made him the Terror of the Wicked, the Delight of the Sober, and the Hope of those who had any hopeful Design in Hand for the Good of the Nation and the Interests of Religion. Accordingly, when the noble Design of carrying a Colony of chosen People into an American Wilderness was by some eminent persons undertaken, this Eminent Person was by the Consent of all chosen for the Moses who must be the Leader of so Great an Undertaking." In far simpler phrase Dr. Fuller, who was at the Bay when Winthrop arrived, wrote to Bradford, "The Governour is a godly, wise, and humble gentleman, and very discreet and of a very fine temper."[2]

Winthrop was in his forty-fourth year, in the full vigor of life and full maturity of a character, which all the years before had deepened, broadened, and sweetened. A devoted son of the Church of England, he never associated himself with dissenters until his coming to this country, but at the

Winthrop.

[1] Prince, *Annals*, II, 11.
[2] *Massachusetts Historical Collections*, I, 3; 74.

same time was markedly Puritan in regard to existing errors. His diary reveals a nature remarkably sensitive to religious influence. While but a lad he wrote in it:[1] "I desire to make it one of my chiefe petitions to have that grace to be poore in spirit: I will ever walk humbly before my God, and meekly, mildly, and gently towards all men; so shall have peace. . . . I doe resolve first to give myselfe, my life, my witt, my healthe, my wealthe to the service of my God and Saviour, who by givinge himselfe for me & to me deserves whatsoever I am or can be, to be at his Commandement and for his glorye." With this as a keynote to his life, he was making continual advances into the realms of spiritual experience. Of such the diary abounds in tokens, displaying faith and love in constant and increasing exercise; while in no line appears, after the fashion of religionists of his day, any censorious judgment of those who differed from him. As a man of affairs, both in business and public office, he had given evidence of marked judgment and ability, so that "both in character and capacity he was one to inspire peculiar confidence."

Because of such character he was solicited by the company in England, himself not one of the original members, to join their adventure not only, but to accept the governorship in America. This he took under advisement, and wrote, May, 1629: "My deare wife, I am veryly persuaded God will bringe some heavye Affliction upon this lande, and that speedylye. . . . If the Lord seeth it will be good for us, He will provide a shelter and a hidinge place for us & others, as a Zoar for Lot."[2] Then he proceeds, after a conscientious manner of consideration peculiar to himself, to set down "*Reasons for the Plantation in New England*";[3] and among them these: "What can be better worke and more honorable and worthy of a Christian than to helpe raise and supporte a particular Church, while it is in its Infancy. It appears to be a worke of God for the good of his Church, in that he hath disposed the heartes of soe many of his wise and faithful servants,

---

[1] *Life of Winthrop*, I, 72.   [2] *Ibid.*, I, 296.   [3] *Ibid.*, I, 309.

both ministers and others, not only to approve, but to interest themselves in it."

With such thought in his mind, it was urged upon him by his associates that he must both go and assume command : and presently he set down " *Particular Considerations in the case of John Winthrop*," [1] writing of himself in the third person : " 1. It is come to that issue as (in all probability) the welfare of the Plantation dependes upon his goeinge, for divers of the Chiefe Undertakers (upon whom the rest depends) will not go without him. 2. He acknowledges a satisfactory callinge. 3. . . . If he should refuse this opportunity, the talent which God hath bestowed upon him for publicke service were like to be buried."

This is an interesting process through which the strong, devout, and loving man came to the conviction that the call to him from God was clear. It accounts for much in his after life of devotion and patience. '

We are not, then, surprised to see him on the Arbella westward bound, and to hear him discourse to his companions in words of rare eloquence and tenderness : [2] " Thus stands the case between God and us. We are entered into a covenant with Him for this work. We have taken out a commission. . . . The only way to avoid shipwreck, is to follow the counsel of Micah, ' *to do justly, to love mercy, and to walk humbly before God.*' For this end we must be knit together in this work as one man. . . . We must hold a familiar commerce together in all meekness, gentleness, patience, and liberality. We must delight in each other ; make other's condition our own ; rejoice together, mourn together, labor and suffer together, always having before our eyes our commission and community in this work, as members of the same body."

There is abundant evidence in the after story that Winthrop faithfully exhibited in his own life the principles thus urged upon his brethren. He was far from sympathizing in

[1] *Life of Winthrop*, I, 327.   [2] *Ibid.*, II, 18.

the intolerance of his companions and joined in its decrees, when so compelled, under the protest of his heart. During the nineteen years of his life in New England he was twelve times chosen governor, and one of the two charges brought against his administration was, that he "had dealt too remissly in point of justice in one or two passages . . . and failed in over much lenity." [1]

This charge was brought before the deputies by Dudley, to whom Winthrop replied that, "in the infancy of plantations justice should be administered with more lenity than in a settled state." The leading magistrates and ministers differed from him, and Winthrop professed himself convinced. [2]

They were a hard-headed and determined set of men, with whom Winthrop had to deal, unwilling to submit to anything which looked like dictation, even from the all powerful ministers. Of this two notable expressions are found in respect to Winthrop's occupation of office. In 1634, Winthrop being governor at the time, John Cotton preached the election sermon and argued against rotation in office, whereupon the deputies at once put Dudley in Winthrop's chair. Again, in 1643, Winthrop being governor again, Ezekiel Rogers preached the election sermon and argued against the reëlection of an incumbent, on the ground that it would tend

---

[1] *Life of Winthrop*, II, 136.

[2] Winthrop in his journal gives an amusing account of the opening of this case ; that he challenged his critic to show wherein he had failed, " and speaking this rather apprehensively, the deputy (Dudley) began to be in a passion and told the governor that, if he were so round, he would be round too. The governor bade him be round, if he would. So the deputy rose up in great fury and passion, and the governor grew very hot also, so as they both fell into bitterness." (Adams, *Three Episodes in Massachusetts History*, I, 377.)

There is a fine touch illustrative of Winthrop's character in another tilt with Dudley, who had written to him an angry letter. Winthrop read the letter and returned it to the bearer saying, " I am not willing to keep such an occasion of provocation by me." This was repeated to Dudley and he, in language as fine, but more unusual with him, sent reply, " Your overcoming yourself has overcome me." (*Winthrop's Life*, II, 102.)

toward the creation of a life office.   To this the deputies responded by immediately reëlecting Winthrop![1]

Another incident may well be noted, for the sake of the utterance which it brought from Winthrop's lips.   In 1643 he was accused of having exceeded his authority in the matter of a trumpery dispute at Hingham, as to who should be captain of a militia company.   Solemn impeachment of the governor was based thereon, and Winthrop, refusing to sit among the magistrates until he was acquitted, made his own defence, with the result of a most honorable dismissal of the charge.   In the course of his speech he phrased as fine a definition of Civil Liberty as ever has been made:

Liberty.

"This liberty is the proper end and object of authority, and cannot subsist without it; and it is a liberty to that only which is good, just, and honest. . . .   This liberty you are to stand for with the hazard (not only of your goods, but) of your lives, if need be. . . .   This liberty is maintained and exercised in a way of subjection to authority; it is the same kind of liberty wherewith Christ hath made us free."[2]

How much the exclusiveness of the Bay went against the grain with Winthrop is suggested by his refusal to sign an order for banishment of "a heretic."   This was brought to him by Dudley, in Winthrop's last illness.   He declined, saying, "I have done too much of that work already."   How he was regarded by the people, among whom he lived and whom he served, is well shown in Cotton's sermon on his death: "A governor who has been unto us a brother; not usurping authority over the Church; often speaking his advice and often contradicted, even by young men and some of low degree; yet not replying, but offering satisfaction also when any supposed offences have arisen: a governor who has been unto us a mother, parent-like distributing his goods to brethren and neighbors, and *gently bearing our infirmities without taking notice of them.*"[3]

[1] *Winthrop's Life*, II, 305.   [3] *Ibid.*, II, 393.

[2] *Ibid.*, II, 330 ; Palfrey, *History of New England*, I, 358.

To this judgment of contemporaries may be fitly added that of posterity. Thus writes Doyle: "Every page in the early history of New England bears witness to the patience, the firmness, the far-seeing wisdom of Winthrop. But to estimate these qualities as they deserve, we must not forget what the men were with whom, and in some measure by whom, he worked. To guard the Commonwealth against the attacks of courtiers, churchmen, and speculators was no small task. But it was an even greater achievement to keep impracticable fanatics, like Dudley and Endicott, within the bounds of reason, and to use for the benefit of the state those headstrong passions which at every turn threatened to rend it asunder." [1] The attentive student of Winthrop and his time can hardly fail of assent to the calm encomium of Young: "In his magnanimity, disinterestedness, and moderation; in his mingled firmness of principle and mildness of temper; in his harmonious character, consistent life, and well-balanced mind, the Father of Massachusetts reminds us of the great Father of his Country, and is the only man in our history worthy to stand as a parallel to Washington." [2]

There is no need of apology for so long excursion in description of Winthrop, for it is well to remind ourselves of a somewhat forgotten greatness. Nor would the picture be complete without some notes of his close associate, Dudley. Dudley. In nearly all respects where Winthrop was broad, patient, wise, and loving, Dudley was his opposite. Irritable, intolerant, narrow-minded, and censorious toward all who differed from him, Dudley stands in the history as a constant foil by which the nobler qualities of Winthrop appear the more illustrious. Jealous of Winthrop's position and influence and impatient of his milder spirit, he was ever on the watch to discover faults where they did not exist, and to impede any efforts of Winthrop's liberal spirit. Human kindness

---

[1] *The English in America — Puritan Colonies*, I, 165.

[2] *Chronicles of Massachusetts*, p. 105. (Published in 1846.)   Weeden, *Social and Economic History of New England*, p. 120.

was left out of his nature, and charity failed to express herself in his religious character. He was equal to approaching the death-bed of his Chief to solicit complicity in an act of spiritual tyranny. In his pocket, after his own death, was found the famous quatrain, supposed to be his own composition : —

> "Let men of God in Courts and Churches watch
> O'er such as do a Toleration hatch ;
> Lest that ill egg bring forth a cockatrice,
> To poison all with heresy and vice."

It is impossible for men of our day to find anything lovable in the character of Dudley, though we cannot fail to respect in him a conscientious tenacity of what he regarded as duty, and a courage insensible of fear. Winthrop describes him as " a man of approved wisdom and godliness, and of much good service to the country."

Such, then, were the two leading spirits in that company, which in the spring of 1630 landed at Salem to reënforce the band of Endicott ; and with their charter in their hands to found an independent, self-governing commonwealth. As before noted, in one respect, and that which specially concerns this narrative, they found the work already done and awaiting their acceptance. The first Church of Massachusetts had been organized, and with it the ecclesiastical polity of the new state established.

To this establishment the new comers not only seem to have made no objection, but rather by immediate concurrence signified their hearty approval.[1] Though not patterned after any prearranged plan and instructions of their own, they recognized in Endicott's work a form of united civil and ecclesiastical government which they were glad to adopt. Confessedly, having left England for the sake of religion, what better scheme could be devised to effect their desire ?

[1] Palfrey, *History of New England,* I, 115 ; Winthrop, *Journal,* I, 13.

We owe to John Cotton the explicit terms in which that governing desire is acknowledged. At the request of the General Court he drew up an "*Abstract of Laws*" for the guidance of magistrates, which he patterned after " the laws of judgement delivered from God to Moses."[1] This abstract he accompanied with an argument of advice, " that *Theocracy*, *i.e.* God's government, might be established as the best form of government, wherein the people that choose rulers are God's people in covenant with Him, that is, members of the Churches." Afterward Cotton, writing to Lord Say and Sele, describes the Government of Massachusetts as " a Theocracy in both, the best form of government in the Commonwealth, as well as in the Church."[2]

In so expressing himself Cotton was but putting in a phrase of definition the formative principle which had already controlled the colonial legislation. The earliest legislative body in the Bay was the court of assistants, under Endicott as governor; and at their initial meeting the first question considered was, " How the ministers shall be mayntained?" This was at once answered by ordering that houses should be built for them, and competent provision be made in supplies and money "at the publicke expense."[3] Three months afterward the court ordered a tax to raise £60 for this purpose. Afterward there are many acts of the legislature having reference to such provision. Thus, in 1637, the people of Newberry having proved remiss, the general court *ordered* the selectmen to levy a tax for the minister's support; and in 1638 enacted a general law that " all inhabitants are lyable to assessment for Church as for State," the tax to be collected by distraint, if necessary. At the very beginning of the government there was by such action imbedded in the constitution one essential feature of an established Church, Church-rates to be levied and collected by the civil officer. There it remained a part of Massachusetts

Church tax.

---

[1] Davenport, *Life of Cotton.*
[2] Hutchinson, *Massachusetts Bay*, I, Appendix.
[3] *Massachusetts Records.*

law for two hundred years, not giving way until long after the political independence of the United States was effected.[1]

An early instance of opposition is related by Hutchinson. One Briscoe, a tanner of Watertown, published in 1644 a pamphlet against the Church tax, arguing that such method of supporting religion was immoral and contrary to justice, and that ministers accepting moneys so raised, disgraced themselves and the cause of religion. For this publication he was summoned before the general court and gravely admonished.

It is worth while to notice, in passing, that this first court of assistants emphasized their care for religion in another way. At the first meeting, having disposed of ministerial support, they cited Morton of Mount Wollaston — or Merry Mount — to answer for his "godless" conduct, and at their next session ordered that he be sent to England, his goods confiscated to pay costs, and his house burned. Presently thereafter they ordered "all cards and dice to be made away with." Their settlement was distinctly religious, and whatsoever legislation was deemed needful to sustain religion and keep the people in religious ways the authorities scrupled not to enact out of any consideration of personal liberty.

Merry Mount.

The next step in the establishment of a State-Church was taken by the first general court, which met on May 18, 1631. At this session applications to be " admitted Freemen " were made by one hundred and ten persons. The applicants were admitted, on taking the oath of allegiance; but the court, as though alarmed by so large an influx of citizens and fearing the consequences of too wide entrance to the franchise, im-

Freemen.

---

[1] Hutchinson (*History of Massachusetts Bay*, I, 427) says : " The ministers of Boston have ever been supported by a free weekly contribution. . . . In the country towns compulsory laws were found to be necessary." This would seem to imply that such laws were an afterthought, which the records show not to have been the case. The exception noted in the Boston Churches was due to their own voluntary provision, and not to any exception from the law, which was general. Had their voluntary contributions failed of the needed amount, they would have found the law compulsory on them, as on others.

mediately took the following action, the importance of which as defining the colonial aim cannot be exaggerated. The act is in these words: " To the end the body of the commons may be preserved of honest and good men, it is ordered and agreed, that, for the time to come, noe man shall be admitted to the freedome of this body polliticke, but such as are members of some of the Churches within the lymitts of the same."

This restriction of the franchise went further than the intent recited in the act, " to preserve the body of the commons of honest and good men." It went further than the requirement of religious character, or profession, on the part of electors, and confined the suffrage to members of a particular *Church approved and supported by the state*. There were " honest and good men" in the colony who were not members in that Church, and could not vote. This class so increased in number that at the time, 1665, when the restriction was somewhat relaxed, it was estimated that they outnumbered the freemen in the ratio of five to one.

Nor could the condition of freemen be obtained by the most positive evidences of Christian character. Neither Episcopalian, nor Presbyterian, nor Baptist, of howsoever exalted spiritual standing, could be a freeman. The only legal evidence that even a saint had honesty and goodness enough to fit him for the sacred duty of voting for a constable was the certificate of some minister that he was a member of a Congregational Church "in good and regular standing." This is precisely the ground occupied by the parliament of England in its acts of uniformity, debarring from all civil privileges and office every man not a member of the Anglican Church, and from the oppression of which these Puritans had come across the sea. The only difference was that parliament established Episcopacy, while the general court of Massachusetts established Congregationalism.[1]

[1] There is one exception to the stringent law of the franchise recorded in the early history of the colony. This is in the case of a Mr. Humphries of

The reasons of such action by the fathers of Massachusetts are not far to seek.　They came into the wilderness to establish for themselves a religious commonwealth, in which both State and Church should be patterned after their own mind, and into which they desired that none should come, who were not in thorough sympathy with themselves on these cardinal points.　They made little of what in modern phrase is called the "solidarity of humanity."　Their asylum was not founded as a refuge for all the oppressed.　The world was wide. There was yet ample room in America: let those who were not of them keep away from them.　"I do take upon me," says the "Simple Cobler of Aggawam," — in words already quoted, — "to be the Herald of New England, so far as to proclaim to the world in the name of the Colony, that all Familists, Antinomians, Anabaptists, and other Enthusiasts shall have free Liberty to keep away from us, and such as will come to be gone as fast as they can, the sooner the better." [1]

There has been made no better defence of this policy of restriction shown, not only in the law of franchise, but also in the laws touching the domicile of strangers, than is found in the "*Considerations*," of Winthrop, of which the following are specially in point: —

"1.　If the place of our co-habitation be our own, then no man hath a *right* to come unto us, &c., without our consent.

"2.　If no man hath a right to our land, government privileges, &c., but by our consent, then it is reason that we should take notice of (them) before we confer any such upon them.

Lynn, who was an assistant for several years.　There was no Church at Lynn when he was made freeman, and he never afterward became a Church-member.　Cotton says that he would have so done, "if there had been opportunity!" (Hutchinson, *History of Massachusetts Bay*, I, 423.)

[1] Force, *Historical Tracts*, III.

" 3. If we are bound to keep off whatsoever appears to tend
to our ruin or damage, then may we lawfully refuse
to receive such whose dispositions suit not with ours,
and whose society (we know) will be hurtful to us.

.   .   .   .

" 7. A family is a little commonwealth and a commonwealth
a great family. Now as a family is not bound to
receive all comers, no more is a commonwealth.
" 8. It is worse to receive a man, whom we must cast out
again, than to deny him admission." [1]

One other step remained to make the establishment com- A State
plete. This was the giving to the magistrates power over Church.
the Churches themselves, and it was accomplished by an act
of the general court in 1635. Already it would seem that
irregularities had occurred in the matter of organizing
Churches, and the court proceeded to ordain a uniformity
and prevent all diversities in ecclesiastical polity. The act
recites: [2] "This Court doeth not, nor will hereafter, approve
of any such companyes of men as shall henceforthe ioyne in
any pretended way of Church fellowship, without they shall
first acquaint the magistrates and the elders of the greater
part of the Churches in this jurisdiction with their intentions,
and have their approbation herein : and noe person, being a
member of any Church which shall hereafter be gathered without the approbation of the magistrates and the greater part
of the Churches, shall be admitted to the ffreedome of this
comonwealthe."

This effectually put into the hands of the civil power
authority over the Church, an authority not only controlling
questions of organization and polity, but assuming inquisi- Inquisitorial
torial power. Indeed, before this act the general court had power.
not hesitated to inquire into the affairs of the local Churches.
Prince relates [3] that one Richard Browne of Watertown had

---

[1] Hutchinson, *Collections,* pp. 68, 69.
[2] *Massachusetts Colonial Records.*   [3] *Annals,* III, 38.

said, that "the Church of Rome was a true Church, basing
his opinion on the fact that the Reformed Churches did not
re-baptize those who came over from Rome." The Church at
Watertown had just chosen Browne for an elder, and the general
court notified the Church that "he was not a proper person for
such office." This took place in 1631. In like exercise of
power the court, as will presently be noted, rebuked the Salem
Church for calling Roger Williams to the pastorate, compelling
the Church to dismiss Williams and to apologize for its conduct.[1]

The court also took upon itself to scrutinize any persons
attempting to preach, forbidding all unauthorized persons,
and also forbidding any one to preach before an unauthorized
society. In 1650 a Mr. Matthews, for preaching to an unauthorized Church, was fined £10.[2] Such actions were based
upon the principle formally adopted by the general court
(1641) that "The civil authority . . . hath power and liberty
to see the peace, ordinances, and rules of Christ observed in
every Church, according to His word. . . . It is the duty of the
Christian magistrate to take care that the people be fed with
wholesome and sound doctrine" (1658).[3] Again in 1660, the
following was enacted: "It being the great duty of this court
(to see) that all places and people within our gates be supplied by an able and faithful ministry of God's holy word . . .
the president of each county court shall duly, from time to
time, give it in charge to the grand juries to present all abuses
and neglects of this kind." Eight years later, the court declared: "The Christian magistrate is bound by the word of
God to preserve the peace, order, and liberty of the Churches
of Christ, and by all due means to promote religion in doctrine
and discipline."[4]

The Massachusetts establishment differed from the State
Church in England and in other colonies in that the law

[1] Hutchinson, *Massachusetts Bay*, I, 423.
[2] Felt, *Ecclesiastical History of New England*, II, 42, 53.
[3] *Massachusetts Colonial Laws*, pp. 100, 101.
[4] *Ibid.*, p. 104.

conferred no right of presentation, save under special circum- Right of presentation. stances. The choice of minister was left to the people; but the law of 1692[1] provided that the county court should "take care that no town is destitute of a minister." In case of any such vacancy, the court should notify the Church to choose; and, if the Church neglected to do so, the court should procure and settle a minister and levy on the town for his support.

Another great contrast is to be noted in the *source* of the Origin. establishment. In England the crown and parliament, without any consultation with the people, built up the fabric of the Anglican Church. The Church was imposed upon the nation by the monarch. A similar fact exists in the history of those colonies in which the Church of England was established. That Church came into possession by a royal rescript, a clause of the charter, or of instructions from the crown or the board of trade. It was imposed on those colonies without any consideration as to whether the inhabitants were in sympathy with it — a royal demand that what religious polity should obtain among them should be that which the king approved. It is true that the house of burgesses in Virginia did by formal act establish the Church of England as the State-Church of the colony, but in so doing they were in effect only recognizing and confirming that which a dozen years before had been ordered by the crown. This determination by the home government, it is also to be observed, was in most instances against the desire of the colonies and the religious preferences of the people. This was eminently the fact in Maryland from the beginning, and afterward became so in Virginia, while not more than one in twenty of the people of New York approved the futile efforts of Cornbury to establish the Church of England in that province.

The contrast presented in Massachusetts is marked. There was studious avoidance of any religious establishment in the

---

[1] *Massachusetts Colonial Laws*, p. 244.

charter, and the crown attempted no dictation on the subject of the Church. But immediately that the planters were settled they supplied the lack for themselves, building up a State-Church on as rigid lines and as sharp requirements of uniformity as those which intrenched the Anglican Church in the English constitution. This was the expression of the popular will of early Massachusetts. The fact cannot receive too great an emphasis. What the people of that day wanted they established. The hardships of the after condition arose, not from any dictation of external authority, but from the incoming of persons who were not of the same mind, and from the growth of population out of sympathy with the purposes and measures of their fathers.

Under the earlier conditions which the more rigid of the second and third generation strove to maintain, there was much legislation, both to support the Church as an establishment, and to conserve the religious character of the com-

Domicile.   munity. Thus, very early, the law of domicile guarded against strangers and required all people to live within easy distance of the meeting-house, so that all could attend wor-

Heresy.   ship.[1] In 1646 the Act against Heresy ordained that any person denying the immortality of the soul, or the resurrection, or sin in the regenerate, or the need of repentance, or the redemption by Christ, or justification through Christ, or the morality of the fourth commandment, or the baptism of infants, or " who shall purposely depart the congregation at the administration of that ordinance," [2] or shall endeavor to seduce others to any of these heresies, should be banished.

Contempt.   In the same year, contemptuous conduct toward the word or preacher was made punishable; for the first offence, by a public reproof from the magistrate and bonds for good behavior; for the second offence, by five shillings fine, or by

[1] Ellis, *Puritan Age*, p. 253 ; Weeden, *Social and Economic History of New England*, pp. 20, 72, 73, 80.

[2] This clause compelled the resignation of Rev. Henry Dunster, the first President of Harvard College (1654), though he was not banished.

"standing on a block four feet high," having on the breast
a placard with the words, —

"An Open and Obstinate Contemner of God's Holy
Ordinances"[1]

One can hardly fail of noting the wide divergence between
this law and its *Preamble*. The statute begins, "Although
no human power be lord over the conscience, yet because
such as bring in damnable heresies . . . ought duly to be
restrained." Evidently, in the Puritan view there was a
human lordship of every conscience save their own! They
demanded for themselves a power which they denied to all
other men.

By the same law non-attendance on divine service was
punished by a fine of five shillings. In 1656 it was enacted
that any person denying any of the books of the Bible should
be whipped or fined, and, if obstinate, banished. The law of
1697 against "Blasphemy and Atheism" is remarkable both
for the ingenuity of its penalties, and as an indication that
only a sense of waning religious power in the magistrate
could so express itself. In the act, which finds both atheism
and blasphemy in "denying the true God," various penalties
are awarded; surety for good behavior, imprisonment for
six months, the pillory, whipping, boring the tongue with a
hot iron, and sitting on the gallows with a rope about the
neck, at the discretion of the court; provided that not more
than two of such penalties be inflicted for one and the same
offence.

[margin: Non-attendance.]

Of course, under the general law Roman Catholics were
not suffered to live in the colony. In 1647 Jesuits were forbidden to enter the colony. If any should come, they were
at once to be banished; if they returned, to be put to death.

[margin: Romanists.]

We find another illustration of the religious and "orthodox" intent in the "Articles of Confederation," which
(1643) bound together the colonies of Massachusetts, Ply-

---

[1] *Massachusetts Colonial Laws*, pp. 101, 102, 120, 129, 302.

mouth, Connecticut, and New Haven in the " New England Confederacy." The preamble recites : " Whereas we all came into these parts of America with one and the same end and aim, viz.; to advance the kingdom of our Lord Jesus Christ and to enjoy the liberty of the Gospel in purity and peace; " and declares as one of the objects of the union, " preserving and propagating the truth and liberties of the gospel." It was defined that only Church members could be commissioners to the federal council. The immediately practical aim of the union was mutual aid in defence against the Indians, but the colonists could not take measures for such a purpose save in the name of religion. Uniformity also, or at least regularity, seems to have been no less of a requirement; for when Rhode Island applied for admission into the confederacy it was refused, because " they ran a different course both in their ministry and in their civil administration." [1]

Thus the religious quality of early Massachusetts was with its State-Church very prominent and emphatic. It more than justified Dudley's language in his letter to the Countess of Lincoln : " If any come hether to plant for worldly ends, that canne live well at home, hee comits an errour of which hee will soon repent him. But if for spirituall, and that noe particular obstacle hinder his removeall, he may find here what may well content him." [2]

It were impossible that in a community so constituted the

ministry should fail of acquiring an immense influence. They did not as such, after the fashion of the " spiritual lords " in parliament, occupy seats in the legislature, but their power was very great and very general. Their advice on all matters of importance, and on many of trivial nature, was sought by the magistrates. Without exception they were men of education and sincere godliness, without fear in the ways of conscience, as ready to suffer as to speak. But for the most

[1] *Massachusetts Colonial Laws*, p. 722 ; Bancroft, *History of United States*, I, 422.

[2] Force, *Historical Tracts*, II, 12.

part they were intensely narrow, unable to conceive that
truth could lodge outside of their own lines, and as bigoted
and harsh as were the spiritual lords from whose tyranny
themselves had fled. Among his censorious brethren the
charity of the gentle Shepherd shows

> " Fair as a star, when only one
> Is shining in the sky."

Morton in his *Memorial*[1] gives a curious illustration of the feeling common among the ministry. When Wilson, the pastor
at Boston, was dying, he was asked what were the special
sins which provoked the displeasure of God against the country. He replied that the chief were Separation, Anabaptism,
and Korahism, defining the last as a rising-up of the people
against their ministers and elders, as though they took too
much upon them. Wilson died in 1667, when the power of
the ministers had begun to be impaired.

It needs to be noted, however, that, while the official dignity and authority of the ministers were very great, there
was nothing therein of a priestly quality. It was solely because of character and ability that they were put into their
sacred office. Every man of them had to be able to render
a reason other than the sacred character of his office, or lose
both place and respect. The functions of their office, with
all its power and privilege, were rigidly conditioned on personal character and ability.[2]

The *Abstract of Laws* drawn up by Cotton was never
adopted by the general court, and all law was within the discretion of the magistrate. In 1641 a code was compiled by Civil code.
Rev. Nathaniel Ward, author of the " *Simple Cobler of Agga-*
wam." This code was unwillingly adopted by the legislature

---

[1] Page 211.

[2] Scottow's *Narrative* (*Massachusetts Historical Collections*, IV, 4 ; 295)
abounds in praises of the early ministry, in some places with elephantine
humor, as in the celebrated " Quaternion, viz : Mr. *Cotton*, Eminent for
Spiritual Clothing, and *Mather* for Caelestial Dyeing, *Hooker* for Soul Fish-
ing, *Stone* for Building up in the Holy Faith."

and named the "Body of Liberties"; the court being compelled to this action by the murmurs of the people, who had become impatient of a situation, which left all penalty to the discretion, and sometimes whimsical caprice, of the courts.[1]

Of the code Winthrop writes in his *Journal* under date of December: " This session established 100 Laws, which were called the Body of Liberties, composed by Mr. Nathaniel Ward, sometime Pastor of the Church at Ipswich." The code differs from Cotton's Abstract materially, save that " in the article entitled *Capital Laws* each clause is supported by texts from the Old Testament."[2] There is no need here of any analysis of this collection of laws, or of quotation, beyond one peculiar regulation as to forming a Church, viz.: " All the people of God within this Jurisdiction, who are not in a Church way, and be orthodox in judgement and not scandalous in life, shall have full liberty to gather themselves into a Church estate: Provided, that they do it in a Christian way, with due observance of the rules of Christ revealed in his word."

This may be looked upon as a step toward liberty, for

---

[1] *Massachusetts Historical Collections*, III, 8 ; 192, 208 ; Palfrey, *History of New England*, I, 279. Some of the penalties awarded under this early anomalous arrangement were notable, and of them a few illustrations are quite in place here. (Hutchinson, *Massachusetts Bay*, I, 436 ; *Massachusetts and Her Early History*, p. 89 ; Ellis, *Puritan Age*, p. 231.) A Captain Stone, for " abusing Mr. Ludlow (a justice of the peace) and calling him *just-ass*, is fined £100, and prohibited coming within the patent without the governor's leave *upon pain of death*." " Mr. Willi. Foster, appearing, was informed that we conceive him not fit to live with us ; therefore he was wished to depart." Ambros. Martin, for calling the Church covenant a "stinking carryon and a human invention," was fined £10 and sent to Mr. Mather for instruction. F. Hutchinson, " for calling the Church of Boston, a whore, a strumpet, and other corrupt tenets," was sentenced to £50 fine, to be imprisoned until paid, and then to be banished on pain of death. " It is ordered that Josias Plastowe shall (for stealing 4 bushels of corn from the Indians) return them 8 back again, be fined £5, and hereafter be called by the name of Josias, and not Mr., as he used to be." (Palfrey, *History of New England*, I, 300.)

[2] *Massachusetts Historical Collections*, II, 8 ; 192, 234.

though the permission here given is from the magistrate with a power of review, and it was possible for a strict constructionist to decide that no non-Congregational form of Church estate was in accordance with the rules of Christ, yet we have it on Winthrop's [1] authority that there was a disposition to concede freedom of Presbyterian worship. This was in keeping with the greater liberality of the code in regard to other matters.[2] But such tendency toward a larger liberty in religion was speedily arrested by the " Presbyterian Cabal," to be noted presently.

The adoption of the Body of Liberties was looked upon as happily settling the civil and ecclesiastical affairs of the Commonwealth. So Winthrop wrote in his " *Small Treatise* " (1644): " It appears that the officers of this body politic have a Rule to walk by in all their administrations, which Rule is the Word of God, and such conclusions and deductions as are or shall be regularly drawn from thence. . . . The fundamentals which God gave to the Commonwealth of Israel were a sufficient rule to them, to guide all their affairs : we having the same with all the additions, explanations, and deductions which have followed, it is not possible we should want a rule in any case, if God give us wisdom to discern it." [3] In much stronger language wrote Cotton, " The order of the Churches and the Commonwealth is now so settled in New England by common consent, that it brings to mind the new heaven and new earth wherein dwelleth righteousness." [4]

But this condition was not arrived at without struggle. Hardly had the first course been laid in the foundation of the new theocratic commonwealth when the troubler of its peace appeared. Roger Williams landed at Boston in February of 1631, and brought with him a bundle of notions which the Puritan founders could ill abide. A protégé of the great Sir

Roger Williams.

---

[1] Bancroft, *History of United States*, I, 437.

[2] *Ibid.*, I, 418.

[3] *Massachusetts and Her Early History*, p. 52.

[4] Bancroft, *History of United States*, I, 368.

Edward Coke, whose word and actions in after years were so trenchant and influential on the side of freedom in the Great Rebellion, he had received from his patron incentives to the most liberal views. Educated at Cambridge and a graduate of Pembroke College, with a singularly active mind and as singular boldness in expression of opinions, he soon attracted to himself the hostile regard of Archbishop Laud, from the reach of whose arm he withdrew into New England. While in England he became a devoted friend of Hooker and Cotton, whom he preceded to America, and who were not able to equal him in extreme liberality of views; and the latter of whom, with his usual facility to coincide with the dominant party, is found assenting to the banishment of his friend.

On Williams's arrival at Boston he at once signalized his peculiarity of mind by refusing to join the Boston Church,[1] because "they had not publicly declared repentance for former communion with the Church of England," and also because the Boston Church had shown a sympathy with persecutors. He also expressed his opinion that the magistrate had no right to punish a breach of the first table of the law, and that his function was limited to those offences which violated only the second table. Despite the singularity of these views, his sweetness of disposition, his marked spirituality of religious character, and his evident ability so won upon the people of Salem that they immediately called him to take the place of teacher, vacated six months before by the death of Higginson.

From the pulpit of the Salem Church, Williams at once began to express these and other opinions quite opposite to those dominant in the Bay. The Boston authorities had already remonstrated with the Salem Church for calling Williams, and when to his first offence he added insistence on, and amplification of, his dangerous and distasteful opinions, their indignation was extreme. He was fearless in denouncing what he regarded as error, and especially the

[1] Arnold, *History of Rhode Island*, I, 20.

fundamental error of the commonwealth in conceding to the magistrate any power over religious matters.

"Everything in the polity of Massachusetts was made subservient to the interest of the State, and that State was virtually and exclusively the Puritan Church."[1] To the average New England Puritan of the day, of course with the implied premise that his Church was the only one that had the truth, it was difficult to make a distinction between the two blended institutions. To such a view the attempt to separate these factors of a godly state, and, more than that, the hardihood of asserting such union to be a sin against God and conscience, took on the gravity of a heresy, alike impious and dangerous to the public weal.

From the mutterings of the storm Williams, after but few months at Salem, deemed it prudent to retire for refuge to Plymouth. There he was received with both kindness and honor. The tolerant Pilgrims, happy in serving God in such way as their conscience approved, content to accord to other men an equal liberty and abstaining from all attempts to forcibly fuse things civil and religious, at once tendered to this first American refugee from religious persecution the place of teacher in their own Church, assistant to the pastor, Ralph Smith. Here Williams remained for two years, laboring most acceptably in his religious office, though, as must be understood from the fearless and conscientious nature of the man, abating nothing in his views of the dignity of the conscience and the natural freedom of the mind. Bradford[2] describes him as "a Man godly and zealous, having many precious Parts, but very unsettled in judgment. . . . His teaching was well approved, for the benefit of which I still bless God, and am thankful to him even for his sharpest Admonitions and Reproofs, so far as they agreed with Truth."

The judicial mind of the Plymouth governor was undoubt-

[1] Arnold, *History of Rhode Island*, I, 33.
[2] Prince, *Annals*, II, 48; Felt, *Ecclesiastical History of New England*, I, 187.

edly correct in its opinion of Williams, who, besides the countless tokens of an almost prophetic insight into the nature of religion in its relation to the communal life and the natural liberty of mind, at the same time made evident an "unsettled judgment" in sundry matters of public concernment, the utterance of which served, not only to increase the opposition of his foes, but also to cloud the real issue involved.

Vagaries. One of these vagaries was his denunciation of the Boston Church for non-repentance of former membership in the English Church. The thought was absurd and its statement could only annoy. Another absurdity was his doctrine that the magistrate ought not to administer the oath to an unregenerate person, on the ground that making oath was an act of worship, which the unregenerate could not perform and the magistrate should not require! This was Williams's objection to an act passed by the legislature of Massachusetts in April, 1634.[1]

While at Plymouth, Williams issued a pamphlet in which he inveighed against the royal patent of Massachusetts as conferring title to lands which the king could not give, and which could only be rightfully obtained by purchase from the Indians. However correct in theory his position might be, as affected the Indian titles, the argument of the pamphlet was considered by the men of the Bay as both disloyal to the king and assailing the foundation of the colony.

Notwithstanding such manifestations, however, the Church of Salem, on the death of Skelton in January, 163¾, called Williams to the vacant pastorate. This call he was quite ready to accept, but, on seeking dismission from the Plymouth Church, he was met by unwillingness to release him. The character and ability of Williams had so won

---

[1] The act, "upon intelligence of some Episcopal and malignant practices against the country," framed an oath, to be made by every male resident not a freeman, promising allegiance and obedience to the colonial government. (Barry, *History of Massachusetts*, I, 271 ; Arnold, *Rhode Island*, I, 27, 30.) It is not unlikely that the "malignant practices" referred to the teachings of Williams.

upon the people that they were much disturbed. At the same time there was doubt as to how far his idiosyncrasies might carry him, and the question was decided by Brewster's suggestion that there were "abler men in the Bay, who could better deal with him, than the men at Plymouth."[1]

Meanwhile, the neighboring ministers, looking with great disfavor on the prospect of Williams's return to Salem, complained to the general court, alleging the disloyalty of his pamphlet. This charge he seems to have met with disclaimers of all disloyal intentions, so that the court felt itself restrained from prohibitive action, though looking upon the course of the Salem Church as "a great contempt of authority." In consequence of this the court refused a petition from Salem for a grant of adjoining land.

Return to Salem.

More adverse action, however, could not be long delayed, as Williams, settled in his charge, was undeterred by authority or by fear from the utterance of his obnoxious sentiments. He was ever gentle in his attitude toward individuals, never resenting personal injuries or returning reproaches, yet unyielding and uncompromising in his zeal for religious liberty. So he found many things to condemn in the surrounding conditions. There was not a principle of the dominant theocracy which he did not antagonize. He denounced all intermeddling of the magistrate with religious matters. "Let any man show me a commission given by the Son of God to civil powers in these spiritual affairs of His Christian kingdom and worship."[2] He objected to restriction of the franchise and office to Church members; to compulsory attendance on religious service; to the civil tax for support of the ministry. The civil power had no administration in matters of heresy. "The straining of men's consciences by the civil power is so far from making men faithful to God or man, that it is the ready way to render them false to both."[3]

---

[1] Morton, *Memorial*, p. 102. [2] *Bloody Tenent*, p. 239.

[3] *Bloody Tenent Still More Bloody*, p. 209; Bancroft, *History of United States*, I, 370–372.

In the meantime, while the magistrates were smarting under such criticism of their chosen methods, occurred at Salem the silly action of Endicott in cutting the cross from the English flag, on the ground that it smacked of popery. With this folly Williams, says Mather in the *Magnalia*, " was but obliquely and remotely concerned." It is not probable that he was concerned in it at all, or had any sympathy with the perpetrator of such foolishness. Two more opposite spirits were not in the colony than Williams and Endicott.

Process against Williams.

But the action precipitated matters. The general court reprimanded Endicott and deprived him of official capacity for a year, and then began measures of reproof to the Church at Salem and its pastor. The Church was notified that their petition for land was denied, because they retained Williams. On this Williams and the Church sent letters of remonstrance to the other Churches asking them to admonish the court for its injustice to Salem. At the next session of the court the Salem delegates were refused seats until they should "give satisfaction about the letters." Against this exclusion Endicott protested, and was at once committed until "he should acknowledge his fault." [1]

The court then summoned Williams to answer for his expressions of opinion and for the letter to the Churches. Williams justified his actions and doctrine, and by the court (October, 1635) was sentenced to banishment within six weeks. Afterward the court extended the time limit until the spring, on account of the inclement season, but attached the condition of complete silence as to his peculiar views.

The Church of Salem was cowed and made humble apology for their letter, on which they received the desired grant of land. Williams was excluded from the pulpit; but in his own house, whither many of his friends resorted, he refused to observe the command to silence and freely uttered his opinions. This was regarded by the magistrates as a flagrant breach of faith and order, especially as "many were

[1] Arnold, *Rhode Island*, I, 34, 35, 38.

much taken with the apprehension of his godliness," and "his opinions were contagious." They resolved to send him to England on a ship about to sail. Williams, unnotified of this intention, was summoned to Boston; but he, apprehending violence, refused to come. The magistrates then sent a boat to Salem with a force sufficient to arrest him and convey him to the ship; but when the company reached Salem their prey had escaped. Forewarned by friends, Williams had fled forth into the wintry wilderness, to find among its savage denizens a refuge from his Christian brethren.[1]

Thus took form the first case of religious persecution by the Puritans of Massachusetts, after the expulsion of the Brownes. It is possible, indeed, to contend that the action against Williams was mainly for teaching doctrine subversive of the civil order. That his teaching had such tendency is beyond dispute. Williams declared himself opposed to the structural principles of the commonwealth. If his doctrine should be allowed, if men should be largely persuaded by it, then presently all the religious defences of the state would be destroyed, the unregenerate would have equal power and privilege with the saints, and the entire fabric of the theocracy would fall to the ground. This is evident, not only as a thing of fear to the authorities of that day, but as a necessary issue from the prevalence of such opinions. To men in power the teaching of Williams sounded like the voice of anarchy.

Justice to the founders of Massachusetts requires that this should be remembered. Given a commonwealth such as they had founded, and a resolution to maintain it in its purity, it is difficult to see how they could do otherwise than expel one who threatened its very existence. While Williams spoke from the religious standpoint and in defence of the God-given rights of conscience — and there is no evidence that he uttered a word designed against the state and social order — yet it is easy to understand that the standpoint of the authorities might be one which regarded chiefly the civil

---

[1] Felt, *Ecclesiastical History of New England*, I, 230–232, 294.

conditions. The question between them was radical. Is a theocracy — a state merged with a Church — right and possible? He said "No." They said "Yes; and such shall be here." After that, there was nothing but expulsion for the non-content — an expulsion which could logically base itself on the alleged disturbance of the public peace and civil order. Much as we admire the wide vision of Williams, so clearly discerning the principles of spiritual freedom; deeply as we are persuaded of the fundamental error in the Massachusetts constitution, we yet cannot deny to their action against him this favorable and, if their theory of the state were right, justifying construction. With it, there still remains the question how far they might go in the repression of a purely religious opinion, which in no true sense involved the fundamental principles of the state.

The answer to this question was not long delayed, and for it the materials were already prepared while Williams was yet undisturbed at Salem. In 1634 there came to Boston that remarkable woman, Anne Hutchinson, whom Mather describes as "a gentlewoman of haughty carriage, a busie spirit, competent wit, and a voluble tongue;" and who with her purely religious teaching created in the colony a far greater disturbance than did Williams.

Hutchinsonian controversy.

It is impossible to be satisfied with this slighting description by Mather. What he said of Mrs. Hutchinson was true; but she was far more and better than that, a person of exceptional and varied ability, friendly and helpful to those about her, able to "minister to body, mind, and spirit." [1] To a very considerable intellectual faculty, acute rather than profound, she added that dangerous sensibility to enthusiasm which easily passes into fanatic vagaries. With an attractive personality, and no small amount of that quality which our modern phrase calls "personal magnetism," she exerted a powerful fascination upon others, especially upon those of her own sex, who looked upon her as a natural confidant.

[1] Ellis, *Puritan Age*, p. 307.

Clearly, this was a dangerous addition to a colony, where the will of the minister and the magistrate affected to be a law to every one for both action and thought.

She was the colonial type of those women of quick religious sympathy in our own day, who gather about them companies of disciples. She began with quiet gatherings of women in her own house for religious discourse, and early fell into the habit of criticising the doctrine of the ministers in their Sunday preaching and Thursday lectures. Her comments were sharp and accompanied with much denunciation of the ministers themselves. There is no need to revive the details of the controversy thence arising, or to attempt to explain the almost unintelligible jargon of much of the discussion, wherein distinctions without differences were multiplied and magnified into absurd importance. The main doctrine of the new prophetess was in three points: 1st, that the covenant of grace had entirely superseded the covenant of works; 2d, that no amount of sanctification or personal holiness could be regarded as evidence of a justified condition (hence the name *Anti-nomian* applied to the controversy); and 3d, that the Holy Spirit *personally* dwells in a justified soul.[1] With these sufficiently startling propositions, as *criteria* for judgment of the ministers and their teachings, she set aside most of their preaching and declared that all the ministers, except Cotton and Wheelwright, were still under the covenant of works and unconverted. The excitement caused by this teaching was beyond measure. The ministers were naturally indignant, and esteemed that in their persons the ark of God had been touched with profane hands. " The town and country were distressed by these subtleties, and every man and woman, who had brains enough to form some imperfect conception of them, inferred and maintained some other point. . . . The fear of God and love of our neighbor seemed to be laid by and out of the question."[2]

---

[1] Morton, *Memorial*, p. 133 ; *Massachusetts Early History*, p. 97.

[2] Hutchinson, *Massachusetts Bay*, I, 57.

Almost the entire community of Boston were carried away by the novelties. John Cotton was favorably disposed toward them, though he did not come out decidedly in their favor; while his colleague Wilson, with the rest of the ministry, was bitterly opposed. With the outraged ministry was ranged the great majority of the general court, who themselves had been pilloried by Mrs. Hutchinson as not in the covenant of grace. To these grave guardians of the state it seemed that the pillars of the commonwealth were shaken, especially when some of Mrs. Hutchinson's feather-brained disciples undertook to show that a person under the covenant of grace would be guilty of sin in obeying the orders of a magistrate or military officer, who was still under the covenant of works! Logically, it were easy to prove that this absurdity was a just deduction from the theocratic principles of the magistracy, but they could neither see it nor allow it.

But among the magistrates themselves Mrs. Hutchinson had some powerful adherents. The chief military personage of the colony, Captain Underhill, was on her side. But her greatest disciple was the governor, Sir Harry Vane, the younger.

Vane.

Vane was one of the noblest characters of his age, though "the subject of widely differing judgments."[1] Cromwell called him "a juggler"; Clarendon, "a man of extraordinary parts, a pleasant wit, a great understanding"; Swift, "a dangerous, enthusiastic beast." Hallam describes him as, "not only incorrupt, but disinterested, inflexible in conforming his public conduct to his principles, and averse to every sanguinary and oppressive measure." Milton in his honor composed one of his finest sonnets:—

> "Vane, young in years, but in sage counsel old,
> Than whom a better senator ne'er held
> The helm of Rome."

His American experience was a short and disappointing episode in his life. Coming to New England shortly after

[1] Ellis, *Puritan Age*, p. 328.

the arrival of Mrs. Hutchinson, his youthful ardor was soon captivated by her religious enthusiasm. The adhesion of so prominent a personage to her views served to add to the popularity in Boston, which his personal qualities and rank had already made for him, and, though but twenty-four years of age, he was made governor at the election of 1636.

For months the colony lived in the midst of an ever growing excitement, as over a seething volcano. The signal for eruption was unintentionally given by a sermon of John Wheelwright, the brother-in-law of Mrs. Hutchinson, who had followed her to America.[1] Though a zealous advocate of her views, he was far removed from the spirit of the agitator. A man of gentle disposition, nothing could have been farther from his thoughts than the making of an uproar. But with so much powder on every side there needed but a small spark to cause an explosion. Judged of at this day the sermon seems a very small matter indeed to create so great a disturbance. It defended the new views, but without acrimony, and criticised some of the public conditions under which the colony was established. This was enough for the magistracy, who construed Wheelwright as counselling violent change in the constitution, and at once arrested him on a charge of sedition. Wheelwright.

On this the steps toward eliminating the disturbers of the community followed rapidly one upon another. A synod of the Church was called to give ecclesiastical judgment on the heresy. This body met at Newtown (Cambridge) in the spring of 1637, and gravely sat itself down to discuss "eighty-two erroneous opinions" taken from the teachings of Mrs. Hutchinson and her brother.[2] Full liberty of discussion was given, with the curious proviso that "no one should be held responsible for the opinions he defended unless he acknowledged them to be his own."[3] The arch heretic and her Synod of 1637.

---

[1] Felt, *Ecclesiastical History of New England*, I, 269.

[2] *Ibid.*, I, 313.

[3] *Wonder-Working Providence of Zion's Saviour.*

brother were examined. " Inquisition was made into men's private judgment, as well as into their declarations and practices." Cotton acknowledged that most of the " opinions " were erroneous, but could not condemn all, and drew upon himself the sharp criticism of some of his brethren. The popular pastor of the Boston Church was in an evil case, with the vast majority of his parishioners on one side of the fence, and that of the ministers and magistrates on the other. After various attempts at compromise he, according to his nature and manner, got himself down where the chief power lay, with more or less of a wrench to his own convictions.[1]

Action of general court. The synod condemned the heretical opinions and reported its action to the general court. That body met shortly after, in May, 1637, at Newtown, " because of the excitement in Boston," and proceeded to elect a governor, putting Winthrop in the room of Vane and showing to the latter scant courtesy in any attempts he made at defence of his position and conduct. In order to forestall other heretical disturbances, the court prohibited the harboring of persons whose religious views were considered dangerous. The bill was opposed by Vane, to whom Winthrop replied, " the intent of the law is to preserve the welfare of the body."[2] This law extended the statute of 1630, which prohibited the settling of any in the colony without leave from the governor and assistants. It is evident also that the proposers of the law were providing for the severity of sentence already designed toward the heretics already with them.

Remonstrance. At this session of the court was presented a " Remonstrance " signed by sixty citizens, most of them residents of Boston and among them two members of the court itself, William Aspinwall and John Coggeshall. The Remonstrance deprecated the action of the synod and besought the court to refrain from interference with Mrs. Hutchinson and

[1] Morton, *Memorial*, p. 133 ; Hutchinson, *Massachusetts Bay*, I, 75.
[2] Barry, *History of Massachusetts*, I, 268.

her friends. This paper roused the anger of the court, as a "speaking evil of dignities" and insubordination. The two deputies were expelled from their seats in the body, and the court called upon all the signers of the paper to acknowledge their fault. Ten of them weakened and desired leave to withdraw their names, while the balance were condemned to be disarmed — a punishment involving at that day no little disgrace and conveying the utterly unjustified implication that they had treasonable intentions.[1] One individual sentence dealt with Stephen Greensmith, "for saying that all the ministers save Wheelwright, Cotton, and perhaps Hooker did teach a covenant of works." He was condemned to a fine of £40, to give £100 bond for good behavior, and to acknowledge his fault in every Church.

At the November session of the general court final action was taken against the leaders. Though a strictly civil body, it really sat as having ecclesiastical, or religious, function, and its whole process against Mrs. Hutchinson and her brother was conditioned upon their religious opinions. Both were banished from the colony. Winthrop's language is: "Finding that two so opposite parties could not contain in the same body, without apparent hazard of ruin to the whole, it was agreed to send away some of the principal."[2]

Banishment.

After this action of the general court, Mrs. Hutchinson was summoned to answer for her errors to the Church, of which she was a member. There also the decision was against her, and Cotton, "fully persuaded that he had been made her stalking horse," was ordered to pronounce the censure![3] "One cannot read the proceedings without feeling that, if only the scene had been changed to an ecclesiastical court in

Church censure.

[1] In the next year, with the Indian war concluded and a large immigration from England, the court restored the arms. (Palfrey, *History of New England*, I, 249.)

[2] Ellis, *Puritan Age*, p. 334; *Life of Winthrop*, I, 245.

[3] Barry, *Massachusetts*, I, 258.

England, the whole trial would have formed an edifying chapter in Puritan martyrology." [1]

So the colony was purged, and by a process which it is impossible to defend; for the arguments of danger to the state, which threw a color of propriety upon the action against Williams, cannot here find force. There was no danger to the state in the views of Mrs. Hutchinson. Given their full sway they would have made a purer theocracy than that of Winthrop and Wilson. The whole proceeding was due to religious intolerance and to the rancor of the ministers, whose spiritual character had been aspersed.

After the expulsion of the heretics the court was able for a season to settle down to other matters, as says the gentle Shepherd of Newtown, " Thus the Lord having delivered the colony from war with Indians and Familists (who arose and fell together), He was pleased to direct the hearts of the magistrates (then keeping Court orderly in our town, because of these stirs at Boston) to think of a College." [2]

Harvard College.

[1] Doyle, *Puritan Colonies*, p. 183. Wheelwright, with several friends, removed and founded the town of Exeter. Aspinwall, who was banished by the court, went with John Clarke and William Coddington to Rhode Island, where they were soon joined by Mrs. Hutchinson. (Adams, *Emancipation of Massachusetts*, pp. 77, 78.) Her son and son-in-law, having ventured to expostulate with the authorities at Boston for the wrongs inflicted on their mother, were thrown into prison for several months. (Bancroft, *United States*, I, 392.) Vane retired from New England in disgust and went home, there to do yeoman's service for liberty and at last to die for her.

[2] *Chronicles of Massachusetts*, p. 550; Palfrey, *History of New England,* I. 247. It is interesting to note that the first movement toward Harvard College was in this stir of religious strife, a sure token of the desire that a godly ministry should be educated in the way of Truth. Says the *Wonder-Working Providence of Zion's Saviour,* " It is as unnatural for a right New England man to live without an able ministry, as for a smith to work his iron without a fire." (Force, *Historical Tracts.*) The royal commissioners of 1664 did not regard the infant Harvard with so much complacency. In their report to the king they wrote (*Colonial History of New York*, III, 112): " At Cambridge they have a wooden colledg. . . . It may be feared that this colledg may afford as many Schismaticks to ye Church and the Corporation as many rebells to ye King as formerly they have done, if not timely prevented."

The next occasion for the exercise of the repressive religious functions of the Massachusetts magistrates arose within
a short time after the exile of the Antinomians. It was the
affair of Gorton, in regard to whose career there is much Gorton.
confusion of statement and much contradictory representation. The record is not clear as to the date or place of
Samuel Gorton's first appearance in New England. Probably he was in Boston at the time of Mrs. Hutchinson's
trial and exile. As though to avoid similar process against
himself, he departed to Plymouth, where he was found void-
ing his peculiar opinions in 1638. Morton describes him as
"a proud and pestilent seducer," [1] given to "all manner of
blasphemies," and freely expressing himself in great contempt for both the civil and ecclesiastical order of the colony.
The man was evidently what in modern parlance would be
called a "crank," goaded by a continual spirit of unrest,
prompting him to assail everything which failed to accord
with his own views.

What those views were it is somewhat difficult to say, beyond the statement that they were utterly averse to the
opinions generally obtaining in the colonies. His writings
are filled with unintelligible rant, in which the clearest things
seem to be a claim of inner illumination by the Spirit, and
condemnation of the union of Church and State. Withal, he
was of a turbulent disposition, at least in the earlier years of
his American life, and seemed to love strife for strife's sake. [2]

It is quite within the demands of justice to suppose that
the action of the Plymouth and Rhode Island authorities
against Gorton were for civil reasons, a fact not so clear in
the action of the Massachusetts magistrates. [3] At Plymouth
his lack of reverence for all constituted authorities exposed
him to the complaint of Ralph Smith, that he " carried on

[1] *Memorial*, p. 135.

[2] Barry, *History of Massachusetts*, I, 262 ; Palfrey, *History of New England*, I, 304.

[3] Felt, *Ecclesiastical History of New England*, I, 392, 403, 453.

mutinously and seditiously." On this complaint he was tried by the court, and sentenced to fine and to banishment within fourteen days. Going to Rhode Island, he very soon made himself obnoxious by his opposition to the authorities, toward whom he used uncivil language so offensive that the court felt compelled to repress it. Before the court he denied its authority. " The Governor, Mr. Coddington, saying in court, 'You that are for the King, lay hold on Gorton' ; he on the other side cried out, ' All you that are for the King, lay hold on Coddington,' — whereupon he was banished the Island." [1] It is not quite certain that the Rhode Island people whipped or imprisoned him. Certainly, they expelled him for disorderly conduct.

Thence he went to Providence Plantations and was received by Williams and permitted to remain, though the latter had no sympathy with his restless disposition and impracticable caprices. He was allowed to settle near Providence, but seems to have given some trouble to Williams and his colony by unjust treatment of the neighboring Indians. [2] The lands on which he had settled were claimed by the Massachusetts government, which, because of complaint by the Indians, summoned Gorton to answer to the court at Boston. To this summons he returned a contemptuous refusal to appear; [3] whereupon the authorities forcibly arrested him and conveyed him to Boston. Here he was brought to trial on " twenty-six blasphemous particulars " obtained from his writings, adjudged guilty, and thrown into prison. Barry says that the ministers were for death, but the magistrates dissented. [4] Gorton himself states that he barely escaped

[1] *Massachusetts Historical Collections*, III, 3 ; 96; Barry, *History of Massachusetts*, I, 264.

[2] Felt, *Ecclesiastical History of New England*, I, 457.

[3] *The Wonder-Working Providence of Zion's Saviour* says : " Samuel Gorton, being the ring-leader of the rout, was so full gorged with dreadful and damnable errors, that soon after the departure of the messenger, he layes aside all civil justice and, instead of returning answer to the matter in hand, he vomits up a whole paper full of beastly Stuff."

[4] *History of Massachusetts*, I, 265.

death. Twenty-six years afterward he sent a petition to the court of commissioners in England, in which he describes the treatment he had received. The years had not dulled his sense of wrong. " They took offence," he wrote, "that we could not close with them in their Church orders, neither could we approve of their civil course in divers respects. . . . They preached us in their pulpits as gross heretics, and men not worthy to live upon the earth. . . . They tried us upon life and death — had resolved upon our death, in case we would not falsify our faith to God and the King. . . . They put it to the major vote whether your petitioners should live or die, our lives escaping by two votes." [1]

However disorderly Gorton may have been, his trial and sentence were for charges of irreligion, though the modern reader would find it hard to gather "blasphemous particulars" from the unmeaning jargon of his hysterical writings. Gorton, in a letter to Morton, whose *Memorial* was published before the former's death, solemnly denies the charge of blasphemy. " I appeal to God, the Judge of all secrets, that there was never such a thought in my heart." [2]

There is no doubt that the man was scandalously and cruelly abused. The treatment was only possible by an authority which regarded departure from the established religious order as sedition against the state. That Gorton either was grossly misunderstood at the first, or sobered by his afflictions became afterward worthy of public confidence and respect, seems abundantly proved by Judge Eddy, Secretary of State for Rhode Island, who wrote, " I have read the records of the colony from the beginning until after the death of Gorton, and I find that he was almost constantly in office, and not an instance of reproach is recorded against him." [3]

[1] *Massachusetts Historical Collections*, II, 8 ; 68.

[2] *Memorial*, p. 138 ; Felt, I, 463.

[3] It was against Gorton that Winslow wrote his *Hypocracie Unmasked*, already referred to, in reply to Gorton's pamphlet " Simplicitie's Defence against Seven-Headed Policy."

The next important spasm and outputting of theocratic intolerance is found in the action against what is called the "Presbyterian Cabal." This name is something of a misnomer, for the movers of it were not specially concerned for Presbytery, but for general liberty of religion and for citizenship without regard to religious faith. The name seems to have arisen from a supposition of sympathy with the movement in the parliament of the day, which was predominantly Presbyterian. So far as we can gather, the ecclesiastical preferences of the cabal were rather with Episcopacy.

In 1646, Dr. Robert Child, Samuel Maverick, William Vassal, Thomas Fowle, and three others petitioned the general courts of Plymouth [1] and Massachusetts for religious freedom and a redress of grievances. Rev. Peter Hubbard of Hingham, a Presbyterian, was either one of the petitioners or in open sympathy with them. The petition complained of several onerous conditions : [2] that the fundamental laws of England were not allowed in the colony; that non-members of the colonial Churches were denied civil rights and privileges, though freeborn Englishmen; and that many sober, righteous, and godly persons, members of Churches in England, were debarred from Christian privileges. The relief prayed for was that the court should, 1st, establish the common law of England; 2d, open the franchise to all Englishmen, who "were quiet, peaceable, and forward with heart, hand, and purse, to promote the public good"; and 3d, "allow divers sober, righteous, and godly men, members of the Church of England, to be taken into your congregations and to enjoy with you all the liberties and ordinances Christ hath purchased ; " or else to have liberty to form Churches of their own. The petition concluded with the statement that,

---

[1] p. 140.

[2] Hutchinson, *History of Massachusetts Bay*, I, 145 ; Hutchinson, *Collections*, pp. 188–196 ; *Massachusetts Historical Collections*, II. 4 ; 107 ; Palfrey, *History of New England*, I, 325 ; Felt, *Ecclesiastical History of New England*, I, 574.

if its prayers should be granted, " we hope to see the now contemned ordinances of God highly prized; the gospel, much darkened, break forth as the sun at noon-day; and Christian Charity and brotherly love, almost frozen, wax warm."

The petitioners had demanded relief from taxes, in case the court should refuse these requests, and threatened an appeal to England. The general court of Massachusetts was greatly offended and cited the petitioners to appear before it, as " not accused for petitioning, but for contemptuous and seditious expressions." Thus, again, non-conformity was sedition, subversive of both Church and State. The petition was refused by the court, with the somewhat contemptuous language: " These remonstrants would be thought to be a representative part of all the non-freemen of the country; but when we have pulled off their vizards, we find them no other than Robert Child, Thomas Fowle, etc." It was intimated to the petitioners that, if they would apologize, their offence would be forgiven. This they refused to do, and they were fined, Mr. Hubbard being mulcted in the sum of £20.

Some of them resolved to go to England with their complaint, a statement of which was drawn up and signed by twenty-five men, non-freemen. The paper was seized by the court and its signers were fined, on the ground that no appeal could be taken to England from the action of the Massachusetts authority.

A statement of the trouble, however, did reach England in the form of a pamphlet with the fantastic title, " *New England's Jonas Cast-Up at London*" (1647).[1] The pamphlet represented the Petition as the Jonas, too heavy for the New England stomach, now cast up at London. It related the story of the petition from the standpoint of Child and his party, and submitted some *Queries* for an English answer; whether all English inhabitants of the colony, having lands,

[1] Force, *Historical Tracts*, IV.

are not freemen; and whether the petitioners ought to be
hindered from "settling in a Church way" according to the
Churches in England. To invite the sympathy of the powers at home, there is a biting allusion to "a book lately
set forth by Edward Winslow against Samuel Gorton, intit-
uled '*Hypocrasie Unmasked*,' in which there is a deep and
subtle plot against the Laws of England and Liberties of
English Subjects, and the Gentlemen who are now suffering
in England."

Winslow was himself in England, as agent for Plymouth,
at the time the pamphlet was there published, and the fact
that the English authorities abstained from any interference
in the matter is attributed by Hutchinson to his prudence
and influence.

The happy (?) conclusion of this Cabal was probably the
occasion for a congratulatory letter of Symonds to Winthrop. Asking, "What seems to be God's end in bringing
His people here?" he furnishes the answer: "1st, To be an
occasion to stir up the two nations to set upon reformation
of religion; 2d, To have liberty and power to set up God's
own ordinances in Church government, and thereby to hold
forth matter of conviction to the Episcopacy and others, that
this way of Church government and civil government may
stand together."[1]

The allegation that the ulterior design of Child and his
associates was political, looking to the overthrow of the colonial government, is quite unsupported by evidence. The
relief asked for by them, if granted, would have undoubtedly
wrought an essential change, but it was a change sought at
the hands of the authorities themselves, and would have
involved no more of revolution than obtains in any case of
reform conceded by the governing authority. Nor can the
charge lie on the ground of the appeal to England, for such
appeal was felt to be the natural right of Englishmen; and
had occasion to resort thereto arisen for the men who con-

[1] Hutchinson, *Collections*, p. 220.

demned Child and Maverick, none would have been quicker than they to avail themselves of its hope of relief.

The immediate consequence of the cabal was the calling of the second synod of the Churches. To the theocratic mind, alarmed by this attempt to modify the sacred institution of an ecclesiastical commonwealth, there appeared a necessity for strengthening its defences; and for this purpose the general court issued a call for the synod. Curiously enough, and most inconsistently with their avowed principles, some of the ministers and Churches took umbrage at this action, as something which the court had not the authority to do.[1] The dissatisfaction was specially expressed in Boston, where " about thirty or forty of the members excepted that the Churches had a right to meet in synod without the intervention of the magistrates."

Cambridge synod.

The court, anxious for the synodical meeting, in order to allay the jealousy in some of the Churches, offered a compromise, directing that " the call should be drawn up in the form of a motion and not of command." Avoiding decision as to the right of the churches to meet in synod without the magistrates' permission, the court resolved: " Although this Court makes no question of their lawful power by the word of God to assemble the Churches, upon occasion of counsel for anything which may concern the practice of the Churches . . . (it is) thought expedient on the present occasion not to make use of that power, but hereby rather declare it to be the desire of the General Court." This deliverance satisfied all but the Boston Churches, which, however, were persuaded by Mr. Norton to send delegates.

The synod met at Cambridge, June, 1647, but after a few days adjourned on account of an epidemic, and did not reassemble until August of the next year. Then, during a session of fourteen days, the synod adopted the Westmin-

[1] *Massachusetts Historical Collections*, II, 1; 196; Ellis, *Puritan Age*, pp. 217–221; Palfrey, *History of New England*, I, 329; Felt, *Ecclesiastical History of New England*, I, 570; II, 5.

ster Confession of Faith, and settled the scheme of government and discipline, according to a Congregational model, in the famous " *Cambridge Platform*." This action was submitted to the general court for approval, which body referred it, in 1649, to the Churches for their opinions. The Churches fully approved and so reported to the general court, whereupon the court by act of 1651 formally ratified the proceedings of the synod, and enacted them into law for the Churches of Massachusetts.

The various steps in this process deserve notice as illustrating the constitution of Church and State. By it the civil legislature appears as the highest authority in the Church. The synod put the finishing touches to the ecclesiastical structure. By formal statute *Congregationalism became Law*, and any attempt to institute another form of worship became a punishable offence.

In the spirit of this constitution the minuter history of the period shows the general court interfering with the business of the Churches on any pretext, of which a few instances may be noted.

Civil interferences.

It appears that, while some non-members of Churches were aggrieved that they were denied the franchise, there were some Church-members not alive to their privileges as such, who, for the purpose of escaping public service, neglected to be made freemen. To meet the latter situation, the general court, 1643,[1] ordered the Churches to deal by way of discipline with such of their members as refuse to take their freedom. In 1650 the Second Church of Boston called Michael Powell to its pastorate. Powell had been a tavern-keeper in Dedham, and a member of the general court. In 1648 he removed to Boston, where he became noted for a "gift in prayer and exhortation." The court forbade his installation on the ground that, while he might be a ruling elder, he was unfit to be pastor, because " lacking in such abilities, learning, and qualifications as are requisite and necessary for an

[1] *Record*, II, 38; *Puritan Age*, p. 214.

able ministry of the people." To this action both Powell and the Church submitted without remonstrance.[1] Indeed, the docile spirit of Powell seems to have been chiefly occupied by a fear lest the authorities might think him capable of insubordination. The imperative tone assumed by them moves him to reply: " My humble request is that you would not have such hard thoughts of me, that I would consent to be ordained without your concurrence." [2]

After the death of Cotton in 1652 the First Church of Boston called John Norton of Ipswich, whom the Ipswich people were unwilling to release. Hence arose a sharp contention between the two Churches, with which the general court interfered. On its own motion, the court called a council of elders and two messengers from each of twelve towns, and paid all expenses out of the public treasury.[3] Again, in 1663, on the death of Norton, the Boston Church called the celebrated John Owen of England, and the court sent an official letter to Owen urging his acceptance.[4]

The purity of doctrine also, as well as the order of the Churches, engaged the attention of the general court. In 1650 they summoned William Pynchon, a magistrate of Springfield, to answer for a book written by him on the atonement.[5] So serious did they consider the matter that they sent to England a " Declaration and Protestation," asserting that they were no party to the book, but "on the contrary, we detest and abhor many of the opinions and assertions therein as false, erroneous, and heretical." The court ordered that the book be burned in the market-place by the hangman, after the next Thursday's lecture, and appointed Mr. Norton to prepare an answer and refutation, for which service he was voted £20. Pynchon's reply to

---

[1] Ellis, *Puritan Age*, p. 220.
[2] *Massachusetts Historical Collections*, III, 1 ; 45.
[3] *Puritan Age*, pp. 223, 263.
[4] Palfrey, *History of New England*, II, 101.
[5] Felt, *Ecclesiastical History of New England*, II, 20, 43.

the summons was so explanatory that the court in May, 1651, "having hopes," allowed him to return home, taking Norton's answer "to consider thereof." In the following October the court was not satisfied, and put Pynchon under bonds of £100 to appear the next May. Tired and disgusted by the persecution, Pynchon returned to England.[1]

In 1651 the court summoned Rev. Marmaduke Matthews of Malden, whom in the preceding year they had fined £10 for preaching in an "unauthorized" congregation, to answer to the charge of "preaching divers erroneous, unsound, and unsafe opinions." In the trial a certain Thomas Line, a member of the Malden Church, testified against Matthews, and for this testimony the Church proceeded to discipline him. Thereupon the general court interfered and forbade the process, bearing "witness with what tenderness and caution he gave his aforesaid testimony," and advising the Church to call a council to "consider the matter."[2]

The case of President Dunster of Harvard is another interesting illustration. Mr. Dunster had become a Baptist, and on this account the general court, in 1654, called on the officers of the College "not to continue in office any teacher unsound in the faith." In 1657 Mr. Dunster was summoned by the court to answer for not having his own child baptized.[3]

The next notorious act of persecution, after Gorton's experience, is noted in the treatment inflicted on Clarke and Holmes, at Lynn. John Clarke was a friend of Mrs. Hutchinson and went with Coddington to Rhode Island. There he became a Baptist and the pastor of the Church at Newport. Obadiah Holmes was originally of Salem, but was thence dismissed to the Congregational Church at Seekonk in the

Clarke and Holmes.

---

[1] Felt, *Ecclesiastical History of New England*, II, 224.

[2] *Massachusetts Historical Collections*, II, 8 ; 325.

[3] Ellis, *Puritan Age*, pp. 397, 402. Ellis relates that Dunster was prosecuted for rising in the Church and protesting against the baptism of a child brought in for that ordinance. But this cannot be cited against the establishment. Such conduct could be punished to-day as disorderly disturbance of religious service.

Plymouth jurisdiction. Coming into contact with Clarke, he was influenced to Baptist views and was baptized at Newport. Returning to Seekonk, he set up there a Baptist Church.[1]

In 1651 Clarke and Holmes went to Lynn, where dwelt certain sympathizers in their Baptist opinions, and held religious services in a private house. For this they were arrested, taken before the magistrates, and compelled to "go to meeting." There Clarke requested permission to speak and, being allowed the privilege, said: "As strangers to each other's inward standing in respect to God, we cannot conjoyn act in faith, and I could not judge that you are gathered together and walk according to the visible order of our Lord." Here he was stopped by the magistrates. Both were sent to Boston and thrown into prison. On trial they were sentenced to a fine of £20 each; to remain in prison until the fine was paid, or "to be well whipt." Clarke paid his fine and was released; but Holmes refused and was "whipped unmercifully." "A sword of steel," said Clarke, "cannot come near or touch the spirit or mind of man."[2]

The tidings of the harsh treatment of these men were soon carried to England, where they created no small amount of criticism and disgust. Clarke himself took care that the story should be exploited in a pamphlet printed in 1652, entitled "*Ill-Newes from New England. A Narrative of New England's Persecution: wherein is declared, That, while Old*

[1] There must have been a number of Baptists already in the place, as in 1649 the general court of Massachusetts wrote a letter to the Plymouth court, complaining that "some sectaries" had been allowed to settle at Seekonk, and praying for unity of action in the two colonies. On the starting of the new Church, 1650, Holmes was cited by the general court of Plymouth, but it does not appear that any further action against him was taken; and Massachusetts was "grieved by the slight response from Plymouth." (Palfrey, *History of New England*, I, 382; Felt, *Ecclesiastical History of New England*, II, 48, 72, 79; Adams, *Emancipation of Massachusetts*, p. 105 *et seq.*)

[2] Bancroft, *History of the United States*, I, 449; Ellis, *Puritan Age*, pp. 387, 390.

England is becoming New, New England is becoming Old."
The title was suggested by the anonymous "*Good Newes
from New England*" (London, 1648), abounding in fulsome
praise of the colonial constitution and referring to Clarke
and his Rhode Island friends in contemptuous terms.[1]

Saltonstall's
letter.

This persecution of Clarke and Holmes drew from Sir
Richard Saltonstall the famous letter to Cotton and Wilson
to which brief reference has been made. "It doth not a little
grieve my spirit," he wrote, "to hear that you fine, whip,
and imprison men for their conscience. . . . We hoped the
Lord would have given you so much light and love there
that you might have been eyes to God's people here, and not
to practice those courses in a wilderness, which you went so
far to prevent. These rigid ways have laid you very low
in the hearts of the saints. I do assure you that I have
heard them pray in the public assemblies that the Lord would
give you meek and humble spirits, not to strive so much for
uniformity, as to keep the unity of the faith in the bond of
peace. When I was in Holland . . . some Christians there . . .
desired me to write to the governor to know if those who
differ from you in opinion . . . might be permitted to live
among you; to which I received this short answer from your
then governor, Mr. Dudley, ' God forbid that our love for the
truth should be grown so cold that we should tolerate error.'
. . . I hope you do not assume to yourselves infallibility of
judgment, when the most learned of the apostles confessed
that he knew but in part and saw but darkly as through a
glass; for God is light, and no further than He doth illumine
us can we see, be our parts and learning never so great."[2]

Cotton's
reply.

The reply of Cotton and Wilson to this noble letter was
in painful contrast to its dignity and spiritual insight. Of
Clarke and Holmes they say: "The imprisonment of either
of them was no detriment. I believed they fared neither of
them better at home, and I am sure that Holmes had not

[1] *Massachusetts Historical Collections*, IV, 2 ; 1, 195.
[2] Hutchinson, *Collections*, pp. 401–404.

been so well clad of many years before. . . . Do you think that God hath crowned the State with so many victories, that they should (suffer) so many miscreants to pluck the crown of sovereignty from Christ's head? . . . and so leave Christ no visible kingdom upon earth? . . . We believe there is a vast difference between men's inventions and God's instances. We fled from men's inventions, to which we should else have been compelled. We compel none to men's inventions. If our ways (rigid ways, as you call them) have laid us low in the hearts of God's people, yea and of the saints (as you stile them), we do not believe it is any part of their Saintship." This, considering all the attendant circumstances, is about the most lamentable expression of Puritan bigotry which the records preserve to us.

In the decades between 1640 and 1660 there was at once a growing discontent among the people with the repressive Discontent. spirit of the theocracy, and also an increasing bitterness of intolerance on the part of the ministers and authorities. In the eyes of those in power any form of dissent became more and more dangerous and disloyal, and they grew the more outspoken in denunciation as the mutterings of discontent became frequent and loud. Norton declared that variety was fatal to religion.[1] "Religion," he said with emphasis, "admits of no eccentric notions." Ward's " *Simple Cobler of Aggawam in America* "[2] was published in 1647. Besides the two or three quotations already made from its pages, the following may serve further to illustrate the ruling spirit of the day: " God doth nowhere in His word tolerate Christian States to give Tolerations to adversaries of His Truth, if they have power in their hands to prevent them. . . . Here is lately brought us a *Magna Charta*, whereof the first Article of Constitution firmly provides free stable-room and litter for all kinds of Consciences, be they never so dirty or jadish. . . . My heart hath naturally detested Tolerations of divers

[1] Bancroft, *History of the United States*, I, 449.
[2] Force, *Historical Tracts*, III.

Religions or of one Religion in segregant shapes. He that unwillingly assents to it, if he examines his heart by daylight, his Conscience will tell him he is either an Atheist, or an Heretick, or an Hypocrite, or at best a captive to some Lust." [1]

The commonwealth.

The success of the people and parliament in England in their struggle with the king could not fail to reflect itself in the minds of many in the colony, where it was felt that, as inhabitants they were deprived of some of the rights of free-born Englishmen, and in the matter of religion they suffered under a law of uniformity no less rigid than that, which in England the parliamentary triumph had set aside. In point of religion it was felt that England was now far more free than Massachusetts, and the malcontents were dissatisfied that in New England they should suffer more restriction than they would at home.

Hence there was a continual outcropping of trouble for the theocratic rulers. The suppression of Williams, Mrs. Hutchinson, Gorton, Child, and Clarke did not bring the hoped-for relief; while the denial of suffrage to all non-members of churches was creating a dangerous feeling in the community, where in 1660 the unenfranchised population was in a large majority.

More repression.

Against tolerance of divergent religious teaching, and to prevent the incoming of foreign unapproved preachers, such as Clarke, the general court, in 1653, enacted "that no person within this jurisdiction shall undertake any constant course of public preaching or propagating, without the approbation of the elders of four the next Churches, or of the County Court." It was also declared that any person maintaining any heterodox or erroneous doctrine should be questioned and censured by the county court. Against this legislation a protest was made to the next session of the general court by the Church and town of Woburn. This was altogether

---

[1] It is amusing to observe how these men all wrote Conscience with a big C, as though of honor, and never scrupled about denying its rights.

a new thing, and might well have been considered as a hand-
writing on the wall.[1]

In 1659 the general court gave legal expression to the deep
Puritan horror of all things savoring of popery, by making   Popery and
the observance of Christmas a punishable offence.   The first   Christmas.
generation of colonists were all of one mind as to the iniquity
of such observance, and no legislation was needed.   But
thirty years had seen no small change in the popular mind.
A process was going on which the more godly viewed as a
fearful degeneration of morals.   The writings of the Mathers
and others of the day abound in lamentation over the growing
"godlessness" of the community.   One of its indications was
the disposition " to keep Christmas," and hence the action of
the legislature.[2]

In 1665 the king, Charles II., demanded the repeal of this
law, but it was not repealed until 1681.   This repeal, however, did not commend the day to the more pious New
England mind, and men, now (1902) not much beyond
middle life, can remember a childhood to which the festivity
of Christmas was forbidden.

To the leaders of Massachusetts policy it seems never
to have suggested itself, that the so-called " relaxation of   Moral
morals " was the natural reaction from the austere and rigid   laxity.
system, which they had founded and were seeking to maintain as the ark of God.   We are not, indeed, to understand
the lamentations about prevalent ungodliness as importing
the same moral condition as such plaints would suggest

1 There have already been noted certain laws of this period, against
Heresy, Contempt of the Word, or of Ministers, Neglect of Worship, and for
Providing a Godly Ministry. See pp. 176, 177.

2 This horror of the great Feast-Day of the Church was long-lived. That
solemn and intolerable prig, Samuel Sewall, whose soul the wearing of wigs
oppressed like a nightmare, tells in his *Diary* of spending a Christmas in the
family burial vault, arranging the positions of the coffins therein, and described it as " a pleasant but awful Treat."   One can hardly avoid the
thought that no small portion of his pleasure arose from the consciousness
that he was desecrating a day which the Church delighted to honor.

to-day.[1] There was no woful and frequent abandonment of morals. Society was sober and decorous. The things which were so severely reprobated were for the most part innocent departures from the stern, unsmiling austerity of primeval Puritanism. The natural pleasures of youth, the gayety of a husking-bee, the merriment of any festival gathering, were considered sinful frivolities and indicative of a culpable lack of religion.

More important and of much graver moment to the integrity of the theocratic system was the fact that, the majority **Non-church** of the male population were outside of the Churches. There **members.** were many children not baptized because their parents were not communicants. Many of the latter, though themselves baptized in infancy, had neglected to become communing members of the Churches, for various reasons; such as a lack of "spiritual change," conscious unfitness, dissent from the Church creed or polity, or addiction to some other form of faith and worship not recognized by the law. In this class were many children and grandchildren of the original settlers, while to their number were added many immigrants of a later day. Every one of this large number of non-Church members, no matter how well educated, wealthy, or fitted for citizenship any of them might be, was excluded from the franchise and ineligible to office.

This constituted a great danger. The unenfranchised majority was giving louder and more frequent expression to their discontent, and it became evident that in some way the law, or its application, must lose a portion of its rigidity.[2] **Half-Way** The expedient adopted, the famous "Half-Way Covenant," **Covenant.** while pacifying murmurs, was the worst thing that could possibly have been devised, sacrificing the purity of the Church and the spirituality of religious profession to the consistency of the civil statute. The proper thing for them to do was to change the freeman's law, which restricted the

[1] Hodge, *History of Presbyterian Church.*
[2] Felt, *Ecclesiastical History of New England,* I, 548; II, 88, 134-141, 154.

franchise to the members of the established Church. An example of the broader base of freedom was before them in the experience of Connecticut, where the right to vote and hold office was never confined to church-members, and where this more liberal citizenship had wrought only to the good and peace of the state.

But to the men of Massachusetts the fundamental principle of their theocracy was too dear and sacred for them to adopt such relief. Whatever should be done, the voter must still be a member of the Church! So the only way to widen the franchise was to open the door of the Church! And this was the expedient adopted, which, while relieving the immediate clamor, inflicted on the Church baleful consequences not removed for nearly one hundred years.

It is not to be understood that there has been preserved any written outline of such purpose on the part of the leaders. We may suppose that, in their zeal for the freeman's law, they had no eyes for the danger to the Church. Nay — more than this — from the fact that in their action they made no mention of the franchise whatever, it may be argued that their chief design was to make the Church easier of ingress, and to bring into its fold many of those who were without, that access to its ordinances might prove to be "means of grace" to them. But the logic of events is too clear to allow the supposition that the effect upon the franchise was absent from their minds; and it seems only just to conclude that this effect was an ulterior, though unannounced, design.

The active agent in this work of expansion was the third synod of the Churches, called to consider the state of religion, which met in Boston in 1662. The special work for which the synod is famous was its deliverance in regard to the "Subjects of Baptism." In this it was declared that, "The infant seed of confederate visible believers are members of the same Church with their parents and, when grown up, are personally under the watch, discipline, and government of the Church." To this was added, "Church members, who

Synod of Boston.

were admitted in minority, understanding the doctrines of
faith, and publicly professing their *assent* thereto ; not scandalous in life, and solemnly owning the covenant, wherein they
give themselves up and their children to the Lord, and subject themselves to the government of Christ in the Church,"
may demand baptism for their children.[1]

There can be no doubt that the doctrine of this deliverance is from a Calvinistic standpoint thoroughly true, and
corrected the error which, in the past, had made participation in the Lord's Supper by the parent a condition for baptism of the child. But the practical evil of the synodical
action was twofold: in making no proper distinction
between baptismal and communicant membership; and, as
the result proved, in conferring on the former all the religious privileges of the latter. There soon followed a great
relaxing of the rules by which the Church had been wont to
"fence the tables," and baptized members were admitted to
the communion without evidence of any spiritual change,
with the thought and hope that access to the sacrament would
be of gracious influence. Thus was constituted the "Half-
Way Covenant," which, really for the satisfaction of a political need, brought into full Church relationship multitudes
who were strangers to vital spiritual experience ; and which
abode in its strength until, in the next century, Edwards
shattered its power and prepared the way for the Great
Awakening.

It is not to be understood, however, that all the religious
leaders of the day were consenting to this action. The synod,
as in duty bound, reported its action to the general court,
which body, in the fall session of 1662, enacted as follows:
"The Court, having read over the result of the synod, judge
meet to recommend the same to the consideration of all the
Churches and people of the jurisdiction, and for this end do
order the printing thereof."[2]

[1] *Massachusetts Historical Collections*, II, 1 ; 196.
[2] *Ibid.*, II, 1 ; 201.

Thereupon arose great controversy. The leaders of the opposition were President Chauncy of Harvard, John Davenport of New Haven, and Increase Mather. These were answered by Allen of Dedham, Richard Mather of Dorchester, and Mitchell of Cambridge, whom Cotton Mather called "the matchless Mitchell." The contest lasted for many years, but the result was that the principle of the synodical deliverance was adopted by the majority of the Churches, while the logical widening of the suffrage was confirmed by the state in the law of 1664, to be hereafter noted. The second synod of Boston, called in 1676, suggested no departure from this broader rule. Its attention was chiefly directed to "the dangers to New England liberty" arising from the *quo warranto* proceedings in England against the Colony Charter, and at the same time to the Confession of Faith. It is to be noted that its decision, confirmatory of the previous adoption of the Westminster symbol, lacked authority until ratified by the general court.[1]

Meanwhile that the dissension was proceeding which issued in the first Boston synod, there came to the Massachusetts rulers a sharp spasm of alarm and cruelty. As we look back upon it, the alarm seems utterly absurd and the cruelty without excuse. Though the faculty of "putting oneself in another's place" enables the judicial mind to look upon the Quaker episode with less sternness of condemnation than such action would demand to-day, yet the children of the Puritans cannot read the story with much patience for their fathers.

Quakers.

In 1647 George Fox began in England his remarkable career. Believing that the work of the Reformation had not gone far enough, he undertook to restore the purity of primitive Christianity. Teaching the doctrine of the Inward Light of the Holy Spirit in man, he would dispense with priest and presbyter and all distinctions between clergy and laity. He taught that tithes were unlawful, that

Fox.

[1] Bancroft, *United States*, II, 121; *Cambridge and Saybrook Platforms*.

oaths were sinful, and that non-resistance was a Christian duty. No person could without sin engage in any military service. The enthusiasm and personal character of Fox drew to him many followers, whose doctrines immediately aroused the hostility of the authorities and subjected "the pestilent sect of Quakers" to all manner of persecution, short of death itself.

At the same time — the seething years of the English Commonwealth — were proclaimed the fanatical vagaries of the Fifth Monarchy men, and of the Muggletonians, whose wild deliverances were in the common apprehension confused with the teachings of Fox. All were classed together. Hence it was that the reports brought to New England of these new religious teachings made no proper distinctions, while at the same time they excited the fears of the Puritans that the "dangerous heresy" might be brought to their people. Moved by that fear, before any of the sectaries had entered the country, the general court in 1654 ordered,[1] that all persons having copies of the books of John Reeves and Ludowick Muggleton, "who pretend to be the two last witnesses and prophets of Jesus Christ, full of blasphemies," should bring or send them to the magistrates, on pain of £10 fine for failure.

This seems to have been regarded as something of a challenge, accepted first by two Quaker women, Mary Fisher and Ann Austin, who came to Boston from Barbadoes in July of 1656. In a few weeks they were followed by nine others; and the whole company, under the impression that God required them to bear witness against the errors of Church and State, proceeded at once to make themselves as offensive as possible to the ministers and magistrates. They were promptly arrested, and being asked by the court, "How they would make it appear that God sent them? after a pause they answered, that they had the same call that Abram had to go out of his country." They were sent to prison and their

---

[1] Hutchinson, *Massachusetts Bay*, I, 169; *Colony Laws*, p. 121.

books were burned. While the governor was passing the jail, Mary Prince called to him from the window: "Woe unto thee! Thou art an oppressor!" The governor sent for her twice and reasoned with her, and two ministers who were present treated her kindly, "to which she returned the grossest railings, reproaching them as hirelings, deceivers of the people, Baal's priests, seed of the serpent, brood of Ishmael, and the like."[1]

This is a fair sample of the conduct of these unwelcome guests, whose behavior was as madness itself compared to the gentle, charitable, and peace-loving Friends of a later day. Their spirit was a frenzy, for which the only proper place was Bedlam. The thought of opposition to their doctrine, the idea of a paid ministry and of other institutions of the civil and religious state, fired them to a strange and ungovernable rage, in which, while they preached against physical resistance, they made of their tongues weapons harder to bear than clubs. Instead of preaching the gospel of peace they degenerated into brawlers and common scolds. There was no official dignity that they did not revile; no sense of social decorum that they did not outrage.[2] One of the women stripped herself naked and walked through the aisles of a crowded meeting-house, and another through the town of Salem, in order to testify against the indecency of the magistrates in whipping women on the bare back. In proportion as they met any opposition their behavior grew more frantic. And, of course, their claim in all was of a divine mission. Stevenson declared that in Shipton, Yorkshire, as he was ploughing, he heard a voice, saying, "I have ordained thee to be a prophet to the nations."

The first comers of the sect to Massachusetts may justly be called "avowed firebrands," not intending permanent settlement, but with the deliberate design of antagonizing the religious and civil institutions of the colony, a design

[1] Hutchinson, *Massachusetts Bay*, I, 196.
[2] Palfrey, *History of New England*, II, 4, 15.

formed and entered upon in a thoroughly quarrelsome spirit. This was doubtless increased in its bitterness by the repressive measures immediately adopted by the magistrates; but, making all allowance for that influence, the spirit of these New England Quakers was much more pugnacious and ungovernable than was that of their brethren in other colonies. Even the tolerant Roger Williams wrote of them: "They are insufferably proud and contemptuous. I have, therefore, publicly declared myself that a due and moderate restraint and punishment of their incivilities, though pretending conscience, is so far from persecution, properly so called, that it is a duty and command of God." [1]

The effect of such an irruption into the colony was that of great alarm. A nearly hysterical fright took possession of the magistrates, as though they saw reason to apprehend that, unless the severest measures were used, the entire community would be demoralized. It is to be noted that all the actions of the magistrates were predicated on the heretical character of the Quakers' doctrine. While much of the inflictions visited upon its teachers would be equalled in any police court of to-day for like disorderly conduct, the chief thought and purpose then was, not to punish turbulent behavior, but to suppress heresy. The legislation against the new sect constantly defines, "a cursed sect of hereticks which are commonly called Quakers," and their doctrine as "a pestilent Heresy." At the October session of the general court in 1656 began a series of laws against them, growing more and more severe and culminating, two years after, in the doom of death on persistent return after banishment.[2]

Under these statutes Quakers, coming into the colony, and before the commission of any offence besides that of coming, were to be thrown into jail, whipped with twenty stripes, and kept at work until transported or banished. Shipmasters bringing any of the sect were to be fined £100. Any person

[1] Ellis, *Puritan Age*, p. 458.
[2] *Laws of Massachusetts Colony*, pp. 121–125.

entertaining, encouraging, or concealing Quakers was to be fined forty shillings "for each hour of entertainment." For the poor sectaries themselves, to fines were added whipping, mutilation, banishment, and death. The doom of death "barely secured enactment by a majority of one," and this only because of the illness of a deputy from Dorchester.[1]

The authorities of Massachusetts urged other colonies to take similar action, but none of them, while fining Quakers and their helpers, adopted such severe measures as those of Massachusetts. The reply of Rhode Island to the application from Boston contained a telling comment on the spirit of the sect, to the effect that in the absence of repressive laws the Quakers did not wish to remain or make many converts in Rhode Island.[2] "But we intend," wrote Arnold, "to commend consideration of their extravagant outgoings to the general assembly."[3]

The commissioners of the Confederacy responded to the desire of Massachusetts by recommending to the several colonies that the Quakers be banished, on pain of suffering severe punishment for return and death for a second return. This recommendation was signed by the younger Winthrop, of Connecticut, very reluctantly ; and he appended to his signature the words, " Looking at the last as a query and not an Act, I subscribe." Winthrop said that he would go on his knees to the magistrates to arrest execution.

There were four Quakers executed in Massachusetts : Executions. William Robinson, Marmaduke Stevenson, Mary Dyer, and William Leddra. Mary Dyer was the wife of William Dyer, the secretary of Rhode Island, who wrote a most pathetic letter to the magistrates at Boston, on receipt of which they released the woman, banishing and committing her to the custody of her husband. The secretary, however, proved powerless to shield his wife from the consequences of her

---

[1] *Puritan Age*, pp. 451, 453.
[2] Barry, *Massachusetts*, I, 365.
[3] Ellis, *Puritan Age*, p. 458.

fanatical folly. In a short time the infatuated woman returned to Boston, saying that she had "felt liberty" to go to Rhode Island, but was under a "religious restraint" to come back. "She denied our law, came to bear witness against it, and could not choose but come and do as formerly." [1]

Stevenson and Robinson had both been previously banished, and returning to Boston declared that they had "come to offer their lives." Robinson, on banishment from Massachusetts, had gone to Virginia, and there spent six months in prison. Hearing of the capital punishment enacted in the Bay, "he felt that the Lord had laid the burden" on him to put the law to trial in his own person. He wrote to Fox and Roff in England: "I came with my companion, Marmaduke Stevenson, to Boston, in obedience to the Lord, to beare our testimony against *there* BLOODY LAW, which they have made. The Lord laid on me, my LIFE to give up, BOSTON'S BLOODY LAWES to try." [2]

These executions took place in 1659. By them the already smouldering disapproval of the people for the severity of the magistrates was fanned into a flame, and the magistrates soon learned that the population at large, though having no sympathy with the Quaker views, were outraged by the inhumanity of the laws against the sect. No more executions were allowed by this rising public sentiment. Even less inflictions were condemned by it, and, one Brend having been whipped unmercifully, the people protested so effectively that the jailer very narrowly escaped punishment for his cruelty. [3] In consequence of this feeling among the people those imprisoned were released, and the general court in 1661 suspended the capital clause of the law. This was a practical repeal. [4] But the court was not ready to concede

[1] Ellis, *Puritan Age*, pp. 461, 469.
[2] *Massachusetts Historical Collections*, IV, 1 ; 154.
[3] *Puritan Age*, p. 442 ; Adams, *Emancipation of Massachusetts*, p. 165.
[4] *Colonial Laws*, p. 125.

liberty to the " cursed sect." In 1662 it reënacted the law
for the whipping of Quakers: and as late as 1675 a law was
passed imposing a fine of £5 on any person found at a Quaker
meeting. This was a dead letter at its enactment — a last
and despairing fling of already impotent bigotry. By this
time there were many Quakers in the colony. "After these
first excursions they became an orderly people, submitting to
the laws, except such as relate to the militia and support of
the ministry." [1] At Salem they were permitted to build their
first meeting-house in peace.

The credit of the relief afforded to the Quakers has usually been supposed due to orders from the king, but a com-
paring of dates shows that the indignant protests of the
people anticipated the royal command.

Soon after the Restoration in England, Edward Burroughs
complained to Charles of the cruelties suffered by his brethren in Massachusetts, and the king issued an order to "forbear to proceed any further, but send such persons to England, with the respective crimes or offences laid to their
charge." [2] John Colman of London wrote to his brother,
Rev. Dr. Colman of Boston: " The Quakers' complaint hath
been heard (by the Privy Council), and the persons who
were imprisoned are ordered to be set at liberty. I hear that
at the hearing the Attorney General reflected on the country very sharply, and said that was not the only instance in
which they had assumed to themselves unwarranted powers." [3]

The general court, having already relaxed its severity, replied to the king in an attempt to justify the past actions:
" Concerning the Quakers, open and capital blasphemers,
open seducers, open enemies to the government, malignant
and assiduous promoters of doctrines directly tending to
subvert both our Church and State . . . their willingly

---

[1] Hutchinson, *Massachusetts Bay*, I, 205.

[2] Barry, *History of Massachusetts*, I, 368; *Massachusetts Historical Collections*, IV, 9; 159.

[3] *Massachusetts Historical Collections*, IV, 2; 35.

rushing themselves thereupon (the sword of the law) was their own act, we with all humility conceive a crime bringing their blood upon their own head. . . . Had they but promised to depart the jurisdiction and not return, we should have been glad of such an opportunity that they should not die." [1]   Again, the court wrote to the lord chamberlain an apologetic letter, in which hatred, shame, and fear are alike heard. " In respect," it reads, " of those pestilent hereticks, the Quakers, who have lately obtained his Majesty's letter requiring us to forbear their punishment; in observance whereof we have suspended execution of our laws against them respecting death or corporal punishment; but this indulgence they do abuse to insolency and seduction of our people, and unless his Majesty strengthen our hands . . . this hopeful plantation is likely in all probability to be destroyed! "   At the same time, 1661, the court wrote to Lord Say and Sele of " the Quakers risen up against us, accusing us to his Majesty and intruding themselves upon us, whose work it is to dissemble their cursed principles, and in a tumultuous and rude manner reproaching all established order, as well civil as ecclesiastical, acting a part as commissioned from hell to ruin the poor Churches and people of God here." [2]

Any judgment upon this lamentable story must regard this alarmed mind of the authorities. There can be no doubt that they seriously entertained a fear that tolerance of the pestilent sect would result in ruin to both commonwealth and Church. To us such fear is the extreme of absurdity, but to them it was real and solemn. This fear was intensified into horror by the Quaker extravagance in action and speech. It could hardly be expected that a Puritan of the day would allow the painting of such portraits as the Quaker put into the following words: " A man that hath a covetous and deceitful rotten heart; lying lips which abound among them, and a

[1] Hutchinson, *Collections*, pp. 325, 327.
[2] *Ibid.*, pp. 357, 360.

smooth, fawning, flattering tongue, and short hair, and a deadly enmity against those that are called Quakers and others that oppose their wrongs; such a hypocrite is a fit man to be a member of any New England Church." [1]

It is impossible, in seeking palliation for the cruelty of the government, to go the length of Dr. Joel Parker,[2] who, almost justifying all its inflictions, argues that the Puritans did not persecute or harass the Quakers, but the latter harassed the former, while the Puritans imposed penalties for the violation of law. The argument is sophistical, for part of the law violated was a limitation on conscience and worship, the spirit of which was persecution. The history also shows that the first Quakers in Boston were arrested immediately on arrival, so soon as it was known that they belonged to the "pestilent sect." At that time the only harassment, of which they had been guilty, was their mere presence in the town. It may be said also that such a greeting was enough to stir up the bitterness of such fanatics, and that, had the magistrates shown a greater forbearance at the beginning of the business, its issue would not have been so sad and disgraceful.

The most that can be said for the magistrates is that their unreasonable fear destroyed their clearness of judgment. On their own statements, while they sought to check disorderly conduct, yet all their inflictions on the Quakers were in the

---

[1] *Massachusetts and Her Early History*, p. 114. It must be conceded, however, that honors were easy for vituperation between the Puritan and the Quaker. Both raked the language for terms which would both sting and express contempt, though it may fairly be said that the Quaker began the battle of words. Some of the titles of anti-Quaker pamphlets are suggestive (Ellis, *Puritan Age*, p. 417): as "*Hell Broke Loose, or an History of the Quaker, both Old and New*"; "*Anti-Christ's Strongest Hold Overturned, or the Foundation of the Religion of the People called Quakers Bared and Razed*"; "*Quakerism the Pathway to Paganism.*" Roger Williams contributed to this library "*George Fox Digg'd out of his Burrowes,*" a play not only on the name of the great original Quaker, but also on his defender and friend, Edward Burroughs. (Felt, *Ecclesiastical History of New England,* II, 543–548, 661.)

[2] *Massachusetts and Her Early History*, p. 426.

name of religion and for the safety of their Church. They did not wish to take life, and greatly preferred that the heretics would be content to remain away from the colony. " We desire their lives absent, rather than their deaths present." " For the security of the flock," said Norton, " we pen up the wolf; but a door is purposely left open, whereby he may depart at his pleasure." [1] Beyond doubt, the decree of death was enacted *in terrorem*, to frighten away the heretics, and we may easily believe that not a member of the general court, at the time of its adoption, considered it possible that an execution under it would occur. When the banished four returned, " those bloody laws to try," the magistrates were not quick to inflict the fatal penalty. This they might have done under a strict construction of the law, as death was the doom of return, without remedy or appeal. But the magistrates besought the culprits to go, and only on their persistent refusal resorted to the extreme. And yet, while it can thus be clearly shown that they did not desire to take life, yet the issue as clearly declares that they were willing to take life for opinion's sake, rather than suffer the flock " to be exposed to the ' pernicious heresy ' of the Quaker ' wolf.' "

Reaction.
This violent dealing, as before hinted, did not accomplish its design. The reaction was powerful on the theocracy itself. Puritanism and Religious Liberty, under the guise of Quakerism, met in a death grapple, and, though four Quakers went to the gallows, the real victory was with the " cursed sect " and the true principles they professed. The revulsion in popular feeling added an indignant bitterness to the sense of the oppressions suffered by many dissenters, such as Childs and Clarke, and to the sense of exclusion from the rights of freemen on the part of many of the people. All these things were seen to be of one pattern, the pattern of an exclusive religionism, to which must be moulded everything civil and religious. From this revelation a large part of the people

[1] Bancroft, *History of the United States*, I, 452.

revolted, and from the death of Leddra the days of the theocracy were numbered. In several forms of institution it yet lasted for one hundred and fifty years, but it took its real death blow from its persecution of the Quakers.[1] After this fatal work, though it indulged at times in the utterance of imperial language,[2] like the law of 1697 against Blasphemy, it yet steadily weakened, until there remained only certain forms of administration, retained rather for convenience than from any estimate of sacred quality in them.

The men of the next generation were heartily ashamed of the Quaker episode. Thus Cotton Mather:[3] "If any man will appear in vindication of it, let him do as he pleases. For my part, I will not." The same man, in 1718, gave a broader expression to regret for the errors of the fathers, marking the happy growth of religious freedom. The occasion was an ordination of pastor in the Baptist Church of Boston, a service in which the three Congregational pastors of the city took part. Cotton Mather preached the sermon and, speaking of religious persecutions, said: "Good men, alas! have done such things as these. New England also has in former times done something of this aspect, which would not now be so well approved: in which, if the brethren, in whose house we are now convened, met with anything too unbrotherly, they now with satisfaction hear us expressing our dislike of everything which looked like persecution in the days that have passed over us."[4]

At the same time that King Charles interfered for the relief of the Quakers, he bethought him of two other classes of men in Massachusetts whose wrongs needed redress. There were freeborn Englishmen in the colony denied the suffrage,[5] and there were men of the Church of England

Suffrage and Episcopacy.

---

[1] Adams, *Emancipation of Massachusetts*, pp. 175–177.
[2] Palfrey, II, 217.
[3] *Magnalia*, VII, 24.
[4] Bacon, *American Christianity*.
[5] *Social and Economic History of New England*, p. 269.

forbidden to worship according to their conscience. In regard to the latter there was a correspondence of special interest, illustrative of the dogged determination of Massachusetts to allow no departure from the established order.[1] In 1662 the king wrote to the colonial legislature, demanding that liberty of Episcopal worship be granted, and that individual Episcopalians be admitted to the Lord's Supper in the Congregational Churches and be afforded the baptism of their children. The reply of the general court recounts the causes of the Puritan departure from England. "We could not live," they say, "without the public worship of God, nor were permitted the public worship without such a yoke of submission and conformities as we could not consent unto without sin. That we might, therefore, enjoy divine worship without human mixtures, without offence to God, man, or our own consciences, with leave, but not without terms, we departed from our country, kindred, and father's houses into this Patmos. . . . The Congregational way is it, wherein we desire our orthodox brethren would bear with us."

The king was not satisfied by this reply and in 1664 sent over Colonel Richard Nichols — an incident of whose coming was the capture of New Amsterdam — and Sir Robert Carre, joining with them George Cartwright and Samuel Maverick as commissioners to visit the colonies and regulate these affairs. Their instructions as to Massachusetts[2] repeat the order, "that such who desire to use the Book of Common Prayer may be permitted so to doe without incurring any penalty, reproach, or disadvantage in his interests ; " and then proceed, "it being very scandalous that any man should be debarred the exercise of his religion, according to ye laws and customs of England, by those who by ye indulgence

Commissioners.

[1] Hutchinson, *Collections*, pp. 328, 379 ; *Massachusetts Historical Collections*, II, 8 ; 72, 74, 78 ; *Colonial History of New York*, III, 54–58, 84, 87, 102, 111.

[2] *Colonial History of New York*, III, 54, 58, 84, 87, 102, 111 ; Palfrey, II, 59.

granted have liberty left to be of what profession in religion they please. . . . Differences of opinion doe not lessen charity to each other, since charity is fundamental in all religion."

Private instructions charged the commissioners, "to be very careful that nothing be said or done, from or by which the people may thinke or imagine that there is any purpose in us to make any alteration in the Church Government, or to introduce any other forme of worshipp among them than that they have chosen; all our exception in that particular being that they doe in truth deny that liberty of conscience to each other." In order to conciliate and avoid suspicion, the commissioners were advised " to frequent their (the colonists') Churches and to be present at their devotions," but also, "that you carry with you some learned and discreet chaplaine, who in your own families will reade the Book of Common prayer and performe your devotion according to the forme established in the Church of England, excepting only in wearing the surplesse, which, haveing never bin seen in those countryes, may conveniently be forborne att this tyme."

Cartwright, in letters from Boston, wrote to Nichols: " They have admitted for freemen three or four men who are not members of the Church, that by it they might evade the King's letter in that poynt. . . . Their private soliciting for voyces against the next election, give me just cause for being jealous of their loyalty." . . . "Here we find the great probability of obstruction. . . . I doe think it will be better to beginne at Connecticote. If we have good successe there, it will be a strong inducement to these to submitt also."

The commissioners reported to the English secretary of state, with evident bitterness of disappointment: — " Those who have declared themselves loyall are very much threatened and in great feare, and have earnestly prest us to sollicit His Majestie for their speedy defence and safety. . . . We desire you to acquaint His Majestie with their desires in this, as also of haveing their children baptized and themselves admitted to the Lord's Supper. . . . They did imprison and barbarously use Mr. Jourdain for baptizing children. . . . Those whom they will not admit to the Communion, they compell to come to their sermons by forcing from them five shillings for every neglect: yet these men thought their own paying of one shilling for not coming to prayers in England was an insupportable tyranny. They have put many Quakers to death. . . . They yet pray constantly for their persecuted brethren in England."

There certainly was small disposition in the Boston authorities to satisfy the king and his commissioners, and when in 1665 the latter returned to the charge, demanding liberty of Episcopal worship, they received for answer from the general court: " Concerning the use of the common prayer book and ecclesiastical privileges, our humble addresses to his majesty have fully declared our main ends in our being voluntary exiles from our dear native country, which we had not chosen at so dear a rate, could we have seen the word of God warranting us to perform our devotions in that way; and to have the same set up here, we conceive it is apparent that it will disturb our peace in our present enjoyments; and we have commended to the ministry and people here the word of the Lord for their rule therein."

This was a sufficiently explicit refusal, and nothing was left to the commissioners but the pleasure of a satirical reply. " We are heartily sorry," they wrote, " to find that by some evil persuasions you have put a greater value upon your own conceptions than upon the wisdom of his majesty and council. . . . The end of the first planters coming hither, as expressed in their address, was the enjoyment of the liberty of their own consciences. . . . We admire, therefore, that you should deny the liberty of conscience to any, and that upon a vain conceit of your own that it will disturb your enjoyments, which the king often hath said it shall not. . . .

We have great reason both to think and say, that the King and his Council and the Church of England understands and follows the rules in God's word as much as this corporation. . . . His majesty does not impose the use of the common prayer book on any, but he understands that liberty of conscience comprehends every man's conscience as well as any." The weight of argument was undoubtedly with the king; and it makes an edifying spectacle to see Charles thus striving for liberty of conscience in Massachusetts at the same time in which he was shooting Covenanters in Scotland. The fact was that his principle of religious liberty was identical with that of the Puritans, a liberty for one's own sect alone. On such ground only he interfered for Episcopalians in New England, while he cared nothing for the non-conformists in old England, nor remonstrated with Virginia for persecuting the Puritans. His arguments and demands were futile to move the men of Massachusetts. Episcopacy remained *religio illicita* in the colony, until, more than twenty years afterward, Governor Andros forced the issue, seizing a Church and holding a service with a military guard.

The king's demand touching the franchise met a far more acquiescent mood in the general court. The matter had, indeed, been practically settled in the issue of the Boston synod, but the court, as though to satisfy the king and also to legalize the popular conclusions from the synod, in 1665 enacted the new law of the franchise, substantially as follows:[1] New law of franchise. " All Englishmen," presenting the certificates of the ministers of the places where they dwell that they are orthodox and not vicious or scandalous in conduct, and also certificates from the selectmen that they are freeholders; or who are in full communion with "some Church among us," and are twenty-four years of age may "present their desires to this court, and have such their desire propounded and put to vote in the general court, to (be admitted to) the freedom of the body politick, by the suffrage of the major part."

[1] *Colonial Laws*, p. 117.

This was a great step forward in the cause of liberty, and though the terms of the law put every several application at the discretion of the general court, it does not appear that such discretion was ever oppressively exercised. With whatever regret the court may have voted the change, they recognized that the popular mind had registered beyond repeal the relaxing of theocratic restrictions. In 1681 the court, in a letter to the king, construes this law as a repeal of the old statute, and denies that now only Church members are admitted freemen. But they conclude their statement with the plaintive sentence, " We humbly conceive it is our liberty by charter to choose whom we will admit into our own company." [1]

The opponents to the theocracy had thus scored two victories, — in this widening of the franchise and in the general condemnation of the treatment of the Quakers. Immediately thereafter the Baptists,[2] the sect of Clarke and Holmes, renewed their efforts, and more successfully, for freedom of worship. They were growing in number steadily. In Plymouth colony the town of Swanzey was settled by Baptist refugees from Massachusetts, and drew no hostile regards from the colonial authorities.[3] In 1665, the general court of Massachusetts, rendered uneasy by the increase of the sect and of their services, cited a number of them to answer for *schism*. On their refusal to give up their services, they were sentenced to disfranchisement and prison. After several months' detention they were released on payment of fines; and a public meeting was called for *discussion and instruction*, which the Baptists were required to attend![4] These were probably the same men whom Hutchinson mentioned by name: Thomas Goold, Thomas Osburne, and John George, who were persecuted for absenting themselves from the es-

Baptists.

---

[1] Ellis, *Puritan Age*, p. 533.
[2] Palfrey, II, 104.
[3] Hutchinson, *Massachusetts Bay*, II, 421.
[4] Ellis, *Puritan Age*, pp. 404–406 ; Hutchinson, *Collections*, p. 399.

tablished Church in Boston! This was in the theocratic stronghold, and showed how bold the new sect had grown.

The action of the court caused much popular agitation and outspoken dissent, and the court was too weak to enforce its will. The issue of the Quaker episode stood as an ominous warning. The Baptists remained in Boston and built their Church. In 1668 the general court attempted to retrieve the lost ground and after describing the " obstinate and turbulent Anabaptists," who count " infant baptism a nullity," sentenced the sect to banishment.

But the law was an idle word, which the court did not dare to enforce. The Baptists had come to stay, and to share with the Quakers the honor of securing liberty of conscience and of worship in Puritan Massachusetts. Though in many ways it was apparent that dissenters from the established order were unwelcome guests, yet we hear no more of fines, whippings, imprisonment, or exile for an alien religious worship.

The union of Church and State, however, was not thereby dissolved. While it thus lost a large measure of its exclusiveness, it continued to affect much action and legislation. This was indicated by the calling of the synod of 1676, whose advice in the perilous crisis of that time, when the king threatened the revocation of the charter, was particularly desired by the general court.[1] It continued to express itself in what remained for a century its chief concern, the public support of the Church, sundry details of which will presently be noted.

The royal movement against the charter occasioned immense agitation in the colony, not only as threatening the foundation of its liberties, but also entailing unavoidable changes in the religious attitude of the state, changes which simply carried on and widened the results of the Quaker and Baptist incidents. The charter was revoked by the king in council, in 1685, and Andros, the first royal governor in Massachusetts, brought with him instructions as to religious mat-

The charter.

[1] Hutchinson, *Collections*, p. 436.

ters in the several colonies grouped under his short-lived sway. The will of the king was communicated to the people in proclamation: "We do here will and require and command that liberty of conscience be allowed to all persons, and that such especially as shall be conformable to the rites of the Church of England be particularly countenanced and encouraged."[1]

All the evidence attainable suggests that there were many Episcopalians in the colony, whose complaints of their uncomfortable surroundings, their beloved service denied them and their prayer book closed, were continually being laid before the king.[2]

Andros.

With the coming of Andros the issue was forced, and that liberty, which had been obtained by themselves for the Quakers and Baptists, was now extorted for the Episcopalians by the strong hand of the royal power. The struggle began with the governor's demand for a Church building, in which services might be held according to the order of the Church of England. The use of the building (the Old South Church) was refused. Judge Sewall records:[3] " A meeting at Mr. Allen's of the Ministers and four of each congregation to consider what answer to give the Governor, and it was agreed that we

---

[1] *Massachusetts Historical Collections*, III, 7 ; 148.

[2] Among the representations of their claims for the king's help an amusing instance is found in Josselyn's *Two Voyages to New England* (*Massachusetts Historical Collections*, III, 3 ; 330) — a contrast between them and the Puritans. "Many hundred souls there," he writes, " be amongst them grown up to men and women's estate that were never Christianized. . . . The grose Goddons, or great masters, as also some of their merchants, are damnable rich . . . inexplicably covetous and proud. They receive your gifts but as an homage or tribute to their transcendency, which is a fault their clergy is also guilty of. . . . The chiefest objects of discipline, true Religion and morality, they want : some are of a Linsey-woolsey disposition, of several professions in religion, all like Ethiopians, white in the teeth only. . . . But mistake me not to general speeches. . . . There are many sincere and religious people amongst them, descried by their charity and humility. . . . Amongst these we may account the Royalists."

[3] Sewall, *Diary*, December 21, 1686.

could not with a good conscience consent that our Meeting Houses should be made use of for the Common Prayer Worship." It was intimated to Andros that such use of the Town House will not be refused, and Sewall notes on the following Christmas day: "The Governor goes to the Town House to service, Forenoon and Afternoon, and Red-Coat going on his right hand and Captain George on his left."

The governor, however, did not propose to rest satisfied with such indirect recognition of Episcopal rights, and what he could not obtain through open means he reached by secret. Determined that the prayer book should find entrance into a religious building of the town, he prevailed on the sexton, either by threat or bribe, to open the Church. Thither, with his staff and sympathizers among the people, he repaired on a Sunday, in full state, for the first full service of the Church of England in Massachusetts.

Episcopal success.

This triumph of Andros broke the spirit of the opposition, which consented to an arrangement admitting the Episcopal service on the Sunday afternoons. Meanwhile steps were at once taken toward building an Episcopal Church. Land being desired for that purpose, it was at first refused. Sewall writes that he "would not set up that which the people came from England to avoid." A lot was soon obtained and King's Chapel erected before Andros left the government.

Encouraged by this success the governor ventured yet another attempt, to place the support of the Episcopal Church and minister on the public charge.[1] Edmund Randolph, one of the king's commissioners, wrote to the archbishop of Canterbury:[2] "We have often moved for an honorable maintenance for our minister, but they tell us, those that hire him must maintain him, as they maintain their own minister, by contributions. . . . I humbly represent to your Grace that the three meeting houses in Boston might pay twenty shillings a week a piece, out of their contributions, towards defraying our Church charges." The cool impudence of

[1] Palfrey, II, 225, 301, 322.   [2] Hutchinson, *Collections*, p. 549.

this closing proposition is like the quiet assumption of the Church of England men in other colonies, notably in New York, that a lodgment by sufferance immediately elevated the English Church into authority and conferred a right to everything in sight. The people of Boston, of course, could not agree with Randolph and Andros. Sewall wrote: "The bishops would have thought it strange to have been asked to contribute towards setting up New England Churches." What made the demand also the more preposterous to the Boston mind was the fact, to which Randolph alludes, that the Boston Churches were exceptional among the Churches of the Colony, in that their expenses were met by voluntary contributions and not by public tax.[1] Despite the governor and Randolph the Episcopal Church of Boston was forced to provide for its own treasury.

Another small cause of friction is related in another letter of Randolph to his grace of Canterbury.[2] The Episcopalians had requested the members of the old Church to let their clerk toll the bell, "for us to meet to go to prayers. Their men told me, in excuse for not doing it, that they had considered and found it intrenched on their liberty of conscience, granted them by his Majesty's present commission, and could in no wise consent to it!" Notwithstanding such small contentions, the soreness of feeling on the part of the Puritan element soon passed away, and it is pleasing to read that, twenty years after, the Boston town-meeting gave additional land to the Church of England, in order to enlarge its building.[3] With this was perfected the emancipation in Massachusetts of that form of religion, which the Puritan conscience had learned to look upon as only a little worse than popery.

Episcopacy allowed.

In 1687 was published the proclamation of religious liberty, designed by James to remove Catholic disabilities. It was received in the colony [4] with various sentiments. Thomas

James's proclamation.

---

[1] Hutchinson, *Collections*, p. 501.   [3] Sewall, *Diary*, August 14, 1710.
[2] *Ibid.*, p. 553.   [4] *Ibid.*, August 24, 1687.

Danforth, an ex-deputy governor, writes suspiciously: "I more dread the consequences thereof than the execution of those penal laws, the only wall against popery, that are now designed to be cashiered. We may without breach of charity conclude the Popish Counsels are laid."[1] Under date of August 25, 1687, Sewall records: "Mr. Mather preaches from the 5th verse of Jude. He praised God for the Liberty good people enjoy in England — said, "'tis marvelous in our eyes." He also relates that Increase Mather proposed a day of thanksgiving, and that Andros forbade — an altogether new experience for the Massachusetts Puritan, whose religious exercises and appointments had hitherto been entirely at his own discretion. Mather also proposed a congratulatory address to the king from the ministers. This he effected, and himself presented the address to James, who received him graciously, and said, "I hope by a Parliament to obtain a *Magna Charta* for Liberty of Conscience."[2]

This hope of James was never accomplished, and he was soon in a position to obtain nothing from a parliament. William, his successor, issued the new charter of Massachusetts, in 1691, by which Plymouth was merged in the larger colony, and it was decreed that "forever hereafter there shall be liberty of conscience allowed, in the worship of God to all Christians (except Papists)."[3] The enlarged colony was New government. made a royal province, with a governor appointed by the crown, and the king's veto on any legislation. All religious restriction on suffrage was removed. This constituted a Suffrage. crippling blow to the Puritan oligarchy, but it marked a decided advance in the cause of liberty. "The freedom of the inhabitants was almost universal,"[4] while all bands upon conscience and worship, except for Roman Catholics, were entirely removed. The liberty of every Protestant sect was

[1] *Massachusetts Historical Collections*, VI, 1 ; 57.
[2] Palfrey, II, 358.
[3] *Colonial Laws*, p. 31.
[4] Bancroft, *United States*, III, 80.

fixed in the fundamental law, and no longer was it the case as in the past, that each should conquer toleration for itself. "We hear no more of the theocracy, where God was alone supreme lawgiver and king." [1]

What remained of the hallowed union of Church and State was found in the public support of the Congregational Church. This institution of tithes, assessed by the civil officer as a public tax, continued until long after the Revolution and not until 1833 did it cease in Massachusetts. There was a deeply rooted conviction that only through such tax could the minister be supported. Cotton Mather, untaught by the experience of the Boston Churches from the beginning, or perhaps thinking only of the country Churches, wrote: "Ministers of the Gospel would have a poor time of it, if they must rely on the free contributions of the people for their maintenance. The laws of the province are the king's laws, the minister is the king's minister, the salary is raised in the king's name and is the king's allowance unto him." [2]

In the interest of this tax for Church support the legislature of the province took action at various times to both continue the tax and to remove the objections of those not of the established Church. Of course, the tax itself was general on the entire population, and every taxpayer was compelled thereby to help in the support of religious worship. Those who had no Church affiliations at all were thus taxed for the support of the Congregational Church. Such indeed was the case with everybody until 1727, when the "Five-Mile Act," similar to one already obtaining in Connecticut, provided that the taxes collected from Episcopalians should be given to their own Episcopal minister, if there was one within five miles, "whose services they attend." . . . This was devised for the relief of Episcopalians, but the logical effect of it was to put the Episcopal Church into the

Support of Church.

Five-Mile Act.

---

[1] Bancroft, *United States*, III, 99; Palfrey, *History of New England*, III, 21, 73.

[2] Quoted from Baird's *Religion in America*, p. 244.

establishment, as supported by public money.[1]   In 1728 the benefit of this act was extended to the Baptists and Quakers; and since the Quakers were opposed on principle to a "paid ministry," in 1731 they were wholly exempted from Church rates.   This exemption, for some unexplained reason, was in 1734 extended to "Anabaptists."   Again in 1735 and 1742 the Five-Mile Act, with extensions of privilege, was repassed for the benefit of the Episcopalians.

The Great Awakening of 1741 came as a disturber of the quiet order of the Churches.   It was not only a quickening of the religious life, but a protest against the low views of requirements for Church membership introduced by the Half-Way Covenant, to which the great majority of the Churches had fallen victims.   It was attended by much excitement and many intrusions into parishes by unauthorized ministers, to the great offence of many of the established clergy.[2]   A result of the revival was seen in the secession of members from the regular Churches, who organized Churches of their own, and for that reason were called Separates.   They desired, but could not obtain, as such, exemption from taxation to support the established Church, and in order to reach their purpose many of the new Churches organized as nominal Baptists, to obtain the benefit of the Act of 1734.   To meet this evasion the legislature in 1752 passed the only act which has reference to the awakening.   This provided that, "No person shall be esteemed to be an Anabaptist, except such as produce a certificate from the minister and two principal members of the Baptist Church;" and that the certifying minister must produce "a certificate from three other Baptist Churches in this, or neighboring provinces, that the minister and his Church are in Baptist fellowship."

The most curious incident in the provincial period exhibits a fruitless effort by the ministers, in 1725, to obtain a synod,

Great Awakening.

---

[1] *Massachusetts Historical Collections*, II, 2; 203, 204; *Colonial Laws*, p. 537.

[2] Palfrey, IV, 79-100.

Synod
needed.

"to recover and establish the faith and order of the gospel." This desire, true to the old institution which subjected the Church to the civil power, was by the hand of Cotton Mather submitted to the legislature. There it caused trouble. The council assented, but the house hesitated and postponed decision for a year, to give "opportunity for instructions from the people." During the year news of the movement reached England and excited the opposition of the bishop of London, who seems to have taken for granted that there was some plot against the newly enfranchised Episcopalians. Through his influence the king's government reprimanded both the legislature and the ministers, and forbade the synod, "as a bad precedent for dissenters." [1]

No event of the time could more strikingly illustrate the change of conditions. While the clergy by their application to the legislature remained faithful to the principle of the theocracy, the hesitation of that body was evidence of weakening regard for the principle on the civil side. At the same time, the quiet submission of both legislature and clergy to the uncalled-for interference of the bishop of London and the peremptory orders of the king, in a matter which really concerned neither of them, is another token of lost vigor in the Puritan attitude. We cannot conceive of the clergy or general court consenting to any such dictation, fifty years before. Still another feature of the incident is the repetition of the assumption that the English Church had acquired superior place in the colony. In the English view, the allowance of one Episcopal Church in Boston turned the established Church of Massachusetts into a congregation of dissenters!

To men of our day it seems strange that the clergy failed to insist upon their desire, or to hold their synod without the permission of the civil power. All accounts agree that there was great need of some influence to counteract the prevailing religious indifference of the time. But for this failure two reasons obtained. One, already hinted, was that relic of the

[1] Bancroft, *United States*, III, 391; Palfrey, III, 420.

theocracy which made the magistrate's summons the only warrant for a Church synod. The Church as yet had not come to an understanding of its own natural autonomy. The other, and as powerful, reason was the loss of prestige and power suffered by the ministers as a class. They no longer possessed that wide influence and authority, which in previous generations had made them almost the virtual rulers of the commonwealth. This fact was due, partly to the growing consciousness that theocratic institutions were not fitted to modern life; partly to the increasing numbers of those people who acknowledged no Church bonds; and partly, perhaps chiefly, to the course pursued by the ministers themselves in certain past crises.

Cotton Mather, writing of a former condition which he would admire to have renewed in his own time, said: "New England being a country whose interests are remarkably inwrapped in ecclesiastical circumstances, ministers ought to concern themselves in politics."[1] In the early day this ministerial concern in politics was so intimate and influential that the voice of the clergy was often the most powerful in the community, at times even coercing magistrates and courts to its dictation. But the power was abused and on occasion became the instrument of cruel bigotry and superstition. Every case of religious persecution was laid at the door of the clergy, and many times justly. They were held chiefly accountable for the severer inflictions, for the whipping of Holmes and the hanging of Quakers.[2] When in the frenzied crusade against the Salem witches the ministers were found pitiless, urging on the magistrates who had begun to feel compassion, the popular sentiment of humanity was outraged, and the revolt against the spiritual authority of the ministerial order became wide and permanent.[3]

---

[1] Quoted by Bancroft, *United States*, III, 74.

[2] Adams, *Emancipation of Massachusetts*, p. 176.

[3] Hutchinson preserves a letter from William Arnold of Rhode Island to the governor of Massachusetts, which, though written long before the time of

The ministers never recovered from this self-dealt blow, and thereafter what a minister said and did was estimated at its intrinsic value, and not endowed with superior influence and authority by reason of his office.[1]

Thus was completed the breaking down of the religious commonwealth in Massachusetts, and the state made ready for that complete severance from the Church which, both as an incident and consequent, accompanied the Revolution and National Independence.

III.   *Connecticut*

The founding of Connecticut was a protest against the ecclesiasticism of Massachusetts.[2]   Though the younger colony insisted on the power and duty of the magistrate to care for religion and the Church, it never attempted to set up a theocracy, and never conditioned civil and political privileges upon personal relation to the Church, save as respected the one office of governor.

The first movements of foundation were under the lead of the younger Winthrop and Hooker, though each acted quite distinctly from the other, and in different parts of the colony that was to be.   The former's first service was of a military character, noted here only because his action brought into existence a name of prominence in the ecclesiastical history of Connecticut.

It needs to be premised that the Dutch at New Amsterdam had already established, though not without objection from

the Salem tragedy, but with evident allusion to the law on witchcraft, anticipates a sentiment common at the date of that awful frenzy.   Referring to certain enemies of Massachusetts and her policy, he describes them as "crying out much against them that putteth people to death for witches ; for, say they, there be no other witches upon earth nor devils, but your own pastors and ministers and such as they are."   (Hutchinson, *Collections*, p. 238.)

[1] Von Holst, *Constitutional History of United States*, II, 227 *et seq.;* IV, 407.

[2] Palfrey, *History of New England*, I, 178–181.

Massachusetts, a fort and trading-post on the Connecticut
River at Hartford.   To this locality the Puritans of the Bay
laid claim, while for the lands lying on Long Island Sound
the king had given a patent to Lord Brooke and Lord Say   Saybrook.
and Sele.   In 1634 it came to the knowledge of these paten-
tees that the Dutch Van Twiller was about to send an expedition to strengthen the Dutch hold on the river, and to take
possession of its mouth.   To meet this effort they fitted out
an opposing force, with the aid of the Massachusetts authorities, and put the younger Winthrop in command.   He was   Winthrop.
not a man of military training or of subsequent military life,
but on this occasion succeeded as well as could any soldier.
Approaching by sea, he reached the mouth of the Connecticut
in "the nick of time," when the ships of Van Twiller were
almost in sight.   He landed, took possession of the Point on
the west side, built a fort, and named the spot "Saybrooke." [1]
So were the Dutch shut out from the heart of New England,
and a name was coined which was destined to have large
place in the New England Churches.   As for Winthrop himself, he returned to Boston.   Twenty years after he cast his
lot with the new colony of Connecticut, to become for many
years its governor, and to guide its fortunes with a sagacity
and prudence not far surpassed by the like virtues of his
father in the government at the Bay.

About the same time with Winthrop's expedition, the
moral impulses which resulted in the founding of Connecticut
were at work in the mind and heart — the broad mind and
tenderly Christian heart — of Thomas Hooker.   A man of   Hooker.
station, education, and refinement, and a sincere Puritan in
his dissent from the "irregularities" of the Church of England, he had experienced such persecution at the hands of
Laud that he fled to Holland.   In 1633 he came to Boston in
the ship Griffin, together with John Cotton, and made so
favorable an impression on the minds of the people that, very

[1] Palfrey credits the coinage of this name to Fenwick. (*Compendious
History of New England*, I, 235.)

soon after arrival, he was chosen pastor of the Church at Newtown (Cambridge). Of him, at the time of his death in 1647, the elder Winthrop wrote in his *Journal:* "Who, for piety, prudence, wisdom, zeal, learning, and what else might make him serviceable in the place and time he lived in, might be compared with men of greatest note; and he shall need no other praise: the fruits of his labors in both Englands shall preserve an honorable and happy remembrance of him forever."

To Hooker, though for the most part in happy concord with his brethren of the Bay, two features of the Massachusetts policy were ungrateful: its restriction of the suffrage, and its spirit of intolerance toward all difference of opinion. His views on the former point made the great difference between him and Winthrop; for, as to the latter, it is quite clear that, had Winthrop been untrammelled by the narrow prejudices of his associates, the early annals of the colony would have recorded few instances of oppression. Hooker never assented to the rule which made membership in the Church a condition Citizenship. of citizenship. He had no sympathy for the theocratic ideal. To his mind it involved a serious peril to the purity of the Church and gross wrong to a very large portion of the community. Where Winthrop argued for the limited franchise that, "the best part is always the least, and of that best part the wiser part is always the lesser;" Hooker answered, "in matters which concern the common good, a general council, chosen by all, to transact businesses which concern all, I conceive most suitable to rule and most safe for relief of the whole." [1] His was the first voice raised in New England for a pure democracy, and, as the result proved, there were many in early Massachusetts to follow his lead.

He had equally positive convictions on the question of Toleration. toleration for religious differences. Such men as Dudley and Ward were an offence to him. He looked with disapproval on the harsh measures of the general court against Williams

[1] Fiske, *Beginnings of New England*, p. 124.

and the Salem Church, and when the Hutchinson controversy committed the authorities to a course of harsh repression and injustice, he concluded to attempt a new foundation, where freedom of mind should have larger scope. This was not because of any agreement with the opinions of Mrs. Hutchinson, but because he held that such opinions were no proper subject for civil action.

With him there were many others in entire sympathy, a large proportion of his own flock at Newtown, and the ex-governor, Haynes, who had pronounced the sentence of banishment on Williams, but who, by some influence, — perhaps that of Hooker himself, — had been led to more liberal views.[1]

In the height of the antinomian controversy, while Boston was ablaze with excitement, the ministry and court grim with determination to repress heresy, and the great heresiarch still defiant and uncondemned, Hooker, Haynes, and a large company, to the number of over an hundred from Newtown, Watertown, and Dorchester, set forth on their journey through the wilderness to the banks of the Connecticut. They took with them all their belongings, driving before them a large herd of cattle, and after prosperous travel settled Hartford, Windsor, and Wethersfield, bent on the establishment of a new commonwealth, in which religion, liberty, and law should dwell together in friendly union.

It is interesting to note that the departure from the Bay was without opposition, and that certain members of the Church of Watertown carried with them letters of dismission to the future Church on the Connecticut, letters formally

---

[1] Either the change in Haynes was great, or in the action against Williams his official position compelled him to be the mouthpiece of a sentence which himself did not approve. Some years after his removal to Connecticut, he wrote to Williams, describing the new colony as "a refuge and receptacle for all sorts of consciences "; and he added, " I am now under a cloud, and my brother Hooker, with the Bay. We have removed from them thus far, and yet they are not satisfied." (*Massachusetts Historical Collections*, I, 280 ; Bancroft, *United States*, II, 56.)

approved by the general court of Massachusetts.[1] Probably
the thought of the Bay authorities was, that the movement
would extend the bounds of their own jurisdiction. Had
they understood that the issue was to be another government
founded on broader principles than their own, it is not unjust
to think that their farewells would have been less complacent.

That the men at the Bay considered the emigration as an
expansion of their own colony, and that the emigrants themselves so looked upon it in the beginning, is made reasonably
clear by the fact, that the first steps toward forming a separate government were not taken until the party had been
nearly two years in their new home. In that period they
looked to Boston as the seat of authority, while at the same
time constant additions were made to their number. By the
spring of 1638 the community contained eight hundred people, and by common consent it was agreed, that the time had
come to cut loose from the Bay and form a separate government. So the three towns of Hartford, Windsor, and
Wethersfield associated together to form "one Public State
or Commonwealth," to which they gave the name of their
beautiful river.[2] A sermon was preached by Hooker, in
which with religious fervor he laid down the principles of a
pure democracy. "The foundation of authority," he said,
"is laid in the free consent of the people. The choice of the
public magistrates belongs unto the people by God's own
allowance. They, who have power to appoint officers and
magistrates, have the right also to set the bounds and limitations of the power and place unto which they call them."[3]

With the frame of government instituted by them in the
constitution, adopted in January, 1639, — "the first written
constitution known to history, creating a government,"— our
concern here is simply to note its bearing on the questions of
religion and the Church. This is very clearly indicated in

*Organiza-
tion.*

---

[1] *Connecticut Colonial Records*, I, 2.
[2] *Ibid.*, I, 21.
[3] Fiske, p. 127 ; *Connecticut Historical Collections*, I, 20, 21.

the announcement of the duty of the civil government to " mayntayn the liberty and purity of the gospel of our Lord Jesus, as also the discipline of the Churches." More formally and at length was it declared by the first general court: — " Forasmuch as the peace and prosperity of the Churches and the members thereof, as well as Civil rights and Liberties, are carefully to be maintained; It is ordered by this Court and decreed, that the Civil Authority here established hath power and liberty to see that the peace, ordinances, and rules of Christ be observed in every Church according to His word." [1] Civil power in the Church.

Whether this order would prove oppressive or not depended on the spirit of the magistrates. It was sufficiently positive in its assertion of civil control to satisfy even such a man as Dudley. It might be made to cover harsh measures of persecution, or it might find its intended aim in the encouragement of a particular polity and faith, without assuming any hostile attitude toward such as differed from that form. This latter construction was the one in the minds of those who announced that fundamental principle of the new commonwealth, and it marks the distinctive peculiarity of the established Church in Connecticut.

They were a homogeneous people who laid the foundations; all of them of Puritan extraction, and persuaded that the " congregational way " was most in harmony with the word of God. From this persuasion there were no dissentients at the beginning, and many years passed before people of another mind settled among them, to put their charity to a test. What they might have done, had there been any attempt in the first year, like that of the Brownes at Salem, to introduce the prayer-book service, it is idle to inquire. When, in after years, the men of Connecticut had to meet the Episcopal question, they were ready with an answer of liberality.

Without formal definition or prescription of the form of Church polity, they simply assumed that the form to which they had become attached in Massachusetts, and which they Church polity.

[1] *Connecticut Colonial Records*, I, 21, 524, 525.

brought with them, would be the model for the Churches in their new colony. This they established as the State-Church, and over it for one hundred and forty years the civil authorities exercised a power, which in its completeness and detail is almost unique in the history of the colonies: a power also — be it noted with emphasis — never exercised with harshness or even ungentleness.

Liberality. This again makes a peculiar feature in the story of the Connecticut Church. The authorities were not on the watch to warn off imaginary invaders. Their ears were not quick to catch the sound of approaching heresy, and they were fully ready to concede the truth that the Christian religion could vitalize other forms of polity and worship than their own. While taking care that Churches of their own order should be founded and maintained, they never decreed the exclusion of other forms of faith and worship. While Massachusetts was banishing Episcopalians, hanging Quakers and jailing Baptists; while New York was witnessing the robbery of Churches for the benefit of a pseudo-Anglican establishment; while Virginia was chasing the Puritans out of her borders; and while these same Puritans were retorting for their wrongs upon the innocent Roman Catholics of Maryland, Connecticut held herself aloof from all repressive measures. The harsh spirit which represses dissent was altogether absent from her founders, notwithstanding the anti-Quaker laws, and we search in vain through her records for a single judicial action, which can fairly be set to the account of religious persecution. Her worst sins against religious liberty were in the exercise of authority over the Church and the assessment upon the entire community for the support of the establishment. In these respects only did her Church laws differ from the full liberty conferred by Williams on Rhode Island, and by Baltimore on Maryland. And even these provisions of law Connecticut, so soon as occasion arose, learned to relax for the relief of dissenting Churches.

The difference just noted was a very broad one in principle. Williams taught that the magistrate in his official station had no power whatever in the Church, that a Church founded and supported by the action of the civil power was an offence to God and man, productive only of confusion and wrong. Hooker held that the care of the Church was the first duty of the magistrate, and that civil laws for the support of a chosen Church were salutary for both Church and State. But he never attempted to blend the two together. He was with Endicott and Winthrop on the broad question of Church establishment; and with Williams in his attitude toward the theocracy. He was with Williams also in hatred of all persecution for opinion, and in holding that the criterion for citizenship should not be the same as for membership in the Church.

The privilege of a freeman was never made in Connecticut a perquisite of religion, nor conditioned on Church membership. For the governor alone was religious profession made a prerequisite for office. "Citizenship was acquired by inhabitancy" (Bancroft), without inquiring as to religious views or Church standing. All the original settlers were freemen, meeting together for their first legislation, the adoption of the constitution, and choice of delegates to the general court. How many of this number were not members of the Church there are no means of telling. Doubtless some of them were such. Afterwards, as the population increased, it was enacted that persons could become freemen only by a general vote of the town.[1] This action was taken in 1643, with clear intent to supply an omission. In 1658 the law defined the conditions of twenty-one years of age and a taxable estate of £30. The law of 1662 further defined that freemen should be "persons of civil, peaceable, and honest conversation," and reduced the property requirement to £20. No trace is to be found of any attempt to add religious character or Church standing to the conditions for the franchise.

Freeman's law.

[1] *Connecticut Colonial Records*, I, 96.

What we note, then, in the story of this colonial establishment is, not the spirit of repression toward variant opinion, but a benevolent and fatherly care and watchfulness over the interests of the Church. The care was intimate, concerning itself with many minor items ; the erection of meeting-houses, the calling and support of ministers, the location and boundary of parishes, the composition of any troubles arising in the affairs of any parish. The care was shown also, not only by the enactment of general laws, but by the action of the general court in an endless number of individual cases.

Care of Churches. Everything touching Church management, any change in Church or in meeting-house, from one end of the commonwealth to the other, was brought to the legislature for its direction or permission. Any wrong suffered by any individual by way of discipline found its echo in the general court. Any disturbance in a Church soon brought the paternal bidding of the court to consider the things which make for peace. To one looking over the colonial records it seems as though there could possibly arise no contingency in Church affairs, which did not appear at some time and some place in Connecticut, and find the general court prompt to examine, to advise, and then, if need be, to command.

In this constant, watchful, all-embracing and paternal care, the ecclesiastical legislation of Connecticut differs from that of all the other colonies. Never used for oppression, it tended directly to build up and strengthen the Churches. The argument for it was very short and simple. The Church was a public charge ; its building erected at public expense ; its minister called by a town-meeting, and the regular support raised by public tax. Over such an institution and arrangement it was considered a thing of necessity that the general government of the colony should extend authority; with this peculiarity, already noted, that it carried its care into smallest details.

Still another feature, easily discernible by even a careless reader of the records, is the high moral purpose of the magis-

trates in the exercise of ecclesiastical power. They seem to
be always considering the good of the Church and the genuine
religious interests of the community. Their zeal for the
Church was never a cloak to hide personal ambition or to
build up magisterial dignity and authority. They used the
state for the real benefit of the Church; never the Church as
a mere appendage of the state. In all the strifes of legislation
and party, they never lost the high sense of the Church's
divine origin and spiritual nature. In the story of most
religious establishments, both in Europe and America, the
Church is often exhibited as a mere instrument, degraded to
further the schemes of a political party. It was never so
seen in Connecticut, save in the strife of disestablishment in
1816–1818. If ever a religious establishment justified itself
as proper and good, this colonial Church of Connecticut may
be cited as its best exponent.

The story is not punctuated, as is that of Massachusetts,
by prosecutions of heretics and jailing of non-conformists. It
has thus less of excitement, but it is interesting in the constant exhibition of legislative paternal care. Every session
abounded with action in Church matters, sometimes sought
for by the people, and frequently originated by the law makers
themselves. While it would be useless to recount here the
endless detail of such legislation, sundry instances may well
be cited as illustrative of the close and minute care over all
Church matters.

To begin with the *Organization of Churches*. This is in
the nature of the case an episcopal, presbyterial, or congregational function. Connecticut was singular among the colonial Organiza-
establishments in reserving it to the legislature. The law tion of
strictly declared that no Church was to be organized without Churches.
the consent of the general court;[1] and then, as through fear
that the requirement might be construed as having reference
solely to Churches of the established order, the law further

[1] Massachusetts lodged the power in the county court and at least four
neighboring churches.

ordained that no "departure or separate form of worship" was to be allowed, without the special permission of the court.[1] Bills for forming new Churches, dividing parishes, and sometimes for uniting them, are of constant occurrence down to the end of the colonial period.

Most of them present nothing more than the routine of a system. Others are of a different sort. Thus, the people of East Hartford prayed for permission to organize a separate Church, alleging as a reason the difficulty of crossing the river to attend service in the Hartford Church; "which difficulty," the legislative report observed, "they could but foresee before they settled where they are, and therefore is of less wayte with us." Despite this criticism, the request was granted, "provided, that all lands owned by East Hartford people on the west side pay rates to the west side minister, and that the people on the east side pay to the west side minister until they have a minister of their own." [2] The people on the east side of New London were refused permission for a new Church, "there not being clear evidence of agreement among them, nor of their ability to afford a minister honorable maintenance." On a similar application from East Norwich the general court appointed a committee to visit the locality and lay out the parish, declaring the court's willingness to grant the petition, "when they shall be arrived to such a capacity as to mayntayne a minister." [3]

Support of ministers.

The *Maintenance of the Ministry* was a very important subject for legislative action. From the beginning the ministerial salary was an item for public tax, assessed by the selectmen and collected by the constable or other special collector. By the law of 1735,[4] in order to meet many complaints from ministers, it was ordered that no minister should be kept out of his salary more than two months after the year had expired. If he were kept out, the selectmen were to take

---

[1] *Records*, I, 311 ; II, 328 ; Weeden, *Social and Economic History of New England*, p. 270.

[2] *Records*, IV, 136.   [3] *Ibid.*, III, 220.   [4] *Ibid.*, VII, 554.

out a warrant directing the constable to levy on the estate of the collector or collectors and pay the minister. If the selectmen should neglect to take out such warrant, they must themselves pay the salary, and also a fine of £5 for each neglect.

The earlier law of 1644, the same with the law of the United Colonies, required that every man should set down what he was willing to pay for the minister; if he refused such subscription, he must be rated by the authorities; if he failed to pay this assessment, the magistrate should collect.[1] Special laws provided for towns with more than one Church, that no inhabitant should fail of paying his proportion, and no minister fail of receiving his stipend.[2]

In 1711 the Rev. John Jones complained to the general court that the Church at Greenwich had not paid him, whereupon the court *ordered* "the committee who called John Jones" (naming them) to collect the £20 due and pay the minister. If they should fail, the sheriff was directed to "distrain upon the body or bodies, goods or chattels of any one or more of the said committee," and pay Mr. Jones.[3] There are three separate acts of the legislature to regulate and compel the payment of salary to Mr. Woodward at Norwich.[4] In 1718 the legislature detached certain portions of the parishes of Middletown and Wethersfield and united them to the Great Swamp Society, forbidding the residents to pay anything to their former ministers, and ordering payment in the new society. The people of West Wethersfield protested against this order, but the lawmakers turned a deaf ear.[5]

Two cases are worthy of note as showing the beginnings of the *voluntary* system, even within the establishment. One Voluntary was in 1758, when the first society of New London, in view system. of there being many poor people in the parish and of the willingness of the richer brethren "that the poor should have the gospel preached to them freely," petitioned the legisla-

[1] *Records*, I, 111. [3] *Ibid.*, V, 282. [5] *Ibid.*, VI, 48, 56.
[2] *Ibid.*, II, 290. [4] *Ibid.*, V, 468, 527, 555.

ture for permission to raise money for Church purposes by assessment on *pews*, and to appoint from among themselves persons to assess and collect. The prayer was granted by the court.[1] The other case came from Meriden in 1768. Mr. Hubbard, a candidate, was deprived of his license by the association on the ground of unsoundness in faith, but the majority of the Meriden Church insisted on retaining him, though not ordained. The minority complained to the general court, which body ordered, that those who are dissatisfied and who enter their names with the town clerk, may be exempt from tax for the support of Mr. Hubbard. They cannot vote in a meeting of that Church, but can organize and tax themselves for the support of another gospel ministry.[2]

Meeting-houses.

The *Meeting-Houses* also furnished the legislature with much care and occasion, at times, for peremptory action. The law made the appointment of the site of the meeting-house a matter for the general court. Such was the custom from the first. [3] In 1731 an act defined that any parish (excepting tolerated dissenters), wishing to build a meeting-house, must apply to the general court " to order and affix the place whereon their meeting house shalle be erected and built." The penalty for building the meeting-house without order and appointment of site by the general court was £100. Usually the legislature simply legalized the site agreed upon by the people, but occasionally it used compulsion.[4]

Thus, there was trouble about the meeting-house in Norwalk [5] (1719). The old house was in great need of repairs, while the people were divided in mind as to renovating the old house or building a new one, and as to the site of the new one, if such should be determined on. So the general court appointed a committee to visit Norwalk to try and compose matters, and to report to the next session of the court. This committee does not seem to have attended to its duty, for at

[1] *Records*, XI, 198.   [2] *Ibid.*, XIII, 108, 259.   [3] *Ibid.*, VII, 334.
[4] The law of 1744 gave the power to the county court. (*Records,* IX, 398.)
[5] *Records*, VI, 114, 147.

the next session no report was made by them, and a new committee was appointed, who should go to Norwalk, hear all parties, inspect all proposed sites, and determine the place for the house, "which place, so determined, shall be the place where the town of Norwalk shall set up their meeting house." Or, if the committee advise repair of the old house, "so it shall be."

A similar and more peremptory action was taken in regard to East Guilford.[1] The people there memorialized the legislature on their need of a new meeting-house, and a committee was appointed. The committee reported their choice of a site for the new house, as "on the green, where the old meeting house now stands, about mid-way between the said old meeting house and Captain Meiggs' Sabbath house, the southeast corner of the said house to be at a stake stuck down by them." This site was "fixed and determined" by act of the court. But some of the people objected and sent another memorial, alleging that the place ordered was out of the centre of the town, and that the "committee were imposed upon by a false plan; and praying that the same may be reviewed, and the place again affixed by a wise, judicious committee." So another committee was appointed and reported the same site, whereupon the court became very emphatic, determined to put up with no more complaint and division, enacting that "the inhabitants shall set up their meeting house in that place . . . and the said inhabitants are to take notice thereof and to conform themselves to this order."

Another entry is worth citation as illustrating both the court's care for meeting-houses and its liberal missionary spirit. In 1719 a bill was passed, "on petition of several," granting a brief for "a publick contribution throughout the colony, to be improved in finishing a building of a meeting house for a Presbyterian Congregation in the city of New York."[2]

[1] *Records*, VIII, 111, 141, 217, 246.
[2] *Ibid.*, VI, 126.

The most dominating feature of the Connecticut system is in the exercise by the legislature of all the functions of a superior *Ecclesiastical Court*, to which appeals could come, and which, by way of review, could interfere for correction of irregularities. "The assembly was not often arbitrary, and did not use more than a fraction of its power. Without taking sides, it acted the part of a pacificator. . . but was ever ready to arrest by its authority any revolutionary or erratic movement, destructive of the purity of the gospel or the welfare of the Churches."[1]

We find cases of appeal by individuals from the discipline of the Churches,[2] with the evident understanding that it was competent for the legislature to review such proceedings and either sustain, or reverse, a Church sentence. There are also cases of legislative dismission of members from one Church to another. In 1741 John Norton of Guilford petitioned the general court for dismission from the fourth society of Guilford, and to be "joyned" to the first society, which petition was granted by formal act. By a like action in 1773 Elkanah Cobb and others were dismissed from the Church of Plainfield, and joined to the first society of Canterbury, "for all the purposes of society and ecclesiastical privileges only, but not for schooling, military, or other purposes."[3] The reasons for these actions are not stated, but it is probable that these individuals were seeking to indulge a preference for a particular minister or Church; and, not finding their former Church willing to gratify them with a dismission, appealed to the legislature, which in response exercised the function of a presbytery or council.

The most frequent exhibitions of such exercise were in connection with Church troubles and quarrels. When such arose the general court, either solicited by the parties or of its own motion, was prompt to interfere. Very early in the

[1] *New Haven Historical Papers*, III, 373.
[2] *Records*, I, 106, 111; III, 183.
[3] *Ibid.*, XIV, 138.

history, the Church at Hartford [1] fell into dissension, for the healing of which the general court devoted much time and advice, with many persuasions and orders, in which was a curious blending of authority with deference to the opinion and influence of Church councils. Mather [2] says of the trouble: "Its true original is almost as obscure as the rise of the Connecticut River. But it proved in its unhappy consequences too like that river in its annual inundations, for it overspread the whole colony of Connecticut. The factions inserted themselves into the smallest as well as the greatest affairs of all the towns round about." The case caused the first innovations on the established order, and the recognition of the right of dissent. As for Hartford, the court also legislated for difficulties in the Church of Wethersfield. [3] In both Churches the trouble was of a moral nature, such as only an ecclesiastical court should be competent to adjudicate.

At Norwalk the people had fallen into sad quarrelling about their meeting-house, and the general court, exercising a spiritual jurisdiction, [4] "recommended (them) to agree and solemnly comitt the decision of this Controversy to the dispose of the Most High, by a lott, which we hope may be that as will sattisfy and quiet the spirits of all the good people of that place, and be a hopeful means to continue and increase their faith and love."

So when trouble came between the two Churches at Windsor, the general court stepped in and ordered the union of the two societies, adding to the order the admonition, "all the good people are required to be ayding and assisting thereto, and not in the least to appose or hinder the same, as they will answer the contrary at their peril." This was in 1680. For two years thereafter the people could not agree upon a minister, when the legislature again interposed

---

[1] *Connecticut Historical Collections*, II, 51–125 ; *Records*, I, 290, 312, 314, 317, 320, 333 ; Felt, *Ecclesiastical History of New England*, II, 192 ; Johnston, *History of Connecticut*, p. 228.

[2] *Magnalia*, III, 2 ; 16. [3] *Colonial Records*, I, 342. [4] *Ibid.*, III, 59.

with an *order* to settle Rev. Samuel Mather, and commanding that "all the people quietly attend Mr. Mather's ministry, and proportionably comunecate to his honnerable mayntenance and incouragement in the work of Christ there."[1] There was similar difficulty at Farmington, and the legislature appointed a committee to choose a minister, commanding the people to receive him as their minister for one year and to pay him the usual salary.[2]

One other such case may be cited for its peculiarity. A large portion of the Church of Norwich had become dissatisfied with the minister, Mr. Wills, and defaulted in payment of salary. Many complaints against, and from, Wills were brought to the general court. Mr. Wills wanted his money, and was afraid that his enemies would lock him out of the Church. The legislature commanded the people to use no violence and to yield the Church to Mr. Wills. Finally an agreement was reached that the minister would resign, if the people would pay him the salary and also compensation for retiring. He fulfilled his part and resigned, and soon complained that the people had not paid him anything. On this the legislature ordered a tax on the society sufficient to pay Mr. Wills £80 for salary and £800 for compensation, and appointed its own committee to levy and collect the money.[3]

Spiritual affairs.

The interest felt in the *Spiritual affairs* of the Church finds frequent and varied expression. The general court constantly regarded itself as responsible for the state of religion in the commonwealth, and for the purity of doctrine. The court sent commissioners to the Boston synod of 1656, the synod of the famous Half-Way Covenant, and sent the action of the synod to all the Churches, requiring the Churches to inform the court of any objections. It asserted its own approval of the action, particularly commending the admission to baptism

Half-Way Covenant.

of the children of "persons having a competency of knowledge, of honest and godly conversation."[4]

---

[1] *Records*, III, 73, 104 ; *New Haven Historical Papers*, III, 371.
[2] *Records*, IV, 382.   [3] *Ibid.*, IX, 337, 380, 397, 480, 571.   [4] *Ibid.*, I, 362, 438.

In 1666 the general court ordered a synod of all the ministers in the colony to meet at Hartford [1] and dispute on certain questions to be submitted by the court, most of them suggested by the Half-Way Covenant; *e.g.* "Whether federal holiness or covenant interest be not the proper ground of baptism." The next year, to meet some objections from sticklers about terms, it changed the name of the proposed convention from "synod" to "assembly," and proposed a general convention of clergy in the three colonies of Connecticut, Massachusetts, and Plymouth, to consider the points. Nothing came of that motion, and the court contented itself with a less ambitious scheme, appointing, in 1668, Messrs. Fitch, Elliott, Bulkley, and Wakeman to meet at Saybrook and "consider of some expedient for our peace in the matters of discipline respecting membership and baptism." [2]

The Connecticut clergy were far from unanimity of opinion on the points involved. The committee met as directed and agreed upon their report, on receipt of which the court declared its approval of the established system, "but yet forasmuch as sundry persons of prudence and piety are otherwise persuaded, this court doth declare that all such persons, being also approved according to law as orthodox and sound in the fundamentals of the Christian religion, may have allowance of their persuasion and profession in Church wayes or assemblies without disturbance." This is the first full note for freedom in Connecticut legislation.

The matters of *Religious Life* received frequent attention from the court, with lamentations over any degeneracy and failure of instructions. From the beginning, attendance on public worship was compulsory, on penalty of five shillings for every absence. This requirement was renewed again and again. [3] In 1702 an act was passed requiring every person to "carefully apply himself on the Lord's day to the duties of

Religious Life.

[1] *New Haven Historical Papers*, III, 374.
[2] *Records*, II, 53, 67, 70, 85, 109.
[3] *New Haven Historical Papers*, III, 399.

religion — to attend public worship in some congregation allowed by law, provided that he conscientiously and conveniently can attend." Similar acts were passed in 1721, 1750, and 1770. The assembly of 1712[1] varied the form of title by an " Act for the better Detecting and more effectual Punishment of Prophaneness and Immorality," notwithstanding which formidable title the only misdemeanor noted is neglect of public worship. This was repeated in 1721. The colony shared in the same tide of religious lukewarmness which caused so much alarm in Puritan Massachusetts, and the Connecticut legislators strove mightily to stem it. In 1675 the council of governor and assistants called a convention of ministers in the counties of Hartford and New Haven, " to make diligent search for those evils amongst us which have stirred up the Lord's anger against us."[2] The proclamation for a fast day in 1680 laments " the decay of love to God and one to another," and urges prayers " that we may become an humble, fruitful, and holy people . . . for the better preservation and propagation of religion."[3]

To reach existing evils intelligently, the general court in 1714 demanded from the general association of ministers " a Report on the State of Religion, touching common sins and neglects," and suggestive of measures to abate them, " that thereby all possible means may be used for our healing and recovering from our degeneracy."[4] The report of the ministers contains a list of common evils,[5] viz. : —

" 1. The want of Bibles.
   2. Great neglect of public worship.
   3. Neglect of Catechizing in sundry places.
   4. Great deficiency in domestical or family government.
   5. Irregularity in commutative justice upon several accounts. (!)
   6. Talebearing and defamation.

[1] *Records*, V, 323 ; VI, 298.   [3] *Ibid.*, III, 64.   [5] Palfrey, II, 285.
[2] *Ibid.*, II, 389.   [4] *Ibid.*, V, 530.

7. Calumniating and contempt of authority and order, both civil and ecclesiastical.

8. Intemperance: with several other things."

The reception of this report was followed by the enactment of stringent orders to selectmen and constables to enforce all laws touching on the points presented; and specially the laws about catechizing, public worship, profane swearing, the distribution of Bibles, and the "Act (of 1709) [1] to prevent Unreasonable Meetings of Young People in the evening after the Sundays and other times."

Meanwhile the general court had all along, without waiting for ministerial initiative, held itself bound to rebuke all improprieties. It had its own views as to what were proper subjects for pulpit notices, and ordered its " secretary to write to Stoneington to manifest to them our dislike of that custome which is used amongst them in publishing their town concernes on the Sabboth day." [2] In 1684 the court took order to rebuke "some provoaking evills, as viz: prophanation of the Sabboth, neglect of cattechiseing of children and servants, and of famaly prayer, young persons shakeing of the government of parents or masters; boarders and inmates neglecting the worship of God in the famalyes where they reside." [3] In 1721 the court passed a law for the election of " Tything-men," two or more in each parish, to "carefully inspect the behaviour of all persons on the Sabbath or Lord's day," and to present any delinquent. [4]

In 1708 the general court took measures, perhaps the most important of all the ecclesiastical actions of that body, to bring order and unity out of the variant opinions and usages in the Churches, for which the Half-Way Covenant was largely responsible. This action was the call of the Saybrook Synod, which resulted in the celebrated Saybrook Platform and the virtual reëstablishment of the Con-

Saybrook Platform.

[1] *Records*, V, 130.   [3] *Ibid.*, III, 148.
[2] *Ibid.*, III, 95.   [4] *Ibid.*, VI, 277.

necticut Congregational Church.[1]   The call, issued at
the spring session of the court, ran: "This assembly, from
their own observation and complaints of many others, being
sensible of the defects of the discipline of the Churches of
this government, hath seen fit to ordain and require, and it
is by the authority of the same ordained and required, that
the ministers of the several counties shall meet together, and
shall appoint two or more of their number to be their delegates, who shall all meet together at Saybrook, at the next
commencement to be held there, to draw a form of ecclesiastical discipline, which shall be offered to this court to be
considered and confirmed by them: and the expense shall be
defrayed out of the treasury of this colony."

The synod met and prepared a report, containing the Confession of Faith and "Heads of Agreement and Regulations
in the administration of Church Discipline," and presented
the same to the court at its October session.   Thus, together
with the work of the Cambridge synod, were formulated the
statements of fundamental Congregational law.   The general court signified its pleasure in the report, enacting as
follows: "This assembly do declare their great approbation,
and do ordain that all the Churches within this government,
that are or shall be thus united in doctrine, worship, and discipline, be and for the future shall be owned and acknowledged
as established by law: *Provided always*, that nothing herein
shall be intended or construed to hinder or prevent any
society or Church, that is or shall be allowed by the laws of
this government, who soberly differ or dissent from the united
Churches hereby established, from exercising worship and discipline in their own way, according to their consciences."
This action of the court was final, and the platform was *not
referred* to the Churches.   It was ordered to be printed and
distributed, and from the legislature itself went forth as the
ecclesiastical constitution of the commonwealth.

[1] *Records*, V, 51, 97, 423 ; Palfrey, III, 341 ; "*Cambridge and Saybrook
Platforms.*"

Solely on this latter account is it matter for discussion here. Its expression of faith and principles of polity do not concern our present purpose. The significant thing is that the civil authority with the word of command imposed it on the Churches, an action of the same import as that by which the parliament imposed the prayer book and prelacy on the Church of England. There was, indeed, this difference, that the Connecticut legislature proposed no harsh restraint and declared no penalties for non-conformity. On the contrary, the act adopting the platform made express provision for permission of dissent, with only the consequence that a dissenting Church could not belong to the establishment — a consequence, in view of other legislation, of no serious importance.

That other legislation made room for many varieties of dissent, with a liberality surpassing that of other establish- Dissent. ments, and with a surprising readiness to concede a broad toleration. This readiness stands in sharp contrast with the grudging concessions of Massachusetts, where every gain of liberty was extorted from unwilling legislators. This contrast, however, needs to be qualified by the reflection that, because of the homogeneity of the people, the crucial questions of toleration did not arise in Connecticut until after the first two generations had passed away. Yet it is reasonable to think that the colony of Hooker never could have exiled Williams or Mrs. Hutchinson. Certainly, they did not approach the severity of Boston in dealing with the Quakers.

This sect gave the first occasion for laws of discrimination among religionists. That enthusiastic people appeared about Quakers. the same time (1656) in all the colonies, all of which except Plymouth and Rhode Island felt called upon to legislate against them. The measures adopted in Connecticut, for repressive character, lagged far behind those of Massachusetts, New Haven, New York, and Virginia. It may be doubted whether the general court would have enacted any laws at all against Quakers, had it not been for the pressure of Massachusetts in the union of the four colonies. As hitherto noted in the sketches of Plymouth and Massachusetts, the Bay colony was anxious for the moral support of the other colonies in its harshness toward that sect. Plymouth declined the action desired, but Connecticut yielded so far as to make a statute of repressive character, but which, like Bottom, "roared like any sucking dove." It used terms designedly opprobrious, — "Quakers, Ranters, Adamites, or such like notorious heretiques," but curiously enough directed the legislation, not against the heretics, but the town entertaining them.[1] The act of 1656 provided that, "no towne within this Jurisdiction shall entertaine (such persons) above the space of fourteen days, upon penalty of £5 *per* weeke for any towne." The act further said, "If the towne please," it could lodge the Quakers in prison until they could be conveniently sent away. Shipmasters were to be mulcted in £20 for bringing Quakers to the colony. The act of 1657 forbade a town giving any "unnecessary entertainment," and corrected a fault of the previous law by defining that the fine must "be paid by that inhabitant who gives the entertainment" to the Quakers. It also imposed an equal fine on any "who shall unnecessarily speak with" the heretics. The next year, the possession of Quaker books was forbidden under penalty of ten shillings to all persons, "except teaching Elders"; and then the court dismissed the whole matter by leaving "to the discretion" of town magistrates the treatment of "any such person found fomenting their wicked Tenets — to punish by fine, imprisonment, or corporeal punishment, as they judge meete."

One can hardly call such legislation very severe, or imagine a much less offensive way of notifying persons that their presence was unwelcome. The discretion and pleasure allowed to local officers — the concession of fourteen days and of *necessary* entertainment, with the studious avoidance of any pen-

[1] *Colonial Records*, I, 283, 303, 308, 324.

alties upon the Quakers themselves beyond the order that they leave the colony — are all tokens of the legislative unwillingness to assume the rôle of the persecutor.

Nor was there any persecution under these acts. With these laws Massachusetts had to be satisfied, and by them the Quakers in Connecticut were practically unmolested. Fifty years afterward (1705), these acts, almost dead letters with their enactment, met a ridiculously solemn resurrection, when Queen Anne in council formally annulled them and drew to them the attention of the Connecticut legislature, requiring their repeal.[1] The general court at its next session accordingly passed an act of repeal; hardly, one must think, without consciousness of the absurdity of the whole proceeding.

The next item showing the Connecticut tendency toward freedom comes in the story of the charter of 1662, which merged New Haven in Connecticut, and also in the correspondence of the king's commissioners to the colonies. In 1661 the general court of Connecticut addressed a petition to the king, reciting that, "they had laid out a great sum for the purchasing a Jurisdiction Right of Mr. George Fenwick, which they were given to understand was derived from true Royal authority by Letters Pattent;"[2] and now expressing their desire that the king would "confer upon them by direct patent their power and privileges."[3] In furtherance of this desire the court sent with the petition their governor, John Winthrop the younger, than whom there was not in New England a more efficient agent.[4] A man of fine scholarship, wide knowledge of books and the world, and withal a person of great refinement and urbanity of manner, he was equally fitted for the colony and the court. He struck the same mood of royal complacency which was equal to the larger demands of Roger Williams, whose visit to London coincided with his

Charter of 1662.

The younger Winthrop.

---

[1] *Records*, II, 546.
[2] Through the patent granted to Lords Brooke and Say and Sele.
[3] *Letters to Connecticut Governors*, p. 37.
[4] Felt, *Ecclesiastical History of New England*, II, 672.

own. Both men obtained from Charles all that they asked, and Winthrop wrote in high spirits from London to the colonial treasurer, John Talcott, on May 13, 1662, " The Charter . . . hath newly passed the great seale, and is as full and large for bounds and privileges as could be desired." [1] He might well be pleased, for the charter confirmed, what had hitherto existed only on sufferance, the privileges of a self-governing republic, subject only to the king's allegiance. It imposed no restraints upon religious preferences, nor demanded the admission of the Church of England, but left the entire question of Church and religion in the power of the colony. Two years afterward the governor and general court, in grateful recognition of the king's bounty, requested his commissioners to represent to the king their sense of "his more abundant grace in re-ratifying our privileges both civil and ecclesiastick . . . (and) our Christian moderation to men of different persuasions." [2]

Royal commissioners.

The royal commissioners to the New England colonies were sent over in 1664. As already noted in our sketch of Massachusetts, their experience in that colony was not very pleasant. They had to deal with men not given to toleration and also struggling for their charter as a man struggles for his life. In Connecticut they met a different reception from men already grateful for a royal favor, and quite justifying the language of Lord Chancellor Clarendon in his letter to Winthrop, announcing their coming : " I know you will give that reception and welcome to the commissioners as is due to the quality they come to you in." [3]

That portion of their instructions which had special reference to Connecticut ran in part: " You shall take the best meanes . . . that you may know the full difference between them and the Massachusetts, both in their Civill and Ecclesi-

---

[1] *Connecticut Historical Collections*, I, 52 ; Palfrey, *History of New England*, II, 40.

[2] *Letters to Connecticut Governors*, p. 61.

[3] *Ibid.*, p. 51.

asticall estate . . . making the same declaration to them, and to all the rest, of your firme resolution to defend and maintain their charter, without the least restraining them in the free exercise of their religion ; but insisting with them, as with the rest, that all the rest who dissent from them, may have the like liberty without undergoing any disadvantages with reference to their civill interest, but that they enjoy the same privileges with the rest." [1]

As already noted, Cartwright wrote from Boston to Nicolls, " I doe think it will be better to beginne at Conecticote." Certainly they found there an accommodating spirit, though it must be conceded that their demands were much less exact and imperious than those made upon Massachusetts. They submitted to the general court several propositions, of which the third required : " That all persons of civil lives may freely enjoy the liberty of their consciences and the worship of God in that way which they think best, provided that this liberty lead not to the disturbance of the public, nor to the hindrance of the maintenance of ministers regularly chosen in each respective parish or township." To this the general court replied : " To the third proposition ; we say, we know not of any one that hath bin troubled by us for attending to his conscience, provided he hath not disturbed the publique." [2]

This indicates small difference between the commissioners and the general court. It is remarkable that the former made no special mention of the Church of England service, nor referred to the use of the book of common prayer, while the provision in their last clause virtually conceded that dissenters, while allowed liberty of their own worship, might yet be taxed for the maintenance of the regular ministry. The demands on Massachusetts were quite different, strenuously insisting on the English Church service, and exemption of Episcopalians from the rates of the establishment. This difference may perhaps be accounted for by several facts. Not

[1] *Colonial History of New York*, II, 55, 87.
[2] *Connecticut Colonial Records*, I, 439.

many Episcopalians had as yet settled in Connecticut, while in Massachusetts they were either numerous or very clamorous. Connecticut also had distinguished itself from the sister colony by consistently following a far more liberal policy, so that, either because of this policy or the want of occasion, no religious antagonisms had voiced themselves in her past. To these must be added the different dispositions toward the king and his commissioners. Roger Wolcott in his *Memorial of Connecticut*[1] says, " They (the commissioners) were ill received at Boston, but courteously in Connecticut." Undoubtedly, the prejudice and suspicion of the one colony, and the affability of the other, had much to do with the temper and demands of the king's agents. For Connecticut they provided no ground of complaint, nor made any further demand for liberty of worship, satisfied with the general disclaimer by the court of all intolerance.

Four years afterward (1669) the general court made that distinct acknowledgment of liberty of opinion and practice within the established Church, already recorded in our account of the Saybrook committee.[2] It is notable for its generous spirit, and for its understanding that even a religious establishment must admit a degree of elasticity in its laws of uniformity — an understanding exceedingly rare at that day.

The proportion of dissent, and the practical religious unanimity of Connecticut in 1680, may be gathered from the annual report of Governor Leete to the board of trade in London.[3] To the board's inquiry as to religious matters the governor replied that there were twenty-six towns and twenty-one Churches, with a minister in every town, whose support was "raysed upon the people by way of rate. . . . Our people in this colony are, some strict Congregational men, others more large Congregational, some moderate Presbyterians; and take the Congregational men

---

[1] *Connecticut Historical Society Collections*, III, 328.   [2] p. 255.

[3] *Colonial Records*, II, 300; *Massachusetts Historical Collections*, IV, 223.

of both sorts, they are the greatest part of the people in the colony. There are four or five *Seven day* men, and about so many more Quakers. Great care is taken for the instruction of the people in the Xtian religion, by ministers cattechizing of them and preaching to them twice every Sabboth dayes, and sometimes on Lecture dayes: and so by masters of famalyes instructing and cattechizing their children and servants, being soe required to doe by law." From such a showing it would appear that there was but small room for either dissent or repression. There is a record of a very transient disturbing element which appeared about 1680, caused by followers of a certain John Rogers,[1] from whom they were called Rogerines.[2] They were half Quaker and half Baptist, "passionate denunciators and defiant," upbraided the judges and the courts, railed at the ministers as hirelings, refused to pay rates, and labored on Sunday. They did not meet the notice and opposition through which such vagaries grow, and have left no distinct trace on the legislation of the colony.

The attempted usurpation of James II. and Andros had no effect upon the religious status of Connecticut, unless we remark that it drove the people to much prayer. The crisis was short and sharp, with something of the dramatic and a touch or two of humor. The king's jealousy succeeded in annulling the Maryland and Massachusetts charters, and demanded through Andros the surrender of the charter of Connecticut. Then occurred the famous incident of the darkened council-chamber, the abstraction of the charter, and its concealment by Captain Wadsworth in the hollow of the oak. Never had dawned upon the colony a time of so great excitement. The first intimation that their charter and their separate colonial existence were in danger had caused an address to the king (1686) in which they said : " We humbly beg and beseech your Ma'tie to continue our intire Province

1 Palfrey, *History of New England*, III, 440.
2 *New Haven Historical Society Papers*, III, 386.

or Government within our known bounds and colony limits."
When in the next year Andros came to Hartford and per-
emptorily demanded the charter, the people added to the
clever abstraction of that instrument so much of prayer for
divine assistance, that the governor was impressed and
worried by it. Wolcott relates: — "One morning he said
to Doctor Hooker, he thought the good people of Connecticut kept many days of fasting and prayer on his account.
'Very likely,' says the doctor, 'for we read that this kind
goeth not out by other means.'" [1]

With the accession of William and Mary the colony was
again more fortunate than Massachusetts and Maryland,
whose forfeited charters were not restored. Connecticut
retained all its liberties, electing its own governor and
assistants, and was supported therein by the king's solicitor-
general, whose opinion, sought by William, was that the
colony was within its legal rights in so doing and its charter
still in force.[2] Thus the colony was permitted to go on in its
own self-determining way, in the story of which we find no
incident for remark here until 1706.

Then appeared the first movements toward organized
dissent from the established order, in the efforts to gather
Episcopacy. an Episcopal Church at Stratford. In that year the Rev.
Mr. Muirson went thither from New York, probably on invitation from some residents of Stratford, preached and baptized twenty-five persons.[3] This roused opposition by some
of the people, but the missionary was not molested. In the
following year he came again, and labored also at Fairfield,
though not without the strenuous urgencies of both magistrates and the regular clergy to the people not to attend his
services. The opposition confined itself to these urgencies,
and did not resort to any violence against the minister. This
was the beginning of the Episcopal Church in Connecticut,

---

[1] *Connecticut Historical Society Collections*, III, 331 ; *Letters to Connecticut Governors*, pp. 170–172.

[2] *Ibid.*, p. 189.   [3] Barber, *Historical Collections*, p. 409.

which soon made room for itself in the colony and in the tolerant consideration of the authorities.

Its effect on the statute book was immediate, for in 1708 the general court, undoubtedly to meet the condition thus arising, enacted its first law concerning " Dissenters from the Established order." [1] This was the year of the Saybrook synod, and it would seem that the court, having settled the affairs of the established Church to its mind, was specially complacent toward such as preferred another way of worship. The act decreed that dissenters should have full liberty of worship, " without any let, hindrance, or molestation whatsoever," provided that they " qualify " as such by entering their names in the county court, " according to the Act of William and Mary." But they were not exempted from paying rates for the support of the established Church. The law is in entire agreement with the " proviso " of the act by which the Saybrook Platform was adopted, and in very similar words.

The legislature of 1708 thus made two distinct declarations of its tolerant mind. It will be noted that by this time the prayer book had conquered liberty for itself in Massachusetts, and in New York the folly of Cornbury was trying to force its use on unwilling people. The peculiarity of Connecticut is that, on the first occasion of its claim, it met a tolerant treatment. The device of qualifying before the county court and obtaining a legal permission is also another peculiarity in this colony, significant not only of toleration but of the governmental intent to keep a controlling hand on religious matters outside of the establishment, as within it. This latter purpose obtained down to the end of the colonial period, a late instance of which may be cited in a petition from Baptists in Lyme, in 1767, praying to be organized into a distinct Church society. The general court approved, and appointed a committee of its own members to visit Lyme and report.[2]

[1] *Records*, V, 50. [2] *Ibid.*, XII, 640.

After the liberal laws of 1708 the religious affairs of the colony were without special incident for narration here until 1722, when the established Church was much moved by the **Cutler and Johnson.** defection of President Timothy Cutler of Yale College, Samuel Johnson, and four other members of the New Haven association. These men startled their Congregational brethren by going together into the Episcopal Church. They became a subject of much ill-natured remark and of much correspondence. Cotton Mather comments very severely on the "new Episcopalians," and declares that Cutler had all the time been a "secret Episcopalian, and a seducer of young men in the ministry."[1] The excitement soon subsided, and the right of the six clergymen to take this step was generally conceded. Out of the incident came what in modern speech would be called a "great boom" for Episcopacy, the infant efforts of which had been somewhat languishing. In the next year (1723) the first Episcopal Church in Connecticut was organized at Stratford, through the agency of Mr. Pigott, a missionary of the Society for the Propagation of the Gospel, and Mr. Johnson was settled as its rector.[2]

Disorders. About the same time, it would appear that some irregularities had become prominent. Taking advantage of the liberal spirit of the authorities, some dissenters had presumed to neglect reporting to the county court, and some persons, "without the least pretence or color of being ordained (as) ministers of the gospel have presumed to gather together in a tumultuous manner and to administer the sacrament of baptism, to the great abuse and prophanation of that holy ordinance." There is no record to show the denomination of these disorderly people. Possibly they were Rogerines. To meet this condition the legislature of 1723 passed an "Act for preventing Disorders in the Worship of God."[3] The act, after reciting the above disorders, insisted that all dissenters

---

[1] *Massachusetts Historical Collections*, II, 2 ; 128, 133.

[2] Barber, *Historical Collections*, p. 409.

[3] *Records*, VI ; *New Haven Historical Papers*, III, 386.

must "qualify" under the law of 1708, and ordained that such persons as "neglect the public worship of God in some lawful congregation, and form themselves into separate companies in private houses, shall each for every offense forfeit the sum of twenty shillings." It denounced a fine of £10 and a whipping on any person, not a minister, who should dare to administer the sacraments. This is the sharpest specimen of Connecticut law on the subject of religion, and the only one in which the whip is resorted to for penalty. It can be accounted for only on the supposition that the disorders had been extreme, and cannot be cited as a departure from the policy of regulated tolerance. But we find no record of the infliction of these penalties.

That this construction is the true one seems provable by the spirit of accommodation exhibited by the authorities in the matter of rate-paying by dissenters. On this theme there Rates. had been much discussion and many appeals for relief, and though the formal legislative action toward that end was not taken until 1727,there are indications that the authorities were not exacting in the cases of orderly and organized dissent. Only so can we understand Governor Talcott's correspondence with the bishop of London.[1] "(There is) one particular," wrote the bishop in 1725, "in which I desire your favor and indulgence to the members of the Church of England, as far as justice and the laws of the country will permit; and that is, that they may not be constrained to contribute to the Independent minister." To this the governor replied: "There is but one Church of England minister (Mr. Johnson of Stratford) in this colony. His people are under no restraint to contribute to the support of any other minister." There are " some few persons in another town," pretending to be of the Church of England, and objecting to rates " in order to escape a small tax." A fair construction of the governor's reply leads to the conclusion, that by a tacit understanding, while all the people were required to contribute to the support

[1] *Talcott Papers; Connecticut Historical Collections*, IV, 53, 65.

of religious service, and while no merely individual dissent in places having no properly organized dissenting Church could exempt from rates ; yet, in places where such a Church was organized and attended, its members were allowed to divert their rates to the support of their own minister.

Very soon after this correspondence occasion was served by an act of oppression for a legal allowance of this liberty.[1] The local magistrates in the town of Fairfield in 1727 refused to allow this diversion of rates, and insisted that the members of the Episcopal Church should pay to the support of the established Church. They carried their insistence to the extreme of putting in jail ten Episcopalians for declining to pay.

An appeal to the legislature by the outraged Episcopalians brought immediate relief in the " Act for the Ease of such as soberly Dissent," of 1727,[2] passed with special regard to the Church of England. The law first declared that all persons of the Church of England, living within the bounds of an established parish, should be taxed for the support of the ministry ; then it ordained, "if there be a society of the Church of England with a rector, so near that any person, who has declared himself a member of the Church of England, can conveniently attend," the collectors, "having indifferently levied the tax as aforesaid, shall deliver the taxes collected of such persons to the minister of the Church of England living near to such persons." The act also allowed the Episcopalians to further tax themselves for an increase of their rector's salary.

This law is closely like the famous "Five-Mile Act" of Massachusetts, passed by a notable coincidence in the same year. It is less exact than the Massachusetts law, which put a limit of five miles on the range of Episcopal affiliations. This difference really amounted to nothing, for both acts put the seal of legal allowance and exemption on the tolerated sect. The Massachusetts act was broader in not confining

Act for Ease of Dissenters.

---

[1] *New Haven Historical Papers*, III, 394.
[2] *Records*, VII, 107.

its favor to the Episcopalians, but extending it to all orderly dissenters. Two years afterward, the Connecticut legislature supplied their omission by extending the benefit of the act to the Quakers and Baptists.[1] As in Massachusetts, so in Connecticut, the technical construction of the act, through its instrumentality of charging the civil officers with the collection of all Church support, incorporated the dissenting Churches into the Church establishment!

So the churches had rest for a while until the rise of that convulsion, known as the Great Awakening. This move- Great ment, the sequel to Whitefield's preaching tours, besides its Awakening. effects of much spiritual quickening, was attended by many most deplorable features. The reaction from the conservatism of the past had resulted in many cases in the wildest extravagances of action and speech. Many of the promoters of the movement were unbridled in their denunciations of the ministers, who could not go with them in the "new measures." They intruded upon parishes, holding irregular services, urging people not to attend the ministry of their pastors, whom they reviled as unconverted. New England was divided among "New Lights" and "Old Lights," while the Presbyterian Church in the middle colonies was split into "Old Side" and "New Side."[2]

To the staid representatives of the Connecticut establishment this assault of excited itinerant and intrusive preachers was a grievous offence. Not only did these preachers embrace every opportunity offered by sympathizers, but they forced themselves into parishes, uninvited and opposed by the settled pastors.

Among the most troublesome of these itinerants was James Davenport, pastor at Southold, Long Island, in whom the balance of mind was unsettled by the revival excitement.[3]

---

[1] *Records*, VII, 237, 257.

[2] Hodge, *History of Presbyterian Church*, Chaps. IV, V; Palfrey, IV, 76–107.

[3] *Talcott Papers; Connecticut Historical Collection*, V, 370.

He came into Connecticut with Whitefield in 1740, and again in 1741 alone, preaching at Stratford, Saybrook, and other places, and used most violent language against the ministers and Churches with " unrestrained liberty of noise and outcry in time of divine service." A bit of correspondence between Colonel Lynde of Saybrook and Governor Talcott may illustrate the mind of the more sober sort.

The colonel wrote to the governor complaining of Davenport's conduct at Saybrook, where he had intruded his service in the parish of the Rev. Mr. Hart, whom he had treated with great disrespect. Lynde as a magistrate had thought of prosecuting him, but applied to the governor for advice. The reply of the latter, under date of September 4, 1741, is grave and severe. " I am surprised," he wrote, " that Mr. Davenport should in so imperious and unwarrientable manner take upon him to condemn any, and Especially our most Eminently pious and Industrious Ministers, to be Carnall &c., which I look upon as usurping the authority of the Most High. And his advice to people not to hearken to their Ministers by him condemned, but to go 10 or 20 miles, and that they had better sett upon private meetings amongst themselves, &c; all which is a violation and open contempt of the Laws of this Colony, and so apparently tends to the breach of the peace of our Religious Sosiaties and subversion of all good orders in Church and State." The governor then called on ministers, people, and magistrates to " use all their Joynt Interest by advice, Influence, and authority, to Incourage what is vertuous and praiseworthy, and to suppress every disorderly and Vile practice and whatsoever tends to the hurt and Reproach of Religion."

So great had the trouble become in a large portion of the colony, that in the fall session of 1741 the assembly summoned the general association of ministers to meet at Guilford in the following November to devise a remedy, " hoping that such a general convention may issue in the accommodation of divisions, settling peace, love, and charity, and promoting the true interests of vital religion."[1] The convention met accordingly, and after discussion found the root of the trouble in the unwarranted intrusion of itinerant preachers **Intrusion.** into parishes, and recommended to the legislature measures to correct that evil. This advice was adopted by the general court, which at its next session, 1742, passed an "Act for regulating Abuses and correcting Disorders in Ecclesiastical Affairs."[2] The act declared : 1st, That any minister, preaching in other than his own parish without the request of the incumbent, or of the officers of the Church, if there were no incumbent, should be denied the support provided by law; 2d, That every member of any association, intruding by licensure or ordination on the province of another association, should be denied support; 3d, That any person, not a settled or ordained minister, preaching in any parish without "express invitation" of the minister of it, or of the officers, should be fined £100; and 4th, That any foreigner or stranger, ordained or not, so offending should be " sent (as a vagrant person) by warrant from any one assistant or justice of the peace, from constable to constable, out of the bounds of this colony." Some foreigners were expelled, but returned again, the next year, when the legislature ordered that they be arrested, fined £100, and again driven away.[3]

One of the preachers sent out of the colony was Davenport, who had had similar treatment at Boston. Complaints of his conduct at Stratford had been lodged with the court. He was summoned to appear before that body, whose deliverance, after examination, ran : "That the acts of Davenport do, and have a natural tendency to, disturb and destroy the peace and order of this government. Yet it further appears to this Assembly that the said Davenport is under the influence of enthusiastical impressions and impulses, and thereby disturbed in the rational faculty of his mind, and therefore to be pitied

[1] *Records*, VIII, 440.
[2] *Ibid.*, VIII, 454.
[3] *Ibid.*, VIII, 570.

and compassionated, and not to be treated as he otherwise might be." With this opinion, the assembly ordered his transportation to his home at Southold.[1]

Another subject of legislative censure was Benjamin Pumroy. He was first summoned before the court with James Davenport, but was discharged. Afterward he was again summoned on a bill of information charging him with preaching that " the late law concerning ecclesiastical affairs was a foundation to encourage persecution . . . was made without reason and contrary to the word of God . . . that great men had fallen in and joyned with those who are on the devil's side and enemies of the kingdom of Christ. . . . There is no colony so privileged as Connecticut was, and now there is no colony so bad for persecuting laws." Pumroy was arraigned before the court, found guilty, and fined £50, with costs at £32 10s. 8d.[2]

Another case was that of the Rev. John Owen, the minister of the Church at Groton, who sympathized with the " New Lights," and freely expressed in his preaching his condemnation of the proceedings of the general court. This was construed by the court as " tending to bring the laws of this government into contempt," on which the arrest of Owen was ordered and his production before the assembly. He appeared, confessed the language alleged, promised amendment, and was discharged on payment of costs.[3]

While there can be no doubt that the conduct which caused this legislation must have been most exasperating to the majority of ministers and magistrates, yet it is equally beyond doubt that both the appeal to the legislature and the law of 1742 were mistakes. Had the ministry been content to possess their souls in patience, the evil fire would soon have burned itself out. The measures taken added to the trouble and made a distinctly backward step in toleration; while the

---

[1] *Records*, VIII, 483. Davenport had previously been tried in Massachusetts and sent out of the colony. Palfrey, IV, 93.

[2] *Records*, VIII, 566 ; IX, 28.   [3] *Ibid.*, VIII, 519 ; IX, 20.

members of dissenting Churches, which had nothing to do with the disturbances, — unless it may be that some individual Episcopalians and Baptists joined their neighbors of the establishment in this resort to government, — were made the chief sufferers by the action. For in 1743 the general court, as though the inroad of intrusive itinerants had been the work of dissenters and the product of its acts of toleration, repealed the act of 1708 "for the Ease of such as Soberly Dissent," and substituted for it another law, according a far less degree of liberty.[1] New law of dissent.

The new law defined that " any of His Majesty's subjects, being protestants, inhabitants of this colony, that shall soberly dissent from the way of worship and ministry established by the laws of this colony . . . may apply themselves to this Assembly for relief . . . (and) may expect the indulgence of this Assembly, having first before this Assembly taken the oaths and subscribed the declaration[2] provided by Act of Parliament in cases of the like nature."

The narrow and crippling nature of this statute is evident at a glance, when compared with the law of 1708. That law put no vexatious or doubtful obstacles in the way of dissenters. It was general and prescribed comparatively easy rules, under which any dissenting congregation, complying therewith, could demand from their own county court recognition of their rights to organization and worship. The new act took away this ease and liberty, and hampered the dissenters with rules in many possible cases difficult of observance. It does not appear that dissenting Churches already organized were necessarily affected by the statute, but the formation of others was made vexatiously difficult. In place of their own county court, the legislature was made the constituting authority. Dissenters applying, though living at the ends of the colony, must appear in person at Hartford, in order to take the oath " before this Assembly." The *right* of organi-

---

[1] *Records*, VIII, 522 ; Palfrey, IV, 112–118.
[2] Against transubstantiation.

zation was changed to a favor, which, though the applicants were bidden to "expect the indulgence" of the assembly, might be denied on any caprice. In place of the general law covering all cases, the new statute becomes particular, compelling a request for legislative action in every individual case.

While this comparison of the two laws shows the retrograde movement noted, at the same time we may not fail to observe what goes far toward justifying the legislature, that by the act of 1743 dissenting Churches were put on a level with those of the establishment. No Congregational Church could be organized without an express act of the general court, so that in fact between 1708 and 1743, the dissenters had a larger liberty than members of the establishment in matters of organization. Though they were crippled by the new law, they were no worse off than their Congregational neighbors, save as respects the requirement of personal appearance before the legislature.

Another feature of the act of 1743 introduced an entirely new element in Connecticut legislation. This is the clause, "being protestants," the effect of which was to deny tolera-

Romanists. tion to Romanists. Under the statute no room was made for Roman Catholic Churches. This is the first instance in which the laws of the colony recognized the distinction between Protestant and Romanist. The explanation of its absence from former legislation is undoubtedly the fact, that no Romanist had settled in the colony in the past years, and no occasion was given for anti-Roman enactments. Nor does it appear that any of the Roman Church were in Connecticut in 1743 in sufficient numbers to cause any alarm. The form and phrases of the statute, with its reference to the king, parliament, and oaths, suggest that the committee which drew the bill had in mind English toleration, and that thus the words, "being protestants," together with the requirement of the oath, crept into the statute without any special intention of emphasis. At the same time one cannot altogether avoid regret that the usually tolerant Connecticut should even, by indirection, appear to have ever joined in the insane cry of " No Popery."

Another law of 1743 cannot be so easily excused. This is an " Act providing Relief against the evil and dangerous Designs of Foreigners and Suspected Persons."[1] The best that can be said for it is that, though it had a decided bearing on religious matters, yet the evident motive of the act was political. It was directed against the Moravians, who were   Moravians. engaged in teaching the Indians of the Housatonic Valley at Sharon and Kent. Their work had extended also across the border into Dutchess County, New York, and in this same year brought upon them the expulsive action of the New York assembly. In both colonies ignorant prejudice and irrational fear of the French had more to do with the actions against them than any religious considerations. Though their work was clearly of the most humane and Christian character, it was whispered that they were Jesuits in the interest of the French of Canada, affecting the minds of their Indian pupils against the English. This was enough to excite the alarm of the surrounding community, and to forward complaints to the general court.

The preaching and teaching also were objected to as a violation of the law of 1742 against intrusion, though it does not appear that they were at all guilty of the intrusion defined in the law, as they labored only among the Indians, attempting no interference in any parish. Such intrusion, indeed, was impossible to their foreign tongue. Perhaps this latter fact may suggest that the legislature thought the law of 1742 not sufficient to cover the case and caused the new act, the title of which has just been recited. The act described " foreigners and suspected persons who sow and spread false and dangerous doctrines of religion amongst us, to stir up discord, to estrange the minds of the Indians from us," and ordered that all such suspected persons " be arrested and taken before the Governor,

[1] *Records*, VIII, 521.

who shall use such meanes as may be proper" to protect the colony from danger.

[1] Under this law three of the Moravians — Mack, Shaw, and Pyrlaens, a highly educated minister — were arrested and examined by the county court at New Milford. They were not able to satisfy the court, and were bound over to appear before the governor. Governor Law examined them three times, and easily satisfied himself that they were not French spies, but doubted whether they might be teachers of "false and dangerous doctrine." Mack gave bonds not to preach in any parish without permission. The protest of Count Zinzendorf will be found related in our story of New York, as also the protection of the British government, which described the Moravians as "brethren introduced to the colonies by Parliament as members of an ancient Protestant Episcopal Church." This did not satisfy the people, who complained that "parliamentary interference was becoming offensive, and that there were too many Episcopalians in Connecticut already." The final result was that the godly work of Moravians in the colony and in New York was broken up, and the teachers forced to seek refuge in Pennsylvania, whither many of their pupils followed them.

After this almost tragic incident, one of the darkest blots on Connecticut colonial legislation, the records contain few matters calling for present remark. To the end of the period, and after, the assembly held fast to its principles of ecclesiastical control. Churches of the establishment still looked to the legislature for organization and support, and dissenters for any desired relief or exemption; while in the exercise of its ecclesiastical functions the assembly showed a return to its former readiness for liberality. Sundry illustrations of both these features may properly be noted.

Separates.   The "Separates," — the "New Lights," — who had withdrawn from the regular Churches and formed separate Con-

[1] Dr. Andrews, *American Church Review*, 1880; Article, *Moravians in the Housatonic Valley.*

gregational Churches, were granted liberty.[1] Those at Milford were in 1750 allowed to organize, and to be exempted from regular Church rates, "so long as they shall regularly attend the worship of God in said separate congregation." In 1760 this Separate Church was transformed into a Presbyterian Church by act of assembly. In 1751 the First Church of New Haven fell into dissension, and the assembly interfered for peace.[2] In 1757 the Baptists of Enfield were exempted from Church rates.[3] Between 1751 and 1772 sixty Churches were organized by the legislature, and many "winter privileges" were granted.[4] (A winter privilege allowed a portion of a parish, so distant from the Church as to make attendance difficult in that season, to employ a minister for themselves during the winter.[5]) In 1767 the second Church of Lyme was reported to the assembly as without a minister for several years. The information came from the New London association, and the assembly appointed a committee to visit Lyme and report. The most remarkable action of the legislature on the subject of religion, not only during this immediate period, but in its entire annals, was an *order*, made at the instance of the English government, that "the Form of Prayer for the Royal Family" (from the English prayer-book) be published and read in all the Churches![6] This action was taken in 1751, a signal illustration of Connecticut liberality and complaisance. *Prayer for the king.*

This may suffice for the narrative of colonial Connecticut in its relation to the Church. Clearly, it occupied a middle ground between theocratic Massachusetts and free Rhode Island. Its distinguishing features were an insistence on governmental control, with as large a liberty as that ideal would permit. When an unaccustomed impulse to repress any dissent took momentary possession, the reserve of good and liberal sense made legislation fall far short of genuine

---

[1] *Records*, IX, 517 ; XI, 402 ; Johnston, *History of Connecticut*, p. 243.
[2] *Ibid.*, X, 43. [4] *Ibid.*, X, XI, XII, XIII. [6] *Ibid.*, X, 65.
[3] *Ibid.*, XI, 54. [5] *Ibid.*, XII, 638.

persecution, while the impulse quickly passed. Confidently it may be said that, among the establishments of the colonies that of Connecticut was by far the best. The absence of the theocratic ideal prevented both that arrogance of the ministry, under which Massachusetts suffered, and the assumption that the state was a mere servant of the Church. Begun under the fostering care of the broad-minded Hooker, the colony for the most part guided itself by his principles, and was fully ready in feeling for the changes of the Revolution, though some details of form remained for forty years thereafter.

IV. *The New Haven Theocracy*

The short-lived effort of the New Haven colony labored to establish a theocracy even more strict than that of Massachusetts, in which every public utterance and action was to be guided by, and an expression of, the divine law. Its civil leader for many years was Theophilus Eaton, one of a company of English merchants, rich and educated, who with decided Puritan principles associated themselves together to follow the Massachusetts colony into the new world. Their spiritual guide was John Davenport, a friend of Hooker and Cotton, settled in a London parish at the time of their emigration and at that time out of sympathy with their motives. A man of great mental force and of high moral education, and withal of great eloquence as a preacher, not long after the departure of his friends from England, he found reason to change his opinions and soon drew upon himself the hostility of Archbishop Laud. He fled to Amsterdam, whence in 1636 he returned to join Eaton and his companions in their American venture.

At Boston.   In the latter part of that year the company arrived at Boston, in the very height of the antinomian controversy. The air was full of contest. Roger Williams had just been banished, and the mind of the ministry and magistracy was evidently bent on excluding Mrs. Hutchinson and silencing her adherents. On points of doctrine involved Davenport and Eaton were in full accord with the authorities at the Bay, but were affected against settlement there by the universal strife. It is probable that their original intention had been to join themselves to the Massachusetts colony, and that the strife at Boston moved them to attempt a new settlement, desiring to found it in peace and without the presence of disturbing elements. So they set themselves to discover a place of habitation which should be their own. Winthrop wrote,[1] "Mr. Eaton and some others of Mr. Davenport's company went to view Quinepiack, with intent to begin a plantation there;" and, after the new colony had left Boston, "all possible means had been used to accommodate them. They had many offers: Charlestown offered largely, Newbury their whole town, the Court any place which was free."

In 1638 Eaton, Davenport, and their companions left Boston, settled about the bay which receives the Quinnipiac, and founded the colony and city of New Haven.[2] Never, not even among the Puritans of Massachusetts, was made another so religious foundation. On the 4th of June, 1639,[3] was held their first "general meeting to consult about settling their civil Government according to God . . . for the establishing of such civil order as might be most pleasing to God, and for the choosing the fittest men for the foundation work of a Church to be gathered." At this meeting it was voted, "no man dissenting," that "the Scriptures do hold forth a perfect rule for the direction and government of all men in all duties, which they are to perform to God and men, as well in the government of families and commonwealths as in matters of the Church."

With this as the cardinal principle to be observed in all arrangements, they proceeded to enter into a "*Fundamental*

[1] *Journal*, I, 237, 259.
[2] Felt, *Ecclesiastical History of New England*, I, 357.
[3] *New Haven Colonial Records*, anno 1639.

Agreement [1] — a covenant solemnly made by the whole assembly: 1st, that the Word of God shall be the only Rule attended unto in ordering the affairs of government;" 2d, that they should "cast themselves into that mould and form of commonwealth which appeareth best, in reference to the securing of the pure and peaceable enjoyment of all Christ His ordinances in the Church according to God"; and 3d (twice voted in this one meeting), "that the free burgesses shall be chosen from Church members, and they only shall choose magistrates and officers among themselves to have the power of transacting all public civil affairs of the Plantation." It was then *ordered* "that all hereafter received as planters shall submit to this fundamental agreement."

Constitution.

Having thus outlined their principle of civil government, they turned to ecclesiastical matters and chose "Seven Pillars" to be the governors of the Church, both the title and number of these officers being suggested by Mr. Davenport from Proverbs ix. 1. "Wisdom hath builded her house; she hath hewn out her seven pillars." These seven pillars, thus primarily appointed to a spiritual office, seem to have been vested also with a supreme civil function ; for in October of the same year they "chose a chief magistrate or Governor, and four deputies to assist in public affairs." The governor then elected was Theophilus Eaton, who was reëlected for many successive years. This first election was regarded as a thing of great solemnity and was preceded by a sermon by Mr. Davenport, "opening two scriptures, Deut. i. 13, and Ex. xviii. 21 "; the advice of Jethro to Moses, "Provide out of all the people able men, such as fear God, men of truth . . . to be rulers;" and Moses' command, "Take you wise men, and understanding, and known among your tribes, and I will make them rulers over you."

Seven pillars.

Presently, the "General Court" was established, consisting at first only of the governor and four deputies, but increased in number by the settlement of other towns. It

[1] *New Haven Historical Papers*, I, 17.

was formally resolved, " that the Duty of the general court Religious function of government. was: 1st, To provide for the maintenance of the purity of religion, and to suppress the contrary; 2d, To declare, publish, and establish . . . the laws for holiness and righteousness which God hath made and given to us in the Scriptures."

So closely did the men of the new colony adhere to the idea of a government directly controlled, as was that of ancient Israel, by God Himself.[1] The endeavor was to revive the old Mosaic forms; and Davenport, whose moulding hand is seen throughout, even went so far as to put himself in the place of the great Law-giver, when he said to the governor, " The cause that is too hard for you, bring it to me and I will hear it." Certainly, Davenport looked upon the work as very good, writing in 1639 to Lady Vere,[2] " The Lord our God hath here bestowed upon us the greatest outward privilege under the sun, to have and enjoy all His ordinances purely dispensed in a Church gathered and constituted according to his owne minde." The author of the *Wonder-working Providence of Zion's Saviour* [3] was no less delighted, writing: " This government of New Haven, although the younger of the foure, yet was she as beautifull as any of this broode of travellers and most minding the end of her coming hither, to keep close to the rule of Christ both in Doctrine and Discipline; and it were to be wished her elder Sister [4] would followe her example."

It would be difficult in a commonwealth so constituted to draw the line between Church and State. Evidently the founders considered the two as identical. Those of their Unity of Church and State. number who afterward crossed the sound and settled on Long Island, the eastern part of which for years was under the jurisdiction, first of New Haven and afterward of Connecticut, illustrated the same principle in the organization of

---

[1] Johnston, *History of Connecticut*, p. 98.
[2] *New Haven Historical Papers*, II, 228.
[3] Force, *Historical Tracts.*
[4] Connecticut.

their towns. Thus "the early history of Southold discloses
no polity or discipline of the Church apart from the government of the town."[1] The entire organization of colony and
towns was strictly religious, beyond anything in history since
the foundations of Israel. The power of the clergy was supreme. The seven pillars of the New Haven Church not
only chose the colonial governor, but were the magistrates
of the town. The same religious magistracy was constituted
in the other towns, as the colony expanded; and these
magistrates judged all causes without the intervention of a
jury. A jury was out of place in early New Haven, because
there was no trace of such an institution in the Mosaic code.
That code was the foundation of all law, and any crime punishable by death under the old Hebrew law was made capital
in New Haven.[2] The famous "Blue Laws" of Connecticut
and New Haven were a fiction of Samuel Peters in 1681, to
satirize the severity of colonial statutes; but while they contained some pretended laws of a ridiculous character, it
cannot be said that the spirit of them was much harsher than
some enactments of the New Haven legislature.

"Blue
Laws."

The general court at its first session in November, 1639,[3]
true to its religious mission, and regarding the matter as of
the first religious moment, took order for building a meeting-
house, which was to be fifty feet square and to cost £500.
All inhabitants were to be called on for voluntary pledges to
support the Church. If any person refused, he should be
assessed by the magistrates; and if payment were delayed,
collection was to be made "as for debt." No other Churches
could be organized, except on approval of the magistrates
and elders. No person, not a Church-member, could be admitted as a freeman of the colony. Absentees from Church

---

[1] *New Haven Historical Papers*, II, 22.

[2] There were nineteen capital offences. This seems many, but in England
so late as 1819 there were two hundred and twenty-three! Johnston, *History
of Connecticut*, p. 106.

[3] *New Haven Colonial Records*, anno 1639.

service were to be fined five shillings. "If any Christian (so-called) behave himself contemptuously toward the Word or the Minister," he was to be punished in the discretion of the magistrates, according to the gravity of the offence. The punishment of heresy was also left to this magisterial discretion, and might be by fine, banishment, or "otherwise." In order to protect the colony from improper additions, no stranger could be permitted to remain without special license from the magistrate, a rule similar to the domicile act of Massachusetts.[1]

In 1643 New Haven entered into the New England Confederacy with Massachusetts, Plymouth, and Connecticut, of which sufficient has been noted in the sketches of the other colonies. But already another "combination" had been formed of much greater importance to New Haven. This was the merging into one "jurisdiction" with New Haven, Stamford, Guilford, and Yennicook. The peculiarity of this combination will be noted as something unique in colo-

New England Confederacy.

"Jurisdiction."

---

[1] These laws are found grouped together in the *Record* under title of *Colonial Laws.*

A few notes of legislative and judicial action will illustrate both the religious character and the particularity of the government. (These items are in the *Record* under years noted.) In 1640 George Spencer, being "profane and disorderly in his whole conversation, and an abettor of others to sin," was whipped and banished. Two years afterward he returned and was hanged at gross immorality. In 1640 "Thomas Chambers being accused of scoffing at religion, it not being sufficiently proved, he was dismissed only with an admonition and caution." In the same year, "Hen. Akerlye was rebuked for building a cellar and selling it without leave." In 1643 is the record that "Goodman Hunt and his wife, for keeping the counsel of William Harding (a very lewd person who was whipped), baking him a pasty and plum cakes, and keeping company with him on the Lord's Day; and she suffering Harding to kiss her, . . .were ordered to be sent out of this town within one month." A pleasanter entry is that of 1640: "Ordered, that our pastor shall have his farm where he desires it, with all the conveniences of upland and meadow and creeks, which the place where he pitches shall afford, though above his proportion, according to his desire." This showed their regard for the parson; and in 1643 they exhibited their care for the meeting-house, in ordering that, "Sister Preston shall sweep and dress the meeting-house every week, and have one shilling a week for her pains."

nial action. In the other colonies, other settlements springing up within the territory of the original plantation became at once, without special action, integral members of the colony or commonwealth. With New Haven the case was different. Eaton and Davenport located their company on land outside of the other colonies and without a patent of their own, though their settlement infringed on the patent of Lords Brooke and Say and Sele. They claimed no territory beyond the lands immediately occupied by themselves. So when the towns of Guilford and Stamford were settled, each began as an independent settlement, under no other jurisdiction than that of the king. It very soon became apparent that such independence was not desirable, and that the towns should combine together under one colonial government. This took place accordingly, under the name of the first settled town, New Haven.

Milford.

The advantages of this union were so obvious that in 1643 Milford desired admittance to the union, but on the application coming before the general court of the enlarged " jurisdiction " it was objected that Milford had six freemen, who were not Church-members.[1] This objection Milford met with the proposal of a compromise to the effect: 1st, that none of the six should be chosen for any office of the " combination," nor vote in the election of magistrates of the combination; 2d, that hereafter none but Church-members should be admitted freemen of Milford; but 3d, the six were to have liberty to act in town business wherein the combination was not interested, and to vote for deputies to the general court, who should always be members of the Church. On this proposition Milford was admitted by a vote of the general court, " not foreseeing any danger in yielding to Milford with the aforesaid cautions."

But the settlement of so important a matter was not to be left to the terms of a compromise, and at the first meeting of the general court after the admission of Milford, the

[1] Felt, *Ecclesiastical History of New England*, I, 517, 521.

"Fundamental Agreement" was formally and solemnly re-adopted as binding upon all. In the next year, the code already enacted in New Haven was made that of the entire jurisdiction, the general court enacting: "That the judicial laws of God, as they were delivered by Moses, and as they are a fence to the moral law, being neither typical nor cere-monial, nor had any reference to Canaan, shall be accounted of moral equity and generally bind all offenders, and be a rule to all the courts in this jurisdiction in their proceedings against offenders, till they be branched out into particulars hereafter."

The only occasion for the exhibition of a persecuting spirit was furnished by the Quakers. There is no reason to sup- Quakers. pose that the pure theocracy of New Haven would have shown much tolerance for dissent from the established Church, or have suffered a Roman Catholic to remain in the colony. But with such the *Records* do not show the govern-ment to have been tried. But the Quaker alarm woke New Haven to a frenzy only second to that of Massachusetts. In 1656 the rumor of the sect's approach brought out the law that "Quakers shall not be suffered in this jurisdiction." Then the court was silent on the subject for two years.

Meanwhile some of the sect had ventured into the colony, and the general court in 1658 delivered itself of a batch of laws, not a whit less severe than those of the Bay, except in the item of capital punishment. Death was not among the penalties, but the enactments were sufficiently indicative of a frantic and intolerant state of mind. The law declared that "whoso shall bring Quakers, or other blasphemous here-ticks, into this jurisdiction shall forfeit the sum of £50." If any Quaker should come on business, he might be allowed to despatch it, attended by a guard, and was to be put out of the jurisdiction when the business was concluded. If he refused the guard, or attempted communication with the people, he was to be imprisoned, severely whipped, and kept at work for a term discretionary with the magistrate. If a Quaker, having once suffered under this law, should come again, he was to be branded with the letter "H" on the hand and jailed. For a third offence the other hand should be branded, and the fourth offence was to be punished by boring the tongue with a hot iron. Quakers "arising from among ourselves" were to be treated as foreign Quakers. Any person bringing Quaker books was fined £5. Entertainment or concealment of a Quaker was punishable by a fine of twenty shillings for every hour's entertainment or concealment. Any person defending the opinions of the Quakers should be fined for the first offence, £2; for the second offence, £4; and for the third offence, he should be imprisoned until it was convenient to send him out of the colony. "Lastly," whoso reviled magistrates or ministers, "as it is usual with Quakers," should be whipped or pay the sum of £5.

Under this comprehensive law a number of Quakers, some foreigners and others, who had "turned Quakers," were prosecuted, whipped, imprisoned, and banished. But they were not many. Nor did many of the sect come into the colony; we may suppose, because of the greater attractions of New York and Boston, in the way of persecution.

Soon after this experience with the Quakers, began the movement which resulted in the loss of individual colonial existence, when New Haven was absorbed by Connecticut. As in Massachusetts, so in New Haven, there had grown a large party dissatisfied with the restriction of the franchise. A considerable number of the men were not members of the Church, and consequently were not allowed to vote, though taxed for purposes of both Church and State. They could not fail to contrast this exclusion from citizenship with the larger liberty of the neighboring colony, where personal character and taxable capacity were the conditions for the suffrage. The stricter element in New Haven considered the government of Connecticut a "Christless rule," but were outnumbered by the party for union, which was composed not only of the non-members of the Church, but also of many

Suffrage.

Discontent.

among those who were Church-members of a more liberal mind.

To Connecticut the annexing of the little colony of New Haven was a very desirable thing, as giving a natural boundary and adding to the colony's population and resources. Thus, when Governor Winthrop applied to the king for a charter, the southern limit sought was the line of the sound from New Amsterdam to Rhode Island. We do not find that any formal resistance by New Haven to the project was made in London. " Many of the people were very willing for the junction. Mr. Davenport preached to them from Judges xxi. 3 (O Lord God of Israel, why is this come to pass in Israel, that there should be to-day one tribe lacking in Israel ?); and that religion might better adopt the controversie, they fasted the people on the known presbyterian plan." [1] But this opposition did not reach to strenuous protest to the king.

Union with Connecticut.

Nor is it probable that, had such been made, it could have had any influence on the result. For the king had a grudge against New Haven, the one of the colonies which had given a secure refuge to the regicides, Goffe and Whalley. Hardly were the festivities of the Restoration over, when Charles set himself to revenge his father's death. The body of Cromwell was exhumed from Westminster Abbey,[2] and those of the dead judges Bradshaw and Ireton from their places of burial, that their heads might be set on Westminster Hall. The living judges fled, and of them the two named came to America, finding in New Haven shelter and concealment from all the search parties sent out by the king. This was remembered against the colony. Indeed, at the very moment of Winthrop's application New Haven was shielding the fugitives, and it is not hard to imagine the king's satisfaction in extinguishing the independence of the colony.[3]

Regicides.

[1] *Connecticut Historical Society*, III, 328 ; Roger Wolcott, *Memorial of Connecticut.*

[2] Stanley, *Westminster Abbey*, I, 223.   [3] Palfrey, II, 43.

On the union with Connecticut — a union accomplished, not by any compromise or agreement of the colonies, but by the king's order — all the peculiarities of New Haven ceased to be. Its theocracy fell, the laws and authority of Connecticut took the place of its own, and religious profession no longer obtained as the condition of citizenship. Some there were who could not content themselves to remain under so changed circumstances. Davenport removed to Boston and succeeded Norton in the First Church.[1] Rev. A. Pierson with his people, who had come from Southold and settled at Branford, took themselves to New Jersey and made on the Passaic a new settlement, which they called New Ark. Their intent was to raise again the theocratic standard, " to restrict all political power to Church members," and so once more illustrate what they considered the only correct principle of a pure government.[2] But this secession was but small, and the most of the New Haven people easily reconciled themselves to being lost in the Church and Commonwealth of Connecticut.

V. *New Hampshire*

The first settlers of New Hampshire were exiles for conscience' sake. As with Rhode Island and Connecticut, the colony owed its beginning to the religious intolerance of the Bay Puritans. John Wheelwright, banished from Massachusetts, repaired with a number of friends to the banks of the Piscataqua, and before the end of 1638 the exiles were joined by a sufficient number to make necessary the institu-
Foundation. tion of the forms of government.[3] They had bestowed themselves in the three settlements of Exeter, Hampton, and Dover, and in 1639 associated themselves in an " *Agreement* " for mutual government and support. The preamble to this

[1] Felt, II, 421.

[2] *New Haven Historical Papers*, I, 5.

[3] Barstow, *History of New Hampshire*, 40–53 ; *New Hampshire Historical Society*, I, 321.

instrument, after asserting the subjection of the plantations to the king, proceeded: " We, his loyal subjects and brethren of the Church in Exeter, . . . considering the holy will of God and our own necessity, that we should not live without wholesome laws and civil government . . . do, in the name of Christ and in the sight of God, combine ourselves together to erect and set up among us such government as shall be, to our best discerning, agreeable to the will of God, . . . binding ourselves solemnly by the grace and help of Christ, and in His name and fear, to submit ourselves to such godly and Christian laws as are established in the realm of England to our best knowledge, and to all other such lawes which shall, upon good grounds, be made and enacted among us according to God, that we may live quietly and peaceably together in all godliness and honesty."

The religious foundation of the new commonwealth was thus very positively declared, though the " Christian Lawes " in the agreement did not copy the strict exclusiveness of Massachusetts. With a breadth of view not surprising in men who had gone through their experience, the settlers admitted the principle that civic privileges should not depend **Franchise.** on the profession of religious faith, and that every respectable man among them should possess the franchise.

The breadth, however, had limitations. It is not correct to say that the founders intended " to reject *in toto* all that regarded the hierarchy and Church establishment." [1] While there was no attempt to institute any hierarchical scrutiny and oppression, and no declaration of a theocratical design, yet the legislation for the Church and the system of tithes, **Religious establishment.** assessed and collected under the civil law, belong to the idea of a religious establishment.

A necessitous concern at the beginning of any new settlement, not only on the part of the people but on that of the civil authorities, was a provision for the support of the Church: and in old grants of townships it was the usual

[1] *New Hampshire Historical Society*, **VI**, 173 ; *Address of Judson Smith.*

custom "to reserve one share, equal to that of any other grantee, for the first settled minister, as his own right; beside a parsonage lot."[1]   To the end of the colonial period, and beyond it, the government exercised authority in regard to the Church, both as to its support and as to the inroads of sects differing from the established order.   There was never, with two exceptions, — though one of these, as the act of the royal governor, can hardly be cited against the colony, — any attempt at persecution, but at the same time New Hampshire was as fully tenacious of the legal forms of civil authority in religious matters as any other colony, not according in terms of law full liberty to all Christian sects until 1819.   What is still more remarkable, New Hampshire alone, among all the states of the American Union, retains to this day in its constitution the old distinctions of Protestant and Christian, as against Romanist, Jew, and infidel, out of which in former days so many oppressions arose.

A short trial of the infant government in the new settle-
Union with Massachusetts. ment disclosed the necessity of union with Massachusetts. As yet New Hampshire was too feeble to stand alone, and the union was formed by mutual agreement in 1641.   The agreement contained "an extraordinary concession" by Massachusetts, that the franchise in New Hampshire should not be limited to Church membership.   So notable a departure from the Bay policy can only be accounted for by a desire to extend colonial boundaries.[2]

From the time of the union until 1679 deputies from the New Hampshire towns were annually elected to the general court of Massachusetts, and, with the one exception noted, the laws of the latter colony obtained in both.   By reason of this union the annals of New Hampshire were stained with the single record of persecution which can be charged against

---

[1] Belknap, *History of New Hampshire*, III, 324.

[2] One immediate result of this union was the removal of Wheelwright, who, not considering himself safe in the jurisdiction of Massachusetts, withdrew to Maine and began the settlement of Wells.

the colony. This was the shameful treatment of three Quaker women in 1659.[1] Under the furious law of Massachusetts the women, Anna Colman, Mary Tompkins, and Alice Ambrose, were condemned to be " whipped from town to town out of the province." The process was begun at Dover, whence the victims were driven under the lash, " through dirt and snow half-a-leg deep," to Hampton and thence to Salisbury. There Walter Barefoot, a magistrate, moved by shame and pity, persuaded the constable to commit the prisoners to him, when he at once released them. As for the women, they returned to Dover and do not seem to have been again molested.[2]

Meanwhile the colony increased. Other towns were settled, chief among which was Portsmouth. Here the first minister was Joshua Moody, destined to persecution and celebrity. By an ordinance of the town, " to encourage him, those who slept, or took tobacco on the Lord's day during service, were doomed to the cage." [3]

In 1679 the union with Massachusetts was dissolved by royal order, partly because of the growth of New Hampshire, but more because of the king's desire to cripple and annoy the Bay colony. New Hampshire was made a distinct province under the royal charter or " Commission." The establishment of the separate government was under the same commissioners, whose errand brought so much disturbance to other New England colonies. In New Hampshire their offices were welcomed by the people, who had desired independence on the Bay. For the new province the instructions to the commissioners in regard to religious matters were identical with those given for the other colonies, viz.: " We

Union dissolved.

---

[1] Barstow, *History of New Hampshire*, p. 73 ; McClintock, *History of New Hampshire*, p. 59 ; *New Hampshire Provincial Papers*, I, 226–243.

[2] Barefoot was afterward of the council of Governor Cranfield, consenting to his unlawful and oppressive measures, and, according to one of the historians, this release of the Quakers was the only worthy public action recorded to his credit !

[3] McClintock, *History of New Hampshire*, p. 71.

do hereby require and command that liberty of conscience shall be allowed unto all protestants; and that such especially, as shall be conformable to the rites of the Church of England, shall be particularly countenanced and encouraged."[1]

The first provincial assembly, in 1680, settled the right of the franchise by a law that "all Englishmen, being Protestants, settled Inhabitants and freeholders, of the age of twenty four years, not viceous in life, but honest, and such as have £20 Ratable estate," should be admitted freemen of the commonwealth. Thus was reënacted the severance of civil and religious privileges. The only religious qualification for a freeman was Protestantism — an exceedingly illiberal restriction in our day, but in 1680 meaning considerable breadth. It is well to note also that the restrictive word "Protestant" wrought no individual wrong, and acted simply as a deterrent of any Romanist immigration. For a hundred years no member of the Church of Rome furnished occasion to question the disposition of New Hampshire. But it is no injustice to suppose that in 1680 men of that faith might have been desired to leave the province. Its citizens shared with their brethren elsewhere a horror of Romanism, and the proclamation for a fast-day in 1681 called upon the people to implore "the divine favor," as for divers blessings, so "against the Popish party throughout the world."[2]

The mind of the new government on the question of Church support found early illustration. It appears that some of the people were disposed to resent the interference of the magistrate with religious affairs, and in 1681 the constable at Dover reported to the council that many had refused to pay rates for the minister, on the ground that the king's commission guaranteed liberty of conscience, and desired directions as to his duty in the case. The answer to this

Freemen.

Romanists.

Church support.

[1] *New Hampshire Provincial Papers,* I, 372–396.
[2] *Provincial Papers,* I, 429.

inquiry was given by a law of the next year, to the effect that the town officers should assess the minister's support on all the taxpayers of the town, and should collect all arrearages by legal process. Refusal to pay was made punishable by imprisonment, until the rates were paid or good security were given.[1]

By a law of 1680, "contempt of God's word or of the ministers" was made punishable by fine or imprisonment; and in 1681 Robert Briney, a servant or apprentice, for absence from Church services, was sentenced to nine stripes, with suspension of sentence on future good behavior.[2]

In 1682 Governor Cranfield arrived with royal instructions, which repeated the language of the charter in regard to religious matters, the scope of which he endeavored to extend far beyond its legitimate construction. Cranfield is described as a most unworthy character — "arbitrary, needy, and rapacious. He made no secret of his object . . . of bettering his condition." A letter of William Vaughan — than whom there was no better man in the colony, and who himself fell under the displeasure of Cranfield for resisting his oppressive schemes — says of him, "He came for money, and money he will get."[3]

Governor Cranfield.

Our only concern with the governor is his absurd and oppressive attempt to force the Church of England on the colony as an establishment. This was purely arbitrary, and without any authorization from the English government, which had never gone beyond the command, that, while allowing "liberty of conscience to all Protestants," such as were of the Church of England should be "particularly countenanced and encouraged." In his orders the governor appealed to "his Majesty's letters sent the Massachusetts," as though these contained an ordinance for establishment. He must have presumed on the supposed ignorance of the

---

[1] *Provincial Papers*, I, 400, 430, 447.

[2] *New Hampshire Historical Society Publication*, VIII, 15, 66.

[3] Barstow, *New Hampshire*, p. 94; *Provincial Papers*, I, 526.

New Hampshire clergy, for these letters to the Bay contained no prescriptions beyond those already noted.[1]

With the exceptions of Andros, Fletcher, and Cornbury in New York, no other royal governor ventured such lengths in the assertion of ecclesiastical power. By an official order Cranfield undertook to change the character of the colonial Churches and assert the supremacy of the Church of England. This order was issued in December of 1683, and required all ministers of the province, after the first of January following, to admit to the Lord's Supper all persons of suitable age and not vicious, to admit the children of such persons to baptism, and, if any one should desire the sacraments according to the rites of the Church of England, to use those rites for the administration. If any minister should refuse to obey this order, he was to be deprived of his salary, and his people were to be freed from the payment of tithes.

Order for English Church.

The ministers paid no attention to this order, whereupon the irate governor summoned "all the ministers in New Hampshire to attend, the Monday following, to give their reasons why they did not administer the sacrament according to his Majesty's letters to the Massachusetts and the statutes (English) in that case." The result of this proposed hearing, if it ever took place, is not recorded, but the governor determined to bring matters to a head in the most summary fashion and selected Moody of Portsmouth, the most prominent of the clergy, as the object of his special wrath.

Moody.

To Moody he issued a special command, that on the next Lord's day he read in his meeting-house the order for conformity. To this command Moody paid no more attention than to the original order, and conducted his service as before. Then, under date of January 15, 168¾, it is recorded that "James Sherlock gives Moody notice in writing, that Cranfield, Barefoot, Chamberlain, and Hincks would receive

[1] *New Hampshire Historical Society*, VIII, 163–237 ; McClintock, *New Hampshire*, p. 104 ; Barstow, *New Hampshire*, pp. 99, 100 ; *Provincial Papers*, I, 482–520.

the sacrament from his hands, according to the liturgy of the Church of England, the next Sunday."

This precise demand was met by Moody with a distinct refusal to obey, whereupon an immediate order was issued for his arrest, "for administering the sacrament contrary to the laws of England, and refusing to administer according to the rites of the Church of England." The case was tried before Barefoot, as justice, and Moody pleaded in his own defence, showing that the laws of England forbade the use of the rites of the Church of England to those not ordained in that Church, and that he could not use the English liturgy without violating the law, and "besides, these statutes were not made for these places, the known end of their removal hither being that they might enjoy liberty in these foreign plantations, and our commission granting liberty of conscience."

The plea was just, but the court, controlled by the governor, set it aside and committed Moody to prison, where he was detained for three months. One account states that he was not released until he promised to leave the province. If this is correct, then it was during the term of imprisonment that occasion was given for the following curious record: "Mr. Joshua Moody, being to take a journey out of the Province, was forced to give a recognizance of £200 to return in three weeks, if alive and well."[1] Not long after this experience Moody left Portsmouth and settled in Boston, where he made himself conspicuous by opposing the witchcraft persecution, comforting the afflicted, and helping some to escape, to the great wrath of Cotton Mather.[2]

So ended the great persecution in New Hampshire, though it would appear that other ministers were subjected to annoyances, for they joined in complaint against Cranfield, that "the Ministers, contrary to his *Majesty's commission*, which grants liberty of conscience to *all Protestants*, have

[1] *New Hampshire Historical Society*, VIII, 237.
[2] Barstow, p. 100.

their dues withheld from them, even those due before Mr. Cranfield came, and are threatened with 6 mo.ˢ *imprisonment* for not administering the sacrament according to the liturgy of the Chh. of England." This and other complaints against Cranfield's course had effect in England. The governor was recalled, and the New Hampshire Churches suffered from no more attempts to convert them to Episcopacy.

In the subsequent years various enactments confirmed the Church, under the old Congregational order, as a *town* establishment.[1] The laws of 1692, 1702, 1714 ordained that, the *freeholders* in each town should choose the minister for the town Church and agree with him for salary, that the selectmen should assess this salary upon the town, and the constable should collect it: "Provided, that this act do not at all interfere with their Majesties' grace and favor in allowing their Subjects liberty of conscience: nor shall any person, under pretence of being of a different persuasion, be excused from paying towards the support of the settled Minister or Ministers of the Towne, but only such as are conscientiously so and constantly attend the publick worship of God on the Lord's day according to their own persuasion." The toleration in this act was more complete than that of the Five-Mile Act of Massachusetts and the similar law in Connecticut. By these statutes the constable collected rates from all, applying those from dissenters to the support of their own ministers, thus making all the Churches a concern of the state. In New Hampshire the law made no provision for the payment of any rates by dissenters, nor concerned itself with the support of dissenting ministers. Those who were excused from the town rates, were at liberty to arrange for and collect the salary of their minister as pleased themselves. But exemption was not so easily obtained in New Hampshire. A dissenter claiming it was compelled to produce proof of conscientious dissent, of regular attendance on

marginal note: Town establishment.

[1] *Provincial Papers*, III, 189; IV, 226, 391, 414; *Johns Hopkins Studies*, X, 89.

public worship, and of payment for its support, while "at every point his evidence was contested by the State."

Beyond this general arrangement of system there was not much legislation on Church matters. Occasionally — departing from the town system — the legislature organized a Church, or divided a parish. In 1724 a bill attempted amendment as to the method of choosing ministers, the intent of which was to give the initiative to the Church itself. The Church was first to choose, and their choice to be submitted to the town. If the majority of freeholders accepted this nominee, he was to be minister. In case of disagreement, the matter must be "Decided by the next three or five adjacent Churches." The bill was deferred to the next session and never became a law, so that its only value here is as an indication of growing sentiment toward the autonomy of the Church.

In 1725 the legislature granted relief in certain matters to the people of Sandy Beach, appending to the grant the condition, "that they are obliged to Maintain an able Orthodox Minister of the Gospell at their own Charges."

The colonial action in regard to *tests* varied.[1] Previously Tests. to 1696 the oath required was simply one of allegiance and fidelity, but in that year the "horrid and detestable conspiracy" against William and Mary moved the legislature to pass a law, requiring "*all male persons* to take the oath appointed by Act of Parliament." This act was the toleration act of 1689, which imposed, in addition to the oath of allegiance and supremacy, a "Declaration" against the pope and all peculiar doctrines of the Roman Church. This requirement was simply the demand of transient excitement, and it does not appear that the oath continued to be exacted, even from office-holders. The legislature of 1727 formulated an oath for office-holders, which was very precise in its loyalty to the House of Hanover and its abjuration of the Stuarts, but made no declaration of faith or against popery. Again in 1752, in

[1] *Provincial Papers*, III, 201; V, 128; *New Hampshire Historical Society*, V, 93.

the time of the French war, when there was a new spasm of fear of popery widespread in the colonies, the legislature itself took " the Oaths and Declaration appointed by Act of Parliament," but did not impose them on the people at large or on other office-holders.

One other item remains, not of legislation, but of action illustrating the prevalent thought that government should concern itself with religious matters.[1] In 1725 the Rev. Hugh Adams, having composed a religious treatise, sent the manuscript to the governor, with the request that the legislature take order for its publication. That body, to whom the governor sent the application, finding that the treatise was " on controversial points of Divinity," voted, that " the Gospell Ministers of this Province take the manuscript into consideration and report, that the Publication thereof may be countenanced or discouraged, and the said manuscript be disposed of as may be most for the Glory of God." The report of the ministers represented that the work was full of errors of doctrine and was " unworthy of the least countenance "; whereupon the legislature thanked the ministers, and ordered that " the manuscript be lodged in the Secretary's office, and no one shall have a copy ! " Thus the lawmakers were conservative and dreaded the introduction of heresy. One can regret the nature of the treatise and report, for the mere desire of seeing what the action would have been on a favorable verdict from the examining ministers. A religious treatise published by a legislature would have been something altogether unique.

Our New Hampshire chapter is thus necessarily short. Religious matters in the province knew little change. The people were mostly of one faith, while the spirit of intolerance was never a popular sentiment among them. With their Church established as a town institution they went into the revolutionary period; and what changes were subsequently made will be noted in the chapter on Final Settlements.

[1] *Provincial Papers*, IV, 172, 192, 412.

VI

CHANGING ESTABLISHMENTS

THE colonies of New York, Maryland, New Jersey, and Georgia form a group by themselves, by reason of the fact that their history is marked by change in the relation of the colonial government to the Church. In all of them there occurred during the colonial period a distinct modification of the ecclesiastical attitude. New York and New Jersey, begun under Dutch auspices and with ecclesiastical subjection to the Reformed Church of Holland, were by the English conquest brought into a peculiar ecclesiastical struggle. Not only was their ancestral Church dislodged from its position, but a prolonged, though unsuccessful, effort of the English government to force upon them an alien establishment was the cause of much trouble and bitterness. Maryland began with almost complete freedom, under a Roman Catholic palatine, but through Puritan uncharitableness and political intrigue was forced into intolerance, and finally subjected to an Anglican establishment. Georgia also was planted with the allowance of liberty, but, on the annulling of its charter by the crown, this liberty gave place to the royal establishment of the Church of England. The history of colonial Georgia is, however, so short, and its beginnings were so near to the time of the Revolution, with the crucial questions of liberty already decided, that its religious story is without much importance in the development of our present theme.

I. *New York*

The story of New York, in relation to the Church and to religious liberty, has some peculiar features without likeness

301

in other colonies, except New Jersey. Throughout the colonial period there either was, or was supposed to be, an established Church, but the Church of early institution was other than the one which the English conquest of New Amsterdam attempted to introduce. In regard to the later establishment there is also the curious fact that, while the English authorities always acted on the supposition that the Church established in New York by the act of 1693 was the Church of England, it yet was not such and legally had no organic relation to the Anglican establishment.

Another notable thing is, that the bounds of this latter establishment were restricted to four counties by the terms of the act, all the rest of the colony being free from the imposition of a State-Church.

Yet one more general feature is in the vacillating conduct of the colonial authorities in regard to religious and ecclesiastical affairs; for the most part easy and tolerant of dissent, and occasionally breaking out in stern language of repression or harsh measures of persecution. There was no set purpose, as in Massachusetts and Virginia, to force one form of worship on the people, a purpose steadily adhered to until relaxation was compelled by the strong growth of dissent. Whether the utmost possible laxity, or a bigoted narrowness, should prevail in the governmental policy depended entirely on the changing caprice, or principle, of governors.

To begin with, when the Dutch West India company set out, under the broad and almost imperial powers of their charter from the states general of Holland, to found their colony on the Hudson, unlike other colonial founders, they made no professions of religious motives. Undoubtedly, the religious troubles in Europe had large influence in peopling the colony. Germany sent Lutherans out of the turmoils of the Thirty Years' War; France sent many of her Huguenot refugees; out of Scotland and intolerant Massachusetts came the disciples of Presbytery; while the Dutch founders brought with them the ordinances of discipline of

Settlement.

the Reformed Church of Holland. The latter were hastened also in their schemes of colonization by the sharp, political antagonisms in the Netherlands growing out of the Arminian debate. Thus it may be truly said that, "the settlement of Manhattan grew directly out of the great continental struggles of Protestantism."[1]

Yet the confessed motive of the undertaking was neither for liberty of conscience nor for the propagation of the gospel among the heathen. So far as the states general were concerned, the motive was political, to give to Holland place and power among the colonizing nations of Europe ; while the West India company occupied its mind with dreams of commercial gain.

At the same time, the thought of, and provision for, religion were not absent from the company's plans. That some provision should be made by government for religious services in the settlement was a necessity of the time. It was taken for granted, both that such arrangement should be made, and that the religious affairs should be under the control of the company. Care for religion.

The first Dutch minister, Jonas Michaelius, was sent out by the company in 1628, for whose support the company made itself responsible. He "built a Church" and formed an organization, with Peter Minuit, the first Dutch governor, as one of its two elders. So far as is reported, the first formal expression of the company's policy in regard to religious matters was made in 1638,[2] in the "Articles for Colonization." These articles were drawn with the aim of attracting emigrants, and were submitted for approval to the states general. The two sections which touch upon religion are as follows : —

" 2. Religion shall be taught and preached there, according to the Confessions and formularies of Union here pub-

[1] Bancroft, *History of the United States*, II, 277.
[2] *Colonial History of New York*, I, 110.

Liberality
of West
India
company.

licly accepted . . . without, however, it being inferred that any person shall be hereby in any wise
constrained or aggrieved in his conscience.

" 8. Each house holder and inhabitant shall bear such tax
and public charge as shall hereafter be considered
proper for the maintenance of clergymen, comforters of the sick, &c."

The intent of a Church establishment, with a rate assessed by
the civil law on every inhabitant, is thus clearly expressed while
there is marked liberality in the allowance of dissent.

Because of this latter feature, it would appear, the articles
failed of approval by the states general; and, two years after,
the direction about the Church was modified to the terms of
positive and exclusive establishment of the national Church
of Holland. The article reads: " No other Religion shall

Reformed
Church
established.

be publicly admitted in New Netherland except the Reformed,
as it is at present preached and practiced by public authority
in the United Netherlands: and for this purpose the Company shall provide and maintain good and suitable preachers,
school-masters, and comforters of the sick." [1] Under this
restricted rule the ecclesiastical affairs of the colony were
ostensibly administered to the end of the Dutch possession,
but showed no indications of harshness until the fiery Stuyvesant came to the governorship. The company assumed the
expense of Church-building and maintenance of the ministry,[2]
the choice and commissioning of whom it claimed as its prerogative — a genuine right of presentation.

It is not to be supposed, however, that the company's out-
lay for these purposes was large. In the whole period of the
Dutch rule not more than ten ministers were sent over, and
there appeared early tokens of desire to shift the burden
of maintenance upon the colonists. This desire, indeed, was

---

[1] *Colonial History of New York*, I, 119.
[2] *Ibid.*, I, 155; XIV, 69, 84.

expressed in the first *articles*, and was put into the agreement of 1629[1] with the "Patroons."

This agreement, which instituted a favored class of men   Patroons. unlike any found in other colonies, conferred upon any, who "within four years would plant a colony of fifty souls," a right to purchase immense tracts of land and to exercise thereon the power of lords of the manor.[2] The agreement recited that, " the Patroons and colonists shall in particular and in the speediest manner endeavor to find out ways and means whereby they may support a minister and school-master, that the service of God and zeal for religion may not grow cool and be neglected among them; and that they do, for the first, procure a comforter for the sick there."

With this desire to get rid of the expense of the establishment, the company was yet unwilling to part with its right of presentation; and on that subject it came promptly into collision with its first patroon upon the Hudson, Kiliaen van Rensselaer. This powerful and rich member of the company had by purchase from the Indians and by patents obtained an enormous estate, extending twenty-four miles on both sides of the Hudson, above and below Fort Orange (Albany), and forty-eight miles east and west. To such a manorial lord as this it seemed but fitting that the choice of a minister in his domain should vest in himself.[3] He therefore agreed with and appointed John Megapolensis as the minister at Fort Orange. To this appointment the company objected strenuously, claiming that the directors alone could make or approve such appointments. The strife between the two parties was continued for several months, and was finally composed by a compromise, which left a doubtful victory to the company, that Van Rensselaer should consent to " the directors approving the appointment, under protest, saving his rights as Patroon."

[1] *Colonial History of New York*, I, 405; O'Callaghan, *New Netherland*, I, 119.

[2] Bancroft, *United States*, II, 281.   [3] O'Callaghan, I, 328.

Sundry other instances of action by the company and by the civil authorities at New Amsterdam may further illustrate their intentional administration of a Church establishment. In 1638 Domine Bogardus, evidently regarding himself as a servant of the company, requested permission to visit Holland, which request the governor and council refused, explaining, "We have deemed it necessary to retain the Minister here, so that the Church of God may increase more and more, day by day." [1]

A similar application was made to the council by Megapolensis in 1649, and refused, on the ground that, "the extreme need of the Church imperatively demands that one minister at least remain in this province, . . . were it only for administering Baptism to the children." [2] The Domine had already been dismissed from Rensselaerwyck and had come to New Amsterdam, on his way to Holland. The council not only refused permission to sail, but formally called him to the Church of New Amsterdam, recently left vacant by the departure of Domine Bogardus. The council reported their

Megapolensis.

determination to retain Megapolensis, "*blanda vi et quasi nolens volens.* Such we resolve to be most necessary for the honor of God, the service of his Church, and the salvation of the people." This action of the governor (Stuyvesant) and council was approved by the directors in Holland, who wrote to Stuyvesant, [3] that they have paid to the Domine's wife 600 florins as six months' salary; that they are taking steps to have published at their expense a religious treatise by Megapolensis; and that they have engaged the Rev. Samuel Drisius, "a very pious man and possessed of great gifts, able to preach in English, Dutch, and French," to go out as an assistant. The directors fixed the salary for Drisius at 100 florins per month and 250 florins annually for subsistence.

Another record — or set of records — exhibits the governor and council attempting to exercise ecclesiastical discipline. [4]

Bogardus.

The subject of it was the same Domine Bogardus, whose

[1] *Colonial History of New York*, XIV, 10.   [2] *Ibid.*, XIV, 116.
[3] *Ibid.*, XIV, 119, 123, 134, 173.   [4] *Ibid.*, XIV, 59, 69, 72, 84.

spiritual services were in 1638 too valuable to lose. Seven years after that date, either the Domine had changed his conduct or the council had altered their opinion of him, for in 1645 Governor Kieft sent to him from the council a formal admonition in writing, " which he would not receive or open, and the paper was returned by the court messenger." Thereupon Bogardus was summoned to answer before the governor and council on various charges of improper and scandalous conduct "unbecoming a Minister." The summons also upbraids him for "your disposition towards the Company, by whom you are paid." To this summons Bogardus replied in writing, refusing to appear, and "abusing them from th~ chair of truth." The council then offered to leave the matter to the decision of Domines Megapolensis and Doughty; but this also Bogardus refused, demanding that the case be deferred until the arrival of the new governor (Stuyvesant), then daily expected.

When Stuyvesant arrived he decided to send the stubborn Stuyvesant. minister home to Holland, together with Kieft, whose administration of civil affairs had been one continued disgrace. The two sailed in the ill-fated *Princess*, which was lost at sea. The directors, in notifying Stuyvesant of the loss, wrote of Bogardus : — "'When the shepherd errs, the sheep go astray,' fitly applies to his case. He with others, has been relieved from rendering his account."

In the same period with these records are others showing the liberal disposition of the authorities at New Amsterdam. Toleration. In 1642 the Rev. F. Doughty, whose expulsion from the Church at Taunton has been narrated in the chapter on Plymouth, came with Richard Smith and others to Long Island, and the company received from the council permission to settle with their minister. It was ordained that "They shall enjoy the free exercise of religion." [1]

Patents were issued in 1642, 1644, and 1645 to different parties of "Englishmen," at New Town, Flushing, and the

[1] O'Callaghan, I, 257 ; *Laws of New Netherland*, p. 27.

"Great Plaines on Long Island," which ordained "the use and exercise of the reformed Religion, which they profess, with the Ecclesiastical Discipline thereunto belonging."[1] The patent to the Flushing settlers specified that they were "to have and Enjoy the Liberty of Conscience according to the Custom and Manner of Holland, without molestation or disturbance from any Magistrate or Magistrates, or any other Ecclesiastical Minister that may pretend Jurisdiccōn over them." In these regulations a full toleration of orderly dissent was undoubtedly intended. So much the "Custom and Manner of Holland" involved, while the reference to the "Reformed Religion which they professe" clearly carries the broad construction of the word "Reformed."

Besides these admissions, other parties were welcomed to the Dutch Colony. Throgmorton and a number of friends, who had left Massachusetts on account of the prosecution of Roger Williams, settled at West Chester with the permission of the council. Sir Henry and Lady Deborah Moody, "who had become imbued with the erroneous doctrine that infant baptism was a sinful ordinance," were, 1645, with Ensign George Baxter and Sergeant James Hubbard permitted by a formal vote of the council to settle at Gravesend, Long Island.[2] The celebrated Ann Hutchinson also found a free asylum among the Dutch, taking up her abode with her younger children in the upper part of Manhattan Island. Not long afterward they all perished in the massacre by the Indians. That the directors approved of such admissions is stated in their letter to Stuyvesant, that they had no objection to Englishmen settling in New Netherland "in reasonable numbers."[3]

Ann Hutchinson.

In 1646 Peter Stuyvesant began his tempestuous reign at

[1] *Laws of New Netherland*, pp. 43, 48 ; *Colonial History of New York*, XIV, 38.

[2] O'Callaghan, I, 258 ; Felt, *Ecclesiastical History of New England*, I, 486; *Laws of New Netherland*, p. 53.

[3] *Colonial History of New York*, XIV, 76.

New Amsterdam. Honest and faithful, never did a man strive more earnestly than he to serve his masters and bring order out of chaos. With a devoted patriotism, never did a man drink a bitterer cup than he when he surrendered to the British. At the same time, the one-legged governor qualified these virtues by narrowness of mind, obstinacy, and a fiery temper. The beginning of his administration was with gentleness and with many indications of his care for the Church, several incidents of which are noted in illustration of the acknowledged dependence of religious affairs on governmental action.

In 1646 the sheriff and others in the new settlement at Flushing applied to the governor and council to "favor them with a pious, learned, and reformed minister, and then to order that each inhabitant shall contribute to such godly work according to his ability."[1] To this the council promised such action "as shall be found to promote peace, union, and tranquillity both in ecclesiastical and civil affairs." The matter having been reported to the company, a reply assured that, "We shall look out for a man fit to attend the Church there." This search does not seem to have been immediately successful, or it may be that a vacancy had occurred, for in 1654 the directors of the company alluded to the matter again, saying: "We have been pleased to see the zeal of several of our inhabitants of a new village on Long Island for the Reformed religion, and, that it may not cool, we have resolved to contribute 600 fl. yearly, and are looking about here for a fit and pious teacher or minister."[2]

In the letter of Stuyvesant, telling of the above request, he also suggested to the directors that Domine Megapolensis should be transferred from Fort Orange to the Church in New Amsterdam, to which they answered with a doubt whether the patroons would consent, and whether the Domine could not be as useful at Rensselaerwyck as elsewhere. Then, in striking contrast with a frequent arbitrariness in

[1] *Colonial History of New York*, XIV, 82, 84.   [2] *Ibid.*, XIV, 252.

such matters, they remarked: "It must also be considered that this plan cannot be well carried out without the consent of the colonists."

Interest in the religious affairs of the colony finds expression in the states general in Holland, which in 1650 resolved that, "New Netherland being now provided with only one clergyman, orders shall be given forthwith for the calling and support of at least three more." [1]

Ministerial support. The matter of support of ministers was the subject of much action both in Holland and New Amsterdam. In 1654 the company wrote to Stuyvesant that, Domine Drisius complained "that he did not get his salary," and rebuked the governor for his carelessness in not securing the payment of the minister.[2] Thereupon the council at New Amsterdam adopted a rule, ordering the *Schepens* (associate justices) in each town to provide for the minister's salary. To this the burgomasters and schepens replied with an agreement to "pay one preacher, one precentor, who is to be schoolmaster, and one beadle." This official array they styled "the ecclesiastical establishment."

There seems to have been some failure on the part of the town officers to fulfil this agreement, as, later in the same year, the governor and council sent the following remarkable notice to them. It asserts that the matter of "Tavern Excise" had been put into the hands of the burgomasters and schepens, "on the promise and under the condition that they would induce, or compel, the *proprietors* to provide means for the support of the preachers." They having failed, the council will now "let the said Excise to the highest bidder"; and the notice concludes: "By these means the Burgomasters and Schepens will be excused and delivered from carrying out their agreement to support one clergyman, one schoolmaster, and one beadle; the intentions and orders of the Lords Directors will be executed; the *jus patronatus* will

---

[1] O'Callaghan, *New Netherland*, II, 134.
[2] *Colonial History of New York*, XIV, 252, 268, 289, 293.

be preserved, and both the clergymen paid and placed above want." No record was made of the success of this ingenious scheme to support the gospel from the proceeds of the liquor business, and to maintain the rights of an established Church.

Sundry records illustrate the attention of the council to the details of the Church, to an extent that deprived ministers and Churches of much self-determining power. A few of such, taken almost at random, are of interest.[1] Thus, in 1654, the council ordered that "Dom. Polhemus should continue at Midwout, and the people have liberty to collect money for building a Church." The people must have met with success in their collection, but they were not to be allowed to spend the funds at their own discretion, for at a subsequent meeting of the council a committee from its own members was appointed to superintend the building of the Church. *Interference.*

To a petition from Brooklyn asking that the minister at Midwout be allowed to preach alternately in Brooklyn, the gracious answer was returned: "The Director General and Council of New Netherland have no objection against Do Johannes Polhemius officiating alternately at both places, wind and weather permitting."[2]

This Domine Polhemus had troubles which he brought to the council.[3] In 1656 he complained that his "house was not fit to live in," and also asked the council to pay him 100 florins on salary account. This the council did, but took no action about his house. Two years afterward, the council paid all arrears of his salary, and ordered the arrest of three men of Brooklyn for refusing to pay 6 guilders each toward the minister's support. One of the three was a Frenchman and the others were Englishmen. The first pleaded that he was a Catholic, and the others that they did not understand Dutch; but each was compelled to pay a fine of 12

[1] *Colonial History of New York*, XIV, 295, 310.
[2] *Ibid.*, p. 338.   [3] *Ibid.*, pp. 370, 377, 411, 414.

guilders.[1]   The Domine's wrongs found their way into the
chambers of the company at Amsterdam, on complaint of
three Holland ministers, and payment was ordered by the
directors.[2]   About the same time the complaint came to the
council that "some Inhabitants of Hempstead refused to
pay" toward the minister's support, and the magistrates of
the town were authorized to "constrain and punish as they
in equity shall think meet."[3]

Toward the middle of Stuyvesant's term there appear
tokens of a more strenuous rule, and determination to uphold
the established Church against all comers.   In 1651 the
Council adopted an ordinance, declaring that the judges must
be "promoters and professors of the Reformed Religion, as it
is at present taught in the Churches of New Netherland, in
conformity to the Word of God and the order of the Synod
of Dordrecht."[4]

The governor was jealous for his own authority also, and,
while watchful that the Churches were faithful in religious
duty, would permit no outbreaking of the clergy into civil
affairs.   Domine Backerus had offended him by some such
manifestations, whereon the peppery Stuyvesant went in
person to the Domine's house and left a written notice, *forbidding* him "to read, or have read, in Church any writing,
petition, or proposal, having relation to the municipal or
general government, whether generally or in particular, before such writing shall be signed by the Director himself, or
the Secretary, by order of Director and Council.   But this is
not to apply to ecclesiastical affairs."[5]   The precise nature of
the minister's offence is not recorded, but the governor's
rebuff seems to have crushed him, for presently he applied
for permission to return to Holland, which was at once

---

[1] O'Callaghan, II, 353.
[2] *Colonial History of New York*, II, 72.
[3] *Ibid.*, XIV, 513.
[4] *Laws of New Netherland*, p. 395.
[5] *Colonial History of New York*, XIV, 114, 115.

granted by the council. Such was the issue of the first attempt in New York to take politics into the pulpit.

Stuyvesant was also of a mind to assert his ecclesiastical authority at a distance from the capital, as in 1657 he wrote to the magistrates of Hempstead, nominating a Mr. Denton to be minister there, and *forbidding* " the return of Rev. Mr. Fordim because he did leave the place, and also the exercise of the ministry without our wish or knowledge, and for no or little reasons." [1] The governor meant to govern in all things, and had small patience with opposition, whether from individuals or Churches, in things secular or religious.[2]

The first dissenters subjected to his annoyance were the Lutherans. Many of these religionists had been attracted to New Amsterdam, and in 1653 petitioned the governor and council for liberty of worship and permission to send for a Lutheran minister.[3] The petition was opposed by the Dutch clergy, and referred to the company in Holland, who, in 1654, replied: " We have decided absolutely to deny the request made by some of our inhabitants, adherents of the Augsburg confession, for a preacher and free exercise of their religion, pursuant to the custom hitherto observed by us and the East India Company, on account of the consequences arising therefrom ; and we recommend to you also not to receive any similar petitions, but rather to turn them off in the most

Lutherans.

---

[1] *Documentary History of New York*, III, 118.

[2] This testy disposition made for him enemies very early in his service at New Amsterdam, a token of which is preserved in a letter, written in 1651, by one Van Dincklage to a Van Donck : " To describe the state of this government to one well acquainted and conversant with it is a work of supererogation ; 'tis to wash a blackamoor. Our great Muscovy Duke goes on as usual, with something of the wolf ; the older he gets, the more inclined he is to bite. He proceeds no longer by words or writings, but by arrests and stripes." (*Colonial History of New York*, I, 453.) This description had reference to Stuyvesant's course in some political disturbances, but it may illustrate the spirit with which he undertook to suppress dissent in religious affairs.

[3] O'Callaghan, *New Netherland*, II, 320 ; *Laws of New Netherland ; Colonial History of New York*, XIV, 252.

civil and least offensive way, and to employ all possible, but moderate, means to induce them to listen and finally join the Reformed Church."

Notwithstanding this rebuff, the Lutherans persisted in their desire, and held religious services in their houses without a minister, by which they excited the governor's wrath, made specially severe by the Lutheran assertion that " Heaven was above law." Some of the offenders he threw into prison, and posted up an " edict" prohibiting any more attempts at their dissenting worship.

Persecution.

In this harsh treatment Stuyvesant doubtless thought himself justified by the directors' refusal to permit freedom of worship ; but it seems that in the meantime they had found reason to modify their decision, notice of which they sent to the governor together with a rebuke for his violence. Under date of June 14, 1656, they wrote : " We should have gladly seen that your Honor had not posted up the transmitted edict against the Lutherans, and had not punished them by imprisonment, . . . inasmuch as it has always been our intention to treat them with all peaceableness and quietness. Wherefor, your Honor shall not cause any more such or similar Edicts to be published without our previous knowledge, but suffer the matter to pass in silence, and permit them their free Worship in their houses."

This is as far as the directors were willing to go for a while; for they wrote to Stuyvesant in 1657,[1] that they would not increase the religious liberty of the Lutherans " beyond the terms of our letter of June of last year." Again in 1658 they signified to the governor their approval of his action in sending out of the colony John Goetwater, a Lutheran minister, who had found his way thither and had attempted ministerial functions.[2]

---

[1] *Colonial History of New York*, XIV, 388.

[2] This approval seems to have been incited by a report from Domines Megapolensis and Drisius to the classis of Amsterdam, which is well worth quotation. (*Documentary History of New York*, III, 69.) They relate that,

In their last letter the directors opened a matter, in which lay the root of Lutheran objections to the established Church. The law required the baptism of all children, while restrict- Baptism. ing the administration of the ordinance to the Reformed minister and in the Reformed Church. Thither were Lutheran parents compelled to take their children for an administration which they resented. The directors counsel " moderation and tolerance " in the enforcement of the law, and ordered the use of " the old formulary of baptism," which they understood to be less offensive to the Lutherans ; and also ordered that " the words '*present here in Church*' (referring to parents) be entirely omitted." [1]

To this subject the directors returned in the next year, severely blaming Domines Megapolensis and Drisius for " making difficulties in regard to the use of the old formula of baptism," and insisting that the Lutherans must " be placated," as otherwise the trouble " might result in the permission to conduct a separate divine service there ; for the Lutherans would very easily obtain the consent of the authorities here (the states general) upon a complaint, and we would have no means of preventing it." In 1660 the directors informed Stuyvesant that they were sending two preachers, Blom and Selyns, both of whom " said that they

" a Lutheran Preacher, Goetwater, arrived, to the great joy of the Lutherans and the especial discontent and disappointment of the congregation of this place ; yea, of the whole land, even the English. We went to the Director General," who summoned Goetwater, and found that he had as credentials only a letter from a Lutheran consistory in Europe to the Lutheran Church in New Amsterdam. The governor ordered him not to preach, even in a private house. The Domines lament, " We already have the snake in our bosom," and urge Stuyvesant to open the consistory's letter, which, oddly enough, he refused to do, but consented to the ministers' demand that Goetwater be sent back in the ship that brought him. " Now this Lutheran parson," the Dutch ministers conclude, " is a man of a godless and scandalous life ; a rolling, rollicking, unseemly carl ; who is more inclined to look into the wine-can than to pore over the Bible, and would rather drink a kan of brandy for two hours than preach one."

[1] *Colonial History*, XIV, 418, 421, 451, 461 ; O'Callaghan, II, 345.

would make no difficulty about the formula of baptism," and they were also sending books containing the old formula to be given to Megapolensis and Drisius, " that they may use it, and carry out our good intentions, which they *must not oppose*."

The incident illustrates quite strikingly the religious powers of a commercial company, and puts in contrast the desire to placate the Lutheran conscience and willingness to coerce that of their own ministers. Still another contrast is exhibited in the same letter, which urged complacency to the Lutherans, by refusing similar regard for the English settlers in the colony. With a notable liberality of mind which their successors of a hundred years later might have copied to their advantage, the two Dutch ministers had urged the sending two English preachers, to be located in the English villages. This the directors refused, on account of " the condition of England," but would try to find among the Dutch candidates some one who could preach English." [1]

Jews.

The next religionists to feel the heavy hand of Stuyvesant were the Jews. [2] In 1654 he wrote to the company, requesting that no Jews be permitted " to infest New Netherland." To this the company answered that the request was " unreasonable and unjust," and that Jews should be permitted to go to the colony, on condition of taking care of their own poor, " without giving the said Jews a claim to the privilege of exercising their religion in a synagogue, or at a gathering. If they desire that, refer them to us."

Stuyvesant, however, was a decided anti-Semite and contrived to put many hardships on the Jews. He refused, " for pregnant reasons," to allow a deed to be given to a Jew, who had bought land in Manhattan ; and forbade the Jews to trade at Fort Orange and South River. For such conduct he was rated sharply by the company, who ordered that the

[1] *Colonial History of New York*, XIV, 451.

[2] *Laws of New Netherland*, p. 193 ; *Colonial History of New York*, XIV, 341, 351.

Jews should have in the colony the same liberties as they possessed in Holland, except that of having a synagogue, and " may exercise in all quietness their religion within their houses."

In the meantime trouble arose for the governor in another quarter.[1] The two ministers of the Dutch had heard that one Wickendam, a Baptist, had been holding unlawful services, and they complained to the council that, " during the absence of Do. Moore from Middlebush, some unqualified persons ventured to hold conventicles, and assumed to preach the gospel, from which nothing could be expected but discord, confusion, and disorder in Church and State." Conventicles.

This complaint drew from the council the stringent " Ordinance against Conventicles," adopted February 1, 1656, which ran: " Some unqualified persons in such Meetings assume the ministerial office, the expounding and explanation of the Holy Word of God, without being called or appointed thereto by ecclesiastical or civil authority, which is in direct contravention and opposition to the general Civil and Ecclesiastical order of our Fatherland, besides that many dangerous Heresies and Schisms are to be apprehended: Therefore, the director general and council . . . absolutely and expressly forbid all such Conventicles and Meetings, whether public or private, differing from the customary, and not only lawful but scripturally founded and ordained, Meetings of the Reformed Divine Service, as this is observed . . . according to the synod of Dordrecht." The penalties imposed by the act were £100 *Flemish* for the preacher and £25 for every attendant.

Under this act William Hallett, sheriff of Flushing, who had allowed such meetings in his house, was deprived of office and fined £50. In default of payment he was to be banished. The preacher, Wickendam, was fined £100 and sent out of the country. Henry Townsend

[1] O'Callaghan, II, 316, 321 ; *Laws of New Netherland; Colonial History of New York*, XIV, 337, 369.

of Rustdorp was convicted of having had "prayer meetings in his house" and condemned to a fine of £8 pounds Flemish; failing which he was to be whipped and banished.

This persecution for irregular worship presently ran into the furious onslaught upon the Quakers, who had appeared in the colony about the same time as the wandering Baptist preacher, and whose proceedings could come under the Conventicle Act. Against the Quakers Stuyvesant was "exceedingly mad." Ten of them came to New Amsterdam from Boston in 1657, and were immediately arrested and jailed.[1] As with the Boston magistrates, the Dutch governor did not propose to wait for any overt act. Their mere presence was an offence and danger.

One of their number, Hodsham, escaped and went to Hempstead, where the magistrates issued a proclamation against him and his services. They arrested him, seized his papers and Bible, and fined two women who had entertained him, and then took all three to New Amsterdam for the disposal of the governor. Stuyvesant threw Hodsham into jail, and had him condemned to two years hard labor, "at the wheel-barrow with a negro." The man either unable or refusing to work, the governor caused him to be beaten unmercifully, several successive days, and to be strung up by his hands with a log tied to his feet. He was finally released because of the intercession of Stuyvesant's sister.

This severity had its natural issue of spreading the persecuted opinions, which found many adherents at Flushing and Jamaica. The council sent (1660) Domine Drisius to Jamaica to "inquire about the Quakers and their friends."[2] Two years afterward, the magistrates of Jamaica reported to Stuyvesant that a majority of the people of the town were adherents of the Quakers.[3] The absurd order was sent to the constables to arrest all such persons.

[1] O'Callaghan, II, 347.   [2] *Colonial History*, XIV, 490.
[3] *Ibid.*, p. 515.

A similar order had been sent (1658) to Flushing, in Flushing. response to which the people of the town presented to the council a remonstrance,[1] refusing to execute the law against the Quakers. "Therefore," they said, "if any of these persons come in love unto us, we can not in conscience lay violent hands upon them, but give them free Egresse and Regresse into our town and houses, as God shall persuade our consciences, and in this we are true subjects both of Church and State, for we are bound by the law of God and man to do good unto all men and evil to no man." This remonstrance was read to the council by the sheriff of Flushing, Tobias Feake, who was at once put in jail, whither Edward Hart, the clerk, was sent to keep him company. Feake was soon released, but Hart was kept three weeks. The magistrates of the town were suspended from office, and Flushing was forbidden to hold town meetings without the special permission of the governor and council. Feake, who had added to his offence touching the remonstrance, that of " lodging some of the abominable sect called Quakers," was removed from the shrievalty and fined 200 guilders. Should he refuse to pay the fine, he was to be banished.

Henry Townsend of Rustdorp, notwithstanding his experience of two years before, continued to have prayer meetings in his house, and joined himself to the Quakers. For this he was fined 300 guilders, and on refusing to pay, was "cast into a miry dungeon." [2] Tilton, the clerk of Gravesend, who had "dared to provide a Quaker woman with lodging," was fined £12 Flemish. In 1661, Henry Townsend, John Townsend, and Tilton were all banished for " harboring Quakers "; [3] and it was ordered that soldiers be quartered on all inhabitants of Rustdorp, who did not promise to have nothing to do with Quakers.

In the next year the authorities resorted to frantic measures of repression. A proclamation was issued forbidding

[1] *Colonial History*, XIV, 402 ; O'Callaghan, II, 351.
[2] O'Callaghan, II, 352.   [3] *Ibid.*, II, 450.

the public exercise of any other than the Reformed religion, "either in houses, barns, ships, or yachts; in the woods or fields," under penalty; for the first offence, of 50 guilders fine; for the second offence, 100 guilders; and for the third, 200 guilders fine, with "arbitrary correction." To import or distribute Quaker books was punishable by a fine of 150 guilders, while to receive such books subjected the recipient to a fine of 50 guilders. All persons arriving at New Amsterdam were to register and take the oath of allegiance, under the penalty of 50 guilders fine and "arbitrary correction." All magistrates conniving at a violation of this ordinance were to be degraded and made incapable of holding office.[1]

Bowne.

  The climax to these high-handed measures was reached through the action and experience of John Bowne of Flushing. One of the most prominent of the citizens of that progressive and liberal-minded little burgh, he does not seem to have been concerned with the Quaker movement until after the issuance of Stuyvesant's proclamation.[2] Then, as though prompted to bear testimony against such persecution, he announced himself a Quaker, and made his house a home for any of the persecuted sect who might come to the town. On this he was arrested and fined £25. He refused to pay and was thrown into prison. He lay in prison several months, and was then sent by the governor to Holland. Doubtless this deportation was considered by Stuyvesant as a final riddance, but it enabled Bowne to bring the issue to a prompt decision by the governor's superiors, and to Stuyvesant's complete discomfiture.

  On arrival in Holland, Bowne at once appealed to the West India Company with the statement of his own wrongs and the sufferings of his fellow-religionists, securing from the company a sharp rebuke to Stuyvesant and a disallowance of all his persecuting measures. Under date of April 16, 1663, the

[1] O'Callaghan, II, 454.

[2] *Ibid.*, II, 454–457; *Colonial History of New York*, XIV, 526.

directors wrote to the governor: "We heartily desire that these and other sectaries had remained away, . . . yet we doubt very much whether we can proceed against them vigorously, without diminishing the population and stopping emigration. In the youth of your existence you ought rather encourage than check the population of the colony. . . . The consciences of men ought to be free and unshackled so long as they continue moderate, peaceable, inoffensive, and not hostile to the government. . . . You may therefore shut your eyes, at least not force people's consciences, but allow every one to have his own belief, so long as he behaves quietly. . . . Such have been the maxims of prudence and toleration, by which the magistrates of this city have been governed; and the consequences have been that the oppressed and persecuted from every country have found among us an asylum from distress. Follow in the same steps, and you will be blessed."

So ended the persecution of the Quakers and all persecution in New Netherland, of which it is evidently to be noted that the spirit of it was altogether Stuyvesant's. It may be regarded as certain that, as his superiors did not approve, so his associates in the colony were not in sympathy with him in his oppressive course, and were coerced into their agreement by the dignity of his office and the violence of his temper. Stuyvesant's fierce bigotry was singular among the Dutchmen of that day, and the reader wonders that he should have been so blind as not to see that his course would be disowned by the company in Holland. Probably, at so great a distance from his masters and left to his own discretion in so many affairs, he grew to regard himself as an autocrat and his own opinions as supreme. By whatever process, he prepared for himself a humiliation public and stinging, such as rarely has been experienced by a governor not dismissed in disgrace.

It is well to remark this personal quality in the harsh religious measures of his term of power. Such measures did not belong to the policy of the government. The founders of the colony, while all in the Reformed communion, and while seeking that their colony should maintain a Reformed establishment, had yet no purpose of coercion toward dissent. They had no theocratic principle to express in legislation, and gave to the religious affairs of New Netherlands the forms of an established Church, simply for the reason that they, with almost all of Christendom of the day, looked upon the state as in every place vested with a care for the Church. Except for Stuyvesant, "running before he was sent," never in the fifty years of Dutch rule in America would any sectary have felt an oppressive hand.

We can well imagine that the reproof from Holland must have been a bitter morsel for the fiery governor to digest, but he had other and more serious troubles to disturb him presently. Not long afterward (1664) the English fleet sailed into the harbor and compelled surrender of the colony, a surrender almost welcomed by many of the people, because of Stuyvesant's despotic ways. So ended the history of New Netherland, giving place to New York, save for the brief return of Dutch power in 1673 and 1674.

Our narrative may here anticipate that period, and, before regarding the incidents of English rule in the ecclesiastical affairs of New York, look at some religious features in the story of that Dutch return. When Evertsen and Colve came to New York in 1673, captured it without a blow and turned it to New Amsterdam again for a little season, they undoubtedly thought that the conquest was to be permanent. With this thought the intention took form to secure also the permanency of the Reformed Church establishment, while at the same time they did not hesitate to give expression to tolerance toward all forms of dissent. In this latter particular the legislature under Colve went further than any of its predecessors.

This care for the establishment at once expressed itself in a renewal of the ordinance of 1651, requiring that all magistrates should be "exclusively of the Reformed Christian

English conquest.

Religion, or at least well affected thereto." This action was repeated in the next year.[1] On these magistrates it was made obligatory that they "shall, each in his quality, take care that the Reformed Christian Religion be maintained in conformity to the Synod of Dordrecht, without permitting any other Sects attempting anything contrary thereto." This order, taken in October, 1673, was repeated in the next month and again enacted in the following January.[2] In consistency with this order the commissioners, sent in 1673 to Fort Nassau and South River, were instructed that their duty was, to take care, "First, that the pure, true Christian Religion, agreeably to the Synod of Dordrecht, shall be taught and maintained in all things as it ought, without suffering any the slightest attempt to be made against it by any other sectaries." The same instruction was sent to the magistrates of Brooklyn and the other towns on Long Island, and of the settlements up the Hudson.[3]

Along with these tokens of a purpose to conserve the Reformed establishment, appear the evidences of a very tolerant spirit.[4] From the legislature of 1673, the delegates from Fort Orange, "lately called Albany," among other conditions demanded, "That conscience shall not be subjected to any constraint, as there are some here of different opinions, who have intermarried, but that every one shall be permitted to go where he pleases to hear the Word of God." To this demand the response was, "Granted; and the Commandant and Magistrates are ordered to pay attention to it." To the towns in the east of Long Island, on their submitting to the reëstablished Dutch rule, there was allowed "Freedom of Conscience in the Word of God and Church discipline." The same was allowed to the settlers on South River, in reply to their petition: and to English settlers in Jersey there was

[1] *Laws of New Netherland*, pp. 473, 515.
[2] *Ibid.*, pp. 476, 485, 512.
[3] *Colonial History of New York*, I, 618, 620, 653.
[4] *Ibid.*, I, 584, 593, 605.

" accorded Freedom of Conscience as the same is permitted
in the Netherlands." [1] But to these towns thus made free in
the exercise of religious worship, it was commanded that their
choice of magistrates should be restricted, according to the
statute, to " such only as are of the Reformed Christian
Religion, or at least well affected thereto." [2]

Notwithstanding an apparent contradiction between these
grants of freedom and some of the stringent terms requiring
the maintenance of the Reformed Church, it is but fair to
presume that no curtailing of the allowed religious liberty
was designed; and that "any attempt against it by other
sectaries " had in view, not the orderly independent services,
but the possibility of invasion by the sectaries on the service
of the established Church.

Of other religious action by Colve's government one item
may be cited for its ferocity.   There had been some disorder
in New Amsterdam and martial law had been proclaimed.
Under such rule it was ordered, with a Puritanical zeal
worthy of early Massachusetts and of Dale's "Lawes Martiall
and Morall " in Virginia, that " Whosoever blasphemes the
name of the Lord, or His holy Word, shall be, for the first
offence, fined and committed three days to prison on bread
and water; and, for the second offence, shall have his tongue
bored with a red hot iron, and he shall furthermore be banished out of this government and the United Provinces, as a
villain." [3]   On one occasion Colve exercised an ecclesiastical
jurisdiction, *degrading* for one year a Lutheran minister,
Fabricius, who had married parties without publishing banns.
After the year he must apply for a special license in order to
preach.   The language used indicates the governor's purpose,
not to silence a sectary, but to suspend a minister from his
spiritual office. [4]   Colve also showed his care for the State-
Church in obtaining from the council an order for the payment out of public funds of all arrears of salary to the widow

[1] *Laws of New Netherland*, p. 467.   [3] *Ibid.*, I, 623.
[2] *Colonial History of New York*, I, 586.   [4] *Ibid.*, I, 693; XII, 512.

of Do. Megapolensis, "about to return to Patria"; and to Do. Samuel Megapolensis, then settled in the colony.[1]

With this pleasing evidence of desire to see justice done, Colve ended his care of the Reformed Church in New Netherland, and presently, surrendering his government, ended also this short Dutch episode. With the peace of 1674 between England and Holland the colony was returned to English hands, and reassumed the name of New York, so to remain under the British rule until the era of American Independence.

With the fall of the Dutch power, fell also the Reformed Church from its position of a State establishment. This, indeed, was the immediate result of Stuyvesant's surrender in 1664, to be made final and complete by the return of the English, ten years later, after their short-lived banishment. *Fall of Reformed establishment.*

This disestablishment of the Dutch Church did not, however, place it on a level with other non-Anglican communions in New York. In the "articles of Capitulation," in 1664, it was specifically agreed that, "The Dutch here shall enjoy the liberty of their Consciences in Divine Worship and Church discipline."[2] The intent of this agreement was that the Reformed Church should enjoy a complete autonomy in its own affairs, and not be subjected to the interference by the magistrates, which other Churches were compelled to submit to until near the end of the colonial period. The principles thus obtaining were in the main respected by the English governors, though some departures will appear. The Dutch themselves were so jealous and watchful for these rights, that, on the resumption of the province by the English, they refused to take the oath of allegiance to the king of England, until assured in writing "that the Articles of Surrender are not in the least broken, or intended to be broken, by any words or expression in the said oath."[3] *Dutch privileges.*

[1] *Colonial History of New York*, I, 722.

[2] *Ibid.*, I, 251 ; O'Callaghan, II, 533.

[3] *Colonial History of New York*, III, 74–76 ; Corwin, *History of Reformed Church*, p. 63. (*American Church History Series*, Vol. IX.)

The agreement at the second surrender to the English was made by Colve and Andros, and each consented to the stipulation of the other. In regard to Church affairs and the rights of the Dutch, Colve insisted "that the Inhabitants of Dutch Nativity may be allowed to retain their customary Church privileges in Divine Service and Church discipline." To this Andros added, " The usual discipline of their Church is to be continued to them as formerly."

To return now to the surrender of 1664, the first English governor, Nicholls, on entrance to office published his " Instructions" from the Duke of York, to whom Charles had given the province. In these were recited, " The Conditions for new planters in the territories of his royal highness, the duke of York." Among these conditions, with an undoubted intent to make the first step toward tolerance of Roman Catholics, it was prescribed that, " In all the territories of his Royal Highness liberty of conscience is allowed, provided such liberty is not converted to licentiousness or the disturbance of others in the exercise of the *protestant* religion. Every *township* is obliged to pay their minister, according to such agreement as they shall make with him, and no man shall refuse his proportion; the minister being elected by the major part of the householders, inhabitants of the town."[1]

The Duke's laws, touching upon Church affairs,[2] further provided that a Church building with a seating capacity for two hundred should be erected in every parish; that the cost of such building and of the support of the minister should be raised by public tax; that "every inhabitant shall contribute to all charges both in Church and State; " that preachers must produce to the governor certificates of ordination by some Protestant bishop or minister, on which *the governor shall induct them* in their pastorates; that the minister must administer the Lord's Supper at least once a year, and must not refuse baptism to a child of Christian parents;

The
" Duke's
Laws."

[1] Smith, *History of New York*, I, 39.
[2] Corwin, *Reformed Church*, pp. 66–68.

"nor shall any person be molested, fined, or imprisoned, for differing in judgment in matters of religion, who professes Christianity."

Besides this breadth of tolerance, unwonted at the time, the instructions and laws of the duke are notable in that they do not surrender civil control over religious affairs. The unique character of this position is in the assumption of civil power of direction over all sects. No individual Church is sought to be thereby established, and the legal effect was to establish religion as such, by whatever Churches it might be represented. The vast majority of the population were, of course, Dutch, and any Church organized by them would be Reformed. Other settlers were expected and came from England in the immediately following years. But the duke's laws do not specify to either nationality the particular Church, only that there must be a Church of some kind in every town. Here is an establishment without a name.

Freedom and establishment.

This further appears in the making Church expenses a public charge, in directing as to *minutiæ* of Church services, in prescribing an examination and approval by the governor of ministerial credentials, and finally in the putting into the governor's hands the right and power of induction.

Such arrangements virtually made the head of the civil government the head also of the Church, not specifically the Reformed or Anglican, but every Church in the province! Theoretically, this situation is without a parallel in the entire history of Church and State. Elsewhere the idea of civil power over the Church always involved the legal preference of one Church, accompanied by either the proscription, or modified tolerance, of all others. Singular as the relation was, it will be seen that the early governors of New York frequently acted upon the supposition of its propriety and validity, up to the time of the abortive endeavors of Fletcher to establish the Church of England.

Nicholls, who published the duke's instructions, noted his first use of ecclesiastical authority by ordering the city to pay

the salary of the Dutch minister.[1] His successor, Lovelace,
extended his protection over the Lutherans in 1666, forbidding
all interference with them, "so long as they live quietly and
in order."[2] In 1670 Lovelace directed that the Church at
Albany (Reformed) should be maintained "as the established
Church," and guaranteed support to any minister who would
come over as assistant to Domine Drisius. This brought
over William Nieuwenhuysen, to whom the promise of maintenance was not well kept.[3] In 1671 Lovelace wrote to the
minister and Church of Southold a letter of reproof for having distressed a Mr. Booth for rates. In so doing the Church
and town magistrates were clearly within the law requiring
every inhabitant to contribute to Church support. But this
Booth was an Episcopalian, in whose defence the governor
was willing to wrest the law, and to upbraid the Church with
their "misuse of the liberty given to their opinion," threatening them also with the loss of that liberty.[4] This was the
first recorded instance of gubernational perversions of law in
favor of episcopacy, which were quite frequent during the
English sway.

It would be tedious, and is altogether needless, to recite all
the instances of interference by the New York governors with
the affairs of the ministry and the Churches, or of their action
against the law in favor of their own preferred Church order.
Sufficient witness of these things will appear in the more
important incidents which illustrate the ruling principle of
the government on religious matters.

The reappearance of English power in 1674 was with the
proclamation of the broadest kind of liberty of opinion.
James's instructions to Governor Andros ran, "You shall
permitt all persons of what Religion soever, quietly to inhabitt
within the precincts of your jurisdiccōn, without giveing them

James's
proclama-
tion of
liberty.

---

[1] Corwin, p. 68.
[2] *Colonial History*, XIV, 626.
[3] *Ibid.*, III, 189 ; Corwin, p. 69.
[4] *Documentary History of New York*, III, 209.

any disturbance or disquiet whatever for, or by reason of, their differing opinions in matters of Religion: Provided they give noe disturbance to ye publique peace, nor doe molest or disquiet others in the free exercise of their religion." [1]

This breadth of toleration has frequently been cited against the memory of James, as something arguing a specious and deceptive intent, in like manner that his efforts toward toleration in England have been charged to an innate falsehood of mind. It is remembered that James was a Romanist, and supposed that he was a bigoted one at that, from which the usual conclusion has been made that this proclamation of liberty of conscience was a mere blind; that under the cover of it he might make an asylum for distressed Catholics in his new dominions. This conclusion drew with it the inference that, when the Catholic representation in the colony should become large enough to permit, he would turn the government into "papistical" hands and withdraw the ordinance of toleration.

All of which supposition may be true, as an outline of the duke's desire. At the same time, it is not a matter of record and is nothing more than a supposition of what might have taken place on the possible occurrence of a situation which was never reached. James made no expression, at least as preserved to us, indicating any such treacherous purpose. What he said and did in the matter was altogether honorable, and far in advance of the toleration accorded by his son-in-law, William, the idol of seventeenth century Protestantism.

Certainly, it is not to be charged to him as a crime or as a proof of treacherous intent, that he sought to make a safe retreat for the oppressed followers of the Church of Rome. Himself a devout Catholic, it would have been strange, and would have been just cause for reproach, if, with this authority over a princely domain, he had not bethought him of the opportunity to afford his co-religionists an asylum. It would not redound to his honor, if he, a Catholic prince, had

Sincerity of James.

[1] *Colonial History*, III, 218.

put into the charter of New York liberties the words, "except Papists," so common with the men of the day, who were loudest in their demands for freedom of conscience. The last of the Stuart kings has enough to answer for at the bar of history, without depriving him of the honorable record made by all his actions in regard to religious freedom in his province of New York, notwithstanding its unlikeness to other portions of his record.

Andros.

Presenta-
tion.

Almost at once that Andros assumed his government in New York, he found occasion to exercise his supposed right of presentation and that in the Reformed Church.[1] A certain Nicholas van Rensselaer, a native of Holland and licentiate of the classis of Amsterdam, but whether related or not to the patroon of Rensselaerwyck does not appear, went to London in the train of Charles II. at the time of the Restoration. He was permitted to preach in London and was ordained a deacon by the bishop of Salisbury. He did not appear in New York until 1674, when, it is probable, he came over with Governor Andros, bringing with him a recommendation from the duke of York to some "benefice" in the province. He was sent by Andros to Albany as colleague to the minister there, with a somewhat peremptory command to receive him as a co-pastor. The governor wrote to the Church that Van Rensselaer had "made his humble request . . . whereunto I have consented. I do hereby desire you to signify the same unto the Parishioners . . . wherein I shall looke upon their compliance as a mark of their respect and good inclinations towards me. 23 July, 1674."

This was a sufficiently imperious message to begin with, at the opening of his administration, in dealing with a Church which had prided itself on submitting to even the Dutch governors only as they were themselves supposed to be submissive to the classis of Amsterdam. The Albany Church declined to receive the candidate, in which refusal minister,

---

[1] Corwin, *Reformed Church*, p. 73; Smith, *History of New York*, I, 49; *Colonial History of New York*, III, 225.

magistrates, and people were agreed. It was denied that he had a right to administer the sacraments in their Church, because he had been episcopally ordained; and he was not permitted to even preach until he promised to submit to the classis.

Andros was incensed, and summoned Nieuwenhuysen, the Albany minister, to answer before him for contempt, with the result of arousing great public indignation both at Albany and at New York. Meanwhile Van Rensselaer preached at Albany and was thrown into jail by the magistrates, for "several dubious words" in his sermon, and thereupon the governor felt still more outraged and issued warrants for the arrest of the magistrates and to put them under £5000 bonds to show cause for their conduct. The celebrated Leisler took part with the offending officers and was imprisoned by order of Andros.

But the governor could not enforce his will. After much commotion he gave up the case altogether, "referring" it, for form's sake, "to the Consistory of the Church of Albany." Inasmuch as the said consistory had already made its opinions very clearly known, this reference was but a euphemism to signify the striking of the governor's flag of presentation to a Reformed Church. So fared the first conflict of an English governor with a Dutch Church, in the complete victory of the latter. As to Van Rensselaer, he was not worth the struggle, and after a year's time the governor compelled him to depart, "for scandalous conduct."

Another ecclesiastical mandate of Andros met with a greater success in 1679, when he *authorized* and *directed* the Dutch clergy of New York to ordain Tesschenmacker to the ministry.[1] In respect to ecclesiastical polity, this demand made the highest flight of spiritual supremacy ever attempted by a colonial governor. It was an attempt to *create an ordaining power*, which in a colony under the Church of England establishment could only be equalled by the appointment

Ordination

---

[1] Corwin, p. 74.

of a bishop, a peculiar prerogative of the crown. For in the polity of the Reformed Church, as in the Anglican, the power of ordination was not resident in the clergy as such. In the Anglican Church only a bishop could ordain, while in the Reformed Church the power belonged to a convened body of ministers and elders, called a classis, formally organized for that purpose and for the care of the Churches.

But in the time of Andros there was no such " Reverend Body " in New York. The care of the Churches in New Netherland had been committed by the states general and the West India company to the classis of Amsterdam. To that body belonged ordination for the Dutch Reformed Church in America; for which rite any man of those Churches, desiring ordination, was forced to go in person to Holland. A like hardship was experienced by the American candidates for Episcopal ordination, who, until after the Revolution, were compelled to voyage to England for the imposition of a bishop's hands.

The singularity, then, and arrogance of Andros's demand were in the attempt to create a spiritual body for the discharge of the highest office in the power of the Church! It is hardly to be supposed that the governor was at all aware of the real gravity of his command. He probably only looked upon it as a matter of convenience, which he as governor had every right to direct. In reality, he could not have presumed much further, unless he had undertaken to ordain the candidate himself.

A still more singular thing about the incident was the complaisance of the Dutch clergy. They, unlike Andros, perfectly well understood the nature of the demand, and that it was a preposterous invasion of one of the Church's most sacred rights. They knew that they could not ordain as clergy; and could not organize themselves into a classis, without express authorization from their superior at Amsterdam; and that any action, which they as a pretended classis might take, would be irregular and void. At the same time, they complied with Andros's demand, organized themselves into a classis, and ordained Tesschenmacker! It is worthy of note that, on report of this action to the classis of Amsterdam, that body, for the sake of peace, ratified the ordination, but did not legalize the classical organization at New York.

So Andros carried his point, and won the greatest (theoretical) ecclesiastical victory ever gained by a colonial governor, with which his success in securing rights of Episcopal worship in Boston is not to be compared. Doubtless, the record of this incident emboldened Governor Nicholson, thirty years later, to demand the ordination of Van Vleck at the hands of Dubois and Antonides, Dutch ministers in his time at New York. But these men were either wiser or less pressed by circumstances than their predecessors, and flatly refused to do the governor's bidding. The governor was sensible enough not to press the matter.[1]

The assembly of 1683,[2] the first after the coming of Governor Dongan, adopted a " Charter of Liberties," in which it was ordained that, " No person professing faith in God by Jesus Christ is to be molested or called in question for any difference of opinion in matters of religion." This is substantially in the language of the duke's instructions to Andros in 1674. The " Charter " goes on to say that " the Churches already in New York do appear to be privileged Churches," their privileges confirmed by the past government

Charter of Liberties.

[1] Smith, *New York*, I, 199.

An amusing instance of governmental interference with religious matters is contained in a letter from Lieutenant Governor Brockholst to the constables at Huntington in 1682. (*Colonial History*, XIV, 765.) He writes that complaints have come to him against Mr. Jones for refusing to baptize children ; and that Jones informs him that he is willing to baptize all children of Christian parents, but that many inhabitants of Huntington are godless and Sabbath-breakers. Whereupon the governor charges the constables to " see that the Lord's Day is well and Solemnly observed by all . . . that it may not longer be A Doubt or Dispute who are Christian Parents."

[2] Corwin, p. 78.

and by the later surrender confirmed again, "Provided also that all other Christian Churches, that shall hereafter come and settle in the province, shall have the same privileges."

There can be no exception taken to such an ordinance. It distinctly declared the mind of the colonists as opposed to any legal preference of any particular Church. Though the great majority of the people were attached to the Reformed Church, they desired that all Churches should be on a level before the law — a thing worthy of all honor, as showing that the Dutchmen of New York had not lost the tolerant spirit which their fathers had brought from Holland.

The broad terms of this charter were approved by the duke of York, but when he became king and the titular head of the Church of England this approval was recalled, and the attempt was made to establish that Church as the State-Church in New York. Thus, James's instructions to Governor Dongan in 1686 said:[1] "You shall take care that God Almighty bee devoutly and duely served throughout your Government, the Book of Common Prayer read each Sunday and Holy day, and the Blessed Sacrament be administered according to the Rites of the Church of England." Various prescriptions were made about Church buildings and ministers, and each one of the latter was to have assigned to him "a competent Proportion of Land for a Glebe and exercise of his Industry." The parishes were "to bee so limited and setled as you shall find most convenient for ye accommodating this good work." The ecclesiastical jurisdiction over the province was lodged in the archbishop of Canterbury, while the governor was vested with the powers of presentation and immediate discipline and removal of the clergy. The governor was forbidden to prefer any minister "to any benefice" without a certificate from the archbishop that he is of the Church of England; and he was empowered to remove any "scandalous" minister and to fill the vacancy at his "discretion."

Church of England.

---

[1] *Colonial History of New York*, III, 372, 373.

These provisions in preference of the Church of England, forced upon James by his accession to the throne, were not designed to act in exclusion of other Churches. Nothing was said toward modifying the liberty granted in the former instructions. This was again allowed, and the door was intentionally left open to the followers of differing forms of religion, "provided they make no disturbance of the public peace." Through this open door various religionists entered the colony and settled without hindrance. Among them were a number of Romanists. Three Jesuit priests are said to have been in New York during Dongan's administration, one of whom is thought to have been teacher of the Latin school opened by the governor.[1]

Dongan's "Report on the State of the Province,"[2] 1687, in reference to religious matters, said: "Here bee not many of the Church of England; few Roman Catholics; abundance of Quaker preachers, men and Women especially; Singing Quakers; Ranting Quakers; Sabbatarians; Anti-Sabbatarians; some Anabaptists; some Independents; some Jews; in short, of all sorts of opinions there are some, and the most part of none at all. The most prevailing opinion is that of the Dutch Calvinists. . . . It is the endeavor of all persons here to bring up the children and servants in the opinion which themselves profess; but this I observe, that they take no care of the conversion of their Slaves. . . . As for the King's natural born subjects that live on Long Island, and other parts of the Government, I find it a hard task to make them pay their Ministers." *Religious state.*

There are no records of serious interference with ecclesiastical affairs on the part of Dongan. Though an avowed Catholic, he showed no strong desire to build up any Church, but devoted himself to his civil duties, in which he proved to be one of the very best of the governors in the province. During his term the influx of Romanists could not have been *Dongan.*

[1] *Documentary History of New York*, III, 73; Smith, *New York*, I, 90.
[2] *Colonial History*, III, 410; *Documentary History*, I, 116.

large, but those who did come were the recipients of his favor. Some of the public officials professed attachment to Rome, and many of "the people trembled for the Protestant cause."[1]

This fear found expression on the fall of James II. and the usurpation by Leisler of the government in New York.[2] On receipt of the news of the Revolution in England, the council at once resolved to "suspend all Roman Catholics from Command and Places of Trust." This resolution turned out just two officers, Major Baxter and Ensign Russell, — not a very formidable number, — who left the province. Leisler ordered the arrest of all "reputed Papists," and forbade the franchise to others than Protestant freemen. The effect of this, however, was only an expression of opinion and desire, for Leisler and his government soon came to ignominious disaster.

In 1689 Governor Sloughter came to New York with instructions from William and Mary, which repeated in regard to Church matters the provisions in James's orders to Dongan, except that the jurisdiction of the colonial Church was transferred from the see of Canterbury to that of London. They were made also in the light of the great toleration act of 1689, which was intended to have force in all the English dominions, and which excluded from favor both Unitarians and Romanists.[3] The like instructions were given to Colonel Fletcher in 1692, when he succeeded to Sloughter, with the addition that he was authorized "to Colate any Person or Persons to any Churches, Chapells, or other Ecclesiastical Benefices . . . as often as any of them shall happen to be void."[4] Like instructions, with scarcely a variation, were given to the successive governors down almost to the Revolution. James set the model for his followers on the throne,

[1] Smith, *New York*, I, 90.

[2] *Documentary History of New York*, II, 21, 41, **244**.

[3] *Colonial History of New York*, III, 688.

[4] *Ibid.*, III, 821, 830.

Leisler.

Romanists.

William and Mary.

none of whom ever detected the folly of supposing the Church of England to be established in New York.[1]

Governor Sloughter's administration does not appear to have interested itself in the advancement of the Church of England, or in religious matters at all; unless we may take as an indication of the latter the expulsion from the assembly of 1691 of two members from Queens, on the ground that they were Quakers.[2] Though the royal instructions insisted on the recognition of the English Church and its orders, its establishment in the colony could not be effected without the formal action of the colonial legislature, which action Sloughter made no effort to procure. The only official representation of the Church was in requiring from all office holders the test oath prescribed by the parliament. This involved the oath of allegiance and supremacy, partaking the sacrament "according to the rites of the Church of England," and signing a declaration against the Roman doctrine of transubstantiation. The application of this oath was enough, without any movement of the governor, to cause the exclusion of Quakers from the legislature and all office. *Sloughter.*

When Fletcher came to the government in 1692, he brought with him either emphatic orders from his superiors, or a determined purpose of his own, to procure the formal establishment of the Church by a colonial statute. His own zeal, indeed, was sufficient to urge him to the effort. His religious bigotry was only equalled by his vain love of power and by a lust for money, which made his government the most corrupt in the annals of the province.[3] The story of his struggles with the assembly is notable as illustrating both his temper and the spirit of the Dutchmen, whom he attempted to coerce. It is also a peculiar instance of that ecclesiastical arrogance which has often made no scruple about grasping more "than the law allows." *Fletcher.*

[1] *Colonial History*, IV, 269, 287; V, 95, 391, etc.
[2] Smith, *New York*, I, 113.
[3] *Colonial History*, IV, 822, 826; Cobb, *Story of the Palatines*, pp. 115, 218.

To the first legislature of his term (1692) Fletcher issued a demand that they take the requisite action to "settle the ministry," using that term to involve the establishment of the Church of England.[1] The assembly, however, did nothing in the matter, greatly to the wrath of the governor, who berated them roundly, and declared that "the same law, which established your privileges, provided for the religion of the Church of England." To the next assembly Fletcher presented the same demand, saying, "I recommended to the former assembly the settling of an able ministry, that the worship of God may be observed among us, for I find that first and great duty very much neglected." This assembly of 1693, more complaisant than the last, relaxed something of its opposition. Unwilling, however, to yield all that the governor wanted, they appointed a committee of eight to devise a scheme, which might possibly satisfy Fletcher and yet avoid the establishment demanded. The result of the committee's labor was a bill for a religious establishment of an entirely nondescript character, the like of which is not to be found elsewhere. The bill was reported to the assembly and became law on the 23d of September, 1693.[2]

The significant portions of the Act are as follows: "In Each of the respective Cities and Counties hereafter mentioned there shall be called, inducted, and established a good, sufficient, Protestant Minister." . . . In the City of New York one: in the County of Richmond one; in the County of Westchester two, one to have care of West Chester, East Chester, Yonkers, and the Manor of Pelham, and one to have the care of Rye, Mamaroneck, and Bedford; and in Queens County two, one for Jamaica and "adjacent towns and farms," and the other for "Hamstead" and adjacent towns. The law also ordained that in the Churches named there should be

Establishment.

Act of 1693.

[1] Corwin, *Reformed Church*, pp. 96–106; Smith, *New York*, I, 128–134.

[2] *Colonial Laws of New York. Colonial History*, IV, 57 ; *Legislative Journal*, pp. 47, 48.

" Wardens and a Vestry," to be chosen by the freeholders summoned by the justices: and that the ministers should be supported by public tax. This act is remarkable for both its requirements and its omissions. There is not a word in the act referring to the Church of England, or to the book of common prayer; there is no requirement of services "according to the rites " of the English Church, nor any acknowledgment of the supremacy of the crown, nor any allowance of patronage to the governor. At the same time, the act restricts its operation to the four counties named, and does not apply to Kingston, Albany, or any part of the province outside of those counties. Nor in those counties does it make the establishment universal. What in legal construction it did, was to establish, not a Church at all, but *six Protestant Ministers* in places named, and these ministers of no specified denomination, save that they must be Protestant. In other towns of these counties and in the case of other ministers needed in these towns, the act did not apply. Thus, while the act did create a Church establishment in the places noted, it yet established neither any Church for the province at large, nor any particular Church for the localities specified. The Reformed Church had as good a legal right to claim the establishment as had the Church of England. This was practically acknowledged at the time by Colonel Lewis Morris, himself a strong Church of England man, in a letter written in 1711.[1] The act, he wrote, " is very loosely worded. The Dissenters claim the benefit of it as well as we : and the Act without much wresting will admit a construction in their favor as well as ours." In fact, it belonged to neither. The only named Church that was ever "established " on the soil of New York was the Reformed Church, which fell with the Dutch power. The arrogant assumption of English cabinets and governors that the Church of England was established in New York, and the common supposition, even to this day, that the Episcopal Church was ever a State-

Not Anglican.

Restricted.

[1] *Colonial History*, V, 320.

Church in the province, are alike unwarranted by the facts.[1]

At the time of the passage of the act Governor Fletcher was well aware of its deficiencies. He returned it to the assembly with instructions to amend, by inserting a clause investing the governor with the right of induction. He suggested that the act should require that ministers be "presented to the governor to be approved and collated." But the assembly thought that they had yielded enough and refused

Fletcher's anger. the amendment; whereupon the governor prorogued them, saying, " If you seem to understand that none can serve without your collation or establishment, you are far mistaken; for I have the power of collating or suspending any minister in my government by their majesties' letters patent: and whilst I stay in the government, I will take care that neither heresy, sedition, schism, nor rebellion be preached among you." But neither anger nor argument could bend the legislature to the governor's will, and he was forced to content himself with the act as it stood.

Almost immediately there arose two occasions which gave

Legislative construction. the assembly opportunity to construe their own act. In 1694 the Rev. John Miller, chaplain to the English soldiers, claimed the benefit of support under the act, on the ground that he was a clergyman of the Church of England stationed in New York. Fletcher at once allowed the claim, but the legislature would not permit. Again, in the following year, it was questioned whether any of the Churches named were restricted in their choice of ministers to clergymen of the Church of England. Five wardens and vestrymen in the city of New York petitioned the legislature on the subject, and the house resolved: " That, the vestrymen and Church wardens have power to call a dissenting protestant minister, and that he is to be paid and maintained as the act directs." This was not pleasing to Fletcher, who argued the absurdity of such opinion on the ground that "there is no Protestant

[1] Hoffman, *Ecclesiastical Law in the State of New York*, p. 7.

Church admits of such officers as Church-wardens and Vestry-men but the Church of England." He could not comprehend that the legislature had created an establishment of their own, and had borrowed these terms to hoodwink him; or that considerably more than the titles of local Church officers were needed to constitute a branch of the Church of England. It was only by indirection, and also by many false statements, that the impression took form that the act of 1693 established the Church of England. Fletcher himself knew to the contrary, but he always afterward talked and acted as though he had gotten the establishment he desired. The course of government likewise, on both sides of the sea, always assumed that the Anglican Church had been established. The ministers and members of the Episcopal Church in New York acted on the same assumption — a most unwarranted perversion of the facts in the case; for the reason that it is perfectly clear, from the succession of events, that the establishing of the Church of England was precisely that thing which the legislature was determined *not* to do. Owing to this perversion, the assembly made many efforts to repeal the act, but were opposed by the governor and council, so that the law remained in force until the Revolution.[1]

As though prompted by the passage of the "Ministry Act" and the construction which the governor seemed determined to put upon it, the consistory of the Reformed Church in New York applied for and obtained in 1696 a charter, confirming the privileges stipulated in the articles of surrender in 1664. Beyond doubt, it was a recollection of those stipulations, together with a desire to propitiate a public indignant at his effort to force the English Church upon the colony, that moved the governor to grant the charter.[2]

Collegiate Church charter.

[1] Corwin, p. 106; *Colonial History*, IV, 427.

[2] Lord Bellomont, who succeeded Fletcher in 1697, writing to the board of trade, described this charter as, "extraordinary, for it is setting up a jurisdiction to fly in the face of government." He also said that Fletcher had accepted "a bribe for it," and that himself had seen in the book of the

Other Dutch Churches in New York and New Jersey received charters in the following year, but such incorporation was consistently refused to all other Churches except the Episcopal. Thus — to anticipate in our narrative — the **Presbyterian.** Presbyterian Church in New York applied for a charter in 1719.[1] The application to the governor was opposed by Trinity Church, and was referred to the board of trade to **Lutheran.** meet a denial. In 1763 the Lutheran Church in New York made a similar application, which was approved by the council, but was referred by the governor to the home government, with "several from Dissenting Congregations for like privileges." What these other Churches were does not appear, but they were all denied, "as his Majesty saw no reason which rendered it necessary."[2] In 1766 the Presbyterian Church renewed its request for a charter by way of petition direct to the king. The action in response to this petition took a curious course.[3] It was referred by the king to the board of trade, and the board sent it back to America, inquiring if there were any objections to the petition, "which in the general and abstracted view of it appears to us to be no ways Improper or unreasonable." Thus the request came up in the provincial council, which body, less anti-Anglican than formerly, resolved, that a judicial decision must first be obtained as to whether "the old English statutes of Uniformity extend to America", and stated, "Except the charters granted to the Church of England, all the instances of such Incorporations within this province (four only in number) are confined to the Dutch, whose claims to this Distinction are grounded on one of the Articles of Capitulation." In the next year the king in council took order dismissing the petition, on the ground that it was "against the king's coro-

Church treasurer, the entry of the purchase of "a considerable service of plate" to be presented to the governor (*Colonial History*, IV, 463), which entry he copied for proof to the board.

[1] *Documentary History*, III, 279.   [2] *Ibid.*, III, 295, 299.
[3] *Ibid.*, III, 302–307 ; *Colonial History*, VIII, 846, 943.

nation oath to preserve the Church of England," and that it was "not expedient upon Principles of General Polity to comply with the Prayer of this Petition, or to give the Presbyterian Church in New York any other Privileges or Immunities than it is entitled to by the Laws of Toleration." The Presbyterians undiscouraged renewed their request in 1775, only to be again refused, though less brusquely.[1]

The whole story of these applications is but one among many illustrations of the perverse tenacity which clung to the false assumption of an Anglican establishment in New York. This assumption is most strikingly exhibited in the charter of Trinity Church. That Church, as though startled by the incorporation of the Dutch Collegiate Church in 1696, and as though having some suspicions of its boasted establishment, in the next year made application for a charter, in which application, as also in the charter itself, the assertion is many times repeated that the act of 1693 had established the Church of England.[2] Not for lack of assertion was the misstatement to fail of credence. *Charter of Trinity.*

The administration of Bellomont did not concern itself very greatly in ecclesiastical matters. This was probably through lack of opportunity, if we may judge from one recorded instance of zeal for the Church of England — his veto of a bill for the settlement of a minister, on the ground that he was a dissenter.[3] His lordship's successor, Lord Cornbury, more than made up for the lack, filling his term with much activity in the cause of the Church, and that in ways of most offensive annoyance and oppression. "Educated at Geneva, he yet loved episcopacy as a religion of the State subordinate to the executive power."[4] A cousin of Queen Anne, to whom he bore a strong resemblance of fea- *Cornbury.*

[1] *Colonial History*, VIII, 572.

[2] *Documentary History*, III. 410 ; *Colonial History*, IV, 1114 ; Corwin, p. 116.

[3] *Colonial History*, IV, 536.

[4] Bancroft, *History of the United States*, III, 60, 62.

ture, he prided himself on the relationship and deemed that it conferred upon him more imperial powers than other governors possessed, especially with regard to Church affairs. His zeal carried him to very extreme actions, and, as though dissatisfied with the already defined powers of his office, led him to forge instructions from England for the purpose of increasing his ecclesiastical prerogatives. (Bancroft.)

He arrived at New York in 1701 and at once proceeded to the exercise of episcopal powers, in a way which none of his predecessors had attempted. They had respected that limitation of the ministry act which had confined its nondescript Church to the four counties of New York, Westchester, Queens, and Richmond. But Cornbury chose to consider that it covered the province. Thus, about the time of his arrival the Church (Reformed) of Kingston became vacant, and the governor undertook to induct there a Mr. Haburne, a Church of England minister, whom he sent to Kingston with order that the people receive him as their minister and provide him with a good house.[1] To these orders the Kingston Church paid small attention.

Attempts to dictate to Kingston.

The next year, Cornbury, to his great indignation, learned that a certain Paul van Vleck had been preaching about the country, "notwithstanding that he had been forbid by his Excellency"; and that he had been called by the Church (Reformed) of Kinderhook, "without any License" to the Church permitting the call. The governor at once ordered the "High Sheriff" of Albany to arrest Van Vleck, and bring him to New York. Four members of the Kinderhook Church having presumed to interfere with a certificate in favor of the candidate, they were included in the order for arrest. The party appeared before the governor in March, 1703, and, not having the stuff that martyrs are made of, "acknowledging their error & submitting themselves thereon, were discharged with a caution to be more careful in future."[2]

Kinder-hook.

About the same time Lord Cornbury appeared as a defender

[1] *Documentary History*, III, 584.   [2] *Ibid.*, III, 539.

of the faith against heresy. John Tallman, one of the justices Heresy. of Queens county was reported to have said that, "the Scriptures were not the rule, they being wrote by sinful men of like passions as we are; and that the holy Scriptures was a rule, but not the rule we should go by." Affidavits of these heretical words were laid before the governor's council and it was ordered that Tallman be removed from office and be prosecuted by the attorney-general.[1]

It were tedious to here recount all the instances of Cornbury's impudent interference with Church affairs and the liberty of religion. His administration was rendered famous by three great cases. These were the celebrated Mackemie case, which came to issue and quick decision in 1707; the Jamaica Church case, and that of Freeman and Antonides, both of which began in 1702 and left a legacy of much annoyance to Cornbury's successors. The main features of each must be briefly noted.

The case of the Jamaica Church was one of barefaced Jamaica spoliation. The town had been settled in 1656, mainly by Church. English people with Presbyterian preferences. They had been made welcome by the Dutch, and by the English conquerors were not disturbed until after the passage of the ministry act.[2] They had set apart land for a glebe and made a parsonage for a minister, and in 1699 had built a fine stone Church, the expense of which was raised by public tax. Meanwhile there had come to the town a number of people of the Church of England, whose cupidity was excited by the fine Church property of their Presbyterian neighbors, an opportunity of securing which for themselves seemed to be offered by the ministry act.

On the passage of that act the organization of the Jamaica Church was so far changed as that its officers (all dissenters) took the names of Wardens and Vestrymen. As such they called and settled Mr. Hubbard,[3] who at the time of the open-

---

[1] *Documentary History*, III, 124.   [3] *Ibid.*, III, 160.
[2] *Ibid.*, III, 135; Smith, *New York*, I, 170, 171.

ing of the trouble was the pastor of the Church and in quiet possession of the parsonage and glebe. In pursuance of the Episcopal desires a Mr. Bartow, a missionary of the "Society for the Propagation of the Gospel in Foreign Parts," came to Jamaica in 1702 or 1703, and concerted measures by which the Episcopal minority might obtain possession of the Church property. [1]On a Sunday, after Hubbard had preached in the morning, Bartow and his followers slipped into the Church, held service, and claimed the building for the use of the Church of England. This was the occasion of what is noted in the records as the Jamaica Riot; for the majority of the town did not choose to submit to the robbery and expelled the intruders by force.

"Riot."

This reclamation of their own was regarded by Cornbury as unlawful violence, and he interfered with his authority to confirm the property in the hands of the Episcopalians. He forbade Hubbard to preach in the Church again, "for in regard it was built by a public tax, it did appertain to the Established Church." This language of Cornbury is a curious specimen of his perversity of opinion — for as matter of fact, under the ministry act, the Church with Hubbard as its pastor was already part of the provincial establishment. Of course, Cornbury's false premise was, that the establishment was Anglican, coupled with another equally false, that any property for religious purposes, paid for at any time by tax, must belong to the Church of England. This latter claim finds place in a memorial from the New York Episcopal clergy to the bishop of London in 1711. They therein allege the public tax as a ground for seizure of the Jamaica Church, while they admit that the great majority of the inhabitants, who paid the tax, and all the vestrymen were "dissenters" and opposed to the perversion of the property.[2]

The governor's measures were prompt and sharp, at once that he heard that the "dissenters" had reobtained their

[1] *Documentary History*, III, 131.
[2] *Ibid.*, III, 143; Hoffman, *Ecclesiastical Law in State of New York*, p. 9.

building. "A representation," wrote Colonel Morris, "was made to my Lord Cornbury that the Jamaica Church and house, being built by publick Act, could belong to none but the Church of England; my Lord gives his Warrant to dispossess the Dissenters, which immediately by Force was done without any Procedure at Law." [1] He also ordered Mr. Hubbard to vacate the parsonage, and, on his declining to move out, the sheriff was ordered to eject him. At the same time he ordered the wardens and vestrymen to secure the glebe for the benefit of the Episcopal minister, and the justices to levy a tax for his support. Cornbury completed his work by inducting a Mr. Urquhart into the violently vacated charge.[2] Well might Mr. Urquhart write to the Society for the Propagation of the Gospel that the governor was "a true nursing father to our infancy here." [3]

This opinion was echoed by all the Church of England clergy in the province, who in their convention of 1704, making report to the bishop of London, remark of Jamaica affairs, "There is a Church of Stone, built by a tax levied on the inhabitants by act of Assembly; and a house and glebe formerly in the possession of the Independent minister, but now in the possession of the present Incumbent by Lord Cornbury's favor." [4] The same report notes with satisfaction that a dissenting Church at New Town, the minister of which had gone away, had been given by the governor to the Episcopalians!

Urquhart remained in possession of the parsonage and use of the Church for six years, though not without much trouble and popular discontent. At the end of that period he died, leaving in the possession of the house his widow and daughter, the latter of whom married McNeish, a "dissenting" minister, who at once took residence in the parsonage and was called to the pastorate of the Church by the wardens and vestrymen, not one of whom was an Episcopalian.[5] Thus

---

[1] *Colonial History*, V, 320. [2] *Documentary History*, III, 128.
[3] *Ibid.*, III, 130. [4] *Ibid.*, p. 75. [5] *Ibid.*, III, 144–160.

the property came again into Presbyterian possession, and there remained.

Their tenure, however, was not without opposition from the Church of England party. In 1710 Governor Hunter gave the living to Rev. Mr. Poyer, one of the missionaries of the society, but the new rector was unable to obtain either Church or house, or yet his salary. The governor wrote to Chief Justice Mompesson to put Mr. Poyer into possession by an order from the court, but the judge replied that possession could not be given "otherwise than by due process of law, without a high crime and misdemeanor." Hunter then urged Poyer to carry the case into court,[1] offering his own purse to meet the costs. But this the minister and his associates were unwilling to do, alleging as their reason that "most of the judges were dissenters." To counterbalance such weight of dissent on the bench, a notable scheme was devised, which took form in a memorial to the queen from the society in London,[2] praying for an order in council, allowing appeals by the clergy from colonial courts, on account of their bias toward dissent, to the governor and council and thence to the queen and privy council. This petition was granted, February 6, 171$\frac{2}{3}$. On this the missionary was directed by the society to go into court. The issue after many delays was a defeat, for the court confirmed the property in Presbyterian hands. This final decision was recorded in 1731, and Governor Cosby intimates that it was procured by bribery of Chief Justice Morris,[3] an altogether gratuitous slander. It does not appear that the Episcopal party made use of appeal to England, and they finally reconciled themselves to the necessity of building a Church of their own at Jamaica. So ended Lord Cornbury's famous attempt to pervert a Presbyterian Church by violence into the possession of the Church of England, after a bitter struggle of thirty years.

---

[1] *Colonial History*, V, 310.

[2] *Documentary History*, III, 163 ; *Colonial History*, V, 345, 352.

[3] *New Jersey Archives*, V, 330.

The second question, on which he put his ecclesiastical power to proof, was that of patronage. The case is chiefly *Patronage.* notable for the bold insistence by one of the parties that the governor had no power of induction among the Dutch Churches. It began in 1702 and with frequent orders, petitions, and counter petitions, filling many pages of the public documents, lasted for twelve years.

In the year noted some of the elders in the Dutch Churches of Brooklyn, Flatbush, Flatlands, and New Utrecht, in which Churches, as a joint pastorate, Domine Antonides was already *Antonides and Free-* laboring, petitioned Lord Cornbury for permission to call the *man.* Rev. Bernardus Freeman of Schenectady.[1] This petition at once aroused great opposition among the other elders and the congregations, on the ground, as was reported to Cornbury, that he " had nothing to doo with it, and it was their privilege to send for what Minister they please, without your Excellency's leave." A town meeting was held and the three petitioning elders were put out of the consistory for applying to the governor. Cornbury then obtained an order of council for the petitioners to appear, and also for the town clerk with the record of the above action.

In the hearing the governor seems to have learned something to the prejudice of Freeman, for he issued an order forbidding a call to him, because he " has misbehaved himself by promoting and encouraging the unhappy divisions." He declared the call of Freeman " not consistent with her Majesty's service "; for which reasons " the said petitioners are hereby required not to call him; but they are left at liberty to send for such Minister as they shall think fitt from Holland or any other place, as hath been customary." This order anticipated a petition from the Schenectady Church, praying the governor not to allow Freeman to be called away.

But, notwithstanding the prohibition of the governor and the desires of the Schenectady Church, Freeman came to New York with a view to labor in the Churches named, and

[1] *Documentary History*, III, 89–111.

by some undisclosed means succeeded in disarming Cornbury's prejudice and in securing from him a license to preach
in the said Churches, " for & During So Long Time as to me
shall Seem meet, and all P'sons are hereby Required to Take
Notice hereof accordingly."

With this license Freeman began preaching at New
Utrecht and presently made occasion for his elders to petition
the governor that he would compel Antonides to surrender the
property and books of the Churches, " whereof Mr. Freeman
is Minister by License from your Excellency." In response
to this prayer Cornbury issued an order to Antonides for the
" delivery of House, Land, Stock, and Books. . . . Whereas
I have licensed, authorized, and appointed Mr. Bernardus
Freeman."

Out of such a situation grew a long-drawn quarrel between
the party of Freeman and the party of Antonides. The
former distinguished themselves by the most obsequious submission to the governor's right of induction and ecclesiastical
control, and went so far as to say in one of their petitions,
" Your Excellency's petitioners are humbly of opinion that
all Ecclesiastical affairs And the Determination of all
things relating thereto in this Province lies solely before
your Lordpp." This they declared to Cornbury, and after
Cornbury's departure from New York they solicited Lieutenant Governor Ingoldsby, " that your Honour will be
pleased, as has been usual, to order that no Dutch Minister
shall preach or exercise his Ministerial ffunctions in this
County, besides Mr. Freeman, until further orders from
Yoʳ Honʳ."

The opposing attitude of Antonides and his party was that
of stout denial of any ecclesiastical power of the governor
over the Dutch Church and its ministry, declaring that
Antonides held his position by the authority of the classis
of Amsterdam, " according to the laws and customs of the
Dutch Church," and " that no such lycense or the other
orders (Cornbury's) were, nor yet are, of any force or validity

in the Dutch Churches of this Province, but Tended to the ruin of the liberty of the said Churches in this Country." In the exercise of such liberty, and such contempt for governmental interference, Antonides boldly disregarded an order not to ordain elders in the Churches, informing the governor that "he can not comply with the order, unless he breaks through the Rules and Discipline of the Dutch Reformed Protestant Church."

Had Cornbury remained in the government such language might have brought the bold minister into bonds, but his successors were of different mind. The term of Lovelace was too short for much service, giving place after a few months to Robert Hunter, who, while a sincere Church of England man, was liberal of mind and of placable disposition. Instead of taking up his predecessor's quarrel, or insisting on any superior ecclesiastical authority, he attempted to exert a moral influence, rather than official power, in establishing peace between the contending factions. This he succeeded in effecting by persuading all the Churches involved to call both Antonides and Freeman to a collegiate pastorate,[1] in 1714.

The most celebrated action of Cornbury against the liberty of worship was his prosecution of Francis Mackemie, the Mackemie. Presbyterian minister whose settlement and service in Virginia have already been noted in the chapter on that colony. In January, 1707, he with another minister, John Hampton, appeared in New York and did his great work therein in the cause of religious liberty.[2] On arrival in New York Mackemie

[1] Strong, *History of Flatbush.*

[2] Smith, *New York*, I, 186; *Massachusetts Historical Collections*, VI, 1; 12; Force, *Historical Tracts*, IV. Pamphlet entitled: —

"MACKEMIE'S TRIAL

"A narrative of a New and Unusual American imprisonment of two Presbyterian ministers, one of them for preaching one SERMON at the City of New York, 1707.

"A specimen of the Cloggs and Fetters with which the Liberties of Dissenters are intangled at New York and Jersey Governments, beyond any places in her Majesty's Dominions."

either sought and obtained permission, or was invited by the Dutch Minister, to preach in the Reformed Church. But Cornbury forbade the service, and the preacher, not insisting on the use of the Church, held service and preached in the house of William Jackson, "with open doors." Hampton preached also on the same Sunday, January 20th, at Newtown.

So bold a defiance aroused the wrath of the governor, who on the 24th of the month issued a warrant for the arrest of both the men, "who have taken upon them to preach in a private house, without having obtained any License for so doing . . . they are gone into Long Island with intent there to spread their pernicious Doctrines and Principles, to the disturbance of the Church by Law established and of the government of this Province."

The warrant was executed and the culprits were brought for examination before the governor, when Mackemie defended his liberty on the toleration act of England. This act Cornbury declared to be without any force in his government, and required the prisoners to give bonds for good behavior and to promise not to preach in New York or New Jersey. Mackemie was willing to give bonds, but refused the promise, and both men were put in jail, where they remained six weeks and four days, during the absence of Chief Justice Mompesson. On the return of the judge they were brought before him on a writ of *habeas corpus*. Hampton was discharged without trial, as "a man of less interest," while Mackemie was liberated under bonds to appear for trial at the next session of the court, the grand jury having found a true bill against him, that "he did take upon him to preach . . . in a Conventicle and Meeting not permitted or allowed by law, under color or excuse of Religion in other manner than according to our Liturgy and practice of the Church of England." On the trial the prosecution relied on the royal *instructions* to Cornbury, rather than on the ministry act, as though conscious that said act, while establishing a Church, yet inflicted no penalties for non-conformity. Mackemie

defended himself, producing licenses from the governors of
Virginia and Maryland, contending that there was nothing
in the English common or statute law to hold him, and nothing in the laws of New York against the liberty he had exercised. As to the governor's ecclesiastical authority, he
argued that it could not exist without the due promulgation
of law.

The plea of Mackemie was so forceful that a jury, "packed
to convict," was won over to his cause and unanimously
acquitted him. The court, however, would not release him
until he had paid all the costs, which, together with his
expenses, amounted to £83, a sufficiently heavy burden ; for
which he must yet have had great compensation in the consciousness that he had fought a great fight and won a great
victory in the cause of human liberty. Never again did a
New York governor attempt to silence any orderly preaching
of the gospel.

To Cornbury the issue of the case brought a bitter mortifi-
cation, and he seems to have been seriously alarmed for the
consequences to himself from the reports of the trial made
by Mr. Mackemie and his friends in England and the
colonies. Writing to the lords of trade in October, 1707, he
denied that Mackemie had applied to him for a license, and
said, " I Intreat your Lordships' protection against this malicious man, who is well known in Virginia and Maryland to
be a Disturber of the Peace and quiet of all places he comes
into : he is a Jack of all Trades, he is a Preacher, a Doctor
of Physic, a Merchant, an Attorney or Counsellor at Law,
and, which is worse of all, a Disturber of Governments."[1] It
does not appear that Mackemie ever took any action against
Cornbury. Nor was it needed to the damage of his lordship's
reputation, which his course had so deeply stained.

With Cornbury's departure from the government of New
York all attempts at coercion upon recognized "dissenting"
churches and ministers ceased. The forms which asserted

[1] *Colonial History of New York*, IV, 1186.

a religious establishment were preserved, but both in England and the colony it had become evident that a forcible conversion of a dissenting Church to the Church of England, as well as harsh treatment of non-conformists, was not advisable. In 1707 the bishop of London, as though alarmed by the violent proceedings of Cornbury, wrote: "The beginning of any new establishment ought to be carried on gradually, which will make all steps easier, and in case of disappointment the matter will not be so grievous."[1]

The successive governors, Hunter, Burnet, Montgomerie, Clinton, Tryon, all received from the king instructions to "collate to benefices," to demand certificates from the bishop of London, and to allow liberty of conscience to all "except Papists."[2] There occur also in the records many applications to the governor for permission to build Churches, even non-conforming Churches, and for protection against intrusion by irregular preachers, and for licenses to preachers.[3] But there were no more interferences with the liberty of preaching by any ministers of recognized denominations. So far as they were concerned, the victory of Mackemie was final.

Hunter.   The troubles of Governor Hunter on ecclesiastical questions came to him from the clergy of his own Church. They had been so elated by Cornbury's efforts to "become a nursing father" to the Church of England, that they resented Hunter's more tolerant and just disposition. When they found that they could no longer use the governor to prosecute their grasping and ambitious schemes, they turned upon him as an enemy, doing much, both in the province and in their representations in England, to harass the administration of the best governor ever sent to New York.

At first they treated him with deference, and in their convention of 1712, assembled by him to "consult about the

---

[1] *Colonial History,* **V,** 29.

[2] *Ibid.,* V, 95, 132, 135, 391.

[3] *Documentary History,* III, 289, 291, 294, 568, 570, 583.

affairs of the Church," they adopted an address [1] expressing "our humble thanks to your Excellency for this opportunity of meeting." They also desired "the establishment of the Church throughout the other Counties of this province, as well as to secure and corroborate it where it is already settled." According to Colonel Morris,[2] in the letter recently noted and which described Hunter's action in Church matters, the governor had given the use of the King's Farm to Trinity parish to hold during the time of his government. This tract, bounded by the present Chambers Street, Broadway, Fulton Street, and the North River, had been granted by Governor Fletcher to Trinity in 1696, but the grant was annulled in 1699. The grant was renewed by Hunter in 1711 for the term above specified, but with this Mr. Vesey, the rector of Trinity, was not satisfied and besought the governor to influence the queen to give the farm in fee to the Church. This the governor refused to do, and thereby brought upon himself the enmity of the clergy. They found fault with him also for his conduct in the Jamaica case, condemning him, as Morris says, "for not dragooning Mr. Poyer into the parsonage." Vesey declared that Hunter was "no Churchman," and prevailed on the clergy to make representations against him to the bishop of London and the board of trade.

Their complaints do not seem to have had large influence on the other side of the sea, while the governor appears to have been well equipped to sustain his part in the battle of words. Two bits of his letters to Secretary Popple of the board of trade are worth quoting for their tone of easy and contemptuous indifference toward the clerical attack. In one he wrote: "If the Society (for the Propagation of the Gospel) take not more care for the future than has been taken hitherto in the choice of their Missionaries, instead of establishing Religion, they'l destroy all Government and good manners." Again, referring to the report that the

---

[1] *Documentary History*, III, 84.   [2] *Colonial History*, V, 320.

bishop of London had appointed Mr. Vesey his commissary in New York, he wrote: "I hope his Lordship has also constituted Talbot his Commissary for the Jerseys & Phillips for Pennsylvania . . . and then I shall know what he means: the best on't is that, though I know no good they have ever done, I know no great hurt they can do at present."

Quakers.

It should be noted that during the period, which our narrative has reached, the Quakers were pressing for a release from disabilities. Since Stuyvesant's time they had suffered no molestation, beyond fines for refusing militia service and disfranchisement for refusal of the oath of allegiance. Many petitions from them to have their scruples in regard to these matters respected were presented to the governor and council.[1] The response of the council was that, "if they would not train, they must pay the penalty." As to their prayer for the ballot, Attorney-General Bradley gave an opinion, that "the English laws concerning Quakers did not extend to the colonies, and that all who refuse to take the Oath should be excluded from the poll." This opinion was rendered in 1734.

Not long afterward the persistence of the petitioners obtained from the assembly an act, giving to Quakers the same rights which they possessed in England.[2] This conferred upon them the right to vote, but made no release from penalty under the militia law. For such release they were compelled to wait many years, nor could the exaction of the penalty be set down to religious persecution. The militia laws bore equally on all citizens as a necessity of state, without regard to religious opinions. It was at every man's option either to train or pay the fine for failure. That the Quaker's conscience compelled him to choose the latter was no hardship by the law, which in this matter made no discriminations. It could be so accounted only in case the

[1] *Documentary History*, III, 605–612.
[2] *Colonial History*, VI, 28.

law had subjected the Quaker alone to fine for refusal of service. But this was never done.

In 1744 occurred a new provocation to religious persecution already noted in our sketch of Connecticut. It is an interesting illustration of the limitations set by men of the day around the idea of liberty. Not yet had the conception of the breadth of that principle taken hold of the mind. Every new departure from stereotyped doctrine and polity was looked upon with suspicion and subjected to judicial inquisition, with more or less of hardship inflicted on its representatives. As with other sects, this was the fate of the Moravians Moravians. in New England and New York. These gentle and devoted people had found places of gospel labor among the Indians in Ulster and Dutchess counties and over the border in Connecticut, presently drawing upon themselves the unfriendly action of the authorities in both colonies, the reason whereof was in no fault of which they had been guilty, but in the shameful ignorance and malice of their neighbors.[1]

Nothing could be more beautiful than the earnest and self-sacrificing spirit with which they applied themselves to their chosen task of teaching the Indians in the truths of the Gospel and the decencies of civilized life. But their neighbors could not understand them. They themselves cared nothing for the Indians. The Moravians were strangers and with a strange tongue, while their religious methods and services differed from those to which their critics were accustomed. It is not at all unlikely, also, that these neighbors did not want a civilized body of Indians settled down among them. Thus, for a variety of reasons, there were soon sent to Governor Clinton and the council petitions against the Moravians and their work, representing that they were disturbers of public order and were suspected of being "disguised Papists." In those days when the French and English were at

[1] *Documentary History of New York*, III, 617–621; *Colonial History of New York*, VI, 269, 279, 311; *Colonial Laws of New York; American Church Review*, "*Moravians in Housatonic Valley*," by Rev. Dr. Andrews.

swords constantly drawn for the dominion of America, and the borders were the scene of frequent massacre and rapine, this suspicion of "Papistry" was very easy to throw at a stranger. We have seen something of it in Virginia and will meet it again in Pennsylvania and Maryland.

In answer to the petitions the Moravian teachers were summoned to New York, and there examined before the governor and council. As the result of this examination it is recorded that the council could "find no fault in them," save that they refused the oaths for conscience' sake. In view of this and the opposition near the scene of their labors, they were ordered to leave the province. Thus, from the narrowest of spirits was broken up a godly work, which only bigotry or malevolence could condemn. The banished Moravians took themselves and many of their converts, first to more liberal-minded Pennsylvania and then to Ohio, where awaited them both a blessed work and the dreadful catastrophe of Gnadenhütten.

Their New York enemies, despite this departure, were not satisfied, and to guard against return secured from the legislature the enactment of the most disgraceful law that defaces the statute book of either colony or state. It is the act **Act against Moravians.** of September 21, 1744, entitled, "An Act for securing his Majesty's government of New York." It purports to guard against French and "popish" influence, but is solely directed to the distress of the pious and guileless Moravians; and ordains that "no vagrant Preacher, Moravian, or disguised Papist, shall Preach or Teach, Either in Public or Private without first taking the Oaths appointed by this Act and obtaining a Lycence from the Governor or Commissioner in Church for the Time being." The penalties of the act were fine, imprisonment, banishment, and, in case of return, "Such Punishment as shall be inflicted by the Justices of the Supreme Court, not extending to Life or Limb."

Against this oppression of his brethren the great Mora- **Zinzendorf.** vian leader, Count Zinzendorf, then in London, protested in

complaint to the lords of trade. He wrote: "By an almost evident instigation of the Calvinist clergy and a mean
sort of people who through their ignoble disposition easily
take occasion thereto, there has arisen an evil Custom of disturbing and burdening honest Men of all Sorts, who have
settled themselves in those Colonies, hoping to enjoy an unrestrained Freedom of Religion. . . . I petition for two Declarations or Orders. The one to keep honest people, as well
strangers in as inhabitants of America, from being chicaned
with and plagued without the least reason and, as it were,
only *de gayeté de Cœur*. The second, that no body, but least
of all the Indians, shall be hindered from joyning with any
Protestant Church whatever, which in his ideas is the most
solid, according to the measures taken for encouraging Foreigners to settle in the British Colonies in America."

This complaint of Zinzendorf, together with another from
M. de Gersdorff "in behalf of himself and the Moravians in
New York," the board of trade referred to Governor Clinton, Governor
inquiring what the Moravians had done to deserve such treat- Clinton.
ment. The reply of the governor indicates the thought in
his mind, that violence of epithet is sufficient to justify the
harshness complained of. He described the Moravians as
"Suspicious, Vagrant, Stroling Preachers," who "debauch
the Minds of the people with Enthusiastical Notions, at least,
and Created Great Scisms & Divisions in the protestant Congregations." They were "suspected of being popish emissaries
and having designs against his Majesty's government." He
denounced the free asylum for such people in Pennsylvania as
"a most pernicious thing." Then he launched out in a dia-
tribe against Whitefield as laboring "with real design to fill
his own Pockets," declaring the Moravians to be of the same
class, who "compassed sea and land to make Proselytes";
from which last assertion it would seem that, though the governor could quote Scripture, he knew not how to apply it.

This letter of Clinton was written in 1746. Only five
years afterward, an item of record shows, both how short-

lived was this spasm of religious bigotry, and how the governor's ecclesiastical authority had waned. It appears that Moravians, undeterred by the hostility of the government, had not ceased coming to the province. A number of them had settled in the city of New York and in 1751 by formal letter notified the governor of their "intention of building a Church in this city."[1] For this building they neither asked nor expected the permission of the governor, and by him no prohibition was interposed.

Moravians build in New York City.

That the pretensions of the civil authority to interference in religious matters had greatly weakened is shown by another incident of Clinton's term of office, which occurred in 1746. About that time there came to New York a certain John Hofgoed, who appears to have been an irregular Lutheran preacher. He applied to the governor for a license, but Clinton refused and forbade him to exercise ministerial functions. This order he disregarded, to the great annoyance of the Lutheran minister and Church in the city, evidently intruding his service where it was not desired. To rid themselves of the infliction, the Lutherans appealed to the governor, praying him " to Interfere in this Behalf and Supress the further proceedings of the said John Lodewick Hofgoed by such Ways and Means as your Excellency in Council shall think fit and proper to be Done." So far as the record goes, it appears that Clinton thought "fit and proper" to do nothing, for no order or prosecution is noted. Hofgoed, however, retired from the city and appeared at Fishkill in 1749, where his attempts to preach and intrude upon the regularly constituted parish caused another petition to the governor, in which the Fishkill people implored him to silence the troublesome minister. To this petition also Clinton turned a deaf ear, showing how the spirit of the time had changed from that of Fletcher or Cornbury, neither of whom would have delayed to clap the delinquent into bonds. It was becoming evident that any minister, who disturbed not the public peace, might

Waning power.

[1] *Documentary History*, III, 621.

exercise his ministry, and that contentions of order in the Churches themselves, touching doctrine and ordination, must be decided by their own authorities without appeal to the civil power.

This remark, of course, does not apply to the established Church, which, by dint of constant perversity of statement, had become entirely of the Church of England. Within this Church the governors continued to exercise a semblance of authority, while, until the opening of the Revolution, there were frequent efforts to advance its interests to the detriment of other Churches in the province. Such efforts, however, it must be noted, came not so much by way of government initiative as by the persistent demand of the Church itself *The establishment.* for the active assistance of the civil power. It will hereafter be shown that this demand, made by a Church representing not more than a fifteenth part of the people [1] and with an arrogance of assertion difficult for " dissenters " to bear, had no small influence in preparing the population for entire separation from the mother country in both ecclesiastical and civil affairs.

But this establishment was forced to content itself with the original limitations of the act of 1693. Though implored by the Episcopal clergy, the government never made any effort to widen its domain beyond the four counties named in that act. The temper of the people at large was too well known to permit the attempt. Indeed, had the people had their way, the Church would have been speedily disestablished. Repeated efforts to secure that end were made by the assembly, to be as often defeated by the governor and council. The status remained until the coming of Independence, when the nameless establishment in New York fell with the royal power.

[1] Smith, *New York*, I, 337.

II. *Maryland*

The contribution of the history of Maryland to the question of Church and State and the related principle of Religious Liberty is a story of peculiar interest and vicissitudes. At different times Maryland faced both ways, for liberty and against it, while the conduct of affairs was in the midst of chronic broils and factions. A proprietary government, it was torn by continual jealousy. A foundation of Roman Catholics in the avowed interests of religious freedom, it was wrested from their grasp and made hostile to both their faith and the rights of conscience.

Calvert.

Its projector, Sir George Calvert, was a personal friend of James I., and one of his secretaries of state. In 1624 he was converted to the Church of Rome and openly confessed the change, resigning at the same time his secretaryship and offering to retire altogether from the government. The king's friendship forbade the latter and retained Calvert in the privy council, and also raised him to the peerage as Lord Baltimore. This friendship was continued by Charles I., on his accession to the throne in 1625, with the result that Baltimore's colonization schemes found a ready and gracious attention on the part of the king.

Not long after the accession of Charles, Baltimore set out with several companions, among whom were three Jesuit priests, White, Copley, and Altham, to take possession of his patent of Avalon in New Foundland, which had been granted to him by James in 1624. The rigor of the climate, during a trial of less than two years, concluded Baltimore to abandon his intention of colonizing that locality, and he sailed southward in search of more promising regions. This search brought him to Virginia, where, as noted in the chapter on Virginia, he was not suffered to remain, because of his declining to take the oath of supremacy. This expulsion took place in 1628, when Baltimore, leaving his wife in Virginia, returned to England to seek a new patent from the king.[1] While in the neighborhood of the colony he had been able to look at the country on both sides of it, and at first selected that to the south of the James River, but concluded to substitute for this in his application the country to the north of the Potomac, which he and his Jesuit friends described as "pleasant to look upon and fitted for the homes of a happy people."

The application for a patent covering the regions of the Chesapeake was made in 1630 and met with the royal favor, though the patent was not issued until 1632. Meanwhile Lord Baltimore had died, and his son Cecil succeeded to his barony and his colonizing plans. Thus, the Maryland patent was issued to the second Lord Baltimore, whose life and zeal were fully engaged in the schemes and desires of his father. *Maryland patent.*

The patent for the designated province — to be called Maryland, in honor of Queen Henrietta Maria — is remarkable for several peculiar features, and for meaning much more than it says on the subject of religion. It was undoubtedly drawn up by Baltimore himself, with a view to permit the exercise of religious freedom. The king is represented as moved "with the laudable and pious desire of extending alike the Christian religion and the territories of the King's Empire," in the pursuance of which desire various rights of genuine sovereignty are conferred on Lord Baltimore. As Carolina, thirty years afterward, Maryland became a palatinate, and its ruler had almost regal powers. He possessed "the Patronages and Advowsons of all Churches, which shall happen to be built, together with licence and faculty of erecting and founding Churches, Chapels, and places of worship . . . and of causing the same to be dedicated and constituted according to the ecclesiastical laws of our Kingdom of England, with all and singular such and as ample rights, privileges, sovereignties &c. . . as any Bishop *Religious freedom.*

---

[1] Johnson, *Foundation of Maryland,* p. 18. (*Maryland Historical Society Publication,* No. 18.)

of Durham, within the Bishoprick or County Palatine of Durham in our Kingdom of England, ever hath." All the powers granted Baltimore was "to hold of the King in free and common socage . . . yielding unto the King and his successors Two Indian Arrows of those parts, to be delivered at the Castle of Windsor every year on Tuesday in Easter week, and also the fifth part of all gold and silver ore that shall happen to be found." This sovereignty is "subject only to one condition, namely; that it should not be such as might prejudice the true Christian Religion or allegiance to the crown."

Church.
This charter is sometimes spoken of as establishing the Church of England in Maryland. But this is not correct. The Church of England is not mentioned in the instrument, while the phrase, "according to the ecclesiastical laws of our Kingdom of England," might mean much or little, as circumstances might vary.[1] Baltimore construed the charter as conferring ecclesiastical supremacy on the proprietary, which he was to exercise according to those laws. This is to say, as those laws made the king head of the English Church, the charter made Baltimore head of the Maryland Church. It did not specifically tell him to conform the Church of Maryland to the English model, but left it in his hand to do as he wished and as he found what Church he desired. Under the terms of the charter it was competent for him to establish Romanism, Episcopacy, Independency, or Presbyterianism. The power of establishment is plainly in the instrument, but its character is undefined.

Professor Petrie[2] specifies three constructions which have been put on this clause: 1. The Churches *must* be of the Church of England; 2. *If* Churches are formed, they *must* be of the Church of England; 3. *If* they are formed, they *may* be of that communion. He argues also that the intent

[1] The Carolina proprietaries, differing from Baltimore, construed the phrase as establishing the Anglican Church.

[2] *Johns Hopkins Studies*, X; " *Church and State*."

of the Charter was to establish that Church. But the reply Intent of is cogent that if such intention had been clear in mind, charter. instructions would have been explicit to fulfil it, as in other colonies. In the absence of any such explicit command, the most that can be made of the clause is a suggestion of the *manner* in which Baltimore should exercise his ecclesiastical power.

One cannot, at the first glance, escape the suspicion of a somewhat disingenuous purpose on the part of the proprietary in this allusion to the ecclesiastical laws of England. The casual reader could easily suppose that the establishment of the English Church was designed. It is possible, though not probable, that the king so supposed. At all events, it looks deceptive. Anderson, who enlarges on the shameful character of such a charter given to a Romanist, quotes Murray as saying, "It was formed for the purpose of blinding the public mind." [1]

The judgment is not unjust. But the circumstances were peculiar, and, if ever a deceptive turn of words is justified, they certainly justified this "blinding" purpose of Baltimore. Himself a devout Roman Catholic, he desired to make a refuge for the persecuted brethren of his own faith, who in England were subjected to countless limitations, fines, and penalties. It was impossible for him to obtain a charter with that desire avowed in the instrument. All England, New England, and Virginia would have been roused to a storm of indignation. At the same time, it was impossible to obtain a charter expressive of the other and as great desire of his heart, to confer on Maryland the boon of complete religious liberty. The English prelate and presbyter, the Massachusetts Puritan and Virginia Churchman, would have been in arms at once. The times were not yet ripe for the "lively experiment," which the second Charles allowed Williams to try in Rhode Island, "that a flourishing civil state may stand and best be maintained, with a full liberty of religious concernments."

[1] *History of the Colonial Church*, II, 113.

All the conditions demanded that the charter should contain some ecclesiastical direction, while Baltimore desired that such direction should be in consistency with both of his dominant purposes, to protect his persecuted brethren and to give freedom to all. Both purposes were noble, and while they mark for us the lofty character of this founder of a state — more lofty because so immensely superior to almost all men of the age — we may be content to set down his deceptive phrase to the shrewdness of the politician. He knew that there was no other way to gain these noble ends than to take into his own hand the direction of the religious affairs of his province, according to the method of the king in England. So Baltimore became under the charter virtual king and head of the Church in Maryland, if he should choose to exercise supremacy.

Baltimore.

If ever there was a man fit for so high a station, certainly Baltimore was such. He " deserves to be ranked among the most wise and benevolent lawgivers of all ages. He was the first in the history of the Christian world to seek for religious security and peace by the practice of justice, and not by the exercise of power." [1] The first Lord Baltimore died before his noble scheme could be realized, but the fundamental law of the colony was shaped by his broad and liberal mind, while his son Cecil proved a worthy follower in his father's steps, to put these plans in execution. It is possible to say, as some have said, that the offer of complete freedom, with which the Baltimores began their colony, was but a guise, under which they sought relief for their co-religionists, in no less comprehensive way to be secured. But it is neither necessary nor just to so judge. Every detail of their directions touching on the subject evince the motives of broad minds, not seeking merely a selfish freedom, but grasping the fundamental principles of human rights. Unlike the Puritan, they did not arrogate to themselves the sole possession of the truth, or claim only for their own views freedom of expression. They

[1] Bancroft, *United States*, I, 244.

held rather to the dignity of the human soul, responsible alone to Him who is Lord of the conscience, and to that Master alone to stand or fall. This they preserved in all conditions; nor did they, like the men of Massachusetts, forget in their accession to power the principles of liberty confessed in their days of hardship. They stand level with Roger Williams in the history of human freedom, and among founders of states worthy to rank with Winthrop, Hooker, and Penn.

The charter,[1] thus given to a Roman Catholic and involving so great possibilities, did not escape criticism; nor did the dubious allusion to the English ecclesiastical laws entirely blind the public mind. Scarcely had the instrument passed the broad seal when objections were heard. These had a Objections. double source, coming from both Protestants and Romanists. The former complained that it gave too great power to the proprietary, all the more to be deprecated because he was a Roman Catholic. The latter objected to Baltimore's schemes on the ground that religious freedom should not be allowed in any community. Strangely enough, this latter objection found more strenuous speech than the former. To the former the king's pleasure was a sufficient answer; while the latter was made to assume the form of a question of conscience; as to whether a sincere Romanist could accept a charter allowing freedom of worship to all varieties of religionists.

The specially singular thing about this Roman contention is, that the charter itself did not decree religious liberty in the new colony, nor contain a line suggestive of its institution there. The entire decision in regard to the religious *status* of Maryland was put at the discretion of Baltimore. So far as its terms could forecast that *status*, inasmuch as the proprietary was a professed Roman Catholic, the Protestant contention that the colony would be Romanist appears far more just. The situation can be explained only by the fact that Baltimore, notwithstanding the "blinding" phrase of the charter, made no secret of his intention. This intention

[1] *Foundation of Maryland*, pp. 15–30.

was frankly expressed in personal conversation, and more publicly in advertisements for adventurers, in which was promised the free exercise of each man's religion. Certainly, this frankness may go far to remove the charge of disingenuous purpose in the charter.

At all events, it was clearly understood by very many that the proprietary did not intend to found the colony within the lines of the Roman faith. In consequence there arose much discussion among the English Roman Catholics, by some of whom it was urged to Baltimore that he ought not, as a true son of the Holy Father, to undertake such a scheme; while others were made to doubt whether they could with good consciences associate themselves with him in the enterprise. In this dilemma Baltimore laid the question before Father Blount, the provincial of the English Jesuits, who set aside the objections and argued for the charter and the colony as designed by its founder. In the course of his paper he used surprising language from such a source, which has no parallel in the utterances of the Romanism of the day. "Conversion," he wrote, "in matters of Religion, if it be forced, should give little satisfaction to a wise state . . . for those, who for worldly respects will breake their faith with God, will do it on a fit occasion much sooner with men." This opinion of their spiritual superior resolved the doubts of Baltimore and his associates, and, as Johnson remarks, may be taken as "proof that the charter of Maryland was then considered and treated as securing liberty of conscience to Roman Catholics; and that the Society of Jesus undertook to further and extend the planting of the colony, with full knowledge that the principle of toleration was to be adopted as one of the fundamental institutions of the province."

Settlement.   The first expedition to the new colony set forth in 1632, and was composed of two hundred and twenty emigrants. Of this number one hundred and twenty-eight were Protestants, who took the oath of supremacy at the time of sailing. The rest of the company were Romanists, among them the three Jesuit friends of Baltimore and twenty gentlemen of position and fortune. At the outset the substantial strength of the colony was thus Roman Catholic, while the great majority of the Protestants were artisans, farmers, and servants. Baltimore remained in England, to there superintend the interests of the colony, and sent his brother, Leonard Calvert, in the capacity of governor.[1]

The expedition had hardly disembarked on the shore of the Chesapeake when it met the beginnings of a trouble, which was to annoy the colony for many years, an opposition in which the lust of gain and religious bigotry had about equal parts. There is no need to recount here the details of the struggle between Clayborne and Baltimore, and the present reference is made only to point out its religious element.[2] This Clayborne was secretary of Virginia and had obtained from the governor of that colony permission to explore Chesapeake Bay, and in 1631 secured a royal license to " traffic in those parts." Under this license he took possession of Kent Island and parts of the shore of the mainland. The new colony with a patent covering these stations naturally seemed to him as an invader of his rights, while the Roman faith of Baltimore could ill be suffered by Clayborne's avowed Puritanism. Nor was it difficult for the secretary of popery-hating Virginia to enlist many sympathizers, to whom the establishment of a Roman Catholic colony as their next door neighbor appeared among all evils the most to be feared and deprecated.[3]

Clayborne.

---

[1] *Foundation of Maryland*, p. 31.

[2] Anderson, *Colonial Church*, II, 89.

[3] This animosity of Clayborne was intensified by an incident related in Captain Yong's *Voyage to Virginia and Delaware Bay* (*Massachusetts Historical Collections*, IV, 9 ; 82, note), 1634. Yong brought out with him his nephew, George Evelin, as an agent for Clayborne's London partners, who by some means induced Clayborne to go to England. During the absence of Clayborne, Evelin, who was a Romanist, took possession of his property and turned over Kent Island and the neighboring station to Calvert, whose object they supposed to be " to make Maryland predominantly Catholic." This

The trouble hence arising had many outbreaks of violence, and culminated in the commonwealth time, as will be noted, in the overthrow of Baltimore's government through the attack of Clayborne and Bennett. That overthrow they tried to justify in their remarkable " Declaration against the Patent of Maryland," which bears date of 1649, and in which there is hardly a word of truth.[1] It charges Baltimore with " professing the establishment of the Romish religion only." It asserts, " They suppressed the poor protestants amongst them, to protect chiefly the Roman Catholic religion in the free exercise of the same. . . . There is not the least mention of a King in all their government . . . as if hee (Baltimore) had been absolute Prince or King. . . . The pattent of Maryland was grounded on noe good foundation, the King beeing misinformed."

That the religious action of the new colony was quite other than this declaration asserts is abundantly proved by the colonial records. The instructions of Baltimore were explicit on the point of liberty, and the early legislation sought the same end. Until 1637 the authority of the governor existed alone, without any legislative assembly or regular system of law. In that year the first assembly met on the summons of Calvert and was composed entirely of Roman Catholics. The three priests were summoned with the other freemen, but excused themselves from attendance. Johnson[2] notes that, from the beginning, no priest or minister has ever sat in a Maryland legislature. This exclusion is continued to this day and finds place in the constitution of the State, which makes ministers ineligible to that position.

First assembly.

Exclusion of clergy.

robbery was enough to rouse Clayborne's resentment, and he made much, not only of his own wrongs, but of this perversion to Roman Catholic possession. " But," says *Leah and Rachel*, " it was not religion, it was not *punctilios* they stood upon ; it was that sweete, that rich, that large country they aymed at." (Force, *Historical Tracts*, " *Leah and Rachel*.")

[1] *Colonial History of New York*, III, 23.

[2] *Foundation of Maryland*, p. 94.

The special business for which the assembly was summoned was to act upon a " Body of Laws " [1] prepared and sent over by Baltimore for legislative adoption. It is not at all probable that either he or Governor Calvert apprehended the reception this code would meet. Doubtless, both of them expected a ready and prompt legislative ratification of the proprietary's will. But such did not take place, and it makes a striking indication of the tendency of American air to breed a spirit of independence to note that this Body of Laws was rejected by the assembly, which appointed a committee to digest and report a code for the consideration of the legislature and then adjourned. After but few days, too few for the preparation of a new code, the assembly met again and received the report of the committee, which presented the same laws that they had rejected before. The action of the assembly was a prompt adoption of the report, and enactment of the " Body of Laws "! Thus early did the American settlers learn how to stickle for a point. They had no objection to the code itself, but to Baltimore's initiative. They would not formally ratify his will. What laws they passed must be their own, and transmitted to governor and proprietary for approval.

Body of Laws.

The first law in regard to the Church passed by the assembly was, " An Act for Church Liberties," which in simple and terse language, strikingly like that of the Great Charter of England, recites, —

" Holy Church within this province shall have and enjoy all her Rights, liberties and Franchises wholly and without Blemish." [2]

Church liberties.

This was in harmony with the mandate of the charter to Baltimore that " nothing should be done contrary to God's Holy Religion." It is quite as notable for what it omits as for what it declares, making no distinctions among the various Christian bodies, each of which claimed to be Holy Church and to represent God's Holy Religion. There can

[1] *Foundation of Maryland,* p. 39.   [2] *Acts of Assembly,* I, 96.

be no doubt, indeed, that these Maryland lawmakers were Romanists to a man; or that, had they been called upon to specify the particular communion which to them was Holy Church, with one voice they would have named the Church of Rome. But this definition they studiously refrained from making, leaving to each citizen of the colony to decide for himself as to what communion he would call Holy Church,

Religious
liberty. and asserting that that Church must be free from all interference by the civil power. This was practical religious liberty.

There is another illustration of this freedom in the oath prescribed (1636) by Baltimore to be taken by all officers of the colony,[1] of which a portion affirmed: — "I will not, by myself or any other, directly or indirectly, trouble, molest, or discountenance any person, professing to believe in Jesus Christ, for, or in respect of, religion; but merely as they shall be found faithful and well-deserving; my aim shall be public unity, and if any person or officer shall molest any person, professing to believe in Jesus Christ, on account of his religion, I will protect the person molested and punish the offender." To cause the spirit of this oath to be observed also among the people, a proclamation was published in the colony, forbidding "all unseasonable disputations in point of religion, tending to the disturbance of the public peace and quiet of the colony, and to the opening of faction in religion." Under this order, William Lewis, a Romanist, was fined five hundred pounds of tobacco for "interfering by opprobrious reproaches with two Protestants."[2]

A still further indication of this liberal intent is to be found in a bit of legislation, against which the Jesuit priests protested vehemently, but for which they were themselves chiefly responsible and were quite unable to prevent.[3] We may note in passing that the Jesuit fathers had immediately

---

[1] Hawks, *Contributions*, II, 27.

[2] *Foundation of Maryland*, pp. 52, 53.

[3] *Ibid.*, p. 56.

applied themselves to earnest missionary work among the Indians, with a very flattering success. Father White was specially diligent and devoted, conquering in a short time the Indian dialect, in which he prepared a catechism, and for the printing of which he imported the first press brought to America.[1]

But they were ambitious of more than this and wished to build up the power of their order. It appears that they, and some other priests who had followed the first three, had early acquired large holdings in Maryland and at the same time urged the old distinction between the civil and the canon Canon law. law, which for centuries had obtained in Europe, and which, subjecting priests to the canon law alone, had produced intolerable wrongs. This same distinction the Maryland priests wished to bring into the colony, and to effect thereby a reference of all cases, in which their order might be concerned, to an ecclesiastical, rather than a civil court. Probably, had they not stirred in the matter, the legislature would not have acted. Their own persistency made clear to the lawmakers the need of a special bulwark of liberty, such as no other colony enacted. To provide that bulwark, this Roman Catholic legislature of 1638, to the great discomfiture of their own spiritual directors, enacted that the laws should be "equally enforced against and concerning all persons, lay and ecclesiastical, without distinction, exemption, or privilege of any."

So was established under Roman Catholic auspices the free colony of Maryland, without a parallel for its idea of religious liberty in all the colonies, except the infant Rhode Island. In it the Roman Catholics found a secure asylum, and "Protestants were sheltered from Protestant intolerance."[2] And there was no hesitation on the part of various sectaries to accept the broad invitation which such a constitution made. Winthrop notes in his *Journal* for 1643 that

[1] Scharf, *History of Maryland*, I, 187–190.
[2] Bancroft, *United States*, I, 248.

Baltimore himself invited the Puritans of Massachusetts, offering lands and privileges, with "full liberty of conscience."[1] No records exist of any emigration to Maryland from New England, but the colony proved a harbor of refuge to the Puritans of Virginia, distressed by the brutal and intolerant Berkeley.

Protestant majority.

The majority of Protestants over Romanists, noted in the first company of colonists, steadily increased. The Jesuit White wrote as early as 1641: "Three parts of the people in four at least are heretics."[2] It is estimated that by 1649 there had come no less than one thousand from Virginia,[3]

Bennett.

and among them was Bennett, the Puritan leader, who specially vexed the soul of Berkeley. This man in Maryland forgot all gratitude for the asylum afforded him and was blind to all decency of conduct, when he lent himself to Clayborne to force the catastrophe of 1654.[4]

The population of the colony thus became overwhelmingly Protestant. For some reason Baltimore's asylum for his coreligionists did not attract very many of them — a fact that may well seem strange. Undoubtedly, he supposed that multitudes of Romanists would flock to this happy refuge from the disabling acts of England; while for the historian it constitutes something of a surprise that so small a number of them sought its freedom and relief. Perhaps, we can find no better explanation of this fact than the supposition that the average Romanist conscience refused to purchase peace by tolerating opposing faiths, and that the offence of Maryland's religious freedom was greater than the attraction of its refuge. But, however the fact may be accounted for, the

[1] Bancroft, *United States*, p. 257.

[2] " *Twenty Cases.*" (*Publication Maryland Historical Society.*)

[3] Fiske, *Old Virginia*, I, 312.

[4] *Leah and Rachel* had a suggestion of fine scorn for the baseness of the conduct of this Bennett and his companions, saying that, " Maryland was courted by them," and that all their requests for liberty of conscience and other privileges were readily granted. We shall see how unworthy of every favor they proved themselves to be.

result of twenty years' colonization found the Roman Catholics in a hopeless minority.

This disparity did not find its counterpart in the official bodies in the colony. Till 1648 Baltimore's appointments to office were almost invariably from among the Romanists, though it may fairly be claimed for him that his criterion of selection was rather personal fitness than religion. A large proportion also of the legislature was of the same faith, due to the fact that nearly every Romanist was a freeman, while only a minority among the Protestants were possessed of the franchise.

Romanist officials.

Though in no act of assembly or of public officers was there any evidence of intention to interfere with the Protestants, yet this situation in itself gave rise to great dissatisfaction among them. They esteemed it a wrong that the majority of the people should be excluded from the management of public affairs, and they knew not at what moment the dominant minority might fling aside its professions of liberality and proceed to oppress the Protestant faith. At the same time the struggle in England between king and parliament found reflection in the colony, adding greatly to the indigenous discontent. Maryland, unlike Virginia, did not exalt loyalty to the king. While the colonial authorities took no part against him, the great Puritan majority of the population were pronounced in their advocacy of his opponents.

In such conditions of discontent Baltimore found it advisable to make some changes to placate the opposition. To this end he remodelled the government in 1648, by displacing a majority of the Roman Catholic officials and appointing Protestants in their rooms. This, with an enlargement of the franchise, put the local government into Protestant hands. He even superseded his own brother, as governor, by the appointment of the Protestant Stone. In addition to this change in personnel he reappointed the oath of office, already noted, with the addition for the governor of the words, " nor will I make any difference of persons in conferring offices, rewards, or favors. . . for, or in respect of, their said Religion." [1]

It was deemed also advisable that the free toleration of the past should receive from the local legislature an emphatic re-affirmation. To this end, and undoubtedly at Baltimore's sug-

Act of Toleration. gestion, the famous " Toleration Act " of 1649 found its place in the statute book.[2] The act is remarkable both in its form and spirit, in its breadth and limitations. Curiously enough, it begins with its exceptions; ordaining death for blasphemy and the denial of the Trinity, and a fine of £5 for speaking "reproachful words of the Virgin Mary, the apostles, or evangelists." Then it imposes a fine of ten shillings for calling any person "by such opprobrious terms as, Heretic, Schismatic, Idolator, Puritan, Independent, Presbyterian, Popish priest, Jesuit, Papist, Lutheran, Calvinist, Anabaptist, Brownist, Antinomian, Barrowist, Roundhead, and Separatist." Having specified these details, the act proceeds: " Whereas the enforcing of the conscience in matters of Religion hath frequently fallen out to be of dangerous consequence in those commonwealths where it hath been practiced, and for the more quiet and peaceable government of this Province, and the better to preserve mutual Love and amity amongst the Inhabitants thereof: Be it therefore also by the Lord Proprietary, with the advice and consent of the Assembly, ordered and enacted (except as in this present act is before declared and set forth) that no person or persons whatever within this Province, . . . professing to believe in Jesus Christ, shall from henceforth be any ways troubled, molested, or discountenanced for, or in respect to, his or her religion, nor in the free exercise thereof within this province, or the islands thereunto belonging, nor in any way compelled to believe or exercise any other religion against his or her consent, so that they be not unfaithful to the lord proprietary, or molest or conspire against the civill government." That the influence of this law might be universal the legislature in 1650 prescribed

[1] *Foundation of Maryland*, pp. 112–114. [2] *Acts of Assembly*, I, 244.

" The Oath of Fidelity for every resident, in which he was made to declare for Libertie of Conscience in point of Religion to himself and all other persons." [1]

While the liberty confirmed by the statute was far greater than obtained in England, it was distinctly lower than that of Rhode Island. In Maryland only Trinitarian Christians were to be tolerated. There was no room under the law for the Unitarian, the Jew, the Infidel, or the Pagan. To our eyes it is narrow, but in the time of its enactment it was exceeding broad — far broader than the great toleration act of William and Mary, forty years later.

With this condition, one would think, the Puritans of Maryland ought to have been satisfied.[2] Though the powers conferred upon Baltimore by the charter were regal, the proprietary had divested himself of many privileges and had consented that all the rights of freeborn Englishmen should belong to his colonists — more rights indeed than they would possess in England. As enumerated by Johnson,[3] they had all the rights of *Magna Charta*: a free legislative assembly; the common law of England; trial by jury; taxation only by act of assembly; immunity from martial law, except in camp and garrison; equal taxation on all, and the liberty of conscience. Besides these great concessions, the recent acts of Baltimore had put the entire government in Protestant hands, with the one exception of the proprietary himself, while he had shown nothing but the fairest and most liberal disposition toward the followers of a faith different from his own. On the religious question there was absolutely nothing for the Puritan to complain of. He had entire freedom of conscience and worship, while there was no State-Church and no Church-rate compelling the support of a religion he did not own.

But this did not satisfy him. Like his brethren in New England, he considered himself alone entitled to liberty. In

---

[1] *Acts of Assembly*, 1650.

[2] *Leah and Rachel;* Force, *Historical Tracts.*

[3] *Foundation of Maryland*, p. 148.

Puritan
ingratitude.

Massachusetts there was this justification of Puritan exclusiveness, that the colony was their own and was founded with
the express intention to build up a commonwealth, in which
a unity of faith should be the great pillar of the state. They
neither invited nor desired religionists of other views, and
any person of different persuasion, entering the Bay colony,
went thither a conscious and unwelcome intruder. We may
condemn as unsound the principle on which the Massachusetts Puritan moulded his state. We may condemn as cruel
the harshness of many of his repressive acts. But we can
never charge him with treachery or ingratitude to his benefactor, nor because of the narrowness of his view fail to see
the stern and honest uprightness of his character.

Far otherwise was it with the Puritan of Maryland, in
whose course there was nothing to commend or excuse it
before the bar of history. Himself, equally with the Roman
Catholic, the object of harsh treatment in England and in
Virginia, he accepted the invitation of a Roman Catholic to
an asylum of liberty for both. In it he suffered no wrong
in his religious rights, and when he complained that he had
not the share in governmental matters, which was appropriate
to him, this also was accorded. On which recognition and
with the first taste of power, he set himself to plot against his
benefactor and against the religionists who had given him a
home and liberty. He played the part of a viper, stinging
the bosom that had warmed him, and made the most disgraceful chapter in the history of Puritanism and of religious
liberty.[1] There were, indeed, political motives on the part
of the Protestants in the Maryland broils; there was jealousy
of Baltimore himself, though his rule had been beneficent
and his policy was enlightened; and there was the old quarrel of Clayborne, now exalted into a struggle for the entire
province. But none of these elements had any power of
excuse for the conduct of the Puritans on the matter of
religion.

[1] Scharf, *History of Maryland*, I, 200.

Their opportunity was furnished by the triumph of the English parliament in England. The downfall of the king, to the Commonwealth. minds of the Maryland malcontents, seemed to require the overthrow of the proprietary.[1] Under the lead of Clayborne and Bennett the Puritan party in 1652 drove out Governor Stone and took possession of the government. Stone attempted armed resistance, but was defeated in pitched battle. The rights of Baltimore were ignored. Ten commissioners were appointed to administer the government and a new assembly was called. This assembly at once acknowledged the Commonwealth and the authority of Cromwell, without any recognition of the proprietary.

Having thus made a revolution in civil affairs, the Puritan party proceeded to reverse the colonial action in regard to Puritan religion. In 1654 an act was passed repealing the toleration intolerance. of 1649.[2] The act explicitly declared that, "None who profess the exercise of the Popish Religion, commonly known by the name of the Roman Catholic Religion, can be protected in this Province." The law went on to accord liberty of dissent from the "predominant religion," but it was not to be "extended to popery, prelacy, or licentiousness of opinion." What was intended by the words, "the predominant religion," does not clearly appear, for amid the variety of opinions formerly made welcome in Maryland no one could be called chief. The phrase suggests that the dream of these conspirators was the establishment of a non-prelatical Church on the pattern of Massachusetts. There can be little doubt that they confidently counted on the approval of Cromwell for this repealing act. They assumed that the protector would sympathize in any effort to dispossess Romanism and prelacy.[3] Their surprise must have been great on receiving from Crom- Cromwell. well a distinct disallowance of the act with the command to set it aside. At the same time Cromwell commanded the com-

[1] Scharf, *History of Maryland*, I, 210–220.
[2] *Acts of Assembly*, I, 340.
[3] Bancroft, *United States*, I, 260.

missioners "not to busy themselves about religion, but to settle the civil government." The assembly was forced to repeal the persecuting act, and the toleration of 1649 was left unchanged. But, though the effort of the Puritan party was thus made void, yet the attempt is sufficiently illustrative of their spirit.

We need not dwell here on the political turmoil which for several years disturbed the province. Baltimore was restored to his rights by Cromwell, but was met by many petty revolutions in his province, with all of which the question of religion was connected, but with none in such a way as to cause special change in the religious history or attitude of the colony. Meanwhile there was a steady increase of the non-Catholic population. The emigration was of all sorts and from every clime. Huguenots, Dutch, Germans, Swedes, Finns, Bohemians,[1] all were found in Maryland. All faiths were represented also, and among them a considerable sprinkling of Quakers, who were allowed full freedom of worship; but about forty of them suffered fines and whippings, because of their refusal of oaths and militia duty.[2] So large had the disproportion grown between the Catholic and Protestant populations by 1675, that the former had sunk to a very small minority. It was estimated that not more than one-twelfth of the people were Romanists, one-sixth of the Church of England, and three-fourths "Puritans." The last must be understood in its broadest sense as including all sects outside the two Churches of Rome and England.[3]

It is not surprising that this great disparity should accentuate a frequent discontent that a province so peopled should be in the possession of a Roman Catholic; while the discontent was increased by Baltimore's return to the early policy of choosing officials from among men of his own faith.

Quakers.

Discontent.

---

[1] Bancroft, *United States*, II, 236.

[2] *Johns Hopkins Studies*, X; " *Church and State in Maryland.*" Indulgence in regard to those scruples was afterward accorded to them in 1688, through the intercession of William Penn.

[3] Fiske, II, 150.

The death of the second Lord Baltimore in 1675, leaving title and province to his son Charles, who was of the same religion as his father and continued his father's colonial policy, gave the signal for new manifestations of opposition. There were complaints of arbitrary administration, into which we need not enter. But a large ground of complaint was in the religion of the proprietary and his colonial officers. This complaint was almost entirely sentimental, for it could not be shown that a single Protestant in the province had suffered in person or fortune on account of his religion, save in exclusion from colonial office. The complaint, however, was sufficient to meet with sympathy in England, where all Romanists were under the ban, and the wretched Oates was turning the cry, "No Popery," into the absurdest shriek of agony that ever split the air. Protestantism in Maryland had become political, and soon after the accession of the third Lord Baltimore, the English ministry issued an order to him that all offices of government in the province must be intrusted exclusively to Protestants. "Thus were the Roman Catholics disfranchised in the province which they had planted."[1]

At the same time a new trouble for Baltimore was being prepared by the ambition of the Church of England. The movement looking toward the establishment of that Church in Maryland seems to have been started by a Rev. Mr. Yeo, laboring in the province, who wrote to the archbishop of Canterbury a piteous appeal in 1675, imploring action for the establishment of the Church.[2] "Here," he wrote, "are ten or twelve counties, and in them at least 20,000 souls, and but three Protestant ministers of the Church of England. The priests are provided for, and the Quakers take care of those that are speakers, but no care is taken to build up Churches of the Protestant religion. The Lord's day is profaned; religion is despised, and all notorious vices are commended; so that it has become a Sodom of uncleanness and a pest-house

Church of England.

[1] Bancroft, *United States*, II, 242.
[2] Hawks, *Contributions*, II, 49.

of iniquity." With such an introduction, Yeo craves the influence of the archbishop with Lord Baltimore toward "some established support for the ministry of the Church of England."

This appeal was sent by the archbishop to the king's ministers and by them referred to the committee on plantations — otherwise called the board of trade. This body called upon Lord Baltimore, then in London, — for Charles, unlike his father, spent much of his life in Maryland, — for explanation. He replied,[1] that there were four ministers of the Church of England in his province; that every one of them had a comfortable support; that in the previous year an individual had bequeathed to the minister in Baltimore county five hundred and fifty acres, and another had conveyed his personal estate to St. Mary's Church for the maintenance of the ministry; and that the various religious tenets of the members of the assembly rendered it difficult to obtain any law establishing one Church.

The king's government were not satisfied with Baltimore's reply, and insisted that provision must be made for the support of the clergy of the Church of England, and the insistence was made more urgent by the clamors of many high officials in the English Church. But the proprietary promised nothing and returned to Maryland, where he administered the government in person until 1684.

In that year, the last of the reign of Charles II., the continuance of complaints from the Maryland malcontents and the threat of a writ of *quo warranto* against his charter,[2] due to the increased pressure of English Churchmen on the government, compelled him to go to England to defend his rights. Charles died before any decisive action was taken, and if Baltimore expected with confidence that the Romanist James would protect him from an unjust Protestant clamor,

[1] *Johns Hopkins Studies*, X ; " *Church and State in Maryland.*"

[2] Scharf, I, 299 ; Hawks, *Contributions*, II, 50 ; Anderson, *Colonial Church*, II, 617.

he was grievously disappointed. The king, though a bigoted Treachery of James II. son of Rome, loved power more than the bonds of religious brotherhood. While he posed as the grantor of religious liberty in New York, he could strike hands with its enemies in Maryland, though he knew that the sufferers by the action were to be men of his own faith. His sole reason was jealousy of the palatine powers possessed by the lords of Maryland, for the sake of which jealousy he was willing to sacrifice the rights and comfort of every Roman Catholic in the province. In the whole story of American colonization there is nothing more preposterous and absurd than the outcry of lying Protestants in Maryland to a Catholic king, and his readiness to listen.

Baltimore pleaded that his administration and that of his father had always been in conformity with the charter and with the laws of England, that he had never failed to show respect and obedience to every royal demand, and that he had in no instance been guilty of conduct which could incur the pain of forfeiture. The plea was just and could be borne out by the most scrutinizing examination of his rule. But it was idle in the ears of James, who gave orders for the writ, which did not come to issue before the treacherous king was himself thrust from power.

The fate of Baltimore fell thus into the hand of William, William III. whose natural sense of justice would have prompted a favorable consideration, had the king understood the situation fully. This, it is safe to say, was not the case. New to the English throne and law, with many matters of highest imperial concern to claim his study and decision, it is not strange that this "Defender of Protestantism" should have failed to detect at a glance that the Roman Catholic lord of a little American principality was belied by his Protestant subjects. It was enough that the province was in an uproar and that the Catholic population was an inconsiderable minority, against whom and the proprietary the Protestant revolution in Maryland was already an accomplished fact.

For during the absence of Baltimore in England his enemies in the province had been busy.[1] Scharf justly observes **Puritan plot.** that " this revolution of 1689 was the result of a panic produced by shameful falsehoods and misrepresentations." At the head of it was a man named John Coode, himself as shameful as the lies which helped him to his short lease of power. A frantic cry of " No Popery " was raised to stir up the people. Stories were circulated, of a popish plot to kill all the Protestants in the province, and of hardships suffered by Protestants in various parts of the colony — not one of which was true. There is not a single recorded instance of Romanist violence against Protestants in the history of the province.

But the stories found wide credence, so that the leaders easily organized an " Association in Arms, for the Defence of the Protestant religion and assisting the Rights of King William and Queen Mary." The demonstration was too forcible for resistance by the officials of Baltimore, who gave way before it. Coode and his associates took possession of the government and issued a proclamation filled with falsehoods. It discoursed of " the injustice and tyranny under which we groan"; declared, that " the Churches which should be consecrated according to the ecclesiastical laws of the kingdom of England have been diverted to the use of popish Idolatry ; " that Protestant children had been subjected to " forcible tutelage in the Roman Catholic religion "; that many Protestants had been thrown into prison " by the Papists "; and that " the priests and Jesuits used all means that the art of malice can suggest to divert the loyalty and obedience of inhabitants from " William and Mary.

This proclamation was designed to do its chief work in England, and was accompanied across the sea by an address to the king and queen from Coode, who extolled his own efforts to have their majesties proclaimed in the province, complained that Baltimore had failed to cause such proclama-

---

[1] Scharf, I, 306–336 ; Hawks, II, 55–63 ; Anderson, II, 618.

tion, and besought the royal aid toward the advancement of the Protestant religion.

Coode also called an assembly, to which no Romanist was to be admitted. To this assembly the freeholders of Calvert county, headed by Sheriff Taney, refused to send delegates, embodying their reasons in a public declaration. For this act of independence Taney was put in jail. Neither this assembly nor one called in the next year, 1690, made any attempt to settle the civil government. The minds of the members seemed completely filled by their frantic hatred of Roman Catholics. They kept dinning the king's ears with their insane bellowings. From six counties went as many addresses to the king, numerously signed, craving " deliverance of your suffering people, whereby our Religious Rights and Liberties may be secured under a Protestant Government." These were answered by five other addresses, as numerously signed by both Protestants and Romanists, denying the statements of the former. There is no room for wonder that the English government was disposed to put an end to such a state of things by assuming direct control of the province ; and all the more that no adequate demonstrations were at hand of the baseless nature of the Protestant complaints.

Coode's assembly.

Charles Carroll, one of the most prominent citizens of the colony, wrote to Baltimore of "this strange rebellion of your ungrateful people, at the wicked instigation of Coode, Jowles," and others, " profligate wretches and men of scandalous lives." But, while this testimony goes far in a later generation to discredit the conspiracy, the religion of its author was enough to prejudice the English authorities against his cause. The outcome of the turmoil was that William voided the charter, dispossessed Baltimore, and took over the government of Maryland as a royal province.

Charter annulled.

There is some satisfaction for the sense of historic justice in noting that the leaders in this " strange rebellion," though they effected their aim against Lord Baltimore, yet did not gain for themselves the prizes they sought.   The government was not committed to them, and Coode especially was left entirely without any marks of the king's favor.[1]   He dropped out of sight for a while, and then reappeared in holy orders, was notorious for scandalous conduct, was tried by a civil court for blasphemy, and fled the province.[2]

The final act of William in revoking the charter of Maryland took place in 1692, when the king sent over Governor Copley to the province.   Copley was an ardent Church of England man,[3] and brought with him several clergymen to aid in settling that Church in the colony.   Soon after arrival the governor summoned an assembly, which with great zeal and promptness passed "An Act for the service of Almighty God and the Establishment of the Protestant Religion within this province."[4]   By this act the Church of England was made the State-Church of Maryland; the justices in each county were directed to lay out the county in parishes; the freeholders in each parish were to choose the vestry; Churches and chapels were ordered to be built; and a tax of forty pounds of tobacco was laid on "each taxable Person" for the support of the clergy.

Church of England established.

If we are to believe contemporary reports, we must conclude that the religious condition of the day was deplorable.[5] One writer — probably one of the clergymen who came over with Copley — wrote: "There is scarce any protestant minister in Maryland.   Now and then an itinerant minister came over of very loose morals and scandalous behaviour, so

Religious condition.

[1] Scharf, I, 309, note; Hawks, II, 63.

[2] Hawks very aptly cites this career of Coode as " affording a striking illustration of the facility with which in that day vice, that deserved a prison, could figure in these unfortunate colonies in the robes of a priest.   It happened in the times when too many thought that any one would suffice to serve the Church in America, and when a willingness on the part of an English clergyman to come to the American plantations was not infrequently viewed as presumptive evidence against his character."

[3] Hawks, II, 65.

[4] Scharf, I, 343, 363, 365; *Acts of Assembly*, IV, 425.

[5] Hawks, II, 76.

that, what with such men's ill examples, the Romish priests' cunning, and the quakers' bigotry, religion was in a manner turned out of doors." The clergy also sent to the bishop of London a statement of a similar tenor. It declares that there were but three clergymen in the province before the governor's coming, and continued, "There was also a sort of wandering pretenders to preaching, that came from New England and other places; who deluded not only the protestant dissenters from our Church, but many of the Churchmen themselves, by their extraordinary prayings and preachments, for which they were admired by the people, and got money of them."

The act of establishment was a distinct loss to the cause of freedom in Maryland, not alone for its institution of a State-Church, but for its bringing in the proscriptions of the English toleration act. The liberty allowed by that act was far less than that of the Maryland law of 1649. The Roman Catholic founders of the colony were put under the ban, and could indulge in the public exercise of their religion only at the risk of fine and imprisonment. Even domestic and private devotions were made causes for hostile remark. Besides this oppression of the Romanist, the non-episcopal worship of Protestants could be exercised only upon sufferance, while every Protestant, not a member of the Church of England, was compelled to support a Church not his own.

This makes the course of the Maryland Puritans all the more notable. Their lying clamor against a "Popish tyranny," which did not exist, fettered the religious liberty they already possessed. Either their Puritan bigotry against the Church of Rome made them blind to the ecclesiastical consequences for themselves; or their affectation of a Puritan character was a mere cloak to cover political malice, indifferent to the religious result. The latter supposition is by far the more just, both from their unscrupulous methods of attack, and the readiness with which they accepted a prelatical establishment. No genuine Puritanism would have submitted to the Anglican burden without a struggle, second only to its resistance to the Church of Rome. But so far as the Maryland Puritans were concerned, we read of no objection to the establishment. On the contrary they welcomed it, as though it had been a deliverer, and promptly established it themselves. The only protest came from the Quakers, who sent a deputation to England and petitioned the assembly, seeking relief from Church taxation as "a burden to their consciences and estates." But the assembly turned a deaf ear, and in England the remonstrances of the Anglican clergy hindered a favorable response.

Immediately that the Church of England came to its establishment in Maryland, it began the same course of vexations toward non-conformists, which distinguished it in Virginia and New York. In 1694 Nicholson succeeded Copley and showed his zeal in much harsh treatment, especially of the Quakers.[1] Various efforts were made to increase and extend the power of the Church.[2] In 1696 the assembly passed a new act of establishment with enlarged powers and reciting: "That his Majesty's subjects of this province shall enjoy all their rights and liberties according to the laws and statutes of the kingdom of England, in all matters and causes where the laws of the province are silent." Against the act the Quakers and Romanists protested, sending an agent to London, and it was disallowed by the king in council, because of the clause above quoted, "which clause is of another nature than that which is set forth by the title to the said law."

Again the Church party in 1700 attempted its purpose by a law, enacting: "That the Book of Common Prayer and the administration of the Sacraments, with the rites and services of the Church, according to the use of the Church of England, the Psalter and Psalms of David, and morning and evening prayer, therein contained, be solemnly read by

Non-con-formity.

[1] Anderson, *Colonial Church*, II, 622.
[2] *Ibid.*, II, 630–631; Hawks, II, 88, 89, 97, 115.

all and every minister or reader in every Church, or other place of public worship, within this province." This act was also disallowed by the king, on the ground that the phrase, "other place of public worship," infringed the act of toleration.

Still another bill was drawn up by Commissary Thomas Bray, approved by the board of trade, sent to Maryland, passed by the assembly in 1700 and approved by the king. *Act of 1700.* By this act the Church was finally settled. In brief, the act provided that every minister of the Church should be inducted by the governor, and should receive forty pounds of tobacco per poll in his parish, and out of this income should pay to his clerk one thousand pounds of tobacco yearly. The sheriffs were to collect the stipends. The vestries, over which the minister was to preside, were to keep the Church property in repair, meeting the expense thereof by *the fines under the act.* If these fines were insufficient, they were empowered to lay a tax not exceeding ten pounds of tobacco *per* poll yearly. The toleration acts of England were extended to Protestant dissenters and Quakers, who were permitted to have meeting-houses, provided the same were certified to, and registered by, the county courts.

Thus did free Maryland pass under bondage. The Puritan exchanged his liberty for a grudging and burdensome toleration, while the Romanist found himself locked out of his own home. The situation makes a curious reverse, the like of which is not to be found elsewhere in the colonies. Not the least curious and expressive feature of the change is the provision that repairs on property should be defrayed by the fines under the act, in its very best light a provision distinctly immoral. The act turns a perfectly innocent thing — nonconformist worship — into a crime, calculates that there will be many violations of the statute, and plans to raise a revenue out of the crime which itself creates. It was no less shameful than oppressive.

We must not fail to note that the author of the bill finally *Bray.* settling the Church came with it into Maryland. Though evidently, from the character of the measure drafted by him, a man of very narrow religious prejudices, yet Bray was in all other respects worthy of the highest commendation — a gentleman, a scholar, of purest personal character, and of unwearied devotion and Christian zeal. Before coming to America he had given evidence of his capacity in founding and organizing the two great English societies, for the "Promotion of Christian Knowledge," and for the "Propagation of the Gospel in Foreign Parts." Chosen by the bishop of London as his commissary to the Church of Maryland, he was a worthy companion to James Blair in Virginia. The two men stood head and shoulders above all the Church of England ministers in America since the day of Whitaker, the "apostle to Virginia." Bray spent many years in Maryland, for a long time the only sweet savor in its Church, laboring with much toil, amid countless discouragements, but with intelligent and unflagging zeal. " He gave nearly all of his earnings to the advancement of religion and the Church in these colonies." [1]

Bray's troubles.

Bray's chief sources of trouble were the character of most of the clergy, and the governor's power of induction to parishes. Bray's own hand in England, taught by English custom, had put that power in the bill of establishment. But he found on acquaintance with American conditions that it was fatal to the Church. The two evils worked together, for the unsavory reputation of the ministry was not to be sweetened by an irreligious governor's appointment of favorites to parishes. All records agree in representing the majority of the Maryland clergy on the same low level with their brethren in Virginia, serving in one province as in the other to nurture resentment, not only against the Church itself, but also against the royal authority, which forced an establishment with such a ministry upon an unwilling people.

The clergy.

We have already noted the effect of this scandal in Virginia. In Maryland it was no less glaring and disabling to

[1] Hawks, II, 79 ; Anderson, II, 623.

the Church, and the popular outcry against it was no less strident. The letters of the few godly men among the clergy to the society and the bishop of London [1] abound in references to it and its terribly disastrous influence on the Church. At nearly every opening of Perry's invaluable compilation the reader will find some allusion. The constant appeal is for better men to be sent from England and for a bishop, the superior need of whose presence is the function of discipline to correct the irregularities of the clergy. Dr. Hawks [2] remarks with sharpness upon the lamentable condition, that while Churchmen were forcing their unwelcome Church on the people and " punishing men for non-conformity, they should not have illustrated their own orthodoxy by a consistent Christian life."

The outcry against clerical indecencies became so strenuous that in 1708 an act was passed by the legislature creating a special court for the trial of derelict ministers. [3] The governor and three other laymen were to constitute the court. To such a court, from which all clerical membership was carefully excluded, was committed the highest functions of spiritual authority, the power to both deprive a culprit of his parish and depose him from the ministry. [4] This court, indeed, was never organized, as the governor, though in sympathy with the object of the act, declined to assent on the ground that he had received no instructions from the king covering such a measure. The assembly declared its intention to persist in action at every session. The clergy became alarmed and sent a remonstrance to the bishop of London, imploring his influence, and describing the measure as " an establishment of Presbyterians." Whether by the bishop's influence or other does not appear, yet the attempt to constitute so anomalous an ecclesiastical court was not continued. Its chief

[1] Bishop Perry, *Historical Collections* (Maryland).
[2] *Ecclesiastical Contributions*, II, 128.
[3] Anderson, III, 283.
[4] This resembles the action of the Carolina legislature in 1704.

value in this narrative is to illustrate the relation which the civil power considered itself to occupy toward the Church.

It found another illustration, sixty-two years later (1770), in a revival of the effort to form a court with spiritual jurisdiction. This new attempt proposed a body composed of the governor, three ministers, and three laymen, the six associates to be appointed by the governor himself. The bill passed the legislature, but Governor Sharp refused assent on the ground that it conflicted with the principles of the Church of England.[1] The evil at which the bill was aimed, although the general character of the clergy slowly improved, continued to plague the Church down to the Revolution. Bray wore himself out in contending against it, and Henderson, his successor in the commissaryship, found a no less discouraging and impossible task.[2]

Induction.

Both of them attributed a great part of their difficulty to the governor's power of presentation and induction, against which there existed no appeal in law. No power could reach a minister whom the governor's favor protected, no matter how shameful his conduct. Even the power which conferred the benefice could not withdraw it, and the governor himself could not remove a minister, who had disgraced his appointment.[3] Bray sought to have the right of induction vested in the commissary, as the official representative of the bishop of London, but was unsuccessful. The power was too valuable for the governor to relinquish.

So thought also the Baltimores when they came to their own again. In 1715 Charles, third Lord Baltimore, died in England, after many ineffectual appeals for the restoration of his proprietary rights, always denied on the ground of his religion.[4] His son Benedict, the fourth Maryland palatine,

Restoration of Baltimore.

turned Protestant and was rewarded by George I. with a renewal of his patent. With his conversion to Protestantism, —a change undoubtedly dictated by policy rather than by

---

[1] Hawks, II, 257.

[2] Anderson, III, 295.

[3] *Ibid.*, III, 281.

[4] Scharf, I, 378.

religious convictions, — he imbibed all the narrow prejudices and arrogancies which distinguished the attitude of the Church of England toward all other religionists. To this somewhat degenerate scion of the noble Roman Catholic house, which established religious freedom in Maryland, the right of patronage in the Church appeared no less valuable than to the royal governors. He clung to it with persistent tenacity and would tolerate no interference with his ecclesiastical power.

He wrote to the bishop of London in 1718, with the ardor of a neophyte: "I have nothing more at heart than the Protestant establishment, and I will do all that in me lies to encourage and favor the Church of England as by law established."[1] At the same time he was very unwilling to yield an iota of his rights as patron throughout the entire province, using them many times to the manifest disadvantage of the Church which he professed to love. The Rev. T. Bacon, who deplored the condition of the Church, wrote in 1750 to the bishop of London: "Lord Baltimore appoints all the clergy, and will not consult either with the bishop of London or the society."[2] And fourteen years later, Dr. Chandler, writing to the bishop a report of a recent tour among the Churches of Maryland, said: "The inhabitants look upon themselves to be in a state of the most cruel oppression with regard to ecclesiastical matters. The Churches are built and liberally endowed entirely at their expense; yet the proprietor claims the sole right of patronage, and causes induction to be made without any regard to the opinions of parishioners. Those who are inducted are frequently known to be bad men even at the very time, and others soon show themselves to be so. After induction they cannot be removed, even by the highest exertion of proprietary power."[3]

Baltimore was unwilling that the clergy should meet together to consult on Church affairs, or to concert any measures looking to relief from their burdens. About 1730 the

---

[1] Perry, *Historical Collections* (Maryland), p. 99.
[2] *Ibid.*, p. 326.   [3] Hawks, II, 249.

bishop of London, moved by the constant complaints from Maryland, and giving way to a surprising impulse of departure from the usual English policy, invited the provincial clergy to choose one of their own number to go over to England and be consecrated as suffragan. The clergy met and selected a Mr. Colebatch for this episcopal dignity, but, when he attempted to leave Maryland for consecration, he was forbidden by the government, which at the same time rebuked the clergy for their action.[1] Thirty years later the clergy renewed their effort for a bishop, and met a similar rebuke. Governor Eden, the last of the proprietary governors, had come over in 1769, and brought a command from Baltimore that the clergy should not be allowed to meet in convention about Church affairs. Meanwhile they had met and adopted a petition for a bishop, which they commended to the governor's influence to obtain a favorable answer. " The only answer received was that of rebuke and insult. Never were they to presume to meet again. . . . The governor told them that the parishes in Maryland were all Donatives, and therefore beyond any control which a bishop could exercise." [2]

Offer of suffragan.

Thus it became clear that there was not much more freedom for the established Church of Maryland than those of non-conformists. Its clergy were indeed stipendiaries of the state, and in the matter of support were much better placed than other ministers. But in regard to the stipend they were subjected to vexations, for which their own irregular conduct was chiefly responsible.[3] There was a struggle of many years' duration between them and the legislature. That body in 1763, " disgusted and wearied by the continued irregularities of the great mass of the clergy," passed an act reducing the ministerial stipend by one-fourth. Such a reduction no body of men would be apt to view with equanimity, and the Maryland clergy were in arms at once, the more clamorous as their character prevented their vision of anything beside their selfish interest. It was at the same

Stipends.

---

[1] Anderson, III, 295.   [2] *Ibid.*, III, 309.   [3] *Ibid.*, III, 308-311.

time with the famous " Parsons' Cause " in Virginia, and the public distress, which gave rise to the Virginia action, was also felt in Maryland as a justification, added to their disgust for the act of the legislature. There was no great trial and judicial decision of the question in a Maryland court, until after 1770, but the war of words was bitter and long.

Indeed, there was not at first much room for appeal to the courts. The Maryland legislators were wiser than the burgesses of Virginia. The latter left the stipends at the old figure, and, to the prejudice of all creditors, fixed the price of tobacco used in paying debts at less than one-third of the true value. The Maryland method was both more direct and thoroughly within the power of the legislature. Without attempting to meddle with prices, the power which had fixed the stipend simply reduced it. But we cannot affect much sympathy with the clergy, for, though their income was reduced, their support was well assured. They were not, as many of their brethren in Virginia, brought into grinding poverty by the blow. Anderson wrote of them : " The position of every clergyman in Maryland was far better than that of their brethren in any other colony. Their complaining alienated sympathy." [1] Dr. Chandler, in his letter of 1764 to the bishop of London, alluding to the clerical complaints, wrote : " The livings generally are worth £300, some of them £500. Very few are so low as £200." [2] It is quite impossible to seriously pity men thus situated, in view of the fact that, even if we suppose Dr. Chandler's figures to represent the stipends before the reduction, yet the reduction left the lowest stipend at an amount higher than the average ministerial salary in this country to-day (1901), while the purchasing power of money, as related to the needs of life, is now much less than in colonial times.

This trouble about the stipends took another form in 1770. [3] In that year the legislature neglected to continue the reduction act of 1763, a neglect which the governor attempted

---

[1] Anderson, III, 307. [2] Hawks, II, 249. [3] *Ibid.*, II, 264-281.

to correct by a proclamation, directing the sheriffs to collect the ministers' salaries at the new rate of thirty pounds of tobacco *per* poll. This action of the governor was condemned by some of the people as an usurpation of power, while the clergy contended that the legislative neglect, through the expiration of the law of 1763, revived that section of the establishing act which assessed forty pounds of tobacco *per* poll for the parsons' stipends.

But this contention of the clergy referring to the establishing act set another party, opposed to the Church, to questioning the legality of the act itself. Though the act was introduced in 1700, final action was not concluded until two years later, and the act was spoken of as the "Act of 1702." The contention of this party was, that the act of 1702 was passed on March 16; that King William died on March 8; that the authority of the legislature elected on the king's writs expired with his life; and, therefore, that the act of 1702 was invalid, and the Church of England had never been established in Maryland!

Here then was a triangular contest in which both Churchmen and non-conformists were engaged. The controversy is known as that of "The Proclamation and Vestry Act," and was never adjusted, save as the Revolution put an end to it and its cause. During its discussion much and bitter strife raged. In many instances people refused to pay under the act of 1702, and the clergy entered suits to recover, on which the decision of the courts was against them. The legislature of 1773 reënacted the provision of reduced stipends, but, in order not to pre-judge the case of the establishment, expressly provided that this action should have no influence in determining the validity of the law of 1702, which must be left for future legal decision. As Dr. Hawks tersely observes, "The American Revolution settled it without the intervention of judge or jury." Certainly, the controversy can be regarded as a prelude to that Revolution and with much of its animating spirit. In Maryland, as in Virginia, the downfall of the establishment "found few to weep over its dishonored corpse." [1]

It remains to note the action of the government toward non-conformists after the establishment of 1702. I have found no records of severe persecution of persons of any faith, though the earlier years of the establishment were full of annoyance. The majority of the population was so overwhelmingly non-episcopal — Baptist, Presbyterian, Huguenot, Methodist, German Reformed — that the legislature never ventured to interfere with their right of worship, though compelling their contributions to the support of the established Church. The Quakers and Roman Catholics were the special objects of animosity, and of these the former found early relief from trouble. *Non-conformists.*

There had come into the province many of the sect, who increased in number constantly. It has been noted that in 1688 they obtained consideration for their scruples concerning militia duty. In 1704 the legislature explicitly conceded their rights to toleration. Twenty years after, 1724, the Quakers having been subjected to great indignity by turbulent disturbance of their meetings, a law was passed to punish such offences, and also to admit a Quaker's affirmation in place of an oath. *Quakers.*

The lot of the Romanists was much more vexatious. They were not driven out of the province; they were not imprisoned or beaten. But they were deprived of all civil rights, prohibited the free exercise of their worship, and fined on any violation of the narrowing laws. Some of the legislation evinces a peculiar malignity of spirit against them. Thus, the law of 1704, " An Act to Prevent the Growth of Popery," forbade a "popish bishop or priest" to exercise his functions in any public service, under a penalty of £50 fine, or six months' imprisonment. If one, once convicted, should be guilty of a second offence, he was to be sent to England for punishment.[2] The only service permitted to the Romanist *Romanists.*

[1] Hawks, II, 117, 174.   [2] Scharf, I, 369, 370; Hawks, II, 117, 142.

was within the limits of a "private family of the Romish communion." The same act laid a tax of twenty shillings on every Irish servant imported, to "prevent the entrance of papists." This provision was renewed in 1714 ; a fine of £5 was imposed for concealing such importation, and certain oaths were ordered for persons on incoming ships, to discover their religious opinions. In 1715 it was enacted that children of a Protestant father and Roman Catholic mother, could, in case of the father's death, be taken from the mother. In case a son in a Romanist family became a Protestant, the father lost control of him and must be compelled to support him. The act of 1716 required the oath of abjuration for all persons elected to office ; and that of 1718 denied the ballot to Romanists unless they abjured their faith.

It is pleasant to note that, despite the virulence of these acts, there was little force to execute them. They were chiefly sound and fury, and this Protestant bigotry was very like "Pope and Pagan" in Bunyan's tale, too stiff in the joints to run after the people at which they snarled. The Roman Catholics, beyond the things noted, suffered no great hardships and no personal persecutions. The fact was that, with all the loud professions of Protestant zeal on the part of the leaders, there was too much love for liberty in the land to countenance severity. Though his brethren suffered in some measure, yet the seed sown by Baltimore had not fallen on entirely barren ground. The heart and head of the people at large were sounder than those of the government. Presently, the Roman Catholics were able unchallenged to assume their rights, and though the colonial legislature never repealed these oppressive laws, they were able in 1763 to build their first Church in Baltimore without opposition.[1]

So must end the peculiar tale of colonial Maryland in its relation to religious freedom. We shall find her well prepared to take her place in the company of states which declared liberty to every soul.

[1] Hawks, II, 246.

III. *New Jersey*

Under the rule of New Netherland the same relation between civil and ecclesiastical affairs was supposed to obtain in New Jersey as we have already noted in Dutch New York. The early occupation of its territory has left permanent monuments of Dutch influence in the many Reformed Churches which flourish in that state. But beyond an occasional and unimportant note it does not appear that the Dutch authorities at New Amsterdam concerned themselves to any great extent about Church affairs in their dominions west of the Hudson. Even the settlement of Quakers in that part of his government did not stir the fiery spirit of Stuyvesant.

Thus our story of New Jersey must begin with the English conquest of 1664. At that time the Dutch had made settlements on the North and South (Delaware) rivers, and in one or two localities in the interior. Newark also had just been founded by Pierson and his Branford flock, who, resenting the "Christless rule" of Connecticut, essayed a "new ark" of that covenant, which defined all civil rights as the perquisites of religion alone. They began with the foundation laid at New Haven, the fundamental rule of Church membership as a condition for the franchise and for office; and through their influence the first colonial assembly, meeting at Elizabethtown in 1668, "transferred the chief features of the New England codes to the statute book of New Jersey." [1]

But the impress of such restrictive legislation was transient. Its bands were sundered almost so soon as they were knit, through the influx of an incoming population over which the extreme Puritanism of New Haven could exercise little control. Into the country between the Hudson and the Delaware there came a steady stream of people not in sympathy with this ideal of a "godly government," men who had struggled and suffered for the rights of conscience and of

[1] Bancroft, *History of United States*, II, 318.

man. Scotch Presbyterians sought in the Jerseys a refuge from the persecutions of Charles. Quakers fled thither from the hostile atmosphere of England and New England. The original Dutch settlers remained to assert continually the freedom which the Reformed faith inculcated. All together made conditions too strong for narrow Puritanism to successfully resist.

There was also arrayed against it the explicit " concession " of the proprietaries, which, after the manner of a fundamental law, guaranteed a complete religious freedom. These proprietaries were Lord Berkeley and Sir George Carteret. On the conquest of New Netherland Charles gave the entire province to his brother James, the duke of York. In expectation of this gift, James had already bargained with Berkeley and Carteret — who were also of the Carolina proprietaries — for the southern portion of the territory which was west of the Hudson. At the fulfilment of this bargain the new owners of the province were ready with their plans for the settlement of their colony, and at once published a scheme, embodying certain principles and stipulations, which they called " Concessions," [1] and by which they desired to attract settlers.

The concessions.

The seventh concession ran : " No person . . . shall be any ways molested, punished, disquieted, or called in question in matters of religious concernments, who do not actually disturb the civil peace of the province ; but all and every such person, or persons, may . . . freely and fully have and enjoy his and their judgments and consciences in matters of religion throughout the province."

This concession does not in words refer to civil rights, but it was understood, as now, that such language involved an entire absence of discrimination as to civil rights because of religion. To so discriminate, whatever might be the amount of civil rights possessed by any portion of the community, would be to " punish and call in question " for religious reasons the excluded portion of the people.

[1] Samuel Smith, *History of New Jersey*, p. 513.

With the reconquest of New York by the English began a new movement in the history of New Jersey.[1] Lord Berkeley, who was old and wished to rid himself of care, sold the western half of the province, for a thousand pounds, to John Fenwick and Edward Byllinge, men of prominence among the English Quakers. With these two William Penn, Gawen Laurie, and Nicholas Lucas soon became associated, and these Quaker proprietaries, desiring not only a place of asylum for their co-religionists but also a territory for their own government, easily made an agreement with Carteret for the division of the province. Thus New Jersey became "The Jerseys," a term which has lasted in common speech down to this day, though the two provinces were reunited by royal decree in 1702.[2]

Quaker purchase.

"The Jerseys."

The Quaker proprietaries of West Jersey wrote to those of their faith, who had already settled in the province: "The CONCESSIONS are such as Friends approve of . . . We lay a foundation for after ages to understand their liberty as Christians and as men, that they may not be brought into bondage, but by their own consent; for we put THE POWER IN THE PEOPLE." This purchase and declaration were made in 1676, and in the following year was published the fundamental agreement of the proprietaries as to the conduct of government in West Jersey.[3]

West Jersey.

This agreement — expanding the terms of the former concession — declared: "No men, nor number of men upon earth, hath power or authority to rule over men's consciences in religious matters; therefore, it is consented, agreed, and ordained, that no person or persons whatsoever within the said province, at any time or times hereafter, shall be any ways, upon any pretense whatsoever, called in question, or in the least punished or hurt, either in person, estate, or privilege, for the sake of his opinion, judgment, faith, or worship towards God in matters of religion; but that all and

Freedom of conscience.

---

[1] Bancroft, *United States*, II, 355–357.
[2] *Ibid.*, III, 48.   [3] Smith, *New Jersey*, p. 529.

every such person and persons may, from time to time and at all times, freely and fully have and enjoy his and their judgments and the exercise of their consciences in matters of religious worship throughout all the said province."

In perfect consistency with this ordination of liberty, the first assembly of West Jersey, in 1681, reiterated its principle, formulated it in a colonial law, and extended its specific **Civil rights.** terms to matters of civil right.[1] This law declared: "Liberty of conscience in matters of faith and worship shall be granted to all people within this Province, who shall live peaceably and quietly therein, and none of the free people of the Province shall be rendered incapable of office in respect to their faith and worship."

With so broad a platform of freedom West Jersey immediately became as a promised land to the followers of Fox, who emigrated from England in large numbers, and whose firm adhesion to the principles of freedom made much trouble for the royal governors and the Church of England party, after the reunion of the Jerseys.

East Jersey. Meanwhile East Jersey had received large numbers of the Scotch, who brought with them their Presbyterian faith and worship. It was not a hopeful outlook for the Church of England men, who labored hard to establish dominance of their own faith. Bray, the commissary to Maryland, complained: "The whole territory is under Presbyterian or Quaker influence. They are left to themselves without priest or altar."[2]

East Jersey was not so liberal as the Quakers in the west. At first, in 1683, the assembly reiterated the language of the **Limitation.** "Concession," but in 1698 limited the liberty of consciences to persons "acknowledgeing one Almighty and Eternal God, and professing faith in Christ Jesus."[3] This was undoubtedly due to the influence of a rigid Scotch religionism, with which

---

[1] Smith, pp. 128, 576.

[2] Anderson, *History Colonial Church*, II, 662.

[3] Smith, *New Jersey*, p. 271; Kent, *Commentaries*.

the sturdy Dutch may have been not entirely out of sympathy. The influence of the feeling seems to have asserted itself even in West Jersey, where in 1693 a bill was introduced into the assembly against non-believers in the Trinity, which appears however to have failed of passage.[1]

The attempt was a departure from Quaker principle, and it is to be set to the credit of West Jersey that the effort failed; and all the more honorable, in that the colony of Penn across the Delaware had been guilty of as signal departure, in making belief in God and Christ a condition of citizenship. This condition was imposed, as will be seen, at the beginning of Pennsylvania and may have been among the reasons for the West Jersey attempt. These facts constitute the only blot on Quaker championship of religious freedom, for with these exceptions it can be noted as the peculiar glory of the Quakers, among the sects of that age, that they remembered in the day of triumph the principle of liberty professed by them in times of persecution.

A much more pleasing illustration of the spirit in West Jersey is found in a letter from the proprietaries in London to the Rev. Thomas Bridges, a minister of the Church of England resident in Bermuda.[2] Mr. Bridges had written in 1692, expressing his desire to settle in West Jersey, and to him the proprietaries declared themselves pleased at the prospect of obtaining for their colony his " religious and civil influence "; and continued, " You may in what situation you please take up Two Thousand Acres, one Thousand to be your own in fee forever, the other to be annexed unto your office and descend unto him who shall succeed you." The governor, Daniel Coxe, also wrote to Mr. Bridges, " You will be rewarded with . . . the Love and Esteeme of those who shall *voluntarily* come under your Pastoral care, with due maintenance: Together with Civill and Christian Respects from others of different perswations." [3]

[1] Smith, p. 417. [2] *New Jersey Archives*, II, 94.
[3] *Ibid.*, II, 96.

Political affairs in both Jerseys were in a chronic state of
turmoil, unmixed with questions about religion or Church,
save in so far as a bitter jealousy of Quaker influence asserted
itself in the quarrels and disputes. The people of both colonies were also jealous of the proprietaries and unwilling to
submit to their requirements, and made so much resistance
that the proprietaries grew weary of their troubled government. In 1699 the proprietaries of East Jersey offered to
surrender their charter to the crown, that their territory
might be combined with New York under one provincial
government. The offer was made with certain conditions,
of which one was the following : [1] —

"X. No Person or Persons whatsoever to be molested
or deprived of any civil Right or Privilege; or rendered
uncapable of holding any Office or Employment in the
Government because of their religious Principles; the
Province being planted by Protestant People of divers
Perswasions, to whom that Liberty was an original encouragement."

Two years afterward, the two colonies united in a joint
petition to the king to be taken under the immediate
government of the crown. Among the proposed conditions
was : —

"XII. That all *Protestants* may be exempt from all penal
Laws relating to Religion, and be capable of being of the Governor's Council and of holding any other Publick Office,
though they do not conform to the discipline of the Church
of England, or scruple to take an Oath." [2] The peculiar form
of this condition indicates the special influences under which
it was drawn. The toleration act of 1689 excluded from public office all non-conformists, hampering them with many
other disabilities. In a province wherein dissenters were almost the entire population, and no Church had yet been
organized of the English communion, it was needful that the
rights of dissent should be clearly acknowledged. Besides

[1] *Archives*, II, 296.   [2] *Ibid.*, II, 404.

this, in view of the fraudulent claim that the Church of England was established in New York by the Act of 1693, the prospect of being united to New York made it the more necessary to protect the non-conforming Jerseymen.

At the same time the influence of the toleration of William is seen in the specific reference to " Protestants " in the proposed condition. This made a distinctly backward step in New Jersey, which hitherto had made no discrimination against Romanists. But in applying to the king for a direct Romanists. royal government, it seems to have been taken for granted, that the liberty demanded must stop short of protecting those whose religion was a crime under English law. It does not appear that Jersey authorities had ever come into contact with Roman Catholic demands, or that any of the Roman faith had ever proposed to settle in the colony. We may consider it, therefore, as probable that this specifying of Protestants was rather for conformity of phrase to the English statute, than for any hostility to Roman Catholics.

The offer and petition were made to William III., but were not acted upon before his death, being left for the disposition of his successor. Among the earlier actions of Anne's reign Anne. was the assumption of the Jersey government. This took place in 1702: the charters of both Jerseys were surrendered and annulled; the united province was received under the direct government of the crown and joined to that of New York, to which joint government the queen sent its first governor in the person of her cousin, Edward Hyde, Lord Cornbury, than whom never was there in the province another " governor so universally detested, nor that so richly deserved the public abhorrence." [1]

But the order in council, assuming the government of New Jersey, made no allusion to the petitioners' conditions, though the substance of them found place in the queen's *in-* Instruc- *structions* to Cornbury, in which no distinction was made be- tions. tween New York or New Jersey. This instrument, in regard

[1] Wm. Smith, *History of New York*, I, 194.

to liberty of religion, used the stereotyped form constantly repeated to every governor: "You are to permit a liberty of conscience to all persons (except papists), so they may be contented with a quiet and peaceable enjoyment of the same, not giving offence or scandal to the government."[1] The instructions also provided for a Quaker's affirmation in place of an oath.

The other items of the instructions referring to religion proceed upon the supposition, either that the Church of England had already been established in New Jersey, or that it could be established by force of the instructions themselves. We have already exhibited the character of the famous "Ministry Act" of 1693 in New York, carefully drawn by

Church of England.

the legislature to avoid recognition of the Church of England, and yet afterward always referred to by governors, the home government, and Episcopalians as having formally established that Church. The act was passed nine years before the appointment of Cornbury to the joint government of the two provinces, and his instructions seem to assume that the governmental union had carried that act over into New Jersey. It is but another illustration of the fraudulent dealing of which the act was the occasion; for, as already shown, its establishment was designed to affect only six towns in the entire province of New York.

At the same time, it is possible that, without regard to the New York act, the home government considered itself competent to establish the Church of England in New Jersey by royal decree; as though the colony, which had sought the direct government of the crown, must accept the queen's pleasure in things ecclesiastical as well as civil. Thus in a province, which did not possess a single Church of the English communion, the governor is vested with ecclesiastical authority.[2] "We . . . authorize and empower you to collate any person, or persons, to any Churches, Chappells, or other Ecclesiastical Benefices within Our said Province, as often as

[1] *Archives*, II, 522.   [2] *Ibid.*, II, 496, 528, 529.

any of them shall happen to be voyd. . . . You shall take special care that God Almighty be devoutly and duly served throughout your government, the book of common prayer, as by law established, read each Sunday and holy day, and the blessed Sacrament be administered according to the rites of the Church of England." The governor was also charged with a care for Church buildings and the support of ministers; to induct no man without a certificate from the bishop of London; to remove any scandalous minister; to constitute ministers members of their own vestries; and to report to the bishop of London, as having colonial ecclesiastical jurisdiction.

The really absurd thing about these instructions is, that the Churches of New Jersey were all of other than the Anglican communion, and the explanation of their purpose is, either the intent to dragoon the Reformed and Presbyterian Churches into conformity, or to confer power over such Episcopal Churches as might thereafter be organized; while behind it all is the evident thought that the royal authority carried the Church of England into the province. It is only thus that we can understand the phrase, " as by law established." The book of common prayer and the Anglican Church were established by law in England, but the only possible way of using those words with reference to New Jersey was with the idea that English Ecclesiastical law covered all parts of English dominion — an idea very easily demonstrable as incorrect.

For in no other colony had this general dominion been thought sufficient for the establishment of the Church. The Virginia Church was established by the colonial assembly; that in Carolina by the charter. The royal authority never affected such power in New England or Pennsylvania; and in New York the angry struggle between Fletcher and the assembly was based on the understanding that an act of the colonial legislature was necessary for establishment. The only other colony, which bears any resemblance in this respect to New Jersey, is Maryland. But in Maryland, when William assumed the direct government of the province, the establishment of the Church, attempted by a specific and detailed order of the king and queen in council having all the force and effect of a charter, was supplemented by an act of the colonial legislature. In New Jersey the peculiar situa-

Church never established in New Jersey. tion was that no such order was made, and that the establishment was simply taken for granted without any law or decree on which to base it. The colonial legislature had never enacted such a law, nor did it afterward supply the deficiency. Bancroft[1] speaks of the Church of England as established in New Jersey in 1702, but the only ground for the statement is in Cornbury's instructions, which in reality assume that which was not true.

The whole treatment of the question has been misleading, for in point of fact the Church of England never was established in New Jersey by either crown or legislature. The contrary claim has not even so much reason as that for the establishment in New York. In both colonies the subsequent incessant claims of the Episcopal clergy and the English authorities to the privileges of establishment involved a perversion of the fact. This perversion was specially gross in New Jersey for the reason that, unlike New York, there was no legislative act whatever to furnish a ground for it.

The absence of an ecclesiastical statute was a sore grievance and conscious weakness to the Church of England party. Occasionally a complaint of it was expressed very plainly. Thus the Rev. Jacob Henderson, a missionary of the Propagation Society, bitterly contrasted the condition of the Church in New Jersey with that in New York.[2] Writing in 1712 he said: "There are two Acts of Assembly for establishing the Church of England in New York, and ministers of the Church of England have always had the six Churches in New York.

---

[1] *History of United States*, III, 48.

[2] *Archives*, IV, 155–161; *Colonial History of New York*, V, 334.

(Both of which statements were mistakes.)   But in New Jersey there are no laws in favor of the Church and but four ministers of the Church of England." [1]

The absence of such law, as of any subsequent attempt to supply one, is to be accounted for by the religious sentiment of the people, so adverse to the idea of establishment as to make even Cornbury sensible that no ecclesiastical statute was immediately possible. He does not seem to have essayed any direct struggle on the question, and certainly did not venture on any so high-handed proceedings as those which characterized his administration in New York. He interested himself for the Church so far as he was able, endeavored unsuccessfully to institute the tithe, and reported at one time with some elation, " There is a Church at Burlington which I have named St. Ann's." [2] But beyond occasional annoyance of no great moment his powers were limited by the overwhelming popular temper. Even his turbulent spirit dared not to openly grapple with the anti-prelatical sentiment of Quaker and Presbyterian. *Cornbury.*

The Quakers, indeed, furnished him and other governors material for much thought and countless complaints. Their numbers and the tenacity of their opinions in opposition to oaths, militia duty, and tithes brought an immense amount of turmoil into New Jersey. Before any hope could exist for a Church establishment the Quakers must first be disfranchised and silenced. The question resulted in a passionate political struggle, but behind it were the religious scruples of *Quaker party.*

---

[1] In this letter Henderson assailed Colonel Morris, the most prominent citizen of New Jersey, as " a professed Churchman, but a man of noe manner of principles or credit, who calls the service of the Church of England a Pageantry, who has Joyned in endeavors to settle a conventicle in New York City." (This probably refers to Morris's approval of the movement to incorporate the Presbyterian Church.) To this letter Morris, paying no attention to the attack on himself, triumphantly replied, " He complains that there are no laws in favor of the Church of England in the Jerseys, which is granted. But does he know of any Law in favor of any other Religion ? "

[2] *Archives*, III, 107.

the Quakers and the ambition of the English Churchmen. Cornbury wrote to the board of trade,[1] 1705, " The Quakers are pretty numerous in this division (West Jersey), and in the time of the Proprietary Government they had all the power in there, and used it very arbitrarily." Part of the reason for the governor's animus is shown in a previous letter:[2] " The Quakers bragged that there should be no Revenue[3] settled, that the Queen had sent them a Governor, but they would keep him poor enough : these and such like reports were spread about, not by the meanest men among them, but by the topping leading Quakers."

[4] Another indication of the spirit of the struggle is in a memorial to the board of trade by three prominent leaders of the anti-Quaker party, Coxe, Dockura, and Sonmans, all of whom at different times stood high in the government. They petitioned for an order from England excluding Quakers from membership in the council and assembly. Among their reasons were : —

" 1. The Quakers were opposed to a militia and to revenue.

" 2. So long as they are in places of power, they awe and frighten many . . . who would otherwise leave that perswasion and come over to the Christian Church.

" 3. Because, refusing to pay Tythes on pretence of Conscience, they will consequently oppose and obstruct the passage of any Act in favor of the said Church, or its settlement.

" 4. Quakers were not admitted to office in England or elsewhere, save in Pennsylvania."

[1] *Archives*, III, 106.

[2] *Ibid.*, III, 70.

[3] This meant salary for the governor. As other colonies, New Jersey did her best to starve out the royal governors. The quarrel was chronic and universal.

[4] *Archives*, III, 82.

5. Lord Cornbury had rightly construed one section of his instructions as admitting Quakers to public office, and this view the memorialists said "manifestly appears to be as false as 'tis scandalous. . . . We hope therefore that the Quakers may be excluded Quakers in office. from the Council, the General Assembly, and all other places of publick trust in the Province." This clearly reveals the motive of some of those opposed to the Quakers, to remove an obstacle to a Church establishment.

Cornbury also, though forced to act according to instructions, yet evidently did not like this admission of Quakers. In a letter of 1704 to the board of trade [1] he complained of them as obstructing the courts by their refusing oaths, and concluded: "I think it would be much more for the service of the queen that none should be admitted into employments, but those who are willing to take the oaths."

The hard fact for Cornbury and the Church party to face was that the Quakers held either the majority or the balance of power, at different times, in the legislature. West Jersey sent in 1705 a delegation entirely Quaker, save for one member; and Lord Cornbury wrote: "Soe long as the Quakers are allowed to be chosen into the Assembly, the service of the Queen and the business of the country must wait upon their humors." [2] Indeed, as time went on, the governor became more and more disgusted with the situation. The "topping Quakers" were ever a burden. His letters abound in flings and complaints. "I have not suffered any Quakers to have any Office in the Government of New York," but in New Jersey, under the queen's commands, "I have put severall of them into employments; but I have always found them obstinate, unwilling to be ruled, never forwarding but still interrupting business: What Quakers would be, had they the Power in their hands, and which they are very fond of,

[1] *Archives*, III, 66.   [2] *Ibid.*, III, 114.

appears very plainly in the Province of Pennsylvania, where noe Man can tell what is his own or how to get what is Justly his due." [1]

Undoubtedly the Quakers were in many things very aggravating. Their placid and quiet obstructiveness was more exasperating than a violent opposition. But they were clearly within their rights, facing a determined effort to debar them from all civil privileges. Save for their conduct in regard to the governor's support, in which matter they had sympathizers in every non-Quaker assembly on the continent, and in their refusal to provide for the defence of the country, it is impossible to find just cause for blame. It was within the province of a good citizen to choose between militia duty and a fine for refusal of it. But one cannot so easily excuse the action of the New Jersey Quakers in regard to the war with Canada and the Indians in 1709. The governor desired troops and money, that the colony might do its part in the general defence; and the assembly, a majority of which were Quakers, passed the following resolution: [2] "The members of this House, being the People called Quakers, have always been, and still are, for Raising money for support of Her Maj[ties] Government: but to raise money for Raising of Soldiers is against their Religious Principles, and for Conscience cannot agree thereto." One cannot excuse that attitude any more than the conduct of the Pennsylvania legislature, fifty years later, in refusing protection to the settlers in the western counties.

There was, then, this amount of justice in the attacks upon the Quakers. To some extent it justified the strictness of Colonel Quary, inspector for the board of trade in the middle colonies, who wrote in 1708: [3] "They are driving at the same game acted in Pennsylvania by their Friends there, who are resolved to allow no prerogative of the Crown, nor any power in a Governor, but will have all power lodged in themselves. . . . This growing evil and mischief requires a

Refuse to defend the colony.

Colonel Quary.

[1] *Archives*, III, 229.   [2] *Ibid.*, III, 470.   [3] *Ibid.*, III, 273.

speedy remedy, else I fear it will spread over the whole continent." It gives some justice also to the language of Lieutenant Governor Ingoldsby in 1709,[1] who attributed the unhappy state of the province to "the Prevalence of a Sort of People amongst us, who, though not above one Sixth part of the Inhabitants of the Province, yet by a Peculiar Address and a Religious Cunning Influence too many well-meaning Men with most Ridiculous and Injurious Principles."[2]

Yet this very language illustrates the spirit with which the Quakers had to contend, in a struggle not only for their civil rights, but against an insidious scheme to impose an unwelcome ecclesiastical establishment on the colony. And it is pleasing to note that they were not without friends outside of their own sect. Colonel Morris wrote to the board of trade[3] of the shameful extortion practised by Cornbury's officers on the Quakers, who refused to pay the militia tax, saying that they distressed "generally above ten times the value, which when they came to expose to sale nobody would buy, so that there is, or lately was, a house at Burlington filled with demonstrations of Quaker obstinacy." He declared that "this extravagant distress from the Quakers had impoverished New Jersie," and then paid his compliments to Lord Cornbury, as "a wretch, who by the whole conduct of his life (here) has evinc't y[t] he has no regard to hon[r] or virtue."

To Colonel Morris was added Governor Hunter in just consideration for the Quakers, and with his entrance to the

Colonel Morris.

Hunter.

---

[1] *Archives*, III, 470.

[2] Ingoldsby, however, quite overdrew the picture at another time (*Archives*, III, 413), writing, "For the Quakers, we meddle not with their Religious Perswasions and have no design to abridge them in any of their liberties and Privileges: But their Insolencies in Government are Intollerable, by their weekly, monthly, quarterly, and yearly meeting (where civil affairs are managed as well as spiritual), their Intelligence from all Foreign Parts, and General Combinations, they become Mischievous and daring, even to the affronting Magistrates and contemning the laws, and Particularly Pride themselves on being able to Cramp and Confound Government."

[3] *Archives*, III, 280.

government of the province their troubles began to cease. Hunter, though a sincere Churchman, was not bigoted. Fair-minded and just, he refused both in New York and New Jersey to use his power at the bidding of the English clergy, and at once detected the iniquity of the scheme in the latter province to disable the Quakers and establish the Church of England. His course in these matters brought upon him the hatred of the clergy, who lost few opportunities of maligning him to the home authorities. The governor, in New Jersey as in New York, does not seem to have been greatly disturbed by these attacks, but showed himself fully able to return their compliments with interest.

In the year (1711), after he came to the government and probably by his encouragement, a bill was passed in the assembly to relieve Quakers from all disabilities. The object was to place in a formal statute an assertion of the privileges, which had been conceded in the queen's instructions, and which the Quakers had been able to retain only by dint of much and constant struggle.[1] Of this action Hunter wrote to the board of trade:[2] "The State of the Province absolutely Requires such, that People being by farr the most numerous and wealthy in the Western Division, and, as I may affirm upon experience, the most Dutyfull."

The bill, however, was thrown out by the council and caused no small excitement among the Church of England party. One of the members of the council wrote to Dockura, then in London, who sent the letter to the board of trade:[3] "Hunter has entirely and passionately espoused the seditious Party of Morris, Johnstone, &c., and united with the Quakers. The Last Bill was Such a Monster that every Part of it was Terrible. It unhinged Our Very Constitution of Government . . . a great Encouragement of Quakerism, or rather its Establishment, and of the most Pernicious Consequences to the Church of England."

[1] *Archives*, IV, 20.   [2] *Ibid.*, IV, 196.
[3] *Ibid.*, IV, 121.

[1]In 1713 the effort was more successfully renewed. The "Act for Relief of the Quakers," enabling them to qualify by affirmation for jury and all other public duty, passed both houses, was approved by the governor and confirmed by the queen. On the accession of King George I., the act was re-affirmed. Its opponents petitioned the king against it, on the astonishing ground that it was "repugnant to the Laws and Statutes of this Realme and the Rights and Libertys of the Subject." The board of trade, considering that the act rather confirmed the rights and liberties of a very large number of his Majesty's subjects, advised the king that it should stand ; and the act accordingly received the royal assent. *Act for relief of Quakers.*

Thus ended in victory for the Jersey Quakers their fifty years' struggle for the full acknowledgment of their rights. There was afterward an occasional outbreak of opposition, but their rights were not again seriously imperilled. The original law was for a term of years, was renewed in 1717, and came up again in 1725 and 1727. On this last occasion Governor Montgomerie opposed renewal, writing to London : [2] "The Quakers do not deserve his Majesty's assent to the act . . . (They) are very insolent and troublesome when they have no favor to ask, but quiet and useful when they have anything depending." But the act stood, the lords of trade writing to the governor that they "allow it to lye-by Probational, and hope the Behaviour of the People will never induce the Crown to Repeal it." It never was disturbed, and thenceforth the most serious annoyance to which the Quakers were subjected was the penalty under the militia act. Party rancor seems to have made the application unnecessarily severe, and Governor Morris, who had criticised the extortion under Cornbury, had to admit in 1740 that under his own administration the distraint was excessive. But, he said, "the Quakers grew fond of what they called suffering." [3]

[1] *Archives*, IV, 334, 342, 343, 367.   [2] *Ibid.*, V, 235, 248.
[3] *Ibid.*, VI, 104.

Besides the incidents recited the colonial archives contain little that relates to the questions of a State-Church and religious liberty. A single case is recorded of voluntary submission to the governor's ecclesiastical authority.[1] This is a petition from people at Woodbridge for permission to build a Church, for "the service of God, after the manner of the Church of England, *as by law established.*" The petition was addressed to Hunter in 1713.

Much space in the record of his administration is filled by his quarrels with the Episcopal ministers, especially Vesey of New York and Talbot of New Jersey. The correspondence is sufficiently amusing and charged with a sly satire, of which Hunter was a master, but it is not germane to this present treatise, save as the spirit of the clerical attacks on the governor is manifestly due to his refusal to forward their illegal schemes for aggrandizing the Church of England at the expense of other Churches. " Meanwhile," wrote Hunter to Secretary Popple of the Board of Trade in 1715, "I have enough to do to keep the peace of the Churches, but Never fear, your friend Jonathan will never yield to 'em, so long as he has the Grace of God and ye prayers of the Saints." [2]

Of course, to the end of the colonial chapter the home government kept up the fiction of an establishment in New Jersey. Every royal governor, even after New Jersey was separated from New York, received the routine instructions as to " liberty of Conscience to all persons (except Papists)," and conferring upon him ecclesiastical powers, which in New Jersey at least amounted to nothing. In 1730 the crown issued a special commission to the bishop of London for ecclesiastical jurisdiction in the colonies, and instructed the governors of New York, New Jersey, Pennsylvania, Maryland, and Virginia " to give all Countenance and due Encouragement to the said Bishop of London, or his Commissaries, in the legal exercise of Such Ecclesiastical Jurisdiction "; and that they " cause the Said Commission (of

[1] *Archives*, IV, 189.   [2] *Ibid.*, IV, 224.

the Bishop of London) to be forthwith Registered in the Publick Records " of the several colonies.[1] But neither commission nor order was able to fasten the Anglican Church upon New Jersey.

At the very end of the period (1771) a Presbyterian movement gave occasion for a curious display of the governmental notion that there either was, or ought to be, a Church of England establishment in New Jersey.[2] The origin of it was an application from the Presbyterian ministers, headed by John Witherspoon, for a charter incorporating a "Fund for the Support of Widows and Children of Presbyterian Clergymen." Governor Franklin was much perplexed by the request and applied to the attorney-general of the colony, who advised sending the petition to England. Then the governor consulted his own council, a majority of which advised giving the charter, on condition that "the said Charter be unexceptionable in Point of Form, and be confined solely to the Purposes of the Charitable Institution therein mentioned, and the said Corporation made accountable to this Board (the council) for the Monies they shall receive and pay." Then the governor referred the question to Justice David Ogden of the supreme court, who approved of giving the charter, but advised the striking out the words describing the Presbyterian clergy as "in communion with the established Church of Scotland,"[3] because it was "improper for his Excellency to recognize by the Charter the Established Church of Scotland, so as to be a Rule, or mask, of distinction of any order of men in New Jersey." Another suggestion of change came in a second report from the attorney-general, who advised striking the word "clergymen" from the petition and substituting "Ministers," or "Teachers," on the ground that "the King can't know, or with Propriety

Presbyterian society.

---

[1] *Archives*, V, 264.

[2] *Ibid.*, X, 339, 340, 350, 359, 400, 404, 407, 409.

[3] This is the only instance I have found in colonial history of appeal to the legal status of the Presbyterian Church of Scotland. (C.)

call, any Men Clergymen, but those of the established Church
of England, at least in England, Ireland, and these colonies."

By this time the governor was in a fine state of confusion,
and referred the petition to the English government. He
alluded to the recent refusal of the king to grant a charter
to the Presbyterian Church of New York, as "not expedient
upon Principles of general Policy"; but at the same time,
willing to do the Presbyterians a favor, he reminded the
home government, that "charters for the like Purpose have
been lately granted to the Clergy of the Established Church
of England." So the petition went to England, where it lay
unanswered for two years. Then in 1773 the governor
inquired what the home authorities meant to do about it, and
received from the Earl of Dartmouth a prompt reply that the
matter would be considered. This was soon followed by the
announcement that the king had granted the petition, and
ordered the governor to pass the charter and affix the seal.
The "incident closed" with a grateful acknowledgment on
the part of the Presbyterian clergy, in October of 1773.

With this may end the sketch of colonial New Jersey.
Long before this date, while still clinging to the fiction of a
tacit establishment, the Church party had given up all hope
of securing by the colonial legislature a recognition of the
Church of England. The clergy of that Church continued
their clamor against the situation, and through their addiction
to the English Church were, with few exceptions, pronounced
in espousal of the king's cause in the revolutionary struggle.
But for the mass of people of all varieties of faith the question of a State-Church was finally and satisfactorily settled,
so that the constitutional definition of full religious liberty
found in New Jersey no statesman to call it in question.

IV. *Georgia*

Our story of Georgia must necessarily be brief. The colony,
opened only two score years before the Revolution, owed its
foundation to the benevolent and gentle heart of Oglethorpe,

whose merciful thought was to form a place of refuge for distressed people of England and persecuted Protestants of Europe.[1] The sufferings of the poor, and especially those in the debtors' jails, appealed to his compassionate spirit, and he determined to provide a relief. The charter for the new colony was granted by George II. in 1732.[2] The charter had the following language in regard to religion : " And for the greater Ease and Encouragement of Our loving Subjects and such others, who shall come to inhabit in Our said Colony, *We do*, by these Presents, for Us, our Heirs and Successors, *grant, establish, and ordain*, That forever hereafter there shall be a LIBERTY OF CONSCIENCE allowed in the *Worship of God* to all Persons . . . within our said Province, and that all such Persons, except *Papists*, shall have *a free exercise of Religion ;* so they be contented with a quiet and peaceable enjoyment of the same, not giving Offence or Scandal to the Government." The instrument also allowed to Quakers a " solemn affirmation " in place of an oath.

Liberty of conscience.

On receiving the charter, Oglethorpe associated with himself twenty others as " Trustees," among whom were five clergymen of the Church of England, and to these four others were afterward added. The English clergy were much interested in the charitable scheme of Oglethorpe, and appeals were made to the Church at large for contributions to assist its work.[3]

The trustees soon issued a statement of their " Design," exposing their purpose to assist distressed Protestants, who were not able to go at their own expense, and " to relieve such unfortunate persons as can not subsist here "; and expressing the hope that " Christianity will be extended by the execution of this design." Neither in the charter nor in the published design was any purpose expressed of establishing

Freedom.

[1] Bancroft, III, 419, 423, 447.

[2] Force, *Historical Tracts*, I, title, *A True and Historical Narrative of the Colony of Georgia.*

[3] Stevens, *History of Georgia*, I, 319.

the Church of England. Nor, strange as it appears, did the lively interest of the English clergy in Oglethorpe's scheme endeavor to supply that lack. The settlers were left free to their religious preferences, with the sole exception of the Roman Catholic.

Oglethorpe and the trustees were not indifferent, however, to the religious interests of their colonists, as appears from their "*Account, Showing the Progress of the Colony of Georgia*,"[1] printed at London in 1741. The account was a reply to the "*True and Historical Narrative*," in which was a sharp attack on Oglethorpe, Canston, and Wesley. The trustees say in their pamphlet that "Lands have been Granted in Trust for Religious Uses, to be cultivated, with the Money arising from Private Beneficience given for that Purpose, in order to settle a Provision upon a Clergyman at Savannah, a Catechist, and a Scholar, Three Hundred Acres." Afterward similar provisions were made for a minister at Frederica, and for a Scotch Minister at New Inverness. But in none of these provisions does it appear that there was any denominational preference on the part of the authorities. The clear inference is that the trustees and colonial government were disposed to help any locality in the provision for a minister of the people's choice. This help was given in the manner of foundation grants, and did not involve a tax for ministerial support.

It were out of place to enter here into the disputes between the trustees and the colonists. They were not on religious or ecclesiastical questions, and were rather charged with mutual jealousies. The zeal of Oglethorpe impoverished himself, and it can be justly said that the colonists were not properly mindful of his generosity. The quarrels resulted in 1752 in the abrogation of the charter and the assumption of direct government by the crown.[2] With that government

Care for religion.

Charter voided. Church of England established.

[1] Force, *Historical Tracts*, I.

[2] Anderson, *History of Colonial Church*, III, 639 ; Stevens, *History of Georgia*, I, 444.

the Church of England entered the colony and was formally established by the colonial legislature of 1758. The colony was divided into eight parishes, and a stipend of £25 allowed to the clergy. In 1769 there were but two Churches of the establishment in the entire colony.

The chief interest of this short narrative of Georgia, in our study, is its beginning with a religious liberty knowing but one restriction, and its finish with an idle attempt to establish a Church, to which as an establishment was fated but a short lease of power. The breaking out of the Revolution destroyed what little semblance of life it ever had.

VII

THE FREE COLONIES

AGAINST the world-wide principle of union between Church and State, which found more or less of power in twelve of the colonial foundations in America, there were three colonies to protest from their beginnings, with no uncertain sound. They were Rhode Island, Pennsylvania, and Delaware.

But there was a marked difference between them. The voice of Rhode Island, under the tutelage of Roger Williams, was far more emphatic than that of the Quaker colonies. It not only decreed a complete severance of state from Church, but forbade to the magistrate any inquiry whatsoever into the views of the citizen on matters of religion. Pennsylvania, — out of which the independent colony of Delaware afterward sprang, — founded and guided by Quaker influence, never attained to so broad a view of religious liberty; for, while denying the propriety of any religious establishment, it still incorporated in its fundamental law an invidious distinction founded on religious opinions — a part of which distinction remains to this day. This distinction is as to belief in the existence of God, upon which was and still is conditioned the right of inhabitancy and citizenship. It is but fair to add, however, that this distinction seems to have been made rather as an expression of opinion and desire on the part of the founders, than as a practical rule of exclusion. No instance of interference with an individual for atheistic opinion is recorded in the colonial history. Nor is it to be supposed that, to-day, the law would challenge an atheist's right to all the privileges of a citizen. Practically, the liberty of the individual in religious matters was from the beginning

422

nearly so well assured in Pennsylvania as in the colony of Williams. To the latter, however, belongs the signal honor of first defining that liberty in constitutional terms, untrammelled by any past or present prejudices, with a breadth of view and fulness of statement unsurpassed by any legal prescriptions of a later day.

I. *Rhode Island*

The history of Rhode Island, so far as concerns religious liberty, is both brief and illustrious. It began with Roger Williams, the fugitive from Massachusetts' ecclesiasticism. Himself the first among philosophers and statesmen, since the day of Constantine, to proclaim the complete freedom of mind and conscience from all civil bonds, he became the founder of the first state in whose fundamental law that freedom was incorporated, not only as a charter of liberty, but as the actual reason and purpose of the state's existence. In this latter particular, indeed, the colony of Rhode Island stands alone, owing its origin, not only to that desire for liberty which brought the Pilgrim and Puritan to New England, but to the set and acknowledged purpose, a purpose confessed by its founders and assented to by the king, " to hold forth a lively experiment, that a most flourishing civil State may stand and best be maintained, with a full liberty of religious concernments." The experiment.

The beginning of it may best be told in the words of Williams himself in a letter to Major Mason of Connecticut, written at Providence under date of June 22, 1670, thirty-four years after Williams's flight from Salem.[1] The occasion of the letter was made by some suggested encroachments by the surrounding colonies on the territory of Rhode Island, and it reviews some of the writer's early experiences. "When I was unkindly and unChristianly, as I believe, driven from my house and land and wife and children (in the midst of New England winter, now about thirty-five years ago) at Letter to Mason.

[1] *Massachusetts Historical Collections*, I, 275.

Salem, that ever honoured Governor, Mr. Winthrop, wrote to me to steer my course to the Nahiganset Bay and Indians, for many high and heavenly and publick ends, incouraging me from the freenes of the place from any English claims or patents. I took his prudent motion as an hint and voice from God, and waving all other thoughts and motions, I steered my course from Salem (though in winter snow which I feel now) unto these parts, wherein I may say *Peniel*, that is, I have seene the face of God. . . . I first pitch't and begun to build and plant at Secunk, now Rehoboth, but I received a letter from my antient friend, Mr. Winslow, then governor of Plymouth, (saying) . . . I was fallen into the edge of their bounds, and they were lothe to displease the Bay, but to remove to the other side of the water, and there I had the country free before me."

Providence. This advice also Williams followed, and named his new settlement PROVIDENCE. But Massasoit claimed that the land about Providence was his and therefore Plymouth's, out of which claim came much disturbance to Williams, until Governor Bradford and others declared, " that I should not be molested and tost up and down againe, while their breath was in their bodies. And surely between those my friends of the Bay and Plymouth I was sorely tost for one fourteen weeks in a bitter winter season, not knowing what bread or bed did meane. . . . God knows that many thousand pounds can not repay the many temporary losses I have sustained. . . . It pleased the Father of Spirits to touch many hearts, dear to Him, with some relentings; amongst which that great and pious soule, Mr. Winslow, melted and kindly visited me at Providence and put a piece of gold into the hands of my wife for our support."

Williams then relates the attempt of Massachusetts to establish a claim upon the land about Providence, and the disallowance thereof by the king, and goes on to declare the main object of the colony : " But here, all over this colonie, a great number of weake and distressed soules scattered are flying hither from Old and New England. The Most High and Only Wise hath in His infinite wisdom provided this country and this corner as a shelter for the poor and persecuted according to their several persuasions. And thus that heavenly man, Mr. Hains, Governour of Connecticut, though he pronounced the sentence of my long banishment against me at Cambridge, yet said unto me in his own house at Hartford, being then in some difference with the Bay, 'I must now confesse to you that the most wise God hath provided and cut out this part of His world for a refuge and receptacle for all kinds of consciences.' "

Nothing could be sharper in contrast than the difference of view between the Puritans of the Bay and the Founder of Rhode Island. " The hostility of the Puritans," says Doyle,[1] " to the Church of England was temporary and conditional. That of Williams was rooted in the nature of the institution. (The former) objected not to a secular control over the Church, but to secular control exercised for what they deemed wrong ends. To Williams a State-Church was an abomination, however it might be administered, and whether it abode in Rome, in England, or in Massachusetts."

Thus to the Puritan of the Bay his own Church, in its purity of doctrine and discipline, represented the supreme function and duty of the state; conformity became a necessary law, and dissent was both criminal and revolutionary. To Williams there were no possible intersections of the Church with the state. The two institutions were as separate and distinct as though their local habitations were divided by the earth's diameter: while the civil law had nothing to say about religion, save that each individual should be left free to the guidance of his own conscience; and the Church, or Churches, should be moulded and controlled by the desires and preferences of those who should voluntarily associate themselves therein.

Williams's own distinctions were clearly drawn, and as

[1] *Puritan Colonies*, I, 155.

noted in our opening chapter — despite some quaintness of expression — cannot be improved in statement. He insisted, far more strenuously than any men of his time, on the essen-

Williams's principle.

tial principle — a principle essential to true religion and true humanity — of the lordship of God alone over the conscience. His opponents declared the principle when striving for their own religious rights, and there stopped. "Yourselves pretend," wrote Williams,[1] "a liberty of conscience; but alas! it is but selfe, the great god Selfe, only to yourselves." Williams asserted the principle to be broad and universal, and to define "liberty for all kinds of consciences."

He thence argued the complete separation of Church from State, both on the ground of pure religion and on that of the radical difference of nature and aim between the two. Thus,[2] " As it would be confusion for the *Church* to censure such *matters* and acts of such persons as belong not to the *Church;* so it is *confusion* for the *State* to punish *spiritual offenses*, for they are not within the *sphear* of a *civil jurisdiction.* . . . The *Civil State* and *Magistrate* are meerly and *essentially civil*, and therefore can not reach (without transgressing the bounds of civility) to judge in matters *spiritual*, which are of another *sphear* and *nature* than *civility* is." He further defines the quality of any action in Church matters by a magistrate as belonging, not to his civil office, but to his personal Church membership: "So far forth as any of this *civil body* are *spiritual*, or act *spiritually*, they and their actions fall under a *spiritual cognizance* and judicature." He then deprecates the serious damage suffered by conscience and religion through the interference of the civil power:

[1] *Puritan Colonies*, p. 281.

[2] *Bloody Tenent Made More Bloody*, pp. 199, 203, 209, 210. This tractate was one of a series. The first, " *The Bloody Tenent of Persecution*," by Williams. This John Cotton answered with " *The Bloody Tenent of Persecution Washed White in the Blood of the Lamb.*" Williams replied with, " *The Bloody Tenent of Persecution Made More Bloody by Mr. Cotton's Attempt to Wash it White.*" (Felt, *Ecclesiastical History of New England*, I, 600, 601.)

" *Civil* and *corporal punishments* do usually cause men to play the *hypocrite* and dissemble in their *Religion*, to turn and return with the tide, as all *experience* in the *nations* of the *world* do testifie now. This *binding* and *rebinding* of *conscience*, contrary or without its own *perswasion*, so weakens and defiles it, that it (as all other faculties) *loseth* its strength and the very nature of a common honest conscience. . . . This *Tenent* of the *Magistrates* keeping the *Church* from *Apostatizing*, by practicing *civil force* upon the *consciences* of men, is so far from preserving *Religion* pure, that it is a mighty *Bulwark* or *Barricado* to keep out all true *Religion*."

Another suggestive utterance is in his letter to Governor Endicott,[1] after the shameful abuse of Clarke and Holmes at Lynn. He imagines Endicott soliloquizing; "I have fought against many several sorts of consciences: is it beyond all possibility and hazard that I have not fought against God, that I have not persecuted Jesus in some of them?" Then he proceeds, "Sir, I must be humbly bold to say, that 'tis impossible for any man or men to maintain their Christ with a sword and worship a true Christ! to fight against all consciences opposite to theirs and not to fight against God in some of them, and to hunt after the precious life of the true Lord Jesus Christ."

Certainly, in Williams's mind there was thus ground enough for the challenge contained in his letter to Major Mason: "I have offered, and doe by these presents, to discuss by disputation . . . these three positions: 1. that forced worship stincks in God's nostrils; 2. that it denies Christ Jesus yet to come; 3. that in these flames about religion, there is no other prudent, Christian way of preserving peace in the world but by permission of differing consciences."

We have no record of any acceptance of this challenge, or of any such public discussion. Had such been possible under the circumstances, we may doubt whether the opponents of

---

[1] Williams, *Letters*, p. 225.

Williams would have been willing to meet him at so close quarters. He was a born fighter, with a superb dialectical skill and an indomitable courage and tenacity, by no means an easy man to face in debate. His insight of spiritual truth was far deeper than that of any contemporary; he detected on the instant any false premise or conclusion, and was both clear and crushing in reply. One cannot read, for instance, his discussion with Cotton without admiring his cogent straightforwardness, or at the same time wondering whether Cotton was not himself conscious of his own weakness in defence.

Yet Williams was far from being a litigious man. Though much of his life was spent in strife, he was no lover of fighting for its own sake. He was of gentle and placable disposition — a personality loving and lovable. The sweetness of that disposition never was soured by the injustice of his foes; he seldom fell into the mistake, so common to moral reformers, of reckoning personal abuse as a proper weapon in the arena of debate; nor does he seem to have ever harbored a single revengeful thought toward those who were prominent in the proceedings against him. Haines is "that heavenly man" and Winthrop, "that ever honoured Governor." With the latter, indeed, he sustained a very tender friendship, writing to him in most affectionate terms.[1] Soon after going to Providence he sought advice from Winthrop in regard to organizing the new plantation, and began: "The frequent experience of your loving ear, ready and open towards me (in what your conscience hath permitted), as also of the excellent spirit of wisdom and prudence wherewith the Father of Lights hath endued you, embolden me to request a word of private advice." Again he wrote: "I still wait upon your love and faithfulness." In another letter: "You request me to be free with you, and therefore blame me not if I answer your request, desiring the like payment from your own dear hand at any time, in any place." And once again: "I wish heartily prosperity to you all,

[1] Williams, *Letters*, pp. 3, 7, 11, 12.

Governor and people, in your civil way, and mourn that you see not your poverty, nakedness, &c in spirituals." When he set out to reply to Cotton, whose pen had not failed in caustic qualities, he began: "I desire my Rejoynder may be as full of *love* as *truth*."

Such equanimity and ability to keep sweet the fountains of friendship, even toward those who had been cruelly adverse, are rare among men. It is pleasing also to note that, despite the intense disapproval of his doctrines, this lovable character was not always without effect upon his foes. Of this there is a curious token in *Scottow's Narrative* :[1] "This child of Light (Williams) walked in Darkness about Forty years . . . yet did not his Root turn into Rottenness. The Root of the Matter abode in him."

Within two years after Williams's settlement at Providence he was joined by various others, who had become dissatisfied with the conditions in the neighboring colonies; and probably by some who came almost directly from England, without staying to try conclusions in the Bay.

Meanwhile another settlement, part of the colony that was soon to be, had been made on the island of Rhode Island, at Aquidneck. Thither had repaired some of the banished followers of Mrs. Hutchinson with other sympathizers, chief among them Coddington and Aspinwall.[2] They were soon followed by the Hutchinsons, and were prompt to make for themselves institutions of free government. In January, 1638, the settlers adopted the following covenant:[3]— Rhode Island settlement.

Ex. 24 : 3, 4.
2 Chron. 11 : 3.
2 Kings 11 : 17.

"We, in the presence of Jehovah, incorporate ourselves into a body politick, and, as He shall help, will submit our persons, lives, and estates unto our Lord Jesus Christ, the King of Kings and Lord of Lords, and to all those perfect and most absolute laws of His, given us in His holy word of truth, to be guided and judged thereby."

[1] *Massachusetts Historical Collections*, I, 281.
[2] Felt, *Ecclesiastical History of New England*, I, 347–351.
[3] *Ibid.*, II, 7 ; 77.

The first act of legislature, passed March 13, 1638, ordered that, " None shall be received as inhabitants or freemen, to build or plant upon the Island, but such as shall be received in by the consent of the body, and do submit to the government that is, or shall be, established according to the word of God." In 1641 this government was legally defined by the legislature as " a Democracy, or popular government," and it was *ordered* that, " none be accounted a delinquent for doctrine, provided that it be not directly repugnant to the government or laws established." At the next session it was "*ordered*, that that law of the last Court, made concerning liberty of conscience in point of doctrine, be perpetuated."

At Providence Williams also was casting about to devise means for the organization of government. He took counsel with Winthrop, and decided that the first thing to be done **Warwick charter.** was to procure a colonial charter. For this he turned to England, intending a personal visit, and wrote to the Massachusetts authorities for permission to embark at Boston, that he might " inoffensively and without molestation pass through your Jurisdiction, as a stranger for a night, to the ship." [1] The desired permission does not appear to have been given, and Williams sailed for England, 1643, probably from Plymouth. The same year, he obtained from the Earl of Warwick a charter for the " Incorporation of the Providence Plantations in the Narraganset Bay in New England." [2] The charter was in 1644 confirmed by the parliament, and with it Williams sailed from England direct to Boston, bringing also an official letter to the general court of Massachusetts.

This letter he relied upon as a protection, and in virtue of the official character it put upon him as a governmental messenger he was suffered to pass unmolested through the colony to Providence. The letter undoubtedly contained some reflections on—if not reproofs for—the past treatment of Williams ; for,[3] " Upon the receipt of the said letter, the

[1] *Massachusetts Historical Collections*, IV, 4 ; 471.
[2] Palfrey, I, 344.   [3] Hubbard, *History of New England.*

governor and Magistrates of the Massachusetts found upon
the examination of their hearts they saw no reason to condemn
themselves for any former proceedings against Mr. Williams:
but for any offices of Christian love and duties of humanity
they were very willing to maintain a mutual correspondency
with him.   But as to his dangerous principles of separation,
unless he can be brought to lay them down, they see no reason why to concede to him, or any so persuaded, free liberty
of ingress or egress, lest any of their people should be drawn
away with his erroneous opinions."

The charter of 1644 was silent on matters of conscience
and worship, probably because Williams did not wish to raise
the question with the English authorities, and also held that
religious liberty was an indefeasible right which no charter
could grant.   There was no objection, however, to the declaration of that right in a statute.   At the first legislative assembly a code of laws was adopted.[1]   The preamble defined the   Code of
form of government as " Democratical, that is to say, A gov-   laws.
ernment held by the free and voluntary consent of all, or the
greater part, of the free inhabitants"; and then proceeded
to declare, as fundamental to that government, the broadest
conceivable liberty of conscience and of worship.   Its notable
words run : " And now to the end that we may give each to
other (notwithstanding our different consciences touching
the truth as it is in Jesus) as good and hopeful assurance as
we are able, touching each man's peaceable and quiet enjoyment of his lawful right and liberty."   Thereon in the act
followed the code of civil law, which concluded with the
words: — "And otherwise than this (what is herein forbidden)
all men may walk as their consciences persuade them, every
one in the name of his GOD.   AND LET THE LAMBS OF THE
MOST HIGH WALK IN THIS COLONY WITHOUT MOLESTATION, IN
THE NAME OF JEHOVAH THEIR GOD, FOR EVER AND EVER." [2]

[1] *Massachusetts Historical Collections*, II, 7 ; 78, 79.

[2] In the *Collections* a footnote by the unknown transcriber of the above
declares, " The men, who at such a time and under such circumstances could

The declaration of so complete freedom was attended in its first years with some disadvantages. Most men of the day could not understand it, unable to make the distinction, which to Williams was clear as the day, between freedom of mind from spiritual tyranny and freedom of conduct from the restraint of civil law. So it fell out that the new plantations,

Dangers.

for a little space, became, not only "a refuge for all sorts of consciences," but a resort for all classes of discontent; a Cave Adullam, to which fled many, who under the cloak of conscience shielded a desire for general lawlessness. The idea of personal liberty was exaggerated into a positive danger to all civil order.

Upon this untoward tendency the enemies of Rhode Island seized with abundant disposition to make the most of it. As already noted, when Rhode Island applied for admission into

New England Confederacy.

the New England Confederacy the request was refused, because "Your present state and condition are full of confusion and danger."[1] We may take it that such charge was readily seized upon by the Massachusetts commissioners, who were supreme in the federal council, to disqualify a colony founded on a principle so opposite to their own. This is the more evident from the further reply, that the island of Rhode Island belonged to Plymouth, and therefore the jurisdiction of that colony must be acknowledged before the applicant could be admitted.

Another indication of this hostile sentiment is contained in a bitter letter from William Arnold, of Pawtucket, to Gov-

Hostility.

ernor Endicott, 1651.[2] It was written with the avowed design to inform the governor of what was "doing in the parts about Providence and Rhode Island," and tells of a movement toward sending Williams to England to obtain a second charter, which should include both settlements. "If they should get them a charter," he wrote, "off it there

frame such a law and undeviatingly adhere to its principles . . . will I reverence, on this side idolatry."

[1] Hutchinson, *Collections*, p. 226.   [2] *Ibid.*, p. 237.

may come some mischeive and trouble upon the whole country, if their project be not prevented in time; for, under the pretence of liberty of conscience, about these partes there comes to lieve all the scume, the runne-awayes of the country, which in tyme for want of better order may bring a heavy burden on the land. . . . We that live heere neere them . . . humbly desire God their purpose may be frustrated. I humbly desire my name may be conceled, lest they will be enraged against me." [1]

Still another token of this unfriendly regard, founded on the stories of Rhode Island disorder, may be quoted for its characteristic expression from the *Wonder-Working Providence of Zion's Saviour*.[2] The passage concludes the account of the Hutchinson episode at Boston, and recounts : " Those sinful erroneous persons, being banished, resorted to a place more Southward . . . where having elbowe-roome enough, none of the Ministers of Christ, nor any other to interrupt their false and deceivable doctrines, they hampered themselves foully with their owne line, and soone shewed the depthlesse ditches that blinde guides lead into. . . . Some of the female sexe . . . from an ardent desire of being famous, especially the grand Mistresse of them all, who ordinarily prated every Sabbath day, till others who thirsted after honor in the same way with herselfe, drew away her Auditors, and then she withdrew herself, her husband and her family also, to a more remote place." [3]

Williams's own reply to the malignant aspersions of his colony, and to those individuals in the colony who presumed

---

[1] This Arnold was one of a small company of four families at Pawtucket, about whom Williams wrote in 1656 officially, as president of Providence Plantation, to the Massachusetts authorities, complaining of their troublesome conduct, and said they were " very far also in religion from you, if you knew all." (Hutchinson, *Collections*, pp. 275-282.)

[2] Force, *Historical Tracts*.

[3] It is true that Mrs. Hutchinson, with some of her family, removed to Manhattan, and there perished in the Indian massacre excited by the foolish Kieft. But there is no reason to suppose her removal due to offended vanity.

that license and disorder were justified by his views of religious liberty, is well expressed in a letter to the magistrates and town of Providence. "That ever I should speak or write a tittle that tends to such an infinite liberty of conscience is a mistake." He then compares the commonwealth to a ship with all sorts of people, Papists, Protestants, Jews, Turks, of whom none should be forced to prayers or worship; but if any should be mutinous and refuse duty or help toward the common charges, or "preach that there ought to be no commanders because all are equal in Christ, I say, the commander may judge, resist, compel, and punish such transgressors, according to their deserts and merits." [1]

The movement, alluded to in Arnold's letter to Endicott, toward obtaining a charter which should merge Providence and Rhode Island in one colony, was the natural outcome from the similar aims and close neighborhood of the two settlements. The desire for this union seems to have found expression, and to have met with general approval, almost immediately on the granting of the Providence charter of 1644. The scheme, however, had some opponents, chief among whom was Coddington, the governor of the island settlement.[2] In 1650 he went to England to forestall the plans of the union, and succeeded in obtaining an order for the separate government of Rhode Island. With this he returned home, and the people at first submitted, but after a few months disowned him and his government and again united with Williams in efforts for the charter. John Clarke was joined with Williams in an embassy to England, whither the two men went in 1651.

New charter.

Williams remained in England for three years, having much converse with Cromwell, Milton, and others, and steadily pressing his suit. For some unexplained reason, unless it be the influence of Coddington, he failed in securing the object of his mission, and in 1654 went back to Provi-

[1] Williams, *Letters*, p. 278.
[2] *Massachusetts Historical Collections*, V, 217.

dence, leaving Clarke as agent for their joint interests. "Plead our cause," he wrote to Clarke in 1658, "in such sort as we may not be compelled to exercise any civil power over men's consciences."

But Cromwell neither granted nor denied the application, and presently his death made room for the restoration of the kingdom. To Charles, therefore, a new petition was pre- Charles II. sented in 1662, and to that king, "who never said a foolish thing, and never did a wise one," save this present action, belongs the honor of granting the broadest charter of human liberties ever issued under a royal seal — a noble exception of wisdom in his deed. The character of it is so averse to all the ordinary principles controlling his government of Great Britain, and the liberties granted by it are so contradictory to his cherished prerogatives, that we can account for his concessions only by one of those inconsistent moods of complacency, to which he gave occasional sway in the earlier years of his reign.

The king seems to have been attracted, not from any love of liberty, but from sheer curiosity, by the novelty of the purpose expressed by the petitioners in that famous sentence, already quoted: "It is much in our hearts to hold forth *a lively experiment, that a most flourishing civil State may stand, and best be maintained, with a full liberty of religious concernments.*" It is a strange thing that the royal mind should be affected favorably to so unheard-of proposition, and stranger still that Clarendon should have exerted himself to obtain for the petitioners the full extent of their desire, and more. Others of the king's ministers opposed the grant, as appears from Williams's letter to Major Mason.[1] He there justly described the charter as "The King's extraordinary favor to this Colony, in which his Majesty declared himself that he would experiment, whether civil government could exist with such liberty of conscience." Thus Charles adopted the petitioners' experiment as his own. Williams proceeds, "This

[1] *Massachusetts Historical Collections*, I, 281.

his Majesty's graunt was startled-at by his Majesty's high officers of State . . . but, fearing the lyon's roaring, they (were) couchant against their wills in obedience to his Majesty's pleasure."

The charter was issued in 1663.[1] Its section on religious matters reads: "No person within the said colony, at any time hereafter, shall be any wise molested, punished, disqualified, or called in question for any difference of opinion in matters of religion : every person may at all times freely and fully enjoy his own judgment and Conscience in matters of religious concernments." Beside this the charter bestowed upon the people of Rhode Island a civil liberty greater than that conceded to any other colony. Even the oath of allegiance was not required; and the demand, that the laws passed by the colonial legislature should be "agreeable to the laws of England," was qualified by a "reference to the constitution of the place and the nature of the people."[2]

Full liberty.   Thus was constituted, and by a king whose tendencies and desires were all toward despotism, a genuine republic — the first thoroughly free government in the world, where the state was left plastic to the moulding will of the citizen; the conscience at liberty to express itself in any way of doctrine and worship; the Church untrammelled by any prescription or preference of the civil law. In this little colony of Rhode Island was first set up this "ensign for the people," the model for that sisterhood of states which was yet to possess the continent.

With such a beginning the further history of religious liberty in Rhode Island presents little matter for comment.[3] The battle was already won, the colony started at the point which the most of her sisters reached only at the Revolution.

The "Great Charter" was received by the people with joy, and the legislature in its first session (1664) organized the

[1] Palfrey, II, 52.

[2] Bancroft, *History of United States*, II, 62–68.

[3] Felt, *Ecclesiastical History of New England*, I, 609.

government anew, repealing all laws inconsistent with the charter, and in its very words establishing religious liberty. In the next year the legislature renewed its declaration, asserting that, "liberty to all persons as to the worship of God had been a principle maintained in the colony from the very beginning thereof; and it was much in their hearts to preserve the same liberty forever."

From this principle the people and government of Rhode Island never departed, and no religionist was ever questioned, or subjected to struggle or distress, in respect to faith and worship. The royal commissioners, who visited New England in 1665, reported of Rhode Island: "They allow liberty of conscience to all who live civilly: they admit of all religions."

In the after history of the colony there appear but two doubtful exceptions to the reign of this perfect freedom, — *Exceptions.* one relating to the Quakers, and the other to Roman Catholics. The alleged action against the Quakers was in a *Quakers.* bill of outlawry, 1665, because they would not bear arms. But this bill, it would appear, never became law, the people in general protesting against it and not suffering its enactment.[1] In the same year the royal commissioners attempted to supply a lack in the charter by demanding the oath of allegiance, but the legislature would concede nothing beyond an engagement of fidelity and obedience to the laws, on pain of forfeiture of the franchise; and, when the Quakers complained that the requirement was irksome, the law was repealed.

There appears in the Revised Statutes a law purporting to have been passed "at some time after 1688," denying citizenship to Roman Catholics.[2] This law Bancroft argues was never the *Romanists.* act of the people, or of the legislature, but that the committee of revisal, preparing the record for printing (the earliest extant copy bearing date of 1744), interpolated this law,

[1] *Massachusetts Historical Collections*, V, 217 ; Bancroft, II, 67.

[2] Fisher, *History of Church*, 479 ; Bancroft, *History of United States*, II, 65 ; Palfrey, *History of New England*, III, 436.

"for which the occasion grew out of English politics." The clause, "passed at some time after 1688," is a footnote in the revision of 1744, and clearly shows that the revisers had before them no official minutes of the act, and were guided by prejudice, or policy, or a memory more or less at fault, or yet, tradition.

Strangely enough, Professor Fiske, in his "*Dutch and Quaker Colonies*,"[1] founds upon this very doubtful bit of legislation a comparison between Rhode Island and Pennsylvania, with regard to their respective attitudes on the question of religious liberty, which is quite disparaging to the former. He not only assumes that the doubtful law was enacted, but makes the surprising statement that in Pennsylvania "all Christian sects stood socially and politically on an equal footing;" and that what Pennsylvania specially "stood for was liberty of conscience." This is robbing Peter to pay Paul, with a vengeance. One might well hesitate to make a stain upon the fair fame of Rhode Island out of a record so dubious and so diverse from all else in her history; while, as to Pennsylvania, it will presently be shown that she never stood for full liberty of conscience, and that through her entire colonial history the Jew and the Socinian were disfranchised, while from 1702 to the Revolution the Roman Catholic was made incapable of holding office.

It remains to be said of this doubtful act that, supposing the law to have been passed, it could have wrought no hardship, for there were no Roman Catholics in the colony. When the first professors of that faith came to Rhode Island, in the persons of the officers and men of the French fleet aiding the colonies in the Revolution, the legislature, "to efface any semblance of opprobrium," at once caused the law to be *expunged*, as not belonging to the record.

Disorders.

In the earlier day there were plenty of people to circulate stories to the discredit of the colony. The magistrates of Boston thought ill of Williams because, while he did not

[1] Vol. II, p. 99.

approve the restlessness of Gorton, he refused to join them in action against him. Williams in his letter to Mason refers to tales told to the king, "that we are prophane people and do not keep the Sabbath . . . But you told him not how we suffer freely all other perswasions, yea, the Common-prayer which yourselves will not suffer . . . Generally all this whole colonie observe the first day; only here and there one out of conscience, another out of covetousness."

It is true that some disorders existed in the earlier years, by reason of which the example of Rhode Island did not exert upon the other colonies the effect that should have attended its illustrious definition and establishment of a perfect liberty.[1] But the actual effects were to be expected. The doctrine was too broad for general comprehension and to many seemed pregnant of destructive license — a conclusion not dispelled by the tendency toward Rhode Island of such persons as found themselves uncomfortable in neighboring colonies.

It may be said also, that for the most of the Rhode Island men themselves the principle was at first too broad. The sense of the individual right inculcated by it went far to weaken the sense of that principle of association which is necessary, with mutual concessions and limitations, to the perpetuity of the institutions of liberty itself. Hence in the colony there was often an altogether unreasonable impatience at the proper restraints of law, and in the Church there was so positive assertion of the individual conscience, that years passed away before the people found a method of voluntary association in which difference of view and unity of action could coexist.[2]

But all these things marked but the ferment caused by a new and vital spirit. The principle had to be learned by degrees in its practical applications. The "lively experiment" had to be put upon its trials, until men should discover

[1] Palfrey, I, 390; II, 110; III, 217, 326.
[2] *Ibid.*, III, 434–437.

that liberty and law must go hand in hand; that faith, freedom, and union are needful to the "civil" and spiritual man.

This lesson little Rhode Island was the first of all states in the world to set herself to learn. She learned and gave it as an object lesson to her sisters and the earth at large. Her experiment was a success. As the result of it, when the Revolution came, shattering the established Church in other colonies, and demanding for them new constitutions suitable to changed conditions, Rhode Island passed into the American Union, still under the old charter of King Charles, to keep it as her fundamental law for two generations afterward.

II. *Pennsylvania and Delaware*

These two colonies may well be considered together. They were originally one until 1702, and afterward showed little difference in their treatment of religious matters. The colony owed its origin to the benevolent, broad-minded, and politic William Penn. As a Quaker, he was devoted to the cause of religious liberty and desired to make for it a secure abiding place. As a statesman, he was well fitted for the task of founding and guiding a commonwealth. Becoming personally interested in American colonization by the purchase of West Jersey in 1674, his ambition expanded to the creation of a distinct and larger colony, of which himself should be the sole proprietor. Though a Quaker of very decided type, he was yet a friend of Charles II. and his brother James, and through this friendship found easy work in obtaining from the king the charter creating the province of Pennsylvania, to which the duke of York added by gift that part of his own American possessions, which had received the name of Delaware.

There can be no doubt that King Charles was aware of Penn's purpose to establish religious liberty in the colony, or,

Penn.

at least, of his desire to retain in his own power the direction
of the colonial attitude on matters of religion. Thus the
charter, which was given in 1681, makes no attempt to decide   Charter.
anything in regard thereto. There is no clause of Church
establishment, and no provision for liberty of conscience.
The only allusion to the Church is the stipulation that, "if
any of the inhabitants to the number of Twenty signify in
writing to the bishop of London their desire for a preacher,
such preacher or preachers as may be sent by him shall be
allowed to reside and exercise their function in the colony,
without any deniall or molestacon whatsoever." [1]

[2] Penn's avowed object in his public "Address" was to
make a "holy experiment," to found a commonwealth on the
corner-stone of freedom. It was like the "lively experiment"   Experiment.
of Roger Williams, except that the Quaker's vision of freedom was somewhat narrower than that of the great founder
of Rhode Island. By a singular infelicity of statement Penn
declared to his friends his desire "to establish a precedent in
government, and to furnish an example." That precedent
had already been existent for forty years in the colony of
Williams, on which Penn's expression was an unjust reflection, not to be fully explained by the early disorders in Rhode
Island by reason of the heterogeneous character of the early
settlers. But Penn's addiction to the cause of liberty was
true and life-long. For it he had suffered, and for this colonizing experiment he ventured his all. "We must give the
liberty we ask," he said. "We cannot be false to our principles. We would have none to suffer for dissent on any
hand." "I abhor two principles in religion," wrote Penn to
a friend, "and pity them that own them; the first is obedience
to authority without conviction; and the other is destroying
them that differ from me for God's sake. Such a religion is
without judgment, though not without teeth."

[1] *Pennsylvania Charter and Laws*, p. 89.
[2] Proud, *History of Pennsylvania*, I, 170; Bancroft, *United States*, II,
361-396.

These views Penn endeavored to express in his regulations for the new colony, though not without some regrettable restrictions. On receipt of his charter, he composed in 1682, while still in England, and there published, a "Frame of Government,"[1] whereof the Preface recites: "We have to the best of our skill contrived and composed the *frame* and *laws* of this government, to the great end of all government, viz.: *to support power in reverence with the people, and to secure the people from abuse of power;* that they may be free by their just obedience, and the magistrates honorable for their just administration; for liberty without obedience is confusion, and obedience without liberty is slavery." Nothing, surely, could be finer or more just than this declaration and definition.

Frame of government.

There is something of a departure from its broad principle in the religious sections of the frame of government. These are:[2] —

Religious restrictions.

"34. That all Treasurers, Judges, Masters of Rolls, Sheriffs, Justices of the Peace, and other officers and persons whatsoever, relating to courts or trials of causes, or any other service in the government; and all Members elected to service in the provincial Council and General Assembly, and all that have right to elect such Members, shall be such as profess faith in Jesus Christ.

"35. That all persons living in this province, who confess and acknowledge the one Almighty and Eternal God to be the Creator, Upholder, and Ruler of the world; and that hold themselves obliged in conscience to live peaceably and justly in civil society, shall in no ways be molested or prejudiced for their religious profession or practice in matters of faith and worship; nor shall they be compelled, at any time, to frequent or maintain any religious worship, place, or ministry whatever."

The first colonial assembly met at Chester in 1682, and

[1] *Pennsylvania Laws;* Proud, Appendix.
[2] *Charter and Laws,* p. 102.

enacted, "The Great Law or Body of Laws"[1] of which the Assembly of 1682. first chapter was "Of Religion." Its prescriptions were in harmony with those of Penn's composition, just cited, but contain peculiarities and additions of a unique character. The chapter begins: —

"Almighty God, being the only Lord of Conscience, "Great Law." father of Lights and Spirits, and the author as well as object of all divine knowledge, faith, and Worship, who only can enlighten the mind and persuade and convince the understanding of people: In due reverence to his Sovereignty over the Souls of Mankind, *Be it enacted*, That no person, now or at any time hereafter, Living in this Province, who shall confess and acknowledge one Almighty God to be the Creator, Upholder and Ruler of the world; And who shall profess him, or herself, Obliged in Conscience to Live peaceably and quietly under the civil government, shall in any case be molested or prejudiced for his, or her, conscientious persuasion or practice. Nor shall hee or shee at any time be compelled to frequent or maintain anie religious worship, place, or Ministry whatever, contrary to his or her mind; but shall freely and fully enjoy, his or her, Christian liberty in that respect, without any Interruption or reflection. And if any person shall deride or abuse any other for his or her different persuasion or practice in matters of religion, such person shall be lookt upon as a Disturber of the peace and be punished accordingly.

"But to the end, That Looseness, irreligion, and Atheism may not Creep in under any pretense of Conscience in this Province, *Be it further enacted*, That according to the example of the primitive Christians, and for the ease of the Creation, Every first day of the week, called the Lord's day, People shall abstain from their usual and common toil and labor, That whether Masters, Parents, Children, or servants, they may the better dispose themselves

[1] *Charter and Laws*, p. 109.

to read the Scriptures of truth at home, or frequent such meetings for religious worship as may best sute their respective persuasions."

Furthermore, the assembly of 1682 defined in Chapter II. the qualifications for office and the franchise, requiring that all civil officers of the Province, all deputies to the assembly, and all electors of deputies, "shall be such as profess and declare that they believe in Jesus Christ to be the Saviour of the world." The assembly declared these laws to be fundamental ; and when they were annulled by William and Mary in 1693, the assembly immediately reënacted them.

From these statutes alone judging, it is evident that the boasted liberty of Pennsylvania was not so broad as has usually been supposed. In the colonies its restrictions were surpassed for narrowness only by Massachusetts, Virginia, and Maryland in the latter half of her colonial government. According to the fundamental law of Pennsylvania, a Jew or any sort of a non-Christian Theist could live in the province, but neither hold office nor vote. For the Atheist or Deist not even a right of residence was conceded by the fundamental law, the expressed desire of which was to prevent atheism and irreligion from " creeping in." A notable feature of the law, differing greatly from other colonial prescriptions, was the complete enfranchisement of Roman Catholics. Under this early constitution a Romanist could both vote and hold office. This exceptional favor was due to the sentiment of Penn, who in England in his arguments and influence had grouped the Romanists with the Quakers, as classes from whom civil disabilities should be removed.

Romanists.

This liberty of the Romanist, however, was not long continued. It was too broad for a province depending largely on royal favor, and too much in opposition to the toleration act of England. The restriction of it was not in the first instance imposed by colonial statute, or in any new definition as to the quality of settlers. It came as a natural consequence of orders from England prescribing the form of oath to be Test oath. taken by office-holders. These orders were from the government of William and Mary, and required that the form of oath used in England, under the toleration act should be used also in Pennsylvania.[1] This order was made in 1693 and was repeated in 1701. The government of Queen Anne in 1703 again repeated the order and embraced "judicial and all other offices."[2] The oath was designed in England as a test, discriminating against Romanists, Jews, and Unitarians. It expressly abjured the Roman doctrines of transubstantiation, the adoration of Mary or other saints, and the sacrifice of the mass; and expressly acknowledged the Triune Godhead of Father, Son, and Holy Spirit, and the divine inspiration of the Scriptures.

Of course, the oath excluded from office every Roman Catholic, Socinian, and Jew, but it does not appear to have been a condition for the right of suffrage. The order imposing it was not grateful to the colonial legislature, or to the proprietor. Much consultation was given to it, but the situation of affairs seemed to require submission. Penn was in England at the time and in hiding. His relations to James II. exposed him to the suspicion of William, while his recent actions in regard to the imprisoned Quakers had brought upon him the maledictions of the people. In order to set them free, there was appeal made to the famous "Declaration of Indulgence" issued by James in 1687, a declaration execrated by every English Protestant as an entering wedge for the introduction of Romanism. According to the general Protestant view it was better to suffer persecution than to accept liberty through such an instrument.[3] Penn and his Penn in England. liberated brethren became marks for passionate denunciation. "Papist," "Jesuit in disguise," were among the milder terms flung at Penn's devoted head; and not long after the acces-

[1] *Pennsylvania Colonial Records*, II, 68.   [2] *Ibid.*, II, 89–96.
[3] *Pennsylvania Historical Magazine*, IX; Stillé on *Religious Tests in Pennsylvania.*

sion of William he was thrown into prison for several months. The action against him went to the extreme of a trial for treason, which resulted in acquittal and discharge from prison. But for some months afterward he found it wise to retire from public observation. While thus in retirement his enemies prevailed on the government to set aside the charter of Pennsylvania and to join its government to that of New York. Instructions to that end were issued to Fletcher, the governor of the latter province, under date of 1693, and carried the order imposing the test oath.

Immediately on Fletcher's assumption of the government, the general assembly addressed to him a petition, reciting the provincial laws already in force and desiring his ratification thereof. Among them were the religious provisions just quoted. The governor's reply was a proclamation requiring all "officers of the province . . . to put in execution the above said laws, until their majesties' pleasure shall be more fully known."[1] This ratification did not do away with the test, which was still required, though inconsistent with the " Laws."

But this union of Pennsylvania and New York was very brief. Penn in some way found means of propitiating William, who in 1694 restored to him the charter and government of the province; and the reinstated proprietor sent out as governor his cousin, William Markham. But Penn could not venture at once on setting aside the test, and accordingly Legislature adopts the test. the first assembly (1696) under Markham, in reëstablishing the proprietary government, passed " A New Act of Settlement," which required the religious tests of the toleration act to be administered to all office-holders.

The situation of Penn was difficult, and it is clear that his assent to such legislation was under a compulsion of circumstances, at the time irresistible. As Stillé says, " The more we study his life and career, the grander and more heroic his character becomes." He had not, indeed, that

[1] *Pennsylvania Historical Magazine*, IX, 188–220.

broad catholicity of view which made Roger Williams the most unique figure in colonial history, but he was far removed from that narrowness which made the boasted toleration of England an instrument of oppression. Evidently he considered the concession of 1696 as only a temporary sop to Cerberus, for on his own return to the colony in 1699 he set himself to put away the hated restriction. This effort he introduced by a series of laws, making a fourth and final " frame of government," among which were two bearing on the question of religion. The one was an " Act concerning Liberty of Conscience " ; and the other an " Act in regard to Attests of certain officers." These were brought in and passed by the legislature in 1700, and their effort was to restore the definitions of the fundamental law of 1682.

The news of this action was ill-received in England, where the queen in council in 1702 annulled it and sent to Pennsylvania peremptory orders, that the religious tests of the toleration act should be restored, and furthermore that every person then in office should subscribe the test on penalty of losing his place. To this order the colonial officers at first demurred, but afterward yielded, to Penn's great indignation.

In an evil hour and with wrong judgment Penn, on the threat of adverse action in London, had taken himself thither in hopes of conciliating the government and so forestalling the order. But this he was unable to do, and was absent from his province at the very moment when his presence was the most needed, in the acute crisis of the cause which he had most at heart. Had he been on the ground he might have braced up the spirits of his colonists to resist the royal demand. As it was, the cause of religious liberty was then lost in Pennsylvania, never in colonial times to reassert itself. In 1703 the entire assembly followed the example of the officers and subscribed the test, and in 1705 passed an act legalizing by colonial legislation all the religious tests demanded by the queen's orders! This act remained in force until 1776. Thus the Quakers went back on their record as champions for human freedom, and established for their chosen colony the principle, which elsewhere they had resisted, that the full enjoyment of civil rights should be confined to professors of a specified religious creed.

At the same time with this submission the legislature took **Quaker affirmation.** special action in relation to affirmation by the Quakers. The new oath seemed to demand a reassertion of their privileges. This act for the relief of Quakers was set aside in 1705 by the queen in council, " not with design to deprive Quakers of that privilege, but solely on account of its making the punishment for false affirming greater than the law of England required for false swearing." [1]

The Quaker attitude toward oaths was a constant annoyance to English authorities, some of whom thought that it portended ruin to the social fabric. This is illustrated in a letter from Lord Cornbury to the board of trade in 1703: " I have some letters from Philadelphia, which inform me that they have lately held Courts of Judicature there, in which they have condemned people to death by Judges that are Quakers, and neither Judges nor Jury under any oath. These proceedings have very much startled the Gentlemen of the Church of England in Pennsylvania." [2] Not until 1725 could a law covering the matter be made satisfactory to both the Quakers and the king. In 1743 religious societies, other than Quakers, were admitted to the benefit of the

[1] Proud, *History of Pennsylvania*, II, 190.

But whatever happened as to the general law concerning oaths, the Quakers were bound to take care of their brethren and were ready to interfere with legislative action for the benefit of any oppressed individual. Thus, in 1704 (*Records*, II, 180) Joseph Yard of Philadelphia complained to the council that the county court had fined him forty shillings for refusing the oath. He prayed for relief, saying that he " could not take one, nor had ever taken one in his Life." The action of the council ordered the fine remitted and the complainant to be " forthwith Reimbursed of the same."

[2] *Colonial History of New York*, IV, 1045.

act; and in 1772 its relief was extended to " any persons "
having scruples against oaths.[1]

The test oath was also administered to persons seeking to
be naturalized in the colony, and the use of it was frequently   Naturaliza-
spoken of as " taking the test."   Thus it appears both in the   tion.
records and in the certificates given to the persons making
oath.   Once the phrase occurs in relation to two members
admitted to the assembly, who made "profession of the
Christian belief and took the test."[2]   Similar notes appear
about persons naturalized, as " having taken the oath
appointed by act of parliament and subscribed the test ";
" having subscribed the Declaration " (against Roman doctrines); " having taken the sacrament of the Lord's Supper
within three months."[3]   This last was so late as 1765.[4]

So far, then, as terms are concerned, Pennsylvania was
much less liberal than most of the colonies, and is not to be
classed with Rhode Island on her broad platform of full
religious liberty.   The one point of close resemblance is in
the absence of a religious establishment.   Pennsylvania
never made any attempts toward establishing a Church.
This fact makes the rigid insistence on religious tests one of
the strangest things in colonial history, for in all other cases
of such insistence the oath has been in the interest of some
State-Church.   With the Quakers of Pennsylvania its demand was in the interests simply of Protestantism.   Protestantism was established, in a sense.   There at least, if not

---

[1] *Pennsylvania Records*, IV, 629 ; X, 42.   [2] *Ibid.*, I, 538.

[3] *Archives*, I, 118 ; III, 692 ; IV, 243.

[4] Another form of oath was devised by the assembly to be taken by the
Palatines, who immigrated to Pennsylvania between 1720 and 1760 in so
large numbers that the local authorities became alarmed lest the foreigners
might " steal the Province from his sacred Majesty, King George."   It is
noticeable that this Palatine oath makes no reference whatever to religious
matters, and pledges only allegiance to the English colonial government.
Even the requirement of the fundamental law as to belief in God and Jesus
Christ is not incorporated. (*Colonial Records*, III, 283.)   Probably, this
Palatine oath may have been added to the other, but the fact does not so
appear on the record.

elsewhere, the Quakers shared the general view of Protestant Christendom, that only Christians of the Protestant persuasion were fit for public office or citizenship.

One noticeable attendant upon this legal supremacy of Protestantism was, so far as the records and archives show, an entire absence of outspoken opposition to its principle. Objection seems to have contented itself with the first official demur of 1705, after which the people rested in quiet content that Romanist, Jew, and Socinian should be denied all civil rights, until the Revolution came and exhibited the meanness of that rule. But even then Pennsylvania could not shake herself loose from all restrictive measures. Nor yet in this year of grace 1902 has she fully done it.

All through the seventy years of proscription no public remonstrances were heard. None seem to have been excited by an invidious law of 1730 for the "Protection of Church Property," which restricted its benefits to Protestant Churches.

It needs, however, to be noted that Pennsylvania never proceeded against persons. There were no instances of **No persecution.** persecution, or of personal hardships for religion's sake, unless exclusion from office can be so termed. Men were not hindered the free exercise of what religion they preferred. Stillé quotes from Hildreth the statement, that the Roman Church of Saint Joseph in Philadelphia was the only place in the thirteen colonies where the mass was allowed to be publicly celebrated prior to the Revolution. In theory, indeed, Pennsylvania, after 1700, lagged behind even the once theocratic Massachusetts, but in her treatment of persons we find no harshness. During the Seven Years' War with the French **Disarming Romanists.** and Indians the assembly passed a law for disarming Roman Catholics, but the motive of the act was not religious oppression, but a fear lest the religious sympathy of the Romanists might cause them to aid the French. The fear was the result of an unjust suspicion, and the law, due to a moment of panic, was never put in force.

Of all the religious legislation in the colonies nothing was more absurd than that against Roman Catholics. One would suppose that the Roman Church was a constant and threatening foe to colonial institutions. The fact was far otherwise. With the opening of the Revolution, it is estimated that there were not more than thirteen hundred Romanists between Canada and Florida. And this is not to be understood as the effect of "anti-papist" laws. For some other reason, not clearly discernible, the people of that faith were not drawn toward America. The opening of Maryland, as a refuge for them from the proscriptions of England, did not attract many. At the beginning of that colony, the majority of settlers were Protestants, and in the following years the disproportion increased steadily, so that by 1700 the Romanists were less than one-sixth of the inhabitants. With all circumstances to attract, and with the sure prospect of possessing the controlling power, the Roman Catholics declined to come in any larger numbers to their own colony. In the face of such a fact, and in face of the still more remarkable fact that, during the half century in which the Romanists governed Maryland, they were not guilty of a single act of religious oppression, the legislation against them was specially unwarranted and base. In the Maryland of the eighteenth century it was the voice of a monstrous ingratitude. In the other colonies it was so needless as to be ridiculous.

Of course, we recognize it as but a reflection from the baleful fires that burned so long in England; and much of the blame for it must be laid at the door of the English government, insisting without reason that the distinctions, which meant so much in English law and society, should be perpetuated in America, where they could not properly apply. This was specially the case in Pennsylvania. The Quakers would never have moved such restrictive measures, if left to themselves; and it is their peculiar disgrace that, unlike themselves, they quailed before the voice of regal authority demanding an action which all their professed principles detested. In so judging, however, it needs always to be

remembered that this invidious legislation was never followed
by oppression of persons for their religion, and that, while
Romanists were excluded from civil rights, yet in the private
and public exercise of their faith they were possessed in
Pennsylvania of larger liberty than in any other colony.
In this regard they were perfectly free. No law " excepted
Papists " from the category of intending inhabitants, or made
the colony dangerous ground for " Popish Priest " or Jesuit.
Coming to Pennsylvania, they were unmolested, and seemed
content to rest under the civil ban, so long as their religious
worship was not forbidden or hindered.

Delaware.   With regard to DELAWARE after its separation from
Pennsylvania, it only remains to note that its records show
much less concern about religious affairs than those of the
parent colony. The law of 1700 in regard to naturalization
made necessary only a "solemn engagement to be true and
faithful to the King and the Proprietary," without any reference to religion. This was passed two years before the separation, but seems to have remained in force in Delaware ; for the
" Laws of Delaware " contain no statute similar to the Pennsylvania act, which subjected would-be citizens to the toleration test. Strangely enough, by a law of 1704 the Delaware
legislature required that test to be taken by " attorneys and
solicitors," in addition to the ordinary oath touching their
duties as members of court, but required it from such officers
only. This was, doubtless, modified by the act of 1719,
which required that " Justices, judges, inquests, and witnesses
(should) qualify themselves according to their conscientious
persuasions respectively." [1]

It would appear that the pressure from England on the
legislation of Delaware was much less than upon that of Pennsylvania, for the laws contain but one instance of discrimination against Romanists. This was an act — 17 George II.
— empowering *Protestant* Churches and societies to receive
and hold real estate.[2] The original requirements of the

[1] *Laws of Delaware*, pp. 53, 56, 65.   [2] *Ibid.*, p. 271.

fundamental law, confining the franchise and office to persons who believed "that Jesus Christ, the Son of God, is the Saviour of the world," was still in force in Delaware after the setting up of its own colonial government; but beyond this Delaware did not much concern itself with inquiring into men's religious opinions, and I find no instance of molestation for conscience' sake.

VIII

COLONIAL BISHOPS

ONE of the most interesting of questions touching the colonial Church and State was that created by the demand for an "American Episcopate." Considered simply as a matter belonging to the constitution and order of the Episcopal Church in the colonies, it would find no proper place in this treatise. That alone is to-day the significance of the episcopate in this country, with which the civil government and other Churches have no legitimate concern. The case was far different in the colonial period, when it was impossible to conceive of the creation of an episcopate without governmental action, or of its existence without more or less dependence on the civil power. Against such aspect were arrayed all the instincts for independence, all the jealousies of other Churches, and all the fears of those colonies in which existed a religious establishment other than the Church of England. The cry for bishops began early in the period, grew more and more urgent as the years went by, caused the most furious and bitter debate in colonial history, and undoubtedly had large influence, especially in the middle colonies, in deciding the popular attitude on the question of political independence.

Need of Bishops.
The demand for colonial bishops grew naturally out of the necessity of the case. Episcopacy without a bishop was an anomaly. It existed at a decided disadvantage, shorn of its proper and needed facilities for the right prosecution of its work. The jurisdiction of a bishop in England was too remote for the healthful conduct of ecclesiastical affairs. Confirmation was impossible, ordination only obtainable at

the risk and expense of an ocean voyage, and discipline destitute of any force. The complaints of the situation on these scores were abundantly justified, and the history of the Church of England in the colonies is full of proof, that this lack of episcopal authority, the essential principle of its polity, resulted in most serious damage.

There was, of course, something of a parallel in the situation of the civil government, over which the supreme jurisdiction vested in the king, to whom appeals came from the colonies, and whose order was competent to set aside colonial legislation and to correct abuses. But the resemblance was only superficial, for the king was represented by governors and other colonial officials, while all the machinery of local government and authority was ample to direct in all ordinary affairs of state. In the colonial Episcopal Church there was nothing to parallel that local government. It was destitute of all spiritual authority. Some of the governors were empowered to induct ministers and to remove for scandalous conduct, but their action in ecclesiastical affairs was not expressive of spiritual aim and power, and was too frequently dictated by personal or party motives.

A much closer likeness to this crippled condition of the Episcopal Church existed in the Reformed Church, by reason of its subjection to the classis of Amsterdam. This subjection continued for one hundred and fifty years, under a constantly increasing sense of its disadvantages, until it became an intolerable burden. So far as ordination and clerical discipline were concerned, the Reformed Church was situated precisely as was the Church of England in the colonies. In the first colonial generation the situation was but natural. The ministers coming to New Netherland were all of German or Dutch birth and education, and properly qualified and ordained before they crossed the sea. But as the colony grew and Churches multiplied, and as candidates of American birth desired to enter the ministry, the necessity of resort to Holland for ordination became a burden of no small weight.

Reformed Church.

Nor did the conquest of New Netherlands by the English make any difference in this matter. The youth of New York or New Jersey, who would enter the Reformed ministry, must go to Holland for sacred orders. Happily for the Church, the necessity for ministerial discipline rarely arose, as there was in the colonies no ecclesiastical authority whatever to call a delinquent Reformed minister to account.

We have already narrated in our sketch of New York the demand made by Governor Andros on two Dutch ministers to ordain a candidate. To do this they organized an irregular classis, which their superior, the classis of Amsterdam, refused to recognize, though, for the sake of peace and charity, it ratified the ordination.[1]

Yet with this close resemblance on ecclesiastical lines the
Difference between the two.
difference between the two was radical. The question in the Reformed Church was purely one of Church order, as affecting the case of discharging its spiritual function. With this neither the government nor the general public had any con-

---

[1] It is appropriate to briefly notice here, as really illustrative of our theme, the issue of affairs in the Reformed Dutch Church. (Corwin, *Manual*, 1869, pp. 6-9; Demarest, *History of Reformed Church*, pp. 86-95.) The first ordination on American soil with approval of the classis of Amsterdam took place in 1736, when the classis authorized two clergymen to ordain John Schuyler. In the following year a plan for a *coetus*, or association, to remain subordinate to the classis, was drawn up by some of the ministers and sent to Holland, but waited there for nine years before the approval of the classis was obtained. There was sharp difference in the colonial Church on the question. A party was formed for separation from the mother Church, which got possession of the *coetus* and ventured to ordain on its own authority. The more conservative elements opposed such action, and a bitter struggle arose which lasted from 1753 to 1771. Through the efforts of John H. Livingston the ecclesiastical authorities in Holland were induced to consent to separation and to an independent organization in the colonies; and the Reformed Protestant Dutch Church in America was in 1772 organized with a synod and five classes. This was only twelve years before the consecration of the first bishop of the Episcopal Church in this country. This little excursus may serve to show that the Episcopal Church was not the only Church in America which suffered because of organic relation to a mother Church across the sea, and to that extent robs the pleas of the English clergymen of their claim of exceptional hardship.

cern. So far as society at large, or other Churches, or legislatures cared, the Reformed Church might have organized a dozen classes independent of Holland, without a single word of protest from outside. For this reason the matter finds place only in the history of the Church itself, and of it the general history of the country knows nothing whatever.

It was far otherwise with the Episcopal Church. This was not the Episcopal Church of the colonies, but an integral portion of the Church of England; a Church created by act of parliament and subject both for faith and discipline to parliament and the crown; its higher dignitaries appointed by the crown and occupying seats in the house of lords; supported by public endowments and taxes; and possessing a very considerable share in the control of political matters. What such a Church did, what was done for or in such a Church, became thus a matter of public concern, and was not confined for legitimate interest to the members of the Church itself. Every Englishman, be he Churchman or Dissenter, was rightly and profoundly interested in many matters affecting such a Church, for they touched not only upon his religious concerns, but also upon his rights as a citizen. *Civil status of Church of England.*

Thus it was in England. And the same necessity for public concern inevitably obtained in the colonies, where the desire and design of the English government of planting the Church of England as an establishment of state had received abundant illustrations. Without reference to the harshness of the English Church to dissenters in England, the colonists had many reasons for public comment and for dread of its encroachments presented by its course in America. They had but to call to mind the Virginia Church, banishing Puritans and persecuting Baptists; the Carolina Churchmen, driving non-conformists from the legislature; the Maryland Church, outlawing that Roman Catholicism, which had given to it a kindly welcome; and the New York Anglican clergy exulting in Cornbury's spoliation of Jamaica Presbyterians, and persisting in the fraudulent claim that the Act of 1693 established the Church of England in their province. With such facts in mind, and every one of them occurring in colonies where the English Churchmen were less than one-fourth of the population, it would have been the sheerest folly for the people at large not to be interested, and not to express their mind about any project of that Church in all matters of its constitution and of its relation to government and the people. Much of the disputation on the part of the English Churchmen expresses surprise that people outside of their Church should consider their application for bishops as a thing with which they had any right to intermeddle. This is the most amusing thing in the entire controversy; for, while pleading — and rightly — that a bishop was essential to the polity and prosperity of their Church, they never fail to give evidence that they still retain in mind the purpose and perquisites of a state-establishment. It was this background of their plea, which made the application a matter for public interest and discussion.

The course of this discussion covered more than one hundred years, though it was not until the last decade that it aroused the interest and opposition of the people at large. Previous to that time the matter was confined to complaints from the better class of the English clergy in the colonies, appeals to the government and to bishops in England, with an occasional expression of favor or disfavor toward the appeal on the part of a colonial governor. We will find interest in noting a few illustrations.

Early demands.

The beginning of the demand seems to have been in the pamphlet " *Virginia's Cure*," [1] presented to the bishop of London in 1661. It pathetically set forth the " unhappy state of the Church in Virginia " due to the greatly scattered state of the population, the destitution of ministers, and the bad character of some of the few clergymen in the colony; and suggested that a bishop was greatly needed, both for the exercise of discipline and for the encouragement and furtherance of

[1] Force, *Historical Tracts*, III.

the Church and its work. In the same year Philip Mallory, a clergyman in Virginia, was sent to England for assistance in "building up the Church in the colony," an important feature in whose plan was the sending of "a bishop, so soon as there should be a city for a see."[1] These representations seem to have made such an impression on the episcopal and governmental mind of England, that the Rev. Alexander Murray was nominated for the bishopric of Virginia, but the matter was not pursued. Murray was not appointed, nor was any bishop sent.[2] Anderson justly says (p. 559), "The Bishops were her (the Church's) natural and true protectors: but they were not permitted in any one colony to watch over her; and hence all her distresses."[3]

In view of the necessity of some Episcopal supervision, the jurisdiction over the colonial Church was lodged, first in the archbishop of Canterbury, and afterward by William III. in the bishop of London, with whom it remained to the end of the colonial period, and whose certificate was made needful for all clergy of the Church of England in those colonies where that Church was, or was supposed to be, established.

Every occupant of the see of London found the duties of his American diocese most troublesome and perplexing. "The care of it," wrote the bishop in correspondence with Dr. Doddridge in 1751, "is supposed to be in the Bishop of London. Sure I am that the care is improperly lodged.

---

[1] Campbell, *History of Virginia*, p. 251.

[2] Anderson, *Colonial Church*, II, 569.

[3] There is an amusing comment on this early effort for a bishop in the records of New Amsterdam. (*Colonial History of New York*, II, 235.) The rumor of it found its way to Holland and suggested to the West India company, that therein might be found an influence toward composing the differences between the Dutch and the colonies east of them. In 1664 the chamber at Amsterdam wrote to Governor Stuyvesant, "We hear from England that the king of England means to establish bishops in America," and expressed the hope that opposition to bishops on the part of the Puritans in New England "will make them friends to the Dutch"! So early did the idea take form that an episcopate created by English law was hostile to American institutions.

For a Bishop to live at one end of the world, and his Church at the other, must make the office very uncomfortable to the Bishop, and in great measure useless to the people." [1]

To meet some of the difficulties of the situation the bishop fell upon the scheme for the appointment of a special kind of agent, to be called a " Commissary." James Blair was constituted commissary for Virginia in 1694; and, a few years after, Thomas Bray was appointed for Maryland. Vesey was also appointed to such office in New York, but the condition of affairs made the appointment of small importance. Blair and Bray were men of devoted piety and earnestness, and the former was the possessor of great force of character and executive ability. The Episcopal Church in Maryland and Virginia owed most of the good that was in them to the wise and watchful care of these two men. Especially is the debt of Virginia to Blair still great for the superb courage and resolution through which, against many obstacles, he secured the foundation of William and Mary College.

Commissary.

But the powers of the commissary were limited. He had no authority beyond that of moral suasion. As the agent of the bishop, inspecting and reporting, he might persuade with greater force than an ordinary minister. But he had no word of command to abate nuisances, to rebuke offenders, or to even institute a process of discipline. He could neither confirm nor ordain, neither induct nor remove ministers. He was limited to inspection, advice, and report — the merest shadow of a bishop. What the church needed was a bishop, and not a commissary.

So thought the Rev. Nicholas Morean, when writing in 1697 to the bishop of Lichford.[2] He commented adversely on the appointment of Blair, because he was a Scotchman, but at the same time admired the character of the man, for he continued: " An eminent Bishop of the same character being sent over here with him, will make Hell tremble and settle the Church of England in these parts forever. . . .

[1] Perry, *Historical Collections — Virginia*, p. 373.   [2] *Ibid.*, p. 31.

If I see a Bishop come over here, I will say, as St. Bernard said in his epistle to Eugenius Tertius, *hic digitus Dei est.*" Some years later, an anonymous letter-writer, discussing the same need, declared: " My Lord Bishop of London's authority, residing there in his Commissary, is notoriously despised and undervalued: his attempts to exercise discipline, even in the worst cases, are hindered by government (colonial), the cases being taken out of his hand and ordered to be prosecuted in civil courts, where they were so slightly handled that they escaped uncondemned." [1]

With like sense of the situation the Rev. Evan Evans wrote from Pennsylvania in 1707, that there was no help for the Church, unless a bishop should be sent, with authority of control over the quarrels and improper conduct of the clergy.[2] Colonel Quary, the agent of the board of trade, and Colonel Heathcote wrote in the same strain of " the great want and need." [3] Another letter from Heathcote to the Propagation Society, in 1705, dwells on the same subject, declares that the English clergy in the northern colonies are good men, and has an amusing fling at the Puritans. Speaking of Massachusetts, he wrote: " They have an abundance of odd laws there to prevent any dissenting from their Church and endeavor to keep the people in as much blindness and unacquaintedness with any other religion as possible: But in a more particular manner *the* Church, looking upon her as the most dangerous enemy they have to grapple withal. I really believe that more than one half of the people in that Government think our Church to be little better than the Papist. And they fail not to improve every little thing against us. But I bless God for it, the Society have robbed them of their best argument, which was the ill lives of our clergy that came unto these parts. And the truth is, I have not seen many good men but of the Society's sending." [4]

---

[1] Perry, *Historical Collections — Virginia*, p. 35.

[2] Perry, *Collections — Pennsylvania*, p. 37.

[3] *Ibid.*, pp. 42–44. [4] *Documentary History of New York*, III, 77.

Clerical
morals.

In this letter the colonel touches upon the great cause of
the almost agonizing cry for a bishop — the misconduct of the
clergy.   The fact of such misconduct has already been noticed
as obtaining, sometimes to a scandalous degree, especially in
Virginia and Maryland, and to a much smaller extent in the
Carolinas.   In the middle colonies and New England the English clergy were not as a class liable to any such stigma.   The
difference may be accounted for by the different conditions in
the contrasted colonies.   In the southern colonies the Church
of England was established by law; in Maryland in 1693,
and in the others from their beginning, and was subject in
many ways to the direct control of the colonial government.
The right of induction vested in the governor, who was very
rarely a person possessed of regard for the spiritual interests
of the Church or people.   Livings were given out of favor.
Adventurers, who had lost place and character in England,
came over to the colonies, where half the parishes were without parsons, and by a little fawning could obtain from governor
and vestry a comfortable location.   After that, no degree of
scandalous behavior could give to the governor a power of
removal.   The ill-living parson remained and held his own
against all remonstrances, unless his misconduct brought him
under censure by the civil law.

It was impossible for such a condition to obtain in the
northern colonies, where, before the introduction of the
Church of England, the sober and elevating influences of
other Churches had long obtained, and where the power of
the governor in ecclesiastical affairs was practically very
small.   In these colonies, with almost no exceptions, the
clergy of the English Church were men of high character and
of spiritual affection for their religious mother, men equal to
sacrifice in order to build up their Church in the midst of
unfriendly surroundings.   It was almost impossible for a
reprobate to obtain a parish, or, having obtained one, it was
impossible that he should long possess it.

I find but one governor giving evidence of anything like

interest in the spiritual and vital interests of the Church. This was Governor Hart of Maryland, "a man of earnest and devout spirit." On his arrival in 1714 he "lost no time in convening the clergy at Annapolis that he might inform himself" about the state of the Church. Presently he reported to the bishop of London that there were many faithful ministers, and "some whose education and morals were a scandal to their profession." "Unless I had a power to remove such as are scandalously notorious, I cannot do effectual service. I am sorry that there are many such here, and I believe nothing will reclaim some of them, until they feel the severities of ecclesiastical censures." The governor joined with Bray and the better men among the clergy in urging the appointment of a bishop.[1]

Governor Hart.

The pressure from the colonies succeeded in producing, about 1707, another slight spasm of interest in England. We find the bishop of London, willing enough to be relieved of his over-sea charge, observing that there "should be a suffragan Bishop in America. An *absolute* Bishop might alarm" the people. But a suffragan, for whose appointment the office of commissary had in a sense prepared them, would excite no fears. It was quite "necessary to go slow" in so important a matter.[2]

There were hopes excited on both sides of the sea. In England the government was urged to send the famous Jonathan Swift, and the dean wrote to Governor Hunter in 1709: "All my hopes now terminate in being made Bishop of Virginia."[3] While one can but sympathize with the colonial Church in its deprivation of episcopal functions, it will not be deplored that the dean's hopes were disappointed. In the colonies the spirits of the clergy were elated. Those of Pennsylvania wrote to the society of their delight in "the

Dean Swift.

[1] Anderson, *Colonial Church*, III, 285; Perry, *Collections — Maryland*, p. 81.

[2] *Colonial History of New York*, V, 29.

[3] Campbell, *History of Virginia*, p. 377.

satisfactory prospect we have of the Honorable Society's successful endeavors for settling Bishops and Bishopricks in these parts." [1]

But all these hopes were vain; no bishop was appointed, and the stream of complaints began again, continuing with more and more of volume, and with ever deepening sense of the need until the end of the colonial period. Perry's *Collections* abound in the most strident cries from the clergy in all the colonies. Dr. Cutler writes (1723) from Massachusetts (pp. 143, 433): "There is no doubt that the interests of religion and the Church of England would flourish with us by the immediate presence and inspection of a Bishop . . . (this) is the universal desire of the Church . . . (and of) many that want hereby to be enlivened and emboldened in their entrance into her communion ;" and again in 1749: "even many sober Dissenters (!) do think a resolute Bishop would be a Blessing, and not a few seem to rejoice at the news encouraging our hopes of it, though others and a still bigger number are ready according to their power to defeat it." Mr. Inglis reports from Delaware (p. 101) the opinion of a voluntary conference of the clergy that they "must have a Bishop. Otherwise the Church will languish and die." Addison of Maryland (p. 334) writes to the bishop of London of the "expediency of establishing episcopacy, without which the Church of England must lose ground." And Craig, writing from Pennsylvania (p. 187), laments the difficulty and expense of going to England for ordination and the consequent scarcity of ministers, and, with a charming subconsciousness that only the Church of England could dispense the pure gospel, concludes that there is "but one way left of removing such a famine of the word, and that is by sending a Bishop to America."

One thing which the English clergy in New England Church rates. promised themselves, as a consequent upon the establishment of bishops, was relief from the legal Church rates. Them-

---

[1] Perry, *Collections — Pennsylvania*, p. 72.

selves non-conformists, they thought it very hard that they should be compelled to bear in New England a burden which all non-conformists in the old country had to submit to. Dr. Cutler was specially outraged by the situation, and in 1727 he joined with six others in a petition to the king against Massachusetts tithes. In a letter to John Delapp he waxed indignant, declaring that "an honest Christian is double taxed, like as a Papist or Recusant."[1] The subject is discussed in the already noted correspondence between the bishop of London and Dr. Doddridge,[2] wherein the latter broadly intimates that the Episcopalian in New England was no worse off and had no more reason to complain than the Presbyterian in England!

The bishop of London and the archbishop of Canterbury were about the only friends that the colonial Church had in England.[3] The latter, Secker, preached the anniversary sermon of the Society for the Propagation of the Gospel in 1740,[4] and pleaded strongly for an American episcopate. He seems to have had the same low estimate of the spiritual condition of the colonies as that expressed by Craig, painting the condition in dark colors. According to his grace there had been "no baptism for twenty years," and no administration of the Lord's Supper for sixty years. "Such was the state in more of the colonies than one, and where it was a little better it was however lamentably bad . . . There are scarce any footsteps of Christianity beyond the very name" (!) In the same discourse he commented on the establishments in New England, and the hardship of tithes exacted from Episcopalians. The sermon was published in America, as well as in England, and drew from Andrew Elliott a caustic review, in which was demonstrated the excessive care of the New

English sentiment.

---

[1] Perry, *Collections — Massachusetts*, pp. 191–264.

[2] Perry, *Collections — Virginia*, pp. 373–375.

[3] Palfrey, *History of New England*, IV, 183.

[4] *Colonial History of New York*, VI, 906; *Massachusetts Historical Society*, II, 2; 190–202.

England colonies to provide religious opportunities to every community, and that the Episcopalians had suffered no hardships whatever since the enactment of the " Five-Mile Act." The discussion had large influence in deepening the feeling of opposition to the establishment of a bishop.

As the numbers of people increased, and the English clergy felt the ever growing burdens of the situation, the representations of their need became ever more urgent, now with a touch of pathos, and again with a stroke of bitterness. The **Johnson.** correspondence of the saintly and venerable Johnson of Stratford has many discussions of the subject. [1]He wrote to Archbishop Secker in 1753, " Give me leave to inform you, That

'As the Church doth hither westward fly,
So Sin doth dog and trace her instantly,'

. . . which makes it extremely melancholy that we cannot be favored with a good Bishop to assist us and go before us in stemming the torrent." At other times Dr. Johnson wrote: [2] " The Freethinkers & Dissenters, who play into one another's hands against the Chh. will never drop their virulence and activity, by all manner of Artifices, till they go near to raze the very Constitution to the foundation, both in Chh. and State." " The Church asks no more than to be upon a par here with her neighbors, and having leave to enjoy the benefit of her own institutions as well as they." " When they enjoy their Presbytery in the full vigor of its discipline, is it not a cruel thing that they should be so bitterly against the Church's enjoying her own form of Government and discipline? She cannot provide for her own children, without their consent to it." In 1766, Dr. Johnson, commenting on two young candidates, who were lost at sea while on a voyage to England for ordination, wrote: " These make up ten valuable lives that have now been lost for want of ordaining

[1] *Colonial History of New York*, VI, 777.

[2] *Ibid.*, VI, 912 ; VII, 373 ; Beardsley, *Episcopal Church of Connecticut*, I, 254.

powers here, out of fifty-four that have gone for ordination . . . I consider the Church here, for want of bishops, in no other light than as being in a state of persecution on that account." Johnson's own son was one of the ten lost. When the news of the bereavement reached him he wrote: [1] "This is now the seventh precious life (most of them the flower of this country) that has been sacrificed to the atheistical politics of this miserable, abandoned age. . . . I confess I should scarce have thought my dear son's life ill bestowed, if it could have been the means of awakening this stupid age to a sense of the necessity of sending bishops." Nothing could go farther than this to illustrate the sense of extreme need entertained by the clergy of the Church of England in the colonies.

After 1760 the discussion and controversy took on a very acute phase. Dr. Mayhew of Boston, in 1763, published a Mayhew. pamphlet against the Society for the Propagation of the Gospel, finding in its charter and conduct what he deemed "a formal design to carry on a spiritual siege of our Churches, with the hope that they will one day submit to a spiritual sovereign;"[2] and expressed the alarm throughout New England, "that all the evils which adhered to the Church in the old world would be transplanted to this" by the appointment of bishops. Rev. Solomon Palmer of Connecticut commented: "The invidious Dr. Mayhew, of base principles and, it is to be feared, a dishonest heart, has raised a dust to blind men's eyes and stir up a popular clamor."[3]

The paper of Dr. Mayhew made a great sensation, and Archbishop Secker thought it of sufficient importance to be honored with a reply from his own pen. Writing to Mr. Duché in 1763 he tells of a new movement for sending bishops, of which he had previously written to Johnson:[4]

---

[1] Beardsley, *Episcopal Church in Connecticut*, I, 184.

[2] *Colonial History of New York*, VI, 906 ; Beardsley, *Episcopal Church in Connecticut*, I, 230.

[3] Beardsley, I, 228.   [4] *Colonial History of New York*, VII, 348.

"This I have long had at heart . . . nor shall I ever abandon the scheme as long as I live." To Duché he said that the scheme had been explained to Lord Egremont, who promised to further it, and that Halifax was in favor of it, but the issue was doubtful; "the more for Dr. Mayhew's late pamphlet. It is written with great virulence, but must be answered with great mildness, else no good will be done."[1] The mild answer of the archbishop appeared in 1764, and sought to allay fears that the appointment of bishops involved anything beyond the order of the Church of England. They were to have no concern in the least with any not of the Church of England; (they were) only to ordain ministers for such as do profess that Church, confirm children, and take the oversight of the Episcopal clergy. It is not desired in the least that they should hold courts to try material or testamentary causes, or be vested with any magisterial authority, or infringe or diminish any privileges or liberties."[2]

But this calm exposition of Episcopal purposes did not propitiate opponents. The Rev. W. Gillchrist wrote from Salem in 1765:[3] "The Gentlemen in this Province are all in a manner professed advocates for universal toleration and liberty of conscience, and yet in direct contravention of this principle the Dissenters avowedly oppose with all their interest a Bishop's being sent over to America. . . . They discover the most partial propensity to their own party, for they stiffly maintain that Spiritual Courts, with such jurisdiction as they have in England, would necessarily follow them, and that their maintenance would be raised by a tax upon America." "Never," wrote Winslow, of Connecticut, "did a malignant spirit of opposition to the Church rage with greater vehemence than of late."[4]

The climax of the dispute came with the controversy

[1] Perry, *Collections — Pennsylvania*, p. 389.
[2] Beardsley, I, 233.
[3] Perry, *Collections — Massachusetts*, p. 519.
[4] Beardsley, I, 214.

between Dr. Chandler of New Jersey and Dr. Chauncey of Boston. The former published in 1767, "*An Appeal to the Public*," in which he entered at great length into the situation and necessities of the Church. Its need of a properly constituted American episcopate is its great theme, cogently presented from the character of the Church polity, the need of watchful discipline, and the exercise of all episcopal functions, and "the unparalleled hardship" of resorting to England for ordination. The appeal was answered by Dr. Chauncey, and in reply to this Dr. Chandler put forth "*The Appeal Defended.*" To this also Dr. Chauncey replied in a pamphlet, which drew from Chandler a third treatise entitled, "*The Appeal Further Defended.*" With this the controversy ended, so far as these writers were concerned. Chandler's Appeal.

But it was not so with the public at large. The appeal was finally attacked in the newspapers, especially in the *New York Gazette* and the *Philadelphia Sentinel*, while almost the entire city of Boston was excited.[1] The difference between the parties was such that it was impossible for them to come to any composition. The very question of the episcopate was a totally different question in the mind of one party from what it was in the mind of the other. To the English clergy it was a question of Church order and discipline, and a perfectly just demand that their Church in America should be properly equipped for its own life and work. To their opponents it was entirely a political question, and matters of Church order and religion entered little into their thought concerning it.

The whole question of a State-Church was involved in it. They knew that a bishop in England was an officer of the state; that the parliament ordained his place and power and the crown had the gift of his preferment, while his maintenance was by public endowment. They remembered what bishops had been in England, and how their fathers had suffered many things at episcopal hands. They knew also that in the Reasons of opposition.

[1] Beardsley, I, 259.

very time of this dispute the non-conformists of England were subjected to many annoyances and disabilities ; and, whether rightly or wrongly, they judged that the institution of an episcopate in America, by an act of parliament and on the nomination of the king, would in the near future be followed by attempts at spiritual tyranny. "It excited," said John Adams,[1] "a general and just apprehension that Bishops, and Dioceses, and Churches, and Priests, and Tythes were to be imposed upon us by Parliament. It was known that neither King, nor Ministry, nor Archbishop could appoint Bishops in America without an act of Parliament; and if Parliament could tax us, they could install the Church of England, with all its Creeds, Articles, Tests, Ceremonies, and Tithes, and prohibit all other Churches as Conventicles and Schism-shops." Thus the question took place among those which brought on the war of the Revolution.

Nothing which the Episcopal party could say, or rather did say, was able to disabuse the public mind of the impression that there was an ulterior design dangerous to liberty. "We can not believe," wrote one disputant,[2] "that he would be long content to be but half a Bishop, to have a nominal Office, without the Powers and Emoluments. You think it hard to be deprived of the Privileges of other Societies, but you may blame the Arbitrary Spirit of your Bishops, who have always infringed on the Estates and Consciences of the People." The fear that bishops would necessarily assume similar relations to the government to those sustained by the English prelates was universal in the non-episcopal community, and it is specially notable that the Episcopal party in all their argument and disclaimers of political designs, evidently thought it possible that such might be the issue. Thus Dr. Chandler in his pathetic appeal, while discussing the non-episcopal objections and denying a desire to establish the Church of England as a State-Church, still finds himself unable to give

Ulterior design.

---

[1] *Colonial History of New York*, VI, 906.
[2] *Letters by an Anti-Episcopalian.*

the guarantee, which alone could have reconciled the people at large to the proposed episcopate.[1]

On the matter of tithes he wrote, that the English laws could "never have any effect here, *until an Act of Parliament shall be made to extend them to us.*" In regard to the public maintenance of the bishops, he disclaimed any intention that such should be established, but in view of the possibility that parliament might so ordain, he continued : "*But should a general tax be laid* . . . supposing we had three Bishops, such a Tax would not amount to more than Four Pence in One Hundred Pounds. And this would be no mighty Hardship upon the Country. He that could think much of giving the Six Thousandth Part of his Income to any Use, which the Legislature of his Country shall assign, deserves not to be considered in the Light of a good Subject or Member of Society. . . . But no such tax is intended, nor I trust will be wanted." Again, on the subject of civil functions he said: " There is not the least Prospect *at present* that Bishops in this Country will acquire any Influence or Power . . . But *should the Government see fit hereafter* to invest them with some degree of civil Power worthy of their Acceptance, *which it is impossible to say they will not* . . . yet as no new powers will be created in Favour of Bishops, it is inconceivable that any would thereby be injured."

Here was the weak point in the appeal and the entire Episcopal argument, and one so fatal that no pleas of the Church's need could offset this suggestive possibility. Had the Episcopal party been able to furnish a guarantee that the Episcopate would be confined strictly to ecclesiastical and spiritual functions in its own Church alone, without possibility that a public maintenance would be assessed, they might probably have disarmed the opposition. But this was not possible. They knew it to be unlikely that the English Parliament would legislate to deprive any bishops, whether at home or in the colonies, of those privileges which for

The weak point.

[1] Chandler, *Appeal*, pp. 105, 107, 110.

centuries had been perquisites of their office. If the Parliament of the day should be so complaisant as to so constitute American bishops, there was no security that a succeeding Parliament might not reverse the action.

Just such an episcopate, shorn of all civil power, was the request of the English clergy of New York and New Jersey, in their address to the government in 1772.[1] They asked for "Bishops with purely Ecclesiastical Powers, without any temporal Authority, and without any Jurisdiction over *Dissenters* of any Denomination. We wish not to interfere with the Rights and Privileges of others, or to abridge the ample *Toleration they already enjoy*. With this Disposition we conceive it to be more than reasonable that we should be indulged with the same religious Privileges which are *granted* to them, *especially considering our Relation to the national establishment*."

This was as far as the Episcopal party could go, in regard to the limitations of the desired episcopate; nor, so far as that was concerned, could their opponents justly ask more. But with that concession the terms by which it was attended were offensive. It was never fitting, north of Maryland, to
" Dissenters." speak of non-Episcopalians as dissenters. In New England the Episcopalians were themselves dissenters. In New York and New Jersey the term involved a claim to an establishment with which the Church of England had legally no connection whatever. Nor were the Churches of the northern colonies willing to admit that they were allowed a toleration. They were to the manor born, and it was the Episcopal Church that was tolerated. The plea also of the "Relation to the National establishment" was such as to prejudice the non-Episcopal mind, which was not ready to agree to anything which based itself on the fact or power of that establishment.

William Smith, the historian of New York, writing about 1770, said: "The Episcopalians are in the proportion of one

[1] *New Jersey Archives*, X, 309.

to fifteen (in New York). . . . The body of the people are for an equal, universal toleration of protestants, and utterly averse to any kind of ecclesiastical establishment. The dissenters, though fearless of each other, are all jealous of the episcopal party, being apprehensive that the countenance they may have from home will foment a lust of dominion and enable them, in process of time, to subjugate and oppress their fellow subjects." [1]

It is notable that this great debate found its place especially in the northern colonies. The southern colonies in which the Church of England was established did not largely concern themselves about it. There had been sent from Maryland and Virginia sundry personal letters expressing a desire for bishops. In Maryland, as noted in the sketch of that colony, a clerical convention, on invitation of the Bishop of London, had nominated for suffragan a Mr. Colebatch, whom the colonial government would not permit to go to England for ordination.[2] But toward the end of the colonial period the southern Church ceased to be greatly agitated on the matter. In 1767 [3] Mr. Neill wrote of Governor Sharpe of Maryland that he "answered all the ends of a bishop, except in conferring orders and confirmation. I wish he had this part of Episcopal authority confirmed upon him. He would make as good a bishop as we could wish for." (!)

In Virginia there was but a very small party in the established Church in favor of having a bishop. How large a part of this indifference was due to the notorious character of many of the clergy there are no means of telling, but it is reasonable to think that men of such character would not be anxious to establish courts for their own discipline. It is clear, however, that this clerical delinquency and the reaction from the "Parson's Cause" had pronounced a majority of the laity in disaffection toward the Church and in opposition

Southern colonies.

---

[1] *History of New York*, I, 337.

[2] Anderson, *Colonial Church*, III, 295.

[3] Perry, *Collections — Pennsylvania*, p. 420.

to any effort for her aggrandizement.   This was strongly expressed in 1771.   In that year the party in favor of having a bishop called a convention to consider the question.   Out of all the clergymen in Virginia only twelve came to the gathering, which, notwithstanding the absurdity of such a body venturing to represent the clergy of the colony, adopted an address to the home government asking for a bishop.   But even this action was not unanimous.   Out of the twelve present four ministers protested, basing their objection on the very proper ground that so small a body could not speak for the Church of Virginia.   The next house of burgesses by formal vote thanked these four for resisting "the pernicious project."   It is evident that in the mind of the legislature it was rather the demand for a bishop, than the smallness of the convention, that excited opposition.[1]

It is not at all difficult to sympathize with both parties to the dispute.   "American Episcopacy without an American bishop was a solecism." (Bancroft.)   That the Church should be possessed of its full polity was a demand for its life.   At the same time, it was impossible for the great mass of the people to regard with equanimity the appointment of an episcopate in the country, unless its relation to the civil government should be radically changed from the English model, and its relation to the Church in England should be completely severed.

The dispute also was inevitably involved in the now pressing political struggle.   Both in Church and State the question was one: whether Parliament should tax the colonies. Dr. Chandler altogether missed the point, when expatiating on the smallness of the tax for Episcopal support.   The tax on tea was insignificant.   The colonial mind was not occupied by the amount of the tax, but the principle of taxation. It refused to pay taxes to the imperial treasury, and to permit the imperial legislature to impose a church order.   Thus, "The claim of a right to establish a Bishop and Episcopal

---

[1] Hawks, *Ecclesiastical Contributions*, p. 126.

courts, without the consent of the colony," was one of the "Grievances" enumerated by a town-meeting of Boston, November, 1772.[1]

That the opposition was entirely political and did not represent sectarianism is capable of abundant proof. The demand came chiefly from the English clergy in the northern colonies, while the great body of their own laity were not in sympathy with them. The Churchmen of Virginia and Maryland were at one with the Congregationalists of New England. No one, into whom had entered anything of the spirit of American freedom, was willing to concede that the royal prerogative extended to the colonial churches. Some things had happened in recent years which men had not forgotten. There still rankled in Massachusetts the king's prohibition of the proposed synod of Congregational ministers in 1725, wherein the lords justices of England claimed for the crown supremacy in all ecclesiastical affairs, which, "being a branch of his prerogative, does take place in the plantations: and synods can not be held, nor is it lawful for the clergy to assemble as in synods, without authority from his Majesty."[2] Nor did the people of New York forget the recent refusal of the king to allow incorporation to the Presbyterian Church, which was bidden to expect no other privileges than those conferred by the toleration act of 1689.

This refusal was singularly impolitic for the interests of the English Church in the colonies. It occurred in 1767, in the height of the Episcopal debate, and could reasonably have no other effect than to intensify opposition to an American episcopate. "That decision," wrote Dr. Chauncey, "was an alarm to all the churches on the continent, giving them solemn notice what they might expect, should Episcopalians ever come to have supremacy in their influence."[3] Under such circumstances, it was impossible to persuade non-Epis-

---

[1] Bancroft, *United States*, VI, 433.

[2] Hodge, *History of Presbyterian Church*, p. 471.

[3] Hodge, *Presbyterian Church*, p. 469.

copalians that the question about bishops was one which need not concern them, or the legitimate interest in which should be confined to the Church of England. Nor is it a strange thing that in the synods of the Presbyterians in New York and Pennsylvania, and of the Congregational churches of Connecticut in 1768 and 1775, "the great and almost the only subject, which occupied their attention, was opposition to the establishment of an American episcopate."[1]   To the same dread of an undesirable elevation and increase of Episcopal power was due the long struggle over the foundation of King's College, which agitated the people of New York.[2] A minor illustration of the encroaching spirit for which the Church of England was feared, is recorded by Smith (I, 349), to the effect that the Episcopal clergy, "for enlarging the sphere of their secular business, attempted by a petition to the late Governor Clinton to engross the privilege of solemnizing all marriages. A great clamor ensued, and the attempt was abortive." Such an attempt seems to the modern mind almost too absurd for belief, but it needs to be remembered, in justice to the clergy, that the effort was in strict accordance with English law. At that time, and for many years after, no marriage could be made in England without the official presence of a clergyman of the national Church. For this reason, the Episcopal ministers of New York, supposing the Church of England to be established in the province, might easily conclude that they should possess all the perquisites of their English brethren.

Still another and powerful factor, in the dispute about bishops, was the attitude of the Episcopal clergy on the questions at issue between the colonies and the English government. *The Memoir of Rev. John Stuart, D.D.*, records, "No class was so uncompromising in its loyalty (to the king) as the clergy of the Church of England in this state (New York); and they in consequence did not fail to expe-

Toryism.

---

[1] Hodge, *History of Presbyterian Church*, p. 449.
[2] Smith, *History of New York*, II, 232–289.

rience the bitter effects of their unwise resolution." [1] From the beginning of the troubles, the English clergy as a class were stout preachers of the doctrine of passive obedience, and condemned all the colonial attempts against parliamentary oppression. In view of the growing spirit of independence, the clergy of New York went so far, in 1760, as to urge in correspondence with Archbishop Secker the abrogation of all provincial charters.[2]

In the midst of the excitement about the stamp act of 1765, seven missionaries of the society in New England joined in a report that the people of the Church of England, and particularly of their own charges, were of "a contrary temper and conduct, esteeming it nothing short of rebellion to speak evil of dignitaries and to avow opposition to this last Act of Parliament." At the same time, Dr. Leaming wrote to the society: "The missionaries in this colony are very serviceable, not only in a religious but in a civil sense." In some northern towns, "most rebellious outrages have been committed, while those towns, where the Church has got footing, have soberly submitted to the civil authority." [3]

The great advocate for an American episcopate, Dr. Chandler, was very pronounced in his adhesion to the royal cause, which he made one with the interest of the Church. In his thought, both must stand or fall together. "Who can be certain," he wrote, "that the present rebellious disposition of the colonies is not intended by Providence as a punishment for that neglect?" (to make the Church a national concern and to send bishops).[4] In 1774, Dr. Chandler published A Friendly Address, asking the question, "What think ye of Congress now?" which so enraged his people at Elizabeth, that he was obliged to leave.[5]

---

[1] Documentary History of New York, IV, 508.

[2] Bancroft, United States, IV, 427.

[3] Beardsley, Episcopal Church in Connecticut, I, 240–241.

[4] Beardsley, I, 245.

[5] Documentary History of New York, III, 637, note.

Another indication of the Episcopal attitude is furnished by a letter of Charles Inglis, assistant rector of Trinity in New York City. It discusses the "State of the Anglo American Church," and among other things declares that "all the society's missionaries proved themselves faithful, loyal subjects in these trying times . . . all the other clergy of our Church have observed the same line of conduct." "An abolition of the Church of England," he continued, "is one of the principal springs of the dissenting leaders' conduct." [1]

The Episcopal clergy found an immediate test of their loyalty in the liturgical prayers for the king. In most of the colonies, the use of those prayers was forbidden by act of legislature, while many of the clergy refused to read the service with the prayers omitted. Inglis wrote that, to hold service and not to pray for the king was against conscience and duty; to pray for the king was to invite destruction; so they shut up their Churches as the only thing to be done. There were a few exceptions to this course out of New York City and Philadelphia. The ability to make a distinction between allegiance to the king and loyalty to the religious needs of their people seems to have been rare. Mr. Tyler of Norwich, Connecticut, was almost singular in defining that "Christ's kingdom is not of this world, and so may exist without the civil power," on which ground he omitted the obnoxious prayer and continued to feed his flock.[2]

With such intense pro-English feeling animating the colonial clergy of the Episcopal Church, it would have been impossible for the people at large to look with favor on the proposition for an episcopate, and the more so as most of the laity of that Church itself were opposed to the scheme. Suspicion of ulterior motives was inevitable. Fear of the Church of England, said John Adams, "contributed as much

[1] *Documentary History of New York*, III, 637-646.
[2] Beardsley, I, 320.

as any other cause to arouse the attention, not only of the inquiring mind, but of the common people, and urged them to close thinking on the constitutional authority of parliament over the colonies." [1]

Of all the circumstances attending this long dispute over colonial bishops the most remarkable is the inaction of the authorities in England. The demand for an episcopate began more than one hundred years before the Revolution, and though repeated every year and with growing urgency, it fell upon deaf ears in England. While the government was particular in many cases that the Church should be established in the colonies, it was steadily indifferent as to its necessities. Even the higher functionaries of the English Church, except the occupants of the sees of London and Canterbury, were equally careless. Says Anderson: "The amount of inert resistance presented in the office of the Secretary for the Colonies was too great to be overcome." [2] Occasionally an excess of urgency would rouse a passing interest of government, only to die out in a few days. [3]

Besides this indifference to religious needs, both the government and the Church of England were jealous of any movement toward colonial independence. The establishment of American bishops would have made the colonial Church practically free of the Church of England, with a subjection to the archiepiscopal see hardly more than nominal. In the colonies also the royal governors were not in favor of the scheme. An American episcopate would rob them of certain

English indifference.

---

[1] *Works of John Adams*, X, 185.

[2] *History of Colonial Church*, III, 571.

[3] What the government was looking for in America was a return for past investment and an unquestioning obedience. This is well illustrated by the famous story of Commissary Blair's efforts to obtain endowment for his college in Virginia. He obtained the charter and a grant of £2000, to which grant of money Attorney-General Seymour objected. To Blair's statements, that the college was designed to educate ministers, and that people in Virginia had souls to be saved as well as people in England, Seymour replied: "Souls! Damn your souls! Make tobacco."

prerogatives, sometimes valuable and always useful for power and dignity. We have noted the refusal of the governor of Maryland to allow Mr. Colebatch to go to England for ordination. So late as 1771, Lord Baltimore showed the same feeling. In that year Hugh Neill wrote of an address to the king adopted by some of the Maryland clergy, asking for a bishop, and told of Baltimore's opposition. " His Excellency received us very coldly, and let us know, by the advice no doubt of his council, that our Livings in Maryland were Donatives, and stood in no need of the aid of Episcopacy. This cast a damp upon many." [1]

This unwillingness of the English authorities in both Church and State to accord the essential need of the Episcopal Church in America expressed itself even after the independence of the colonies was conceded. At the same time all opposition to an episcopate ceased in America, so soon as that independence made clear the fact, that all political danger from the institution was eliminated. Adams, who had heartily opposed in the past, now, as minister of the United States in London, as heartily urged that bishops should be sent, though the urgency, of course, was only in his personal capacity. The difficulty in England arose from a sulky resentment which could not reconcile itself to the separation from the colonies. For three years Seabury, White, and Prevoost waited in England till the bishops of the English Church could recover magnanimity enough to ordain them. Finally Seabury's patience was exhausted, and he obtained ordination at the hands of the non-juring bishop of Aberdeen. This was something of an object lesson, and the archbishop of Canterbury, seeing that the American brethren could not be excluded from ordination, at last consented with an ill grace to consecrate White and Prevoost.[2]

On the new bishops' return to America they found no voices of opposition. All reason for it had disappeared. The question

[1] Perry, *Collections — Maryland*, p. 342.
[2] Bacon, *American Christianity*, p. 211.

of Church and State in America had been decided for all time, and the people knew that an episcopate had in it no elements to affect the civil powers or religious liberty. There was, indeed, early in 1785, a warm discussion in one of the Boston newspapers on the propriety of admitting bishops into Massachusetts, but it was an idle discussion and only served to draw upon the opponent the public ridicule.[1]

[1] McMaster, *History of People of the United States,* I, 33, note.

IX

THE PERIOD OF THE REVOLUTION

WITH the dawn of the Revolution all the colonies were substantially ready for the adoption of measures, which should make the severance of Church from State complete. Though each had gone through an experience peculiar to itself, in some instances presenting marked contrasts to the others, all were practically together in the general desire for a religious liberty entirely untrammelled by the civil law, in which the terms *conformity* and *dissent* would become forever inapplicable.

Some of the individual contrasts and peculiarities may well be recalled in brief review. To *Rhode Island* belongs the singular honor of completing the colonial era as it began. Starting with the definition of the largest liberty possible within the limits of social order, Rhode Island never receded from its fundamental principle and never admitted into statute or practice any spirit of repression. Its "lively experiment" found its way to a perfect success, fulfilling its early promise without the slightest deviation from the principle of its great founder.

In this respect the history of *Pennsylvania*, as already seen, stands in sharp contrast. We have already noted that the common understanding, that the colony of Penn was the chosen home of religious liberty, is very far from the truth. This it never was with its fundamental law limiting inhabitancy to believers in Almighty God, and confining both the franchise and office to believers in "Jesus Christ as the Saviour of the world"; and under pressure from England, excluding Romanists and disbelievers in the doctrine of the

Rhode
Island.

Penn-
sylvania.

Trinity. Thus this colony entered the revolutionary period with a restrictive legislation unsurpassed by that of any other. No act of persecution, indeed, stains the records of Pennsylvania; nor can we suppose that, beyond this deprivation of civil rights, there was ever any danger that any person could be disturbed for reasons of religion. This fact in itself makes it still more remarkable that, so far as terms of law made definitions, there was less liberty in Pennsylvania than in theocratic Massachusetts and conforming Virginia. After 1665, Massachusetts made no so sharp inquiry into personal religious belief as a condition for the franchise; while Virginia, though prohibiting non-conformist worship until compelled to tolerate, yet never bound the franchise to individual faith.

In *Massachusetts* the beautiful dream of a state which Massachusetts. should be as a City of God — an ideal so ardently loved and tenaciously held by the early Puritans — had vanished out of mind, more than one hundred years before the struggle for independence. While the form of the Church establishment remained, and the civil law made provision for its support, all bars to dissenting worship were down, and all dissenters could direct their rates to the Church of their choice.

Virginia had conceded a less degree of liberty. The principle Virginia. of establishment, less from religious reasons than from considerations of state policy, retained to the end a strong grasp on the *official* mind. Each dissenting persuasion had been forced to conquer liberty for itself. The exception in favor of the Presbyterians did not make the way open for the Baptists, who were beaten and imprisoned at the very time when the continental congress was about to assemble. The fate of the Methodists was much more auspicious because of their affiliation with the English Church. Together with these conditions, the state of the general public mind was in strong contrast. Three-fourths of the people were outside of the established Church. But that Church numbered among its adherents the majority of the aristocratic portion of the people, of whom, however, many of the leading minds disapproved the principle upon which the Church was based. They were also disgusted by the immoral character of many of the clergy. They had not forgotten the "Parsons' Cause," which arrayed the clergy against the people, and they deeply resented the attitude of the clergy on the questions at issue between the colonies and parliament.

In regard to this latter feature the clerical statistics are very significant. At the opening of the struggle there were in Virginia ninety-five parishes and ninety-one ministers of the established Church. At the end of the war twenty-three parishes had become extinct, and thirty-four were vacant; while only twenty-eight of the clergy remained in the colony.[1] At least two-thirds of the clergy adhered to the king and found themselves out of place in patriotic Virginia.

Still another element entered into the question in this colony. By a curious anomaly, a large portion of the Presbyterians, while dissenting from the established order and worship, yet approved and desired a civil law which should provide for the maintenance of religion. This desire was formally presented in the legislature and entered strongly into the general discussion.

Thus various circumstances gave peculiar interest to the final settlement in Virginia. Indeed, the chief interest in all the union centred there; there the issue was at this time more sharply drawn than elsewhere, and the answer was more clearly and positively pronounced. In the other colonies the end of establishments came as a natural consequent upon national independence, and without much discussion. To this statement, however, there were two exceptions, found in the retention of Church rates in Massachusetts and Connecticut until long after the opening of the nineteenth century.

Meanwhile, another and most powerful influence on the whole question of Church and State had been making itself

[1] Hawks, *Ecclesiastical Contributions*, I, 153 ; Anderson, *Colonial Church*, III, 274.

felt. This was the influence of Jonathan Edwards, who, Edwards.
more than any other man, settled the principle which fully
justified to the American mind the complete severance of the
state from ecclesiastical functions or concern. Of his influence there were two marked peculiarities; the first of which
was, that he introduced into the question an ele..ent entirely
new to the discussion. Until Edwards's day that discussion
had known but two parties : the state, asserting control over
religious life; and the mind, asserting liberty of thought.
Between the two the Church was in constant danger of losing
either its freedom or its purity. Edwards lifted up the dignity of the Church itself, the eternal City of God, divinely City of God.
founded and nourished by divine grace. Over it no human
authority could hold sway. Into it no man could enter save
as the grace of God opened for him the door. Thus, the
Church was greater than the state, and in an entirely different sphere. It was not of this world and could not be subject to the kingdoms of this world. It was the holy household
of the saints, where faith, love, and a spiritual mind, drawing
their reason and life from the word of God and nurtured by
the Holy Spirit, must characterize all its members. With
such a constitution human policy and laws can have nothing
to do, and a Church under the direction of the state becomes
absurd and impossible.

The other peculiarity of Edwards's influence was in the fact
that it was exerted indirectly. In this respect he occupies.
a singular position among reformers. Other men, who have
wrought great changes in human affairs, — such as Luther,
Knox, Howard, Wilberforce, — give us no reason for doubt
that the things they accomplished were those they had in
view. Edwards, far beyond all men of his time, smote the
staggering blow which made ecclesiastical establishments
impossible in America,[1] but we have no proof that he meant
to do anything of the kind. In all his printed works there is
not a single direct attempt to discuss the question of Church

[1] Allen, *Life of Edwards.*

and State, and but one treatise, on the "Qualifications of Church-Members," which makes room for the subject even as a side issue. It is one of the many evidences of Edwards's profound influence on the minds of men — more profound than that of any other man since Luther — that by the enunciation of a religious doctrine, purely for the sake of religion, he should have revolutionized the minds of his countrymen as to the propriety of a civil institution of the Church.

Edwards was neither a professed statesman nor an agitator in public affairs. He was distinctly a theologian and preacher. Born in 1703, he early gave proof of marvellous intellectual powers, delighting to exercise themselves in the two fields of nature and revelation. Of most acute analytical mind and far reasoning powers, had he given his life to science, he would have rivalled the fame of Bacon or Cuvier. As it was, turning to theology, he made a place for his name along with those of Augustine and Calvin.

Nor was he a theorist alone. Having a religious consciousness that seems fitly described by the old record of Enoch, who "walked with God," his saintliness of character exerted an influence no less powerful and lasting than that of his intellectual power. Indeed, it may be said that his greatest influence on men was by reason of this marvellous religious personality. His entire being was permeated by the thought of God and His constant presence, while in pure holiness was his supreme delight. He had a genius for spirituality, which elevated and controlled all his thought, and made his life radiant of goodness. Though theological systems change under the influx of purer and larger light, so that the theological world has laid aside some of the doctrines on which Edwards strenuously insisted, yet this colossal personality endures, a constant object of reverence, and "the man himself grows greater and greater."[1]

When Edwards came to his charge in Northampton there faced him the special work made needful by the low religious

[1] Weeden, *Social and Economic History of New England*, II, 700-706.

condition of the time. The Half-Way Covenant had wrought its inevitable degradation of the Church. A wretched compromise between political expediency and religion, it had introduced into the Church a large number of people, who, though of outward morality, were utter strangers to vital piety. Against the evils of this condition Edwards struggled with all the energy of his mind and spirit.

Unlike the majority of preachers in his time and our own, he did not make direct attack upon the obnoxious covenant, as such, nor fulminate against special and individual sins. He went deeper and, after the manner of the gospel itself, exposed the principles of righteousness; sure, when received, to bring in their train correction of moral and religious ills. There were two chords continually struck by him: the sovereignty of the infinitely holy God, who could not look upon sin without abhorrence; and the exceeding sinfulness of man, who was helpless without divine grace. Man was entirely dependent upon God, and God's grace alone could bring a soul into spiritual life and to the privileges of the Church, into which he could rightly come only through the avenue of sincere repentance and regeneration by the Spirit of God.

While Edwards remained silent on the relation of the civil law to the Church, his trumpet gave no uncertain sound as to the divine charter of the Church and the absolute necessity for its purity. " Christ and His Church," he said, "like bridegroom and bride, rejoice in each other as having a special propriety in each other. All things are Christ's, but He has a special propriety in His Church. There is nothing in Heaven or earth among all the creations, that is His in that excellent manner that the Church is His, . . . His portion and inheritance." [1] As to membership in the Church, he plainly taught that it should be based only on gracious characteristics.[2] " It is not only . . . moral sincerity, which is the Scripture qualification of admission

---

[1] Edwards, *Works*, III, 567.　　[2] *Ibid.*, I, 104–109.

into the Christian Church, but . . . regeneration and renovation of heart." "None ought to be admitted to the privileges of adult persons in the Church of Christ, but such as make a profession of real piety."

His sentiment as to the custom which had come in vogue under the Half-Way Covenant was strongly adverse, describing it as injuring the Church, a "mere form and ceremony, as subscribing religious articles seems to have done in England; and, as it is to be feared, *owning the covenant*, as it is called, has too much done in New England; it being a prevailing custom for persons to neglect this until they come to be married, and then to do it for their credit's sake and that their children may be baptized."[1] "The effect of this method of proceeding in the Churches of New England, which have fallen into it, is this—some are received, under the notion of their being *visible* saints or *professing* saints, who yet at the same time are open *professors* of heinous *wickedness;* I mean the wickedness of living in known impenitence and unbelief. . . . They do not profess to be as yet *born again*, but look on themselves as really *unconverted*, as having never unfeignedly accepted of Christ. . . . And accordingly it is known all over the town where they live, that they make no pretensions to any *sanctifying grace* already obtained; nor of consequence are they looked upon as other than unconverted persons. Now, can this be judged the comely *order* of the gospel? Or shall God be supposed the *author* of such confusion?"[2]

Once more:[3] "The Church is represented in Scripture as the *household of God*. They are in a peculiar manner intrusted with the care of His name and honor in the world, the interests of His kingdom, the care of His jewels and most precious things: and would not common sense teach an earthly prince not to admit into his household such as he had no reason to look upon as friends and loyal subjects in their hearts?"

[1] Edwards, *Works*, I, 115.   [2] *Ibid.*, I, 189.   [3] *Ibid.*, I, 231.

With such principles, the dominant factor in the question of Church and State is neither civil polity nor individual liberty, but that which is higher than both, the Church of the living God, the Ark of the everlasting covenant which no man must touch with unhallowed hands. Into this Church none can enter save those whom God's grace shall "call." Over such a divinely constituted thing it becomes forever impossible that human governors and legislators shall attempt control. It is forever the imperial City of God, where grace alone shall reign and God's word is the only law.

It does not appear that Edwards himself by any direct argument applied these consequents to existing religious establishments. Occupied with zeal for the religious elevation of his people, his intent was to so preach that souls should be converted and the Church made pure. He welcomed the "Great Awakening" as fulfilling the chief desire of his heart. But at the same time he put into the hand of his countrymen the key, which was to solve their greatest, and the age-long, problem. There was, indeed, widespread revolt against the old theory of Augustine, but not until Edwards spoke were men able to demonstrate its falsity. Augustine, Hooker, Williams, and Edwards — all spoke controlling words: Augustine, for a Church mistakenly longing for the buttress of human law; Hooker, for a comprehensiveness that reduced religion to nationality; Williams, for the inalienable rights of the human conscience; and Edwards, best of all, for God's sole prerogative in the Kingdom of Grace and in the Church, "which He had purchased with His own blood." It is only in the understanding that the principles of Edwards had profoundly affected the minds of his generation, that we can account for the ready and almost universal acceptance of the measures for disestablishment in America.

Of the events attending those measures it is first in place to note a congressional action, which illustrated the progress Congress. of liberty. This was the effort made by the colonial congress in 1774 to enlist the province of Quebec in resistance to England. The immense majority of the people of that province were Roman Catholics, but it was greatly desired that they should make common cause with the revolting colonies. To this end the congress adopted a "masterly address, drawn by Dickinson," inviting their adhesion to the colonial cause, and in which "all old religious jealousies were condemned as low-minded infirmities." [1] This was the sole national reference to the subject of religion, until the Convention of 1787 embedded in the Federal Constitution the principle of full religious liberty.

Virginia.
In *Virginia*, the whole question of establishment and liberty was forced on the immediate attention of the new state by the actual presence of that religious persecution noted in our sketch of that colony. In the counties of Orange, Spotsylvania, and Culpepper Baptist preachers were beaten and

Madison.
imprisoned. On January 27, 1774, Madison wrote to Bradford: [2] "That diabolical, hell-conceived principle of persecution rages among some. . . . There are at this time in the adjacent county not less than five or six well-meaning men in close jail, for publishing their religious sentiments, which in the main are very orthodox. . . . I have squabbled and scolded, abused and ridiculed so long about it, that I am without common patience. So I must beg you to pity me, and pray for liberty of conscience to all." This well illustrates the spirit of the man, to whom, even more than to Jefferson, Virginia was indebted for her clear definition of religious rights.

Convention.
The state convention met in 1776, and received many petitions from various parts of the state, expressing in different phrases the widespread desire for relief from all burdens on conscience and worship. [3] They asked "protection in the full exercise of their modes of worship," exemption from "pay-

[1] Bancroft, *United States*, VII, 159.
[2] Rives, *Madison*, I, 44.
[3] Hawks, *Ecclesiastical Contributions*, I, 139.

ment of all taxes for any Church whatever," the disestablishment of the Church of England, and the removal of all
restraints on the "right of private judgment." The presbytery of Hanover presented an elaborate memorial, demanding the repeal of all laws of establishment or religious preference; that all sects should be equally protected, and that
the maintenance of the Churches should be left to voluntary
contributions. "We conceive," said the memorial, "that
when our blessed Saviour declares His kingdom not of this
world, He renounces all dependence on state power. . . .
We are persuaded that, if mankind were left in quiet possession of their unalienable rights and privileges, Christianity,
as in the days of the apostles, would continue to prevail and
flourish in the greatest purity by its own native excellence
and under the all-disposing providence of God." [1] In these
petitions all varieties of religious persuasion were represented, with the exception of the Church of England and
Methodists. The latter had not as yet separated from the
Church, and joined the Episcopalians in petitioning against
all measures of disestablishment.

The convention, formally severing political relations to
England, set about the organization of a state government,
and adopted the famous BILL OF RIGHTS.[2] The bill was
drawn by George Mason, but the sixteenth section, referring
to religion, was proposed by Patrick Henry. The draft of
the section presented by Henry read : "That Religion, or the
duty that we owe our Creator, and the manner of discharging
it, can be directed only by reason and conviction, and not by
force or violence ; and, therefore (that all men should enjoy
the fullest toleration in the exercise of religion according to
the dictates of conscience, unpunished and unrestrained by the
magistrate, unless under color of religion any man disturb
the peace, the happiness, or safety of society ; and), that it is

Bill of
Rights.

[1] Schaff, "*Religious Liberty*," *American Historical Association*, 1887–1888.
[2] Hening, *Statutes*, IX, 111 ; Rives, *Madison*, I, 140 ; *American Historical Association*, 1886–1887, p. 23.

the mutual duty of all to practice Christian forbearance, love, and charity towards each other."

To that portion of the section here put in brackets Madison objected, on the ground that there was a " dangerous implication " in the word *toleration*, as well as in the clause referring to the magistrate. " Toleration belonged to a system where was an established Church, and where a certain liberty of worship was granted, not of right, but of grace; while the interposition of the magistrate might annul the grant." The argument of Madison effected the striking out of this obnoxious portion and substituting for it the sentence, " all men are equally entitled to the full and free exercise of religion, according to the dictates of conscience." He also secured the addition of a restraining clause: " No man, or class of men, ought on account of religion to be invested with peculiar emoluments or privileges, nor subjected to any penalties or disabilities, unless under color of religion the preservation of equal liberty and the existence of the State are manifestly endangered." Thus the definition of the Virginia Bill of Rights took its final shape, expressing the best conception of religious liberty that had as yet found utterance outside of Rhode Island. Rives justly says : " The amendment by Madison itself forms an era in the history of American liberty. In discarding a term hitherto consecrated in some degree as a symbol of liberty, but intrinsically fallacious, it erected a new and loftier platform for the fabric of religious freedom."

This was the beginning of disestablishment, and laid down the broad principle according to which, one after another, the various perquisites of the Church of England in Virginia were in the following years taken away by law, until the work was completed in the " Declaratory Act " of 1785. The legislature of 1776, meeting soon after the convention, proceeded at once to give partial effect to the action of the latter in a law exempting dissenters from the support of the Church established by law.[1] Another act suspended the laws which fixed

Acts of legislature.

[1] Hening, IX, 164.

the salary of the clergy, but did not disturb the Church in the possession of the glebes. This act of suspension was repeated at each successive session until 1779.[1]

These acts and many petitions for and against the establishment gave rise to long and impassioned debate. Edmund Pendleton, the speaker, was a strenuous advocate for establishment, and was ably seconded by Robert Carter Nicholas. Jefferson was their great opponent and carried the assembly with him.[2] Jefferson in his *Autobiography* describes the debates as "the severest struggles in which I have ever been engaged. . . . Although the majority of our citizens are dissenters, a majority of the legislature were Churchmen. Among them, however, were some reasonable and liberal men, who enabled us on some points to obtain feeble majorities. . . . In the bill now passed was inserted an express reservation of the question, Whether a general assessment should not be established by law on every one to the support of the pastor of his choice." This was disputed "from session to session until 1779, when the question against a general assessment was finally carried, and the establishment of the Anglican Church entirely put down."[3]

The agency of Jefferson in the movement toward disestablishment was that of a leader.   His description of the previous condition of "religious slavery," which had obtained in Virginia, is almost impassioned, and abounds in sentences which have become proverbial.[4] "It is error alone that needs the support of government. Truth can stand by itself." "Government has nothing to do with opinion." "Comprehension makes hypocrites, not converts." "Why subject it (religion) to coercion? To produce uniformity. But is uniformity of opinion desirable? No more than of face and of stature. Difference of opinion is an advantage in religion; the several sects perform the office of a *Censor Morum* over each other."

The work was not completed by the legislature of 1776.

[1] Hening, IX, 312, 469, 579.   [3] Jefferson, *Works*, I, 39.
[2] Howison, *Virginia*, II, 187.   [4] *Notes on Virginia*, pp. 262-264, 266, 267.

The Church of England was still spoken of as established. Some of its perquisites remained. The clergy of that Church alone could marry without a special license; while the vestry still remained in possession of civil functions. Down to 1781 legislation was concerned with vestries, and with dividing and uniting parishes. Instances of such action are found scattered through the ninth volume of Hening. Two other actions are worth noting.[1] One was the exclusion by the constitution of 1776 of all ministers from membership in the legislature or privy council. The other was a law allowing members of " some religious societies, particularly Methodists and Baptists, to serve (in the army) under officers of like faith."

In 1779, the question of ministers' salaries was met by an act repealing all acts providing salaries, save as affecting arrearages.[2] An act of 1780 created the office of overseer of the poor, to succeed to the powers and duties of vestries touching the poor, as under former laws.[3] In the same year dissenting ministers, Quakers, and Mennonites were empowered to celebrate marriages, without license or publication of banns.[4]

Effects.   The immediate effect of disestablishment was disastrous to the Episcopal Church. Most of its clergy were deprived of support, and, as many of them were loyal to the king and continued to pray for the royal family, they were subjected to much trouble and danger.[5] The more thoughtful of the Church, and those who sympathized with the colonial cause, sought to retrieve its fortunes by obtaining incorporation by the state. This they secured in an act of 1784 for " Incorporating the Protestant Episcopal Church."[6] The act contained a curious proviso that if the revenue of any Church exceeded £800, the fact was to be reported to the general assembly. But the act was short-lived. The proviso savored of civil interference with the Church, and gave to the Episco-

---

[1] Hening, IX, 117–348.
[2] Ibid., X, 197.
[3] Ibid., X, 288.
[4] Ibid., X, 302, 381.
[5] Hawks, *Ecclesiastical Contributions*, I, 139.
[6] Hening, XI, 532.

pal Church a legislative preference.   On this account the act was almost immediately repealed, and made place for another act which annulled all laws favoring the Church of England, dissolved all vestries as related to the state, and left to the Church itself the entire regulation of its own affairs.[1]   This was final and complete disestablishment, and from the passage of the act the State-Church of Virginia ceased to exist.

At the same time of the passage of this act, the legislature was urged to provide " for the support of some sort of wor- Support of ship." [2]   Many petitions were presented praying for a general religion. assessment for the support of religious teachers, and many opposing the prayer and asking " that no steps be taken in aid of religion, but that it be left to its own superior and successful influence."   The committee to which the petitions were referred brought in a " Bill for establishing a provision for teachers of the Christian religion."   Their report emphasized two principles : 1st, That the state ought to give support to the general diffusion of Christianity ; and 2d, That the state ought not to give any preëminence among differing sects. With these in view, the bill provided for a general assessment by civil authority, and allowed each ratepayer to indicate the Church which should receive the amount of his tax.   In this latter respect the proposed law resembled the enactments in New England for the relief of those not of the " established order."   The bill was approved by Washington, Henry, R. H. Lee, and Marshall, and strongly opposed by Madison and Jefferson.   " Chiefly through the influence of Patrick Henry " (Hawks) it passed to the second reading, when final action was postponed, that the popular mind might be discovered.   For this purpose it was ordered that the bill be printed for general distribution, and the people be desired to send up to the next legislature the expression of their opinions.

The effect of this appeal to the people was a flood of pe-

[1] Hening, XI, 536.
[2] Hawks, I, 156–173 ; Rives, *Madison*, I, 561–633.

titions, both for and against the bill, presented to the legislature of 1785. In their petitions the advocates for the bill dwelt upon the "decay of public morals," and with regard to it the Episcopal and Presbyterian clergy found their first point of union. Of course the former were expected to favor the bill, but the support of the latter was a surprise. Madison so regarded the address from the "united clergy of the Presbyterian Church — that a general assessment ought to be extended *to those who profess* the public worship of the Deity." Madison wrote to Monroe: "The Episcopal people are generally for it, though I think the zeal of some of them has cooled. The laity of the other sects are generally unanimous on the other side. So are all the clergy except the Presbyterians, who seem as ready to set up an establishment which is to take them in as they were to pull down that which shut them out. I do not know a more shameful contrast than might be found in their memorials on the latter and former occasions." This critic of Presbyterian inconsistency took pleasure in one memorial "from certain inhabitants of the county of Rockbridge (apparently Presbyterian laymen) deprecating the interference of the legislature in aid of religion as unequal, impolitic, and beyond their power." In another place he wrote, "In the present form it (the bill) excludes all but Christian sects. The Presbyterian clergy have remonstrated against any narrow principles, but indirectly favor a more comprehensive establishment."

The effect of the measure, if it had passed into law, would have been to establish Christianity as the religion of the state, making all Christian Churches stipendiaries on legislative support, and thus, by reason of the public tax involved, oppressing all non-Christians, whether Jews or infidels. This suited neither Madison nor Jefferson, who desired the civil law to entirely refrain from all discriminations, and to accord an equal liberty to all varieties of religious belief and unbelief.

In the midst of the discussion Madison, at the instance of

Mason and others and for a direct appeal to the people, drew up his famous "Memorial and Remonstrance," in which he argued, on the basis of the Bill of Rights, that religion did not come within the cognizance of government, for either the support of worship or inquiry into individual faith. This remonstrance, being circulated among the people for signature, was returned to the legislature with so overwhelming demonstration of popular opinion that the pending bill was at once abandoned without further struggle. *" Memorial and Remonstrance."*

On this the champions of liberty, not satisfied with a merely negative victory, proceeded to secure such action as would render impossible all future attempts at civil interference with religion. Immediately on the failure of the bill for support of religious teachers, there was brought up the "Declaratory Act," which was drawn up by Jefferson and ably advocated by Madison. The act deservedly ranks among the great charters of human liberty.[1] It was made law in October, 1785, and is entitled "*An Act Establishing Religious Freedom.*" Jefferson says, " I prepared the act in 1777, but it was not reported to the assembly till 1779, and not passed until 1785, and then by the efforts of Mr. Madison." [2] It thus appears that this great measure lay on the table of the assembly throughout the vexing debates of the past six years, waiting until the discussions should prepare the legislature for the adoption of its broad principles. *Declaratory Act.*

When it came up for final action, according to Jefferson,[3] it "still met with opposition, but with some mutilations in the preamble it was finally passed." This preamble dwelt on the injustice and immorality of all interference by the magistrate with the religion of the individual, and of all civil regulation of ecclesiastical affairs, as contrary to the spirit of Christianity and its Author. Jefferson records : " A singular proposition proved that its protection was meant to be universal. Where the preamble declares that coercion is a

[1] Hening, *Statutes*, XII, 84.
[2] *Works*, I, 174.   [3] *Ibid.*, I, 45.

departure from the plan of the holy author of our religion, an amendment was proposed by inserting the words, 'Jesus Christ,' so that it should read, 'The plan of Jesus Christ, the holy author, &c.' The insertion was rejected by a great majority, in proof that they meant to comprehend within the mantle of its protection the Jew and the Gentile, the Christian and Mahometan, the Hindu and Infidel of every denomination." [1]

After the exhibition of principles in the preamble the act proceeds: —

"*Be it enacted* by the General Assembly, That no man shall be compelled to frequent or support any religious worship, place, or ministry whatever; nor shall be enforced, restrained, molested, or burthened in his body or goods, nor shall otherwise suffer on account of his religious opinions or belief; but that all men shall be free to profess, and by argument to maintain, their opinions in matters of religion, and that the same shall in no wise diminish, enlarge, or affect their civil capacities."

A curious attendant upon this act arose from the consciousness that it was legislative, and not a part of the fundamental constitution. To meet this condition, and the possibility of a future repeal, the assembly adopted another section, which was rather a declaration of opinion than an enactment of law. After disclaiming, in view of the equal powers of future assemblies, that the act was passed as irrevocable, the section asserts: "yet we are free to declare, and do declare, that the rights hereby asserted are of the natural rights of mankind, and that, if any act shall hereafter be passed to repeal the

---

[1] This description is largely responsible for the widely circulated slander that Jefferson himself was an infidel, which in future years gave so much of bitterness to political discussion. Dr. Hawks (*Ecclesiastical Contributions*, I, 173) says: "There is reason in his case to believe that, under cover of an attack upon a religious establishment, a blow was aimed at Christianity itself. . . . It was not necessary in securing such protection to degrade, not the establishment, but Christianity itself to a level with the voluptuous Mohammedan, or the worship of Juggernaut." (!)

present or to narrow its operation, such act will be an infringement of natural right."

So Virginia settled for herself the principle of religious
freedom on the broadest possible basis ; and, two years after,
in the celebrated "Ordinance of 1787," extended it to the Ordinance
Northwestern Territory, by the section : — "No person, de- of 1787.
meaning himself in a peaceable and orderly manner, shall
ever be molested on account of his mode of worship or religious sentiments, in the said territory." The necessary readjustment of affairs, owing to the claims of the Episcopal
Church to the property of the old State-Church, and also to
various constructions of the law and of legislative power
under it, entailed future legislative and judicial action, which
will be noted hereafter. At present we turn to the action of
the other colonies during the period of the Revolution.

In none of them was there such various and sustained discussion as in Virginia. In most of them a few words of constitutional provision, with more or less of freedom, settled the
question for the time. That which is most marked by the
comparison of the different actions is the varying degree of
ability to understand the true nature of religious freedom.
No other colony, save Rhode Island, equalled Virginia's broad
and comprehensive statement, while some of them fell far
short of that standard.

In *New Hampshire* the constitution of 1776 made no pro- New Hamp-
vision in regard to religious matters. A state convention in shire.
1779 submitted another constitution to the people, which was
not adopted, but its utterance on the rights of conscience may
be noted here as indicating the growth of sentiment. The
section read : " The future legislation of this state shall make
no laws to infringe the rights of Conscience, or any other
of the natural, unalterable Rights of Men, or contrary to the
laws of GOD, or against the *Protestant* religion." [1] Another
convention in 1781 adopted a Bill of Rights similar to that
of the Massachusetts convention of 1780, and in an address

[1] *New Hampshire Historical Society*, V, 155.

thereon remarked : " We have endeavored to ascertain and define the most important and essential rights of man. We have distinguished between alienable and unalienable rights. For the former of which men may receive an equivalent; for the latter, or the *rights of conscience*, they can receive none : The world itself being wholly inadequate to the purchase. ' For what is a man profited, though he should gain the whole world and lose his own soul ? ' The various modes of worship among mankind are founded in their various sentiments and beliefs concerning the Great Object of all religious worship and adoration . . . therefore, to Him alone, and not to man, are they accountable for them."

This seems to reach far enough, but in spite of it, the constitution of 1781, as also that of 1784, left unchanged the old colonial law which made the Church a town institution and its support a matter of public tax, and discriminated also in favor of the Protestant religion.[1]

Massachusetts. In *Massachusetts* the first state constitution was formed in 1780, in which the Bill of Rights contained the following language : " As the happiness of a people, and the good order and preservation of civil government, essentially depend upon piety, religion, and morality, . . . the legislature shall from time to time authorize and require the several towns and parishes . . . to make suitable provision, at their own expense, for the institution of the public worship of God." [2] Thus the state retained the old colonial principle which gave to the Church a civil status. Every ratepayer was, as in the past fifty years, allowed to indicate his preference as to the Church which should be benefited by his tax, while those, who had no choice, were required to pay taxes for the support of the State Congregational Church. In the end, it will be seen that, the system worked special damage to the Church thus preferred by the law.

In *Connecticut* and *Rhode Island* no state constitutions

---

[1] *New Hampshire Historical Society*, V, 175.
[2] *Religion in America*, p. 256.

were formed. Without formal action the colonies passed into Connecticut and Rhode Island. states of the American Union under their old charters, and no changes were made affecting the civic relations of the Church. Rhode Island continued in the way of the broad liberty which had obtained from its foundation; while Connecticut retained its State-Church until the second decade of the nineteenth century. The records of Connecticut contain religious and ecclesiastical legislation during and after the revolutionary period.[1] An act in 1778 exempted *Separates* (though Congregationalists) from taxes for support of the *established* Church. Many Churches and "societies" were authorized at different times. In 1784 was passed an "Act for securing the Rights of Conscience." The law enacted, that no persons *professing the Christian religion*, who soberly dissented from the worship and ministry *established* by law, and *attended worship* by themselves, should incur a penalty by not attending the established worship: that *Christians* of every denomination, who attended and *helped maintain* worship according to their consciences, should not be taxed for the support of other worship; that those who did not belong to any other society were to be taxed for the support of the State-Church; and that all *Protestant* dissenters should have liberty to use the same powers for maintaining their respective societies as belonged to societies established by law.

The effect of this last provision was to continue the colonial practice by which all church support was collected by town officers and distributed according to the indicated preferences of the taxpayers. The act is further notable as restricting liberty to Protestants, and insisting that every person should attend and help maintain some form of Christian worship. The liberty of Connecticut did not yet make room for the Jew or the Romanist, and lagged far behind the new-found freedom of Virginia.

The action in *New York* makes but a short tale. The peo- New York. ple of the colony, in the proportion of fifteen to one, were

---

[1] *Connecticut State Records*, I, 11 ; *New Haven Historical Papers*, III, 400.

opposed to all forms of civil restriction on religion, and disowned the fiction so sedulously maintained by the government, that the act of 1693 had established the Anglican
Church. The nameless Church instituted by that act went
down with the first assault of war: and the state convention of 1777 guarded the rights of conscience and religious
worship from interference by the civil power. The 35th
Article expressly abrogated all laws and parts of law, common or statute, which "might be construed to establish or
maintain any particular denomination of Christians or their
ministers." The 30th Article ordained that "The free exercise and enjoyment of religious profession and worship, without discrimination or preference, shall forever hereafter be
allowed within this State to all mankind." The legislature
of 1784 repealed the "Settling Act" of 1693 and all subsequent acts "which do grant certain emoluments and privileges to the Episcopal Church."

The liberty thus asserted was, however, qualified by two
restrictions. The one was a provision that all persons naturalized by the State should take an oath of abjuration of all
foreign allegiance and subjection in all matters, "ecclesiastical as well as civil." There can be but one interpretation of
the ecclesiastical reference. [1] It was intended to exclude

Romanists. Roman Catholics from citizenship. The other restriction
was the exclusion of clergymen from public office, on the
ground that they "ought not to be diverted from their great
duties of the service of God and the care of souls." This,
the 31st Article, was an infringement upon the rights of a
certain class of men on account of religion, while the reason
alleged was one of which a political convention could not
properly take cognizance.[2] Later New York constitutions
did away with both these restrictions.

New Jersey. The *New Jersey* constitution of 1776 decreed to every one
"the inestimable privilege of worshipping God according to
the dictates of his own conscience, but at the same time

[1] Story, § 114.   [2] Baird, *Religion in America*, p. 268.

imposed a religious test for office, which was confined to
"persons professing a belief in the faith of any *Protestant
sect*."[1]

The constitution adopted by *Pennsylvania* in 1776 declared Penn-
that "all men have a natural and inalienable right to worship sylvania.
God, according to the dictates of their own conscience and
understanding." But while denying all civil interference
with worship and all public taxation for religion, the constitution restricted civil rights to persons "*who acknowledge the
being of a God.*" In addition to this, the oath imposed for
all office-holders required them to affirm, "I do believe in
one God, the Creator and Governor of the Universe, the
rewarder of the good and the punisher of the wicked; and I
do acknowledge the Scriptures of the Old and New Testaments to be given by divine inspiration."[2] Against these
restrictions Franklin fought earnestly in the convention, but Franklin.
he was forced to content himself with the abandonment of
the more severe test against Roman doctrine. Certainly, in
spite of the spirit of its great founder, Pennsylvania had not
yet learned the lesson of full liberty of mind.

And *Delaware* was a close parallel. Its constitution of Delaware.
1776 declared that "all persons *professing the Christian* religion ought forever to enjoy equal rights and privileges," and
in the oath of office put a declaration of faith in the doctrine
of the Trinity and in the divine inspiration of the Scriptures.
This was narrower than Pennsylvania.

The *Maryland* convention of 1775 took the first step Maryland.
toward freedom in the extension of the franchise to "all
freemen having an estate of £40, without religious distinction."[3] But this absence of distinction was applicable only
to differences within the Christian religion. This was specially defined by the Bill of Rights in 1777,[4] which specifies
those "persons professing the *Christian religion* (as) equally

[1] Baird, *Religion in America*, p. 268.
[2] Baird, p. 270; *American Historical Association*, 1887–1888, p. 208.
[3] Bancroft, VIII, 78.   [4] *Maryland Laws.*

entitled to protection in their religious liberty." The bill forbids compelling any persons to attend or support any particular form of worship, and then says, "yet the legislature *may* in their discretion lay a general tax for the support of the Christian religion, leaving to each individual the power" of indicating the direction of his own tax, to any church *or to the poor*. By a happy clause the bill avoided an issue, which afterward plagued Virginia, decreeing that "the property now held by the Church of England" should remain theirs forever; and consulted charity in ordering that the clergy of that Church should be paid until the following November.

This was the Maryland act of disestablishment, and in addition to the removal of the State-Church it made also distinct advance in enfranchising Roman Catholics, for whom as yet New England, outside of Rhode Island, had made no room. The constitution copied New York in excluding clergymen from the legislature, and for office imposed an oath of allegiance and of belief in the Christian religion. A unique incident in Maryland was the appointment of a form of public prayer for the new government. The majority of the clergy of the Church of England refused to use the form, and were required to pay a "treble tax" or leave the country. The most of them chose the latter alternative, and their Churches were closed or used by other religious bodies.[1]

North Carolina.
The constitution of *North Carolina* used a negative form — in that respect peculiar — to the effect that, " No person who shall deny the being of God, or the truth of the *Protestant* religion, or the divine authority of either the Old or New Testament, or shall hold religious opinions incompatible with the freedom or safety of the State, shall be capable of holding any office or place of trust in the civil government of this State." Beyond this definition of religious qualification for office, the state made no further deliverance on the subject of religion, save the guarantee of freedom of conscience. The

[1] Hawks, *Ecclesiastical Contributions*, II, 283.

old establishment died of inanition, and no provision was made to support any Church or religious teaching.

The constitutional action of *South Carolina* was a most curious mingling of political and religious ideas, having in part the ordinary expressions of civil law, and in other part assuming the attitude and motive of a superior spiritual court or confession of faith. The constitution of 1776 contained no religious provisions, but the omission was more than supplied by the constitution of 1778.[1] Its first provision having reference to religion was one excluding from the office of governor, lieutenant governor, and membership in the privy council or legislature all clergymen, "until two years after demitting the ministry."

Chapter XXXVIII. enters into most extensive definitions, as follows : "All persons and religious societies, who acknowledge that there is one God, and a future state of reward and punishment, and that God is publicly to be worshipped, shall be freely *tolerated*. The Christian Protestant religion shall be deemed, and is hereby constituted and declared to be the established religion of this State. All denominations of protestants in this State . . . shall enjoy equal religious and civil privileges." The chapter ordains the security of ownership by the Episcopal Churches in the property already held by them, and provides for incorporating other religious bodies, "whenever fifteen male persons, not under twenty-one years of age," shall agree together for religious worship. Each such society "shall have agreed to and subscribed in a book the following five articles, without which no agreement or union of men, upon pretence of religion, shall entitle them to be incorporated and esteemed as a Church of the established religion of this State : —

"1. That there is one Eternal God and a future state of reward and punishment.

"2. That God is publicly to be worshipped.

---

[1] *South Carolina Statutes*, I, 142-145.

South Carolina.

Christianity established.

" 3. That the Christian Religion is the true religion.

" 4. That the Holy Scriptures of the old and new Testaments are of divine inspiration, and are the rules of faith and practice.

" 5. That it is lawful and the duty of every man, being thereunto called by those who govern, to bear witness to the truth."

The chapter then ordains that pastors must be chosen by the majority of the Church, and that no minister can enter upon a pastorate until he has subscribed a declaration, " that he is determined by God's grace out of the Holy Scriptures to instruct the people committed to his charge, and to teach nothing as required or necessary to eternal salvation, but that which he shall be persuaded may be concluded and proved from the Scriptures ; that he will use both public and private admonitions, as well to the sick as to the whole within his care, as need shall require and occasion shall be given ; and that he will be diligent in prayers and in reading of the Scriptures, and in such studies as help to the knowledge of the same ; that he will be diligent to frame and fashion his own self and his family according to the doctrine of Christ, and to make both himself and them, as much as in him lieth, wholesome examples and patterns to the flock of Christ ; that he will maintain and set forward, as much as he can, quietness, peace and love among all people, and especially among those that are, and shall be, committed to his charge."

There is nothing like this in any other state provision. It strongly resembles the provision for toleration in the colonial law of Carolina, but carries it much further, while its concern for pastoral purity and faithfulness is far more in the spirit of episcopal jurisdiction than that of civil legislation. It makes a curious revival in Carolina, of the puritanic forms of early Massachusetts. At the same time, these South Carolina Puritans of the Revolution were more liberal than the Massachusetts of their day. This *establishment* of the Christian religion, and this concern for pastoral faithfulness, must be regarded as little more than expressions of opinion and desire. Beyond exclusion from office, non-Christians were not subjected to imposition; no penalties were carried by the terms of the constitution, while that instrument expressly ordained that: "No person shall by law be obliged to pay towards maintenance and support of a religious worship, that he does not freely join in, or has not voluntarily engaged to support."

In *Georgia* the constitution of 1777 briefly declared freedom of conscience, but required that "all members of the legislature shall be of the Protestant religion."[1] Georgia.

It will thus be observed that, when the American Union was formed, there was great variety of legal expression on the subject of religion and its civic relations in the different states. By brief grouping of them it appears, that in only two out of the thirteen was full and perfect freedom conceded by law. These were Rhode Island and Virginia. Six of the states, viz., New Hampshire, Connecticut, New Jersey, the two Carolinas, and Georgia insisted on Protestantism. Two were content with the Christian religion; Delaware and Maryland. Four, Pennsylvania, Delaware, and the Carolinas, required assent to the divine inspiration of the Bible. Two, Pennsylvania and South Carolina, demanded a belief in heaven and hell. Three, New York, Maryland, and South Carolina, excluded ministers from civil office. Two, Pennsylvania and South Carolina, emphasized belief in one eternal God. One, Delaware, required assent to the doctrine of the Trinity. And five, New Hampshire, Massachusetts, Connecticut, Maryland, and South Carolina, adhered to a religious establishment. In one, South Carolina, the obnoxious term *toleration* found a constitutional place.

But with this great variety of legal expression the unanimity of sentiment for full liberty was soon made manifest in the adoption of the *Federal Constitution*. That instrument, submitted to the states by the convention of 1787, contained Constitution of United States.

[1] Baird, *Religion in America*, p. 272.

the following sole utterance on the subject of religion : " VI. 3. No religious test shall ever be required as a qualification to any office or public trust under the United States."

When the constitution came before the state conventions, this section gave rise to much debate. On the one hand, it was not regarded as furnishing a sufficient guarantee of religious freedom ; and on the other, it was feared as giving entrance to a liberty which might endanger the commonwealth. New York, New Hampshire, Virginia, and North Carolina insisted on a larger statement for religious liberty. The minority in the Pennsylvania convention wished to reject the constitution until such larger guarantee was incorporated. A similar demand was made in Virginia by Patrick Henry. But Madison prevailed on the convention to adopt the constitution on his personal pledge to obtain the amendment afterward made, carrying his point by a majority of eight in a vote of one hundred and sixty-eight.

In Massachusetts alone was a dread of liberty expressed. Major Lusk "shuddered at the idea that Roman Catholics, Papists, and Pagans might be introduced into office and that Popery and the Inquisition may be established in America." "Who," answered the Rev. Mr. Shute, "shall be excluded from natural trusts ? Whatever answer bigotry may suggest, the dictates of candor and equity, I conceive, will be, *None.* Far from limiting my charity and confidence to men of my own denomination in religion, I believe there are worthy characters among men of every denomination — among Quakers, Baptists, the Church of England, the Papists, and even among those who have no other guide in the way to virtue and heaven, than the dictates of natural religion." [1] The spirit of Puritanism must have travelled a long way to permit such an utterance by the lips of one of its established clergy.

The first Congress of the United States found among its

[1] Elliott, *Debates*, II, 119–148 ; *American Historical Association*, 1886–1887, pp. 27, 120, 405, 414.

duties the consideration of various amendments demanded by different state conventions. Madison maintained that those who had opposed the constitution, disliked it only because it failed in effectual provisions against encroachments on particular rights. Among these were the rights of conscience. Of the ten amendments proposed by the congress, sent down to the states, by them adopted, and so made part of the national constitution, the first is in these words: "Congress shall make no law respecting an establishment of religion, or prohibiting the free exercise thereof." First Amendment.

This amendment and the section already quoted are the only utterances of the federal constitution on the subject of religion. Their brevity is in marked contrast with the diffuse and elaborate verbiage of many of the state constitutions. But they cover the entire ground, and pronounce the national government for the largest liberty of conscience and worship, and restrain the national magistracy from all interference in "matters of religious concernment."

Thus from the beginning of national life, the United States ordained throughout the land, so far as its constitutional power could reach, full liberty of mind, conscience, and worship.

X

FINAL SETTLEMENTS

THE circumstances and constituents of the national government necessitated limitations of its law of liberty. Its provisions applied only in the federal sphere and had no force of law against a religious establishment in any of the states. The constitution conferred on the general government the right and duty to maintain in every state a republican form of government, but it bestowed no right of interference with the institutions of a religious character which any state might choose to establish, so long as the moral safety and the integrity of the nation were not involved. If, for example, one of the states should set aside its present form of government and set up a monarchy, the national government under the constitution would be required to prevent such action. But if one of the states, even to-day, should change its own constitution and set up a State-Church, with the peculiar perquisites and power of an establishment, and should put such Church upon the public treasury for support, the general government has no power to prevent it.

For this reason, the adoption of the federal constitution did not abolish the various restrictions and establishments which obtained in different states. Each state was free to do as it willed in regard to Church, individual liberty of worship, establishment, religious taxation, and religious tests. They carried over into their future statehood the special institutions obtaining in 1789, and used their own time and method of making what changes they desired. For this cause, though full freedom was the law of the nation, yet in some parts of the union illiberal and oppressive restrictions obtained for many years, attended by more or less of struggle, until the last vestige of old distinctions was swept away: if, indeed, it can be said that they are all gone, even yet.[1] Some of those struggles should here be noted.

In *Virginia*, notwithstanding the broad terms of the " Bill of Rights " and the " Act for Religious Freedom," there were two sources of trouble. The first was an apparent inability of lawmakers to altogether emancipate themselves from past customs. Bills were passed for incorporating the Episcopal Church as a denomination, which was considered by some of the people as an indication of state preference. Occasional legislation referring to " dissenters " and vestries caused the same comment. To end the debate thence arising the legislature of 1798–1799 passed an act for the repeal of every law in seeming contravention of the bill of rights, the constitution, and the act for establishing religious freedom, on the ground that " the several acts presently recited do admit the Church established under the regal government to have continued so subsequently to the constitution."[2] This gave the establishment the final *coup de grace*, and was in keeping with a decision of the Virginia Court of Appeals (*Kemper* vs. *Hawkins*, 1793) that the bill of rights was a part of the constitution, and that all laws contrary to it were null and void.

The other source of trouble in Church affairs was the glebe land. The glebes had been given to the Church of England Glebe lands. established in Virginia. After disestablishment the Episcopal Church, rightly considering itself as the successor and heir of the Church of England, laid claim to the lands. Had the Virginia convention of 1776 been as wise in this matter as the men of Maryland and South Carolina, the justice of the claim would have been acknowledged in law. But that body said nothing on the subject, leaving the question open for the contentions of cupidity and sectarian jealousy. In the absence of any legal definition of ownership, the claim of the Episco-

[1] McMaster, *History of the People of the United States*, III, 149.
[2] Shepherd, *Statutes at Large*, II, 149.

pal Church was not quietly acquiesced in. Every year brought to the legislature memorials from rival Churches, contending that possession of the glebes by the Episcopal Church constituted a legal advantage of one denomination over others. Finally the legislature of 1802 passed an act to sell those glebe lands which were vacant, but not to disturb any incumbents. The proceeds of the sale were to be applied to the payment of parish debts, and the remainder to be distributed to the poor. This act was contested by the Episcopal Church in the chancellor's court, and there sustained. In the court of appeals the bench was equally divided, and the chancellor's decision stood. The law came up again in the court of appeals in 1840, when the act was unanimously sustained by the five judges. " Not until then," says Howison, " was the divorce between Church and State in Virginia complete." [1]

The established Church of *Connecticut* [2] existed for a full quarter century after the national constitution was adopted, and its continuance and claims entered largely into political differences and struggles. In both this state and Massachusetts the Federalists espoused the cause of the establishment, which thus became a special object of hatred by the Republicans. The conservatives were tenacious of the privileges of the State-Church and unwilling to extend the liberties of dissenters. In 1791 Connecticut even narrowed those liberties by the requirement that the dissenters must file certificates of dissent and membership in a dissenting Church, in order to be exempt from the state tithe. During the next twenty years the feeling in the opposing parties became exceedingly bitter. The Federalists confounded liberty with Jeffersonism, and Jeffersonism with infidelity and all the horrors of the French Revolution, which would be repeated in Connecticut, if the Church were overthrown. But the tide was too strong

---

[1] Howison, *History of Virginia*, II, 396–405.

[2] *New Haven Historical Papers*, III, 401–402 ; Schouler, *History of United States*, III, 52–53 ; *Johns Hopkins Studies*, X, 99.

for them, and, in order to save themselves, they passed an act in 1816 to repeal the penalty for non-attendance upon Church, a very small concession to the party which had vowed death to the establishment. In 1817 the conservatives fell from power. Oliver Wolcott was chosen governor by a coalition of all opponents to the State-Church.[1] All the dissenting Churches made common cause with the Republicans against the conservative dynasty. The legislature of that year passed an act that any person of any Christian denomination should have full power to change his Church relations at will, and that every Christian society should have power to tax its own members only.

The legislature also called a convention to frame a constitution. This body met in 1818, framed a constitution to take the place of the old colonial charter, and set in that fundamental law provisions which destroyed all religious establishment. It ordained "that the exercise and enjoyment of religious profession and worship, without distinction, shall be forever free to all persons in this state. No preference shall be given by any law to any *Christian* sect or mode of worship." No person should be compelled to join or support any Church, society, or religious association. Each and all should enjoy equal rights, powers, and privileges. These provisions were intended to establish full liberty, but as the clause touching *preference* mentioned the Christian religion and might give rise to the construction that the freedom intended was designed only for Christian Churches, an after legislature expressly construed the benefits of this freedom as including Jews.

Connecticut disestablishment.

The change seemed to many of the conservatives as the beginning of the day of doom. The venerable Timothy Dwight, the president of Yale, deprecated it until his death. It involved much readjustment of affairs, attended by more or less of trouble, but in a few years the wisdom and righteousness of the new system justified themselves

[1] Johnston, *History of Connecticut*, p. 352.

to even those who had been stanchest in defence of the establishment.

Massachu-
setts.

The struggle in *Massachusetts* was more protracted. There was the same political adoption of the Church question as in Connecticut, perhaps with a shade less of bitterness, while to this was added another element which threatened the very existence of the old Puritan Church. [1] The strife began promptly on the adoption of the constitution of 1780, which some of the dissenters construed as exempting them from filing certificates of dissent and from payment of tithes. To test the claim a Mr. Balkom of Attleboro, in 1781, refused to pay and, the tax having been collected by levy, brought suit for its recovery. The case went against him in the justice's court, but on appeal to the county court the sentence was reversed. This should have settled the question for the State, but it did not, and the old custom still generally obtained.

Some years afterward, a Mr. Murray, a Universalist minister, brought suit for recovery of tithes paid by his parishioners. In defence the State's attorney argued that "a minister, who denied the eternal punishment of the wicked, was not a teacher of piety, religion, and morality," within the meaning of the constitution! But the court gave decision for Murray, and in 1799 the legislature passed an act allowing such suits for recovery, from which act a later decision of the supreme court took much of its life by deciding that ministers of unincorporated societies were not *public* teachers, and therefore could not claim the privileges of the law.

Unitarian-
ism.

Meanwhile the Unitarian defection was gathering force and under the law had an immense advantage, so soon as it could persuade a majority of citizens to its views. The law made the Church a town institution, and gave the choice of minister to the town meeting. It was thus easily possible for the town meeting to override the orthodox portion of the community. This danger made itself evident in the great

[1] Schouler, II, 252; III, 222; *Johns Hopkins Studies*, X, 99–104.

Dedham case, the issue of which was so momentous for the Church of Massachusetts.

The majority of the Dedham Church were orthodox, while the majority of the town were of Unitarian proclivities. In 1818 the minister of the Church resigned, and the town chose a Unitarian as his successor. The Church refused to assent to this choice, and the case was carried to the supreme court, which decided that the constitution " gives to towns, not to Churches, the right to elect the minister in the last resort." This decision gave the Church perquisites and property to the Unitarians, and the Orthodox were forced to make a new Church for themselves on the voluntary system. A like result followed in very many places, and the old Puritan Church found itself turned out of house and home by the very powers it had contrived to give it lasting security. This was the death-blow to the long-moribund theocracy. The constitutional convention of 1820, following the erection of the State of Maine, attempted to meet the religious question, but through the opposition of the conservative element succeeded only in the abolition of religious tests for office. In 1833 the Church was finally disestablished. Tithes were **Disestablishment.** abolished, the voluntary system made universal in the state, and the towns discharged from all concern and power for Church affairs.

After the national settlement the attitude of *Pennsylvania* **Pennsylvania.** toward religious liberty was marked by both enlargement and restriction.[1] The constitution of 1790 abolished the religious test for office. This was a great advance. But a backward step was taken, when to " acknowledgment of Almighty God" there was added the belief in " a future state of rewards and punishments," as a prerequisite to the freedom of religion conceded by the state. This was repeated in the constitution of 1837, and remains in the fundamental law to-day.

[1] *Pennsylvania Laws; American Historical Association,* 1887-1888, p. 462 ; *Sergeant and Rawles,* XI, 394.

The state has never repealed the law of 1700, which imposed a penalty upon any who should "wilfully, premeditatedly, and despitefully blaspheme, or speak lightly or profanely of Almighty God, Christ Jesus, the Holy Spirit, or the Scriptures of Truth." The decision of the supreme court, in 1824, in the celebrated case of *Updegraph* vs. *the Commonwealth* — a case arising from words spoken in public debate — declared that the law was still in force.

New Hampshire.

Before the eighteenth century ended *New Hampshire* abolished the religious qualification for the office of governor, but it continued to "authorize the *towns* to provide for the support of *Protestant* teachers." This archaic authorization has long been idle and absurd. No town, as such, has acted upon it within this century, but it still remains in the bill of rights, one of the few surviving relics in the United States of the idea of a state establishment of religion. The same section (6) of the bill of rights contains the words: "Every denomination of *Protestant Christians*, demeaning themselves quietly and as good subjects of the state, shall be equally under the protection of the law." Thus the constitution distinguished against the Roman Catholic, and, on strict construction, put a Jewish congregation outside of the protection of the law. Repeated efforts have been made to strike out the words *Protestant* and *Christian*, but unsuccessfully. They still remain in the revised constitution of 1889. The proposed change seemed to many as though its adoption would be a "repeal of the Protestant Christian religion," and make the state unchristian! So the illiberal technicality remains to misrepresent the true spirit of the state, which in the use of such restriction is alone in the union. [1] New Hampshire, indeed, was slow in recognizing the rights of dissenters. Separate acts of legislation in 1792, 1804, 1805, and 1817 gave exemptions to Episcopalians, Baptists, Universalists, and Methodists, providing that each should be

[1] *Johns Hopkins Studies,* X, 90.

"considered as a distinct denomination, with privileges as such." Finally, a "toleration act" was passed in 1819, which gave freedom to all *Christian* sects.

Delaware[1] soon abandoned its demand for belief in the Delaware. Trinity, and by its constitution of 1831 abolished religious tests. The *South Carolina* constitution of 1790 put aside its South elaborate provisions as to Churches, ministers, and a *Prot-* Carolina. *estant* establishment. By this action it enfranchised Roman Catholics, and in set terms provided for religious freedom, "without distinction or preference." But it still maintained the exclusion of clergymen from public office.[2]

The first state to be admitted to the Union, after the original thirteen, was *Vermont*, the settlers of which had Vermont. shared the prevailing sentiments of New England. Because of this the state life began with civil prescriptions for religion. The law of 1783 had already put the Church on the town care and tax, with some relief for dissenters. A law of 1801 ordained that every person of adult age and a legal voter should be considered as of the religious opinion represented in the town Church, and as such should be liable to taxation for the Church support, unless he should deliver in writing a declaration that he did not agree in religious opinion with the majority of the inhabitants of the town. This caused much opposition, and in 1807 the system was abandoned, the care of the Church taken from the town, tithes abolished, and religion and worship made entirely voluntary.

It is not necessary to pursue our study into the details of later changes in state constitutions, or to reproduce the religious sections adopted by the many commonwealths which now make up the American Union. The states added to the union of the original thirteen largely copied the models set before them in these earlier constitutions, especially following in preamble and bill of rights the exact

[1] McMaster, *History of the People of the United States*, III, 149.
[2] *South Carolina Statutes*, I, 188–191.

verbiage of the older instruments. A comparison of their provisions on certain lines will fully meet the need of the question here.

State constitutions compared.

As one illustration of similarity it may be noted that thirty-one constitutions use in their preambles the phrase "grateful to Almighty God." Three of them, Virginia, Louisiana, and Texas, substitute for this the words "invoking the favor and guidance — or the blessing — of Almighty God." All the constitutions have the name of God in some place, either the preamble or the section on religious worship, with the exception of Michigan and West Virginia. The constitutions of these two states have neither preamble, nor mention of God anywhere in the instrument, but the freedom of conscience and worship is emphatically decreed. No constitution contains the name of Christ. It will be noted that neither God nor Christ is named in the constitution of the United States.

[1] In regard to the expression of liberty all the states are at one in decreeing its full exercise, but there are interesting differences and similarities of statement. Twenty-six states declare that it is the privilege of "every man to worship God according to the dictates of his own conscience." Eleven say that "the free enjoyment of religious sentiments and forms of worship shall ever be held sacred." Five assert a "duty of the legislature to pass laws for the protection" of religious freedom. Nineteen declare that "no human authority ought to control, or interfere with, the rights of conscience." Nine ordain that "no person may be molested in person or estate on account of religion."

In qualification of this liberty, thirteen states define that it is "not to excuse licentiousness or justify practices inconsistent with the peace and safety" of society; seven say that it is "not to excuse disturbance of the public peace"; three, that it is "not to justify practices inconsistent with the

---

[1] All the following comparisons are taken from Stimson's *American Statute Law.*

rights of others "; and three require that "no person may disturb others in worship."

With respect to the relation of individuals to the Church and of the Church to the civil law, twenty-four states forbid compulsory attendance or support of any Church; one (New Hampshire) says that "no person of one sect may be compelled to support a minister of another;" and one (New Jersey) forbids compulsion of any person to attend worship "contrary to his own faith." Five states forbid "an established Church"; twenty-nine forbid the civil government to show any "preference" for any one sect, and three, any "subordination" of one sect to another. Two states, Delaware and Vermont, have it in their constitutions that "every sect ought to observe the Lord's day and keep up some sort of religious worship."

In the matter of support fourteen states forbid the appropriation of money from the state treasury for the support of sectarian institutions. Seven include municipal treasuries in the prohibition. Six apply the prohibition to any *property* of the state; and four, to any property of any municipality. Two states, Michigan and Oregon, carry this principle so far as to forbid the appropriation of public money to pay for the services of chaplains to the legislature.

In one thing a sharp contrast is notable. New Hampshire says that the legislature may authorize *towns* and parishes to provide for the support of religious teachers; Massachusetts and Missouri confine this authorization to *parishes;* the Maine constitution gives this power to "religious societies," without the intervention of the legislature; while Virginia and West Virginia forbid the legislature to take any such action. Religious tests are generally forbidden. Twenty-seven states declare that no religious test shall be required for office; eighteen add to this "for any public trust." Four states include voting as exempt from tests. Six forbid religious test for jury duty, and seventeen for witnesses, while two (Oregon and Wyoming) forbid the questioning of a witness in court as to his religious belief. Eleven states declare that no man can " be deprived of any civil right on account of religious sentiments."

Exceptions. Finally, there are to be observed a few exceptions and limitations. In five states, Arkansas, Mississippi, Texas, and the two Carolinas, no person can hold office " who *denies* the being of Almighty God or the existence of a Supreme Being." Arkansas also makes such a denier of God incompetent as a witness. Pennsylvania and Tennessee restrict office to such as " believe in God and a future state of reward and punishment." Maryland requires this belief in a juror or witness, but for the office-holder demands only a belief in God. Of these eight states thus requiring some religious qualification, Mississippi and Tennessee, by a curious inconsistency, forbid all religious tests as qualifications for office.

Maryland is the only state in the union which still requires the sanction of the Church, or a religious service, to create the *status* of marriage.

The points on which all the state constitutions are at one are as follows : —

1. No legislature can pass a law establishing religion, or a Church. To effect such purpose a change in the constitution would be required.
2. No person can be compelled by law to attend any form of religious service; or, —
3. To contribute to the support of any such service or Church.
4. No restraint can be put by law on the free exercise of religion ; or, —
5. On the free expression and promulgation of religious belief. *Provided* always, that this freedom " shall not be so construed as to excuse acts of licentiousness, or to justify practices inconsistent with the peace and safety of the State."

Such was the progress, and such are the results of nearly three hundred years of endeavor. So far as affected individual liberty, most of the colonies had either conceded full freedom of religion or allowed its enjoyment without legal enactment, long before the Revolution, though several of them maintained some of the features of a State-Church. The political upheaval of 1776 brought the overthrow of the colonial establishments, save as the Church rates still continued for thirty, forty, and fifty years in New Hampshire, Connecticut, and Massachusetts. With the abolition of these, in the last century, but few vestiges were left in America of that old idea of union between Church and State, which had ruled Christendom from the time of Constantine, and is yet regnant in almost every country of Europe.

Thus it is the peculiar merit and glory of this American people that they were the first, and as yet the only one, among the nations to embody the principle of Religious Liberty in the fundamental law. Not toleration, but equality, puts all religions in the same relation to the law, under which there can be no preferences of one before another. The only relation between the Church and state is that of mutual respect. Over the Church the state does "not profess to have any jurisdiction whatever, except so far as is necessary to protect the civil rights of others, and to preserve the public peace. . . . Equity will not determine questions of faith, doctrine, or schism, unless necessarily involved in the enforcement of ascertained trusts."[1] Over the state, the Church affects no authority to exercise dictation. Its influence is solely moral; free to express opinion in regard to any matters of civic interest and to apply thereto the principles of God's word, it is yet destitute of all constraining power, save such as arises from the persuasion of the individual mind and the creation of that public opinion, which in America is the court of last resort.

The few limitations that yet remain in some of the state

[1] Cooley, *Constitutional Limitations*, p. 572.

constitutions — such as the requirement of belief in God, and the retention of the word "Protestant" in the constitution of New Hampshire — are practically devoid of force, lifeless as the fossils in the rock, monuments simply of a system which has passed. The rejection of a witness solely on account of his belief in religious matters would be nowhere in the land possible to-day. Nor could a governor of Pennsylvania be unseated, if he should fall into unbelief in God and a future state of rewards and punishment. Nor yet could a Hebrew congregation fail of "protection under the law" in New Hampshire, though the constitution does not concede it. Practically, religious liberty is complete, involving, to the individual, no curtailment of civil right or privilege; to the Church, no interference with its faith, order, or spiritual function; and to the various Churches, no discrimination or preference by law of one before another.

Objections.   This American religious liberty has been assailed from two standpoints. One opponent objects that it is not complete, the other that it is unchristian. A few brief remarks on both these objections may fitly close this treatise.

Incomplete.   The former objection of incompleteness finds its reasons in such things as, the exemption of Church property from taxation; laws for the protection of the sabbath and against blasphemy; proclamation for days of thanksgiving and fast; and anti-Mormon legislation. Any lengthened discussion of these reasons is here impossible, and it is alone needful to note that the justification of all such legislative action resides, not in the demands of religion nor in the competition of one form of religion with another, but solely in the demands of social order, safety, and prosperity.

If there be any truths clearly demonstrated by the history of nations, among them is the fact that irreligion is the sure precursor of social decay and ruin. A godless community is doomed. A town without a Church is the chosen home of vice and crime. A society that recognizes no divine relation is rotten to the core. Hence, the law recognizes the existence and influence of the Church as a *social* institution, necessary to the safety of society itself, and for the same reason that it lays no taxes on its schools and charitable foundations, it exempts the Churches from taxation. It is true that in some instances this principle has been abused, and that it would be well to make general the limitation, obtaining in some states, which exempts only such Church property as is in actual use for religious service, and not a source of income.

But the principle is just, and the argument that this exemption adds to the taxes of those who have no relation to the Church, and is thus an invasion of their religious liberty, is in reality futile. It would be true, were the exemption made for the Church's sake. It loses all force when the exemption is made for the good of society. In this view the objector has no more reason for opposition than a childless man would have against the school tax, or a man would have against a tax for building a bridge, on the ground that he did not want to cross the stream or could row himself over.

In like manner the experience of mankind has demonstrated that the institutions of morality are essential to the preservation of social safety, and that no requirement of liberty demands that the lust and licentiousness of men shall be given free rein. Men are not to be allowed "under pretence of religion" to indulge in riot and wantonness; to offend the general religious sentiment of mankind by their blasphemous speech or their vicious life; to disturb others in their religious worship by unseemly uproar; to undermine the foundations of social morality; or to poison by immorality the fountain of youth. Liberty is never license, and all liberty is only free when it is regulated by law. When there shall be "no king in Israel, and every man shall do what is right in his own eyes," then will society go to pieces.

Says Judge Cooley:[1] "While thus careful to establish, protect, and defend religious freedom and equality, the Ameri-

---

[1] *Constitutional Limitations*, pp. 578–581.

can constitutions contain no provisions which prohibit the authorities from such solemn recognition of a superintending Providence in public transactions and exercises as the general religious sentiment of mankind inspires. . . . (They regard), without discrimination, religious worship and religious institutions as conservators of the public morals, and valuable, if not indispensable, assistants in the preservation of the public order. . . . Profane and blasphemous things are properly punished as crimes against society, since they are offences to the general public sense, and have a direct tendency to undermine the moral support of the laws."

This then is the central principle which must govern all legislation touching religion or morality: that its specific aim must be for the general good of society. The state has no call to make men religious or moral, but its highest duty is to take care that society shall not be disintegrated by irreligion and immorality. While the American principle declares religious freedom, it yet does not put irreligion in the place of power.

And this brings to view the second objection, that the American constitutions are unchristian. This founds itself on the absence from the constitution of the United States of the names of God and Christ, as also from some of the state constitutions. As already noted, all but two of the latter contain the name of God, while the constitution of New Hampshire contains also the words "Protestant" and "Christian." According to the argument of the objector, New Hampshire must be the only Christian state in the Union.

Unchristian.

The argument is specious, appealing only to a superficial religious sentiment, and the long-sustained effort to obtain a religious amendment of the federal constitution has been alike idle and unnecessary. The religious quality of a people is not determinable by phrases of law, but by the spirit and life. If the American people should insert the divine names in the constitution, that would not keep them from turning to infidelity, or make them a Christian nation after such perversion. New Hampshire is no more Protestant or Christian, with those terms in her constitution, than is Massachusetts without them. Michigan, which excludes the name of Deity from her fundamental law, is no less religious than New York, which is "grateful to Almighty God."

If we would seek the religion of the American nation, we must look into their life, custom, and institutions. Looking on these things — the innumerable Christian temples and institutions of Christian charity, the days of annual thanksgiving, the prayers in legislative halls, the Bible in the courts, the constant resort in legislation and judicature to religious and Christian principles — we may safely declare that, if the American people be not a Christian nation, there is none upon the earth. Sixty years ago wrote De Tocqueville: " There is no country in the whole world in which the Christian religion retains a greater influence over the souls of men than in America. By regulating domestic life it regulates the state. Religion is the foremost of the institutions of the country. I am certain that the Americans hold religion to be indispensable to the maintenance of republican institutions." On this opinion of the acute Frenchman, the Swiss Schaff commented, fifty years later: " I fully agree with De Tocqueville. I came to the same conclusion shortly after my immigration to America in 1844, and I have been confirmed in it by an experience of forty-three years and a dozen visits to Europe." [1]

This opinion has been shared by every statesman and every jurist who has discoursed on the subject. Marshall, Webster, Waite, and a host of others could all join in the language of Cooley, " In a certain sense and for certain purposes it is true that Christianity is part of the law of the land." [2] It is impossible to fix the stigma of unchristian on the American nation.

Furthermore, it may be successfully maintained that, far

---

[1] *American Historical Association*, 1886–1887, p. 473.

[2] *Constitutional Limitations*, p. 579.

from being unchristian, this principle of American religious liberty is of the nature of pure Christianity, and represents the most Christian attitude that a civil government can take with reference to the religion of the people. At the first glance, indeed, and to the eye which chiefly regards externals, this statement seems untrue. In such view, it will be asked, "Is not confession of Christ more Christian than silence?" To such mind there seems a positive gain for righteousness when the governmental expression and action put on the outward forms of religion. This judgment would hold that England, with its legally recognized religious establishment, is a more Christian nation than America.

Of which judgment it may be truly said that it confounds national duties with individual. For the individual the confession of Christ is certainly more Christian than silence. But from this proposition we may not conclude that the same thing is true for a nation. The personal confession affects only the individual who makes it. The constituency is simple, without the possibility of a divided mind. With a nation it is otherwise. There may be a constituency of millions, for whose variety no single confession of faith can speak. Though a majority might be Christian, there yet would be a minority, for whom such confession would be false.

The difficulty is not overcome by the principle of majority rule, for, while that is a wise and just principle for the conduct of civil affairs, it can have no place in the decision of faith. There may be a general consensus of opinion, which only a very small minority of the people oppose; but so long as this small minority do oppose it, the governmental confession of it involves for them a misrepresentation and injustice. It is thus practically impossible for a government to make a confession of faith which shall be at once true and just to all its subjects, who are equally entitled to its protection, and a respect for whose rights in the smallest particular is of the essence of Christian morality.

We need not here dwell on the distinction of Roger Williams — noted in the first chapter — between the totally different aims of the civil state and the Church. "Civility and Religion" are entirely distinct, and not to be confounded. Nor shall one interfere with the other, save as religious conviction in the mind of the citizen may decide his action in regard to civil duties. This underlies the conception of religious liberty, and it is distinctly Christian. Only so far forth as the individual citizens shall be actuated by religious or Christian motives can the government be religious or Christian. No mere form of words put into the fundamental law can alter that condition, and no legal constraint can make that Christian which is not such.

Finally, this American principle, by which the government abstains from all religious function, leaving the utmost liberty of religion and worship to the people, is in perfect harmony with the utterances of the great Founder of Christianity. The things of God and of Cæsar are diverse. The fear of God urges to honor the king, but the king's command cannot constrain to the fear and service of God. The kingdom of God is within the heart, and is neither conditioned nor sustained by civil enactments. These cannot introduce a man into that kingdom, nor make him fit for entrance. Christ Himself declared, "My kingdom is not of this world," not patterned after the fashion of this world's kingdoms, not built on their foundations, nor defended by their arms. With the existence, the spread and the support of this kingdom of Christ, therefore, the governments of earth have nothing to do, save as they refuse to interfere with its freedom, and as they guide their own conduct by its principles of divine righteousness. Into that kingdom of Christ men enter as individuals, not as nations, in all the freedom of personal action, unconstrained by external force and subject only to the influence of spiritual motives reaching to mind and heart.

It is impossible to imagine a distinction more radical or broader than that between things of this spiritual nature and the functions of civil government. To God alone is the man responsible for his religious views and practice. Under God only the man is ruler in his own mind and soul. This autonomy of the soul even God Himself recognizes and respects, not compelling by external force, but appealing to reason, conscience, and affection. Herein is the divine foundation for Religious Liberty. Its enactment by the American constitutions is but a recognition of a law of God written in the nature of truth and of man. As such it is to be reckoned as their echo of the divine will, and fully as Christian an utterance as ever fell from the lips of government.

INDEX

Aberdeen, Bishop of, 480.
Abstract of Laws, Cotton's, 169, 179.
Adams, Rev. Hugh, 200.
Adams, Rev. James, 128.
Adams, John, 470, 478, 480.
Addison, Rev. Mr., 464.
"Agreement" for government in New Hampshire, 290.
Akerlye, Hen., 285 note.
Albany, 323, 330, 339.
Albemarle, Lord, 115.
Albigenses, 45.
Allen, Rev. Mr., 213.
Altham (Jesuit), 366.
Ambrose, 30.
Amsterdam, classis of, 332, 350, 455, 456.
"Anabaptist law" in Massachusetts, 235.
Anabaptists, 50, 63–65, 229.
Anagni, 44.
Andros, Governor, 225, 229, 265, 326, 328, 330, 331, 456.
Annapolis, 463.
Anne, Queen, 261, 279, 343, 405, 445.
Anthony, Joseph, 113.
Antinomian controversy, 188.
Antonides, Domine, 333, 349–351.
"Apostle to Virginia," 76, 391.
Appeal to the Public, Chandler's, 469.
Aquidneck, 139, 429.
"Arbitrary Correction," 320.
Archdale, Joseph, 125, 127.
Argal, Governor, 79.
Arius, 32.
Arminius, 52, 303.
Arnold, William, 239 note, 432.
Articles, Thirty-nine, 55.
Ashley, Lord, 115.
Aspinwall, William, 192, 429.
"Association in Arms" (Md.), 384.
Athanasius, 32.
Atheist in Pennsylvania, 444.
Attleboro (Mass.), 515.

Augsburg, 39, 49.
Augustine, 33, 36, 489.
Austin, Ann, 214.
Avalon, 362.
"Awakening, The Great," 235, 271.

Backerius, Domine, 312.
Bacon, Lord, 134.
Bacon, Rev. T., 393.
Balkom, Rev. Mr., 514.
Baltimore, 1st Lord, 82, 362.
Baltimore, 2d Lord, 244, 363, 370–372, 374, 378, 380, 381.
Baltimore, 3d Lord, 381–385, 392.
Baltimore, 4th Lord, 392, 393, 480.
Bancroft, Archbishop, 84.
Bancroft, George, quoted, 1, 19, 79, 91, 139, 233, 366, 373, 474.
Baptism of children, 306, 315, 333 note.
Baptists in Rhode Island, 64; in Virginia, 100, 111, 457, 480; in Carolina, 118; in Massachusetts, 204, 228, 235, 244.
Barefoot, Walter, 293, 296.
Barrow, 60.
Bartow, Rev. Mr., 346.
Baxter, Ensign, 308.
Baxter, Major, 336.
Bedford (N.Y.), 338.
Belgic Confession, 52.
Bellomont, Lord, 341 note, 343.
Bennett, Major General, 91.
Bennett, Philip, 85.
Bennett, Richard, 85, 370, 374, 379.
Berkeley, Lord, 115, 401.
Berkeley, Sir William, 14, 86, 90, 91, 96, 97, 115, 374.
Beverly, 98.
Bishops, Colonial, 94, 391, 394, Chapter VIII.
Blackstone, quoted, 55.
Blackstone, William, 149.
Blair, Commissary James, 101, 105, 126, 391, 461, 479.

529